CW00829617

Family Power

Since the seventeenth century, scholars have argued that kinship as an organizing principle and political order are antithetical. This book shows that this was simply not the case. Kinship, as a principle of legitimacy and in the shape of dynasties, was fundamental to political order. Throughout the last one and a half millennia of European and Middle Eastern history, elite families and polities evolved in symbiosis. By demonstrating this symbiosis as a basis for successful polities, Peter Haldén unravels long-standing theories of the state and of modernity. Most social scientists focus on coercion as a central facet of the state, and indeed of power. Instead, Haldén argues that much more attention must be given to collaboration, consent and common identity and institutions as elements of political order. He also demonstrates that democracy and individualism are not necessary features of modernity.

Peter Haldén is Associate Professor in the Department of Security, Strategy and Leadership at the Swedish Defence University, Stockholm.

Family Power

Kinship, War and Political Orders in Eurasia, 500–2018

Peter Haldén
Swedish Defence University

CAMBRIDGE
UNIVERSITY PRESS

CAMBRIDGE
UNIVERSITY PRESS

University Printing House, Cambridge CB2 8BS, United Kingdom

One Liberty Plaza, 20th Floor, New York, NY 10006, USA

477 Williamstown Road, Port Melbourne, VIC 3207, Australia

314–321, 3rd Floor, Plot 3, Splendor Forum, Jasola District Centre,
New Delhi – 110025, India

79 Anson Road, #06–04/06, Singapore 079906

Cambridge University Press is part of the University of Cambridge.

It furthers the University's mission by disseminating knowledge in the pursuit of
education, learning, and research at the highest international levels of excellence.

www.cambridge.org
Information on this title: www.cambridge.org/9781108495929
DOI: 10.1017/9781108863612

© Peter Haldén 2020

First published 2020

Printed in the United Kingdom by TJ International Ltd, Padstow Cornwall

A catalogue record for this publication is available from the British Library.

Library of Congress Cataloging-in-Publication Data
NAMES: Haldén, Peter, author.
TITLE: Family power : kinship, war and political orders in Eurasia, 500–2018 / Peter
Haldén, Swedish Defence University.
DESCRIPTION: Cambridge, United Kingdom : Cambridge University Press, 2020. |
Includes bibliographical references and index.
IDENTIFIERS: LCCN 2019050546 | ISBN 9781108495929 (hardback) | ISBN
9781108811095 (paperback) | ISBN 9781108863612 (epub)
SUBJECTS: LCSH: Kings and rulers – History. | Royal houses – History. | Aristocracy (Social
class) – History. | Kinship – Political aspects – History. | Military history.
CLASSIFICATION: LCC D107 .H34 2020 | DDC 950–dc23
LC record available at https://lccn.loc.gov/2019050546

ISBN 978-1-108-49592-9 Hardback

CONTENTS

PREFACE AND ACKNOWLEDGEMENTS

Like so many other books, this one began in bewilderment and ended in emancipation. In my studies of Somalia, I had noticed how much of the blame for the country's woes is heaped upon its clans. From the beginning, this struck me as odd and a bit misplaced. Casting my gaze wider, I noticed that blaming clans, families and tribes – in other words different kinds of kinship structures – was not restricted to observers of Somali politics but a refrain that was often repeated by Western/ Northern observers of politics and societies in countries that were radically different and often, at the time, poorer and more violent than their own. As the years went by, it struck me as increasingly strange, until I realized why. Looking back into European history, my original field of research, I saw families and clans everywhere, not on the out-skirts of society, prowling the edges of civilization as bands of marau-ders but deeply enmeshed in the sinews of power and indeed in the very fabric of society. Aristocratic and royal families not only dominated society but ruled societies, and in some cases even constituted them, for centuries. Initially, I thought that a familiar double standard was at work in the denigration of kinship outside of Europe. Looking into the matter for a paper originally presented at the Department of Peace and Conflict Research at the University of Uppsala in 2012, I found out that kinship-based groups were generally either criticized or made invisible in comparative studies of the development of political order in Europe. Jan Willem Honig's appreciative but critical comments made me realize that I was onto something. Gradually, I found out that much of what social scientists (and to some extent many citizens) think about European history was characterized by a kind of amnesia about our own past. Some narratives wanted to write aristocrats and monarchs out of the history of political order altogether, others wanted to portray them as villains of the story, certainly dominating political order but not contributing to it. I set out to correct these two narratives that have largely dominated, perhaps not all histories but many of them and certainly the most widely read ones.

In providing what I think is a more comprehensive view of past societies, not only of Europe but of other parts of the world, I also wanted to provide something of a rehabilitation. Not a moral rehabilitation in the usual sense of the word. I doubt that I would feel sympathy towards most of the people dealt with in this book on a personal level, but they were no fools and their societies were not faulty, flawed or incomplete versions of our own. I believe that one important task of historical studies is to resist the chauvinism that comes to us in the shape of various '-centrisms'. The two -centrisms that I have in mind are 'tempocentrism', Stephen Hobden's valuable term for presentism and the belief in the superiority of our own time, and 'Eurocentrism', the implicit or explicit belief in the superiority of European (and by extension North American) culture. It is not rare to see them hand in hand. It is possible to object to tempo- and Eurocentrism on many grounds but I think one of the most important is that they, alone or in combination, wreak havoc on our self-image by providing fuel for hubris. One of the many emancipatory effects of historical and sociological research is that it may produce deliverance from hubris.

When writing a book over several years, one naturally becomes indebted to a number of people. Jan Angstrom supported the project wholeheartedly for many long years, always offering friendly critique, suggestions and encouragement. Mattias Albert was kind to host me as a visiting researcher at the University of Bielefeld during the final phases of completing this book. The environment at the Institute for World Society and the excellent library of the University of Bielefeld gave me excellent stimulus, peace of mind and help in this task. I would also like to thank the following for their inspiration, support, comments and friendship: Jens Bartelson, Kjell Engelbrekt, Mats Hallenberg, Ilmari Käihkö, Lars Bo Kaspersen, Richard Ned Lebow, Sofia Ledberg, Kristin Ljungqvist, Dan Öberg, Alex Pritchard, Tobias Werron, Biörn Tjallen,

Mats Utas and Andreas Vasilache. I would like to give special thanks to Carole Sargent for invaluable help with my book proposal. I would like to thank Alice Stoakley for her great work with copy editing my book and helping me sort out obscure details such as Mongolian spelling and correcting the ambiguities of my syntax. Finally, I am deeply grateful to John Haslam of Cambridge University Press for his support of this project and for being a pleasure to work with.

I am also indebted to the staff at the Anna Lindh Library and The Library of the National Heritage Board in Stockholm and the Dag Hammarsköld Library in Uppsala for their helpfulness in supplying me with material for this book and for arranging countless (literally) interlibrary loans. As always, any mistakes or errors are entirely my fault and responsibility. I would also like to thank Taylor & Francis Group for the right to use parts of an article that was originally published as Peter Haldén (2014) 'Reconceptualizing State Formation as Collective Power: Representation in Electoral Monarchies', *Journal of Political Power*, 7(1), 127–47, www.tandfon line.com/doi/abs/10.1080/2158379X.2014.889404. Selections from this article appear in Chapters 4 and 11.

Last but certainly not least I would like to thank my family for everything, particularly for enduring monologues about Franks, Mongols and all the other people featured in this book – and of course for showing on a daily basis the power of kinship.

CHRONOLOGY

476	The last Roman Emperor of the West, Romulus Augustus, is deposed.
496	Clovis, King of the Franks converts to Christianity.
568	The Lombards invade Italy.
588	The Lombard Kingdom is established in Italy.
622	The Prophet Muhammad flees to Medina.
632	The Prophet Muhammad dies. Muslim conquests begin beyond Arabia.
661	The Umayyad Caliphate is established in Damascus.
732	Muslim conquests in the West end with defeat at the Battle of Tours.
750	The end of the Umayyad Caliphate as the Abbasid caliphate is established in Bagdad.
751	Peppin, Mayor of the Palace, deposes the last king of the Merovingian dynasty, founds the Pippinid, later called Carolingian, dynasty.
773–4	The Carolingian Franks conquer Lombard Italy.
793	Viking attacks on Western Europe begin.
800	Charlemagne is crowned Emperor by the Pope, revival of the Empire in the West.
814	Charlemagne dies.
843	Tripartite division of the Carolingian Empire in the Treaty of Verdun.
911	Hrolfr (Rollo) of the Northmen is baptized and dubbed Count of Normandy.
955	Otto I defeats the Hungarians at Lechfeld, establishes the Ottonian dynasty in East Francia and assumes the title of Emperor.
987	Hugh Capet becomes King of France, founds the Capetian Dynasty.
1037	The Great Seljuk Empire is established in Central Asia and so is the Sultanate of Rhûm in Anatolia.
1066	Battle of Hastings, Norman Conquest of England.

1152	Marriage of Eleanor of Aquitaine and Henry I of England establishes the so-called Angevin empire.
1206	Temüjin (Genghis Khan) unites the Mongols, begins conquest of Eurasia.
1215	The Magna Carta is signed.
1258	The Mongols conquer Bagdad, depose and kill the last Abbasid caliph.
1259	Division of the Mongol Empire.
1264–7	Death of Simon de Montfort in England.
1299	Osman I founds the Ottoman Empire.
1310–25	Great Magnate revolt of Hungary.
1337–1453	The 'Hundred Years' War' between the Kings of England and France.
1348	The Black Plague ravages Europe.
1358	The Jacquerie, a peasant revolt in France.
1381	The 'Great English Rising'.
1385	Union of Krewo joins Poland and Lithuania in a personal union.
1452	The House of Habsburg acquires the title of Holy Roman Emperor for the first time.
1453	The Ottoman Empire conquers Constantinople. The Byzantine Empire falls.
1455–85	The 'War of the Roses' between the two branches of the House of Plantagenet.
1474–7	The Burgundian Wars. The State of Burgundy is dissolved.
1492	America is discovered by the Europeans.
1519	Charles V of Habsburg unites the possessions of the two branches of the Habsburg dynasty.
1523	The Vasa dynasty is founded in Sweden.
1526	The Ottoman Empire conquers Hungary after the Battle of Mohàcs.
1529	The Ottomans lay siege to Vienna.
1544	Sweden becomes a hereditary monarchy.
1562	French Wars of Religion and Wars of the Valois Succession begin.
1569	Poland-Lithuania enters into a personal union through the Union of Lublin.
1584	The 'Times of Troubles' in Russia begin.

1589	The House of Bourbon is established as the royal dynasty of France.
1598	French Wars of Religion and Wars of the Valois Succession end.
1613	The 'Times of Troubles' in Russia end. The House of Romanov becomes the royal dynasty of Russia.
1618–48	The Thirty Years' War in the Holy Roman Empire.
1642–51	The Civil Wars in England during which King James II is executed and a republic (Commonwealth) is established.
1660	The Commonwealth of England is overthrown.
1688	The Glorious Revolution in England.
1700–13	War of the Spanish Succession.
1740–8	War of the Austrian Succession.
1776	Revolution in America.
1783	The American republic is proclaimed.
1789	Revolution in France.
1793	Execution of King Louis XVI and Queen Marie Antoinette of France.
1799	Napoleon Bonaparte becomes First Consul.
1804	Napoleon Bonaparte proclaims himself Emperor of the French.
1806	Holy Roman Empire of the German Nation is dissolved. Empire of Austria proclaimed.
1812	Napoleonic France invades Russia.
1815	Napoleon Bonaparte is ultimately defeated. The Congress of Vienna restores the House of Bourbon, creates German Confederation and establishes the 'Monarchical Principle' as a cornerstone of the Vienna system in Europe.
1830	Revolutions in Belgium and France.
1832	The Great Reform Act extends suffrage in Britain.
1848	Revolutions in France, German Confederation, Hungary and Prussia.
1866	Estate-based Diet dissolved in Sweden. Creation of a two-chamber parliament.
1870–1	Franco-Prussian War. Proclamation of the unified German Empire.
1911	The Parliament Act reforms the House of Lords in Britain.

1914	Assassination of Archduke Franz Ferdinand of Austria. World War One begins.
1917	Revolution in Russia. Czar Nicholas II of Russia abdicates. End of the aristocracy and monarchy in Russia.
1918	End of World War One. Kaiser Wilhelm II of Germany abdicates. The Romanov family is executed. End of the monarchy in Austria, Germany, Hungary. Democracy established in Austria and Germany.
1920	The Treaty of Sèvres dissolves the Ottoman Empire.
1922	The last Ottoman caliph, Mehmet VI, is deposed and the Ottoman Caliphate ends.
1922	Proclamation of the Soviet Union.
1932	Proclamation of the Kingdom of Saudi Arabia.
1952–3	Revolution in Egypt, end of the monarchy.
1960	Proclamation of the Republic of Somalia.
1969	Revolution in Libya, end of the monarchy. Siad Barre seizes power in Somalia.
1973	Revolution in Afghanistan, end of the monarchy.
1977–8	Ogaden War in Somalia, start of the civil war.
1979	Revolution in Iran, the Islamic Republic is proclaimed.
1991	Fall of the Soviet Union. End of the rule of Siad Barre in Somalia. The state of Somaliland is proclaimed.
2017	Prince Muhammad Bin Salman proclaimed Crown Prince in Saudi Arabia.

1 INTRODUCTION

Arguments

This book demonstrates that elite families and political order evolved in symbiosis throughout European and Middle Eastern history. Kinship groups like noble clans and royal dynasties were preconditions of stability and legitimacy of political orders. There is a tradition in political theory, anthropology and sociology spanning four centuries that claims that kinship is incompatible with political order. This tradition argues that kinship-based elements either disappeared before the emergence of political orders or were the foes of political order until the emergence of modernity. In contrast to this tradition, I show that neither political order in general nor the state in particular evolved in opposition to kinship groups or to kinship-based principles of legitimacy. Some scholars, like Anderson (2003:19–23) and Oakley (2006), emphasize that dynasties and therefore kinship was central to older political orders. However, the place of kinship in the history of political order remains largely untheorized.

By retelling the development of the state this book pinpoints exactly how kinship-based groups can both support and undermine political order. Contrary to the claims of modernization theorists, a kinship society is not a threat to either political order in general or more specifically the modern state. It is, however, an impediment to democracy.

Because so many leading philosophers and social scientists, from Hobbes, Locke and Rousseau to Marx, Durkheim and Weber, have considered kinship both the enemy and boundary criterion of political order, demonstrating that it has been at the centre of political order unravels a number of ideas about political order, states and modernity. Since kinship – both as a form of organization and a form of legitimacy – has been a blank spot in research on political order much of the theories on the subject have been built around a void. The arguments of this book reinterpret historical developments and social theory, and provide a reassessment of contemporary conflicts and policies. The book (a) makes a macro-sociological account of the role of kinship groups in the development of political order, (b) draws conclusions of the importance of the historical argument for the crisis of order and democracy in parts of today's developing world and (c) draws conclusions of the long historical argument for state theory.

The argument of this book pushes against several ideas in conventional state theory and state formation theory. In several works, 'the state' is used as a catch-all term for political order (Tilly, 1990). In contrast, I argue that 'political order' is a wider term and the state is but one version of political order. Since interdependence rather than conflict characterized the relation between powerful kinship groups and the political order, I conclude that political science and sociology have overemphasized the coercive aspect of the state and social systems and the centrality of a monopoly of violence for the existence of political order. I offer a new understanding of successful political orders by emphasizing co-operation with power elites in a common framework.[1]

Since the nineteenth century, modernization theorists have drawn a watertight distinction between kinship and politics in the colonial (and later 'developing') parts of the world and in Europe's past. Traits that have been identified as alien to modernity's self-image have been ignored or portrayed as obstacles. Conversely, traits that in retrospect could be identified as modern have been elevated and praised. Inspired by the postcolonial reinterpretations of central Asian and African polity formation this book embarks on a similar, and perhaps also, after a fashion, postcolonial, reinterpretation of the history of European polity formation.

This book analyses the development of politics in Europe, the Middle East and the Ottoman Empire from the early Middle Ages to the present. The formalization of aristocratic houses and their embedding

---

[1] Chapter 11 presents a synthesis between conflict and consent theories of social systems.

into a public sphere during the high Middle Ages was essential to European state formation. I show that one of the constitutive causes for successful state-building in Europe was that elite kinship groups were organized and formalized as aristocracies and thus able to integrate with the political order before the big rise in state-building in the seventeenth century.[2] In periods and places where elite kindreds were diffuse, political orders also tended to be diffuse. Organized and public elite kindreds, however, went hand in hand with organized political orders. Thus, focusing on how elite kinship groups were embedded in political orders allows us to understand not only how the state developed but also what political order is. Doing so in turn allows us to understand how to build stable polities today.

To understand what made Europe special, it must be compared to developments elsewhere. In the Middle East, the presence of strong kinship groups that were not formalized or integrated into a political system made the formation of durable polities difficult. The Ottoman Empire represents a halfway house polity between the European and the Middle Eastern cases, with strong kinship groups that were coupled to the imperial centre but not to each other. In a system without embedding institutions, the lineage may become a form for 'exit'; in systems with embedding institutions, the lineage instead may become a form for 'voice' as well as for 'loyalty' (Hirschmann, 2004 [1970]). In early European history, the honour of the lineage fused with an early form of patriotism and obligation to the common good and to the king.

Comparing Arabic, European and Turkic societies gives greater insights into the long-term causes of state stability and fragility than would studying each individually. All societies faced a similar predicament: kinship-based elite groups had political and military power and legitimacy. Rulers that tried to 'break' the power of kinship groups by force, decree and engineered elite circulation provoked rebellion and promoted disintegration. In contrast, political systems with the will, ability and institutions to embed kinship-based groups generally evolved into durable and powerful formations. Building on recent advances in European and Ottoman history, I show that neither European nor Ottoman rulers were hostile to kinship-based elites; rather they were partners in the business of rule. In contrast, this book demonstrates that elite families and political order evolved in symbiosis

---

[2] For an explanation of constitutive causation, see Wendt, 1999:83–8.

throughout European and Middle Eastern history. Kinship groups like noble clans and royal dynasties were preconditions of stability and legitimacy of political orders. The state did not evolve in opposition to kinship groups or to kinship-based principles of legitimacy.

Toolkit

The trademark of social science is the use of theory. However, in this work I do not use a pre-formed theoretical corpus. Instead, I use a theoretical vocabulary drawn from a range of sources in anthropology, political science and sociology. Below I discuss the two main concepts of this book, political order and kinship.

Political Order

I use the word order in the sense of an arrangement of rules and relations.[3] A political order, then, is the authoritative arrangement of human relations and common matters (Mann, 1986:1–33; Onuf, 1989:195). The social world consists of many kinds of relations and interactions, but a political order imposes a normative direction oriented towards central values, a hierarchy of relations. A political order is thus an arrangement of rules and relations that bind interactions into a certain shape. 'Political order' is a broad term that bridges several divides that are often used as starting points of analysis in modern social science: state and society, public and private, and politics and religion. Politics, in this broad reading, relates to the common aspects of a figuration and thus encompasses the allocation of resources, the capability to designate friends and enemies (and thus matters of war and peace), and the rules regulating action and identity. My source of inspiration for this definition is the Roman term *res publica*, which was defined as the common matters as opposed to private ones (Mager, 1984:552). Politics is that which concerns the entire community, however defined. This understanding does not entail any kind of democracy; decisions about the community can be taken by a small group of people. The idea that politics is about communal affairs points towards the idea that a political order requires some degree of self-description; an explicit idea of a collective. It is not a spontaneous or

---

[3] The following section builds on a framework that I developed in Haldén, 2011:18–30.

implicit structure of which its members are unaware. An implicit order that has to be uncovered rather would be a 'social' one. A political order requires some form of corporate existence that lives on although individual members may die (Kantorowicz, 1997 [1957]).

Like all social systems, political orders require that boundaries can be drawn. Political order also involves, in some way or another, the potentiality for collective violence. Carl Schmitt captured both aspects when he defined the core of politics as the distinction between friend and enemy. The enemy in this sense is the public enemy (*hostis*), namely the enemy of all, the entire collectivity (Schmitt, 2007:26). Schmitt goes on to say that '[w]ar is neither the aim, nor the purpose nor the very content of politics. But as an ever present possibility it is the leading presupposition which determines a characteristic way [of] human action and thinking and thereby a specific political behavior' (Schmitt, 2007:34). I stated above that politics cannot be reduced to coercion and the capacity for and exercise of violence, but these elements are part of politics and cannot be absent from a political order.

Political orders have shapes, and they are oriented towards a certain normative goal or sets of values (Reus-Smit, 1999). Edward Shils argued that societies have centres that consist of values and beliefs. He argued that: '[i]t is the center of the order of symbols, of values and beliefs, which govern the society' (Shils, 1982:93). It does not exhaust or encompass all values and beliefs of the society but it consists of the values that are pursued and affirmed by the elites of the subsystems of society (Shils, 1982:95). In the societies that this book analyses, the idea that power and social stratification was, on the whole, legitimately hereditary was an important part of the central values. This understanding encompasses both 'politics' and 'society' since social stratification was eminently political. Shils argues that this centre does not touch everyone, and people who are touched by it are so to different degrees. In older societies, only a small minority participated actively in politics. However, all were in some way cognizant of the political order and touched by the central values upon which it rested. David Graeber and Marshall Sahlins argue that human societies exist in a hierarchy that encompasses cosmic forces and powers (Shils, 1982:27; Graeber and Sahlins, 2017:2). This is reflected in the fact that political legitimacy in all older societies was achieved by anchoring the polity to supernatural powers. It is also reflected in the fact that all hereditary power groups rule by means of charismatic qualities. Or, as Gaetano Mosca put it:

'Hereditary aristocracies often come to vaunt supernatural origins, or at least origins different from, or superior to, those of the governed classes' (Mosca, 1939:62). Naturally, there are always dissidents who have 'a very intense and active connection with the center, with the symbols of the central value system, but whose connection is passionately negative' (Shils, 1982:100). Although there was substantial discord in these societies, the number of people that were 'passionately negative' to this order of things was, for most of history, small.

My understanding of political order can be clarified by contrasting it with a sovereign state. Most definitions of what a state is centre explicitly or implicitly on war. The most accepted definition was formulated by Max Weber: ' [. . .] a compulsory political organization with continuous operations will be called a "state" insofar as [it] successfully upholds the claim to the monopoly of the legitimate use of physical force in the enforcement of its order' (Weber, 1978:54). In contrast, a monopoly of violence, residing in a single centre, is not a requirement of a political order. Also, the stress on a permanent community as the core of a political order is distinct from an understanding of the state that emphasizes organizational capabilities like taxation, capturing capital, coercing and warfare. In my understanding a state is a kind of political order, one that binds interactions in a certain shape. But a political order does not have to monopolize the means of violence. Only the sovereign state, which is but one kind of political order, does so.

All socio-political systems can be described and analysed as forms of rule – a scheme that allows us to sidestep the conceptual primacy of the sovereign state (Haldén, 2011). Empires, 'feudal' organizations, estate-based polities, modern states and modern systems of states can all be understood as forms of rule/different political orders. Each form of rule contains the following elements: (1) the nature of the members, (2) their relation to each other, (3) their relation to the centre and (4) their relation to external actors and institutions. A political order must have a centre, a definition of who its members are, their relation to each other and their relations to outsiders. The composition of institutions determines relations between the members of a form of rule. Order is created by the combination of rules with authority that gives the rules a unified direction. Scripts and institutions define a form of rule by giving it a purpose, a raison d'être, constructing the identities of the members and the relations to each other.

Institutions give shape to patterns of action and determine the character of relations between the members of the form of rule. Systems determine action in different ways because they are different contexts of intersubjective meanings. Institutions, in turn, consist of concepts that give the institution meaning. The introduction of new concepts and categories thus opens new ways of acting and also closes down previous ones. At this point it must be pointed out that forms of rule/political orders are not deterministic, rules can be followed and rules can be broken.

Kinship

This book studies kinship-based elites, groups who have a certain cohesion based on their biological or fictive kinship ties, their position and resources are transmitted through inheritance and they maintain their resources partly through kinship ties with other groups and who legitimate their claims to rule on the basis of descent. From opposite ends of the political spectrum, both Mosca (1939:51, 60–2) and Therborn (2008) emphasize that all societies are dominated by elites, many of which have been hereditary. Second, I focus on the idea that descent is a basis or even the primary basis of legitimate rule in the political order.

Kinship is usually considered a 'primordial' relation and sometimes as a natural, rather than a social, fact (Searle, 1996). Older generations of anthropologists treated kinship as consisting of fixed structures that bound their inhabitants (Kuper, 1982; Levi-Strauss, 1995; Peletz, 1995). I will not follow these lines of reasoning. Instead I will treat kinship as a socially constructed relation that is historically and culturally variable (Sahlins, 2011a, 2011b). For example, the ancient Romans treated adopted children on the same basis, and sometimes better than, natural children. This is evident from the practice of emperors to adopt their successors. By contrast, in high medieval and early modern Europe, royal children born out of wedlock were illegitimate and could not inherit the throne – but achieved high positions under assumed names. Yet another example could be cited from the tenth century, when all sons born of Viking kings were considered legitimate, regardless of the status of their mother.

Kinship is not an 'independent variable' or separate factor. The concepts, practices and institutions regulating kinship and descent always exist in a figuration together with other concepts, practices and institutions (Sahlins, 2011a:13). Kinship was (and in some places and cases, still is) an important part of politics.[4] Concepts, institutions and practices associated with kinship, such as marriage, inheritance, descent and heritage, existed in the same figuration as concepts associated with rule, such as the common good, property rights and the ways that the polity was conceptualized (e.g., realm, empire, sultanate, caliphate). As the empirical chapters will demonstrate, kinship and political order were not only interdependent but co-constitutive.

Thus political and religio-political decisions shape kinship relations. Families can be made more or less hierarchical, more or less standardized and regulated. Families can be stratified internally and social strata can be organized, formally and informally, on the basis of kinship. Law codes, both ancient and recent, often lay down the law for inheritance and other family relations. Such decisions concern, as feminist scholars have argued, not a subsystem (e.g., family law) but they are deeply political. Internal family stratification and the ordering of families in a system of rank in the cases that this book analyses, have political consequences in the sense of Harold Lasswell's famous definition: 'Who gets what, when, how' – not only of the family's assets but of the assets of the political order (Lasswell, 1958). Variations in the political order created entirely different conditions for identity and action. Or, as Hirschmann put it, whether major kinship groups would aim for strategies of 'exit', 'voice' or 'loyalty' (Hirschman, 2004).

As will become evident in later chapters, the capacity to order, regulate and organize kinship, particularly elite kinship relations and forms, was a considerable advantage with regard to polity formation. I am talking here about the invention of nobilities as formalized and public systems (rather than more or less regular practices). This was a major innovation that helped European polities to solidify. Another invention was the evolution of stable rules of inheritance that stabilized royal and noble successions of power.

This book studies societies where status, rank, membership in political bodies, property and often control over military capabilities was transmitted through inheritance and political alliances are facilitated – but not determined – by biological relations. In such societies controlling family formation becomes a paramount means of

---

[4] For the term figuration, see Elias, 2012.

controlling that society. Control over the most powerful families, including the royal one, was important. This was achieved by controlling the delimitation and definition of the family, reproduction, gendered divisions of labour and gender status, and rules of inheritance and general rules of marriage as well as allowing, prohibiting and advancing specific marriages. Such means amount to what Foucault called 'biopolitics': 'Biopolitics has to do with the administration of lives and livelihoods via discursive "rules" that establish and regulate bodily activities such as birth, death, gender, marriage, work, health, illness, sanity, rationality and so on' (Sylvester, 2013:69). In the societies that this book studies, the management, either personally (e.g., by kings, queens, sultans and servants) or by administrative means, of the lives and bodies of people was essential to management of the political system.

Political decisions and emergent evolutionary processes thus impact on kinship systems, which generates feedback effects on the political orders. For example, stabilization of rules of succession and the formation of main and cadet branches of royal houses made politics more regular and ended the tendency for internal wars of succession that characterized the Middle Ages – but they also generated international wars of succession that characterized the early modern period. However, kinship is also fluid and open to modification and negotiation by actors on a micro level. For Lévi-Strauss, a guiding principle is the idea that societies have an underlying structure that directs everything, much like languages have grammar. However, albeit important, grammar is not set in stone. It can be changed, played with and broken to create advantages (Barnard 2000:128, 176). For example, in medieval Europe people were not bound by patrilineality, the idea that descent is counted on the father's side. People often chose to emphasize their ancestry on their mother's or their father's side, depending on which one gave the most status, wealth and resources (Althoff, 2004). Actors within the same group can switch back and forth between different practices of marriage, inheritance and succession.

Today, many of us tend to assume that clans and tribes are well defined and cohesive and that they bind members unambiguously and strongly. In fact, many societies display a considerable degree of fluidity and ambiguity with regard to kinship. The fluidity and overlapping nature of group identity is a feature of what Ernst Gellner called 'agro-literate societies'. In such societies a person can belong to several different groups and use the full range of connections, identities and possibilities of action open to them (Gellner, 2008 [1983]:13, 1998:146). The very ambiguity of belonging may be a considerable asset since it allows a person to 'navigate' and adapt their behaviour to the circumstances as they arise. Since this possibility is an asset that many recognize and want to be able to use there are few systemic incentives to regulate, formalize and simplify the standards of belonging. I am certainly not claiming that this is a feature of all kinship groups everywhere and at all times. In some times and places, such as early to high medieval Europe, kinship (as regards the nobility) had this fluid character. Later, in the sixteenth and seventeenth centuries, belonging and the system of nobility became more tightly regulated and bureaucratized as part of the formation of the state. What is important to recognize, however, is that although the system of political kinship groups changed and became more enmeshed in the state (as we know it; it was previously enmeshed in a system of rule that was not a state) it did not become obsolete or unimportant. Political kinship remained part of the form of rule for centuries to come.

Previous Research

Ultimately the disconnection between several academic disciplines and fields of study produced the subject matter of this book. As such, the book stands at the crossroads between anthropology, comparative history, political science, sociology and war studies. From fairy tales and myths, we know that crossroads can be perilous, but they are also places where insights can be gained. To avoid the former and gain the latter I will orient the reader as to how the different strands of research are connected. It will be evident in Chapter 2 that the division between kinship and political order to some extent represents a division of labour between anthropology and political science.

This book approaches a theoretical and empirical problem that has fallen prey to the fault lines between several disciplines. Political scientists have long neglected the issues of kinship and descent, treating them as belonging to a pre-political stage. I show that they were central to political life for millennia. Anthropologists have generally neglected politics and the state. Yet both have fundamentally shaped a key topic of anthropology: kinship.

One of the strongest themes in state formation research is the so-called warfare thesis – the idea that organization for and the pursuit of warfare were the main drivers in the formation of states in European history. It is also one of the most established and, until recently, almost taken for granted theories in historical sociology at large. Charles Tilly is the most famous proponent of the 'warfare thesis' but a version of it was formulated before him by Otto Hintze and others, such as Thomas Ertman, have subsequently elaborated upon it (Hintze, 1962b; Tilly, 1990; Ertman, 1997; Kaspersen, Strandsbjerg and Teschke, 2017). Charles Tilly's focus is on the later medieval/early modern period and specifically asks how it came about that most European polities became 'nation-states' and not city-states or forms of fragmented sovereignty. The warfare thesis has a strong emphasis on coercion and indeed defines it as one of the drivers and central pillars of the state. A more extended argument concerning the link between war and elaborate forms of social organization has been made by Sinisa Malesevic (2017) who argues that the two have been connected and mutually constitutive since late Neolithic times. I agree that war has been highly important in the formation not only of the state, but of political order as such. However, I disagree with the idea that coercion is the core of political order. Tilly claims in an early paper that state-making was akin to organized crime (Tilly, 1985). I believe that they were very different, indeed antithetical, since the state, or rather political order, relies on legitimacy and – as I will show – on collaboration and consent as well as the capacity for coercion – something that crime by definition never can do. Tilly and several other scholars highlight the role of warfare as a means of weeding out non-viable entities and as a means of accumulation of material resources and organizational capacities. I do think that warfare was highly important for these reasons but not for these reasons only. Warfare also had the intended and unintended effects of creating collective meaning and community, in bonding people together and creating cohesion on a macro-social level. This is dealt with further in Chapters 4 and 11 but it has hitherto been neglected in historical sociologies of state formation. Wars also (re)produce what Edward Shils calls the 'central values' of a polity and highlight them through the production of legitimating discourses before, during and after wars. There are of course always dissenters and debates on wars, and their cohesive effect is neither comprehensive, all-encompassing or uncontested. This book is not an extensive statement regarding the exact role of war in polity formation but tries to outline the first steps towards a perspective that considers the immaterial effects more thoroughly.

Facing in another direction, this book connects historical scholarship with the social sciences. It does so in three principal ways. First, although comparative works on Eurasian polities is a growing research field (Árnason and Wittrock, 2004; Allsen, 2006; Bang and Kołodziejczyk, 2012) there have been no major comparative Eurasian studies of the relation between kinship and political order based on the idea that the two have been symbiotic and not contradictory. The book uses the new historical findings about the relation between hereditary elites and the state in several different contexts to tell a new story about the development of political order. Older theories of state formation are, for the most part, connected to a view of the early modern state as an absolutist one that dominated other centres of power.[5] This view is now considered outdated in historical scholarship but the revisionist story has not been taken into account by the social sciences. Together with the evidence from other periods and places that co-operation and embedding is a far more successful pattern than domination and coercion, I use the synthesized historical evidence to destabilize and reformulate theories of political order and power.

My book consists of a comparative study of historical periods and polities that, barring some notable exceptions (Crone, 1980; Oakley, 2006; Gellner, 2008; Sellin, 2011), are rarely studied together by historians. Connecting different periods has the advantages of highlighting continuities and discontinuities simultaneously. Within a longer historical timeframe we can discern more precisely what changes and how. Several major strands of scholarship are premised on the idea of major, epochal transformations such as the much-debated 'medieval-to-modern' shift (Ruggie, 1993; Teschke 2003:166ff). Another is the idea of state formation as a process of take-off where earlier stages are decisively left behind, like the stages of the launching of a space rocket. A third is the research that deals with the evolution of the modern international system in International Relations Theory. The idea of a break with the past is deeply embedded in the idea of modernity and as such it is both a description of a particular age (e.g., 1800 onwards) and a normative aspiration formulated at regular intervals during that age. However, the normative aspirations have tended to colour the

---

[5] See Chapter 5.

descriptions of the period c.1800–c.2000. In order to provide a more accurate description of continuities through time, a long perspective in time is necessary. A long-time perspective is also a way to bypass the tendency to reduce the history of political order to state formation. It allows us to peripheralize the state and see it both as a particular instance of a more general phenomenon and as embedded in an environment, both historically and contemporary. A long-time perspective allows questions such as: In what kind of organizational environment did the state originate? What general category is the state a case of? What continuities survive into the state and act through the state? Furthermore, the long-time perspective is the only way to make an important argument in anthropology and demonstrate that the ideal type of the egalitarian and segmentary 'tribe' is not meaningful to apply to European history.

Over the years, macro-sociologists have produced valuable insights by engaging in comparative studies of different civilizations. Several times, European cases and developments have been compared to their counterparts in China and Japan, highlighting important contrasts and similarities (Hintze, 1962c; Bloch, 1989; Hui, 2005; Fukuyama, 2012). I continue this research agenda further by making comparisons with cases from the Muslim world, something that has rarely been done in contemporary scholarship. Two exceptions are Hall's *Powers and Liberties* and Crone's *Pre-Industrial Societies* (Crone, 1980, 1989; Hall, 1986). Comparisons between European and Middle Eastern polities tend to highlight structural differences between the two in order to explain the singularity of the latter. In contrast, I demonstrate that Arab, European and Turkic societies faced similar predicaments regarding strong hereditary elites but dealt with them through different institutions and policies.

An effect of the separation between historians and social scientists is that when historians employ social science concepts they sometimes use outdated ones. Over the last three decades, International Relations scholars have made great advances in deconstructing and historicizing concepts like the state and sovereignty and even proposed alternatives, like polities and political society (Onuf, 1989; Ferguson and Mansbach, 1996, 2008). However, many historians still use the state as a transhistorical macro concept. Thus, this book aims to provide historical scholarship with a conceptual language that does not take the unitary, modern, sovereign state as its starting point.

Some readers may ask themselves to what discipline this book belongs. Does it belong to anthropology, historical sociology, political science or war studies? The book touches upon all of these disciplines and the reader may classify it with the help of them according to their interests. If they want to know how and why people have fought wars in older European history and in the Middle East and North Africa region today, or if a reader wants to know how political order has been shaped, then this is a book for them. Although I intend this book for several audiences, I must caution that one cannot read it exclusively from the confines of any discipline. If one wants to know how, with whom and why people wage wars, one cannot ignore political order. Conversely, if one is interested in how political orders evolve and are maintained, it is impossible to ignore warfare and armed forces. Thus, this book does not only move between disciplines but aims to unite historical sociology, political science and war studies.

Design

All studies can be criticized on the basis of what the author has chosen to deal with and what has been left out. The more wide-ranging the study or the more ambitious the propositions, hypotheses or claims of the author, the more leeway is given to criticism. If kinship is such a universal phenomenon (albeit in very different forms) and political order should be understood in such a wide way, why are so many cultures left out of this study? Why does the study not deal with China, famous for its lineages and for its unique and robust political order? Given the considerable focus on European civilization(s), why have I chosen not to include Rome with its senatorial and equestrian aristocracy, its imperial dynasties and remarkably powerful state? Or classical Greece that knew both kingship and aristocracy as well as groundbreaking political thinking? All these cases would have been valuable to study, particularly in a world history context. However, every book entails a trade-off between breadth and depth and I have chosen to opt for the latter over the former. It would have been possible to deal with all these cultures as well as the ones that I have chosen but it would have meant skimming the surface. It would have been a very good book but a different one.

Within the broad category of Europe, some periods, people and institutions feature more prominently than others. I have chosen them to illustrate my general argument. My account deals more intensively with England, France and the Holy Roman Empire than it does with Russia, Poland-Lithuania or Sweden. There are overlaps and inconsistencies over time in my 'units' of analysis. In the chapters on the Middle Ages, Europe is understood mainly as the Latin West, excluding Byzantium and most of the Slav polities. Russia is brought into Europe in Chapter 5 to reflect the country's gravitation towards Western cultural models. The category of the 'Islamic World' is constructed in a similar way, like a radial concept around the core area (Lakoff, 1987). My focus is on the Levant and the core Arab countries – particularly in Chapter 2. The narrative then moves and expands geographically, partly to reflect the expansion of Islam itself, to encompass the Persian and Turkic worlds further east and eventually to the north of the Arab core as the Ottomans establish their empire in the thirteenth century. I also venture further to the east-north-east and discuss some of the Turkic and Persian-speaking peoples of Central Asia.

The languages that I can read restrict my study and therefore the kind of scholarship and sources I have been able to access. Since I have been limited to English, French, German and the Scandinavian languages, the study possibly suffers from certain shortcomings and pitfalls. Primary sources feature more in the chapters on European history than in those on Arab, Ottoman and Turkic history as well as in those on the contemporary Middle East. I have tried to compensate for my shortcomings by consulting historiographical works directly dealing with national scholarship in the respective languages. Unfortunately, a work of this nature must rely heavily on secondary literature. However, some primary sources have been utilized, particularly concerning political and legal thought.

I also eliminated two other approaches in my choice of method. This book does not chart what families were important at a certain time and place and their internal and external relations. Several important contributions have been made using this approach, called prosopography, for example Gerd Tellenbach's studies of the Carolingian imperial aristocracy (Tellenbach, 1939). However, such analyses are difficult to make over long distances in time and space. Instead, this book is devoted to analysing patterns of practices and systems and the ideas about groups of elite families and their positions in political orders. A prominent trait in the empirical studies made in this book is that individual families and kindreds fade away but the systems on which they were based and which they formed a part of remained over very long periods of time. Thus, 'elite circulation', as has been often discussed by elite theorists, took place over the centuries, but in a rather stable framework (Mosca, 1939:65–8; Pareto, 1968). Individual families, even royal ones, were dispensable but the practice of elite families seems to have been indispensable in political orders. I do not study kinship or family structure as such in these societies. Since this book is about the history of political order and not about the history of family structures only those families and kinds of families relevant to rule are included. I have chosen not to study non-noble elites, for example, patrician families, their political power, position in the political order and kinship connection. This has been a choice in favour of a more synthetic account and against a more comprehensive or encyclopaedic approach.

The European part of my narrative ends with World War One, when monarchy and aristocracy were banished from the political orders of Europe and Russia. As I mention in Chapter 6, however, one could argue that kinship remained within the political order but in a different shape. With the rise of nationalism in the nineteenth century, thinkers began to conceptualize the political order, indeed the social order, through kinship metaphors. Nations were constructed through bonds of imagined as well as biological kinship. The latter was supported by notions of racialism and Darwinian sociobiology. The budding welfare states of the nineteenth and twentieth centuries were also characterized by paternalistic ideas that were indebted to ideas of kinship and even as the international realm was characterized less by real bonds of monarchical kinship, metaphors of brotherhood and thus of kinship began to appear in the texts and minds of intellectuals. Exciting and pertinent as these phenomena may be, I have decided not to include them in this book, primarily for reasons of space. A later book might be devoted to the phenomenon of metaphorical and sociobiological ideas of kinship and political order in modern times.

Organization

The rest of the book proceeds in the following way. It consists of three main parts: Chapters 1 and 2 present the conceptual foundations of the book. Chapters 3, 4, 5 and 6 deal with European history between 500 and 1900. Chapters 7, 8, 9 and 10 deal with Arabic, Ottoman and Turko-Mongol history and with the contemporary Middle East, respectively. Chapter 11 summarizes the book and outlines the consequences of the empirical analysis for social and political theory. All chapters follow a simple plan: I inquire to what proportion symbiosis or conflict between political order and kinship can be found in the era. I analyse the forms of symbiosis that can be identified with regard to concepts/ semantics, institutions and practices. I also analyse the role of kinship-based elites in the organization and conduct of war.

In Chapter 2 I demonstrate how old the idea that families do not belong to political orders is in Western thinking. This idea has dominated anthropology, political science and sociology. Despite its popularity, the idea of an opposition between kinship and states is built on problematic notions about the state and kinship and it ignores empirical evidence. The ambition to describe kinship-based groups as obstacles to political development began with early modern thinkers inspired by natural law but it was reinforced in the nineteenth century by sociologists and anthropologists. Understanding how the expulsion of kinship from our ideas of political order was essentially a political project, not the result of academic analysis, helps us to view European and Middle Eastern history with fresh eyes.

Chapter 3 analyses an era in European history often portrayed as a time when families, not political structures, ruled. In contrast, I demonstrate that noble kinship groups and networks were integrated into institutions and ideas of a common political order. Dependence worked both ways. Kings were dependent upon major noble networks and nobles were legitimated by their roles as public actors and public warriors. Towards the end of this period, we also see the growth of a sense of responsibility for the common polity, the realm, even in the absence of kings. The chapter concludes that there was no principled opposition between kinship groups and the polity, between the aristocracy and the king – rather they were mutually dependent. However, since kinship groups were so informal, political institutions were also very informal and elusive. This teaches us that formalization of families was a key to the formalization of political structures.

Chapter 4 studies the period 1000–1500 in Europe. During this period, both elite kinship groups and polities became formalized, conceptually as well as legally. Since interdependence continued, we can surmise a connection between the formalization and stabilization of elite families and the growth of more stable and durable polities. Gradually, 'exit' ceased to be a viable strategy, giving way to 'voice' and 'loyalty'. During the high Middle Ages kin groups changed from sprawling networks to more regulated families, partly since monogamy became the only acceptable form of marriage, partly since inheritance rights began to tend towards primogeniture – the practice that only the firstborn son inherits titles and land. When families became more hierarchical, the nobility as a group became formalized and hierarchical. As the ruling strata of society became public, visible and relatively transparent, more durable political institutions could be formed. Thus, the findings of this chapter support the correlation between formalized elite families and formalized polities. During the high Middle Ages, kings and queens devoted considerable energies to ruling their realms through the nobility, for example by approving and arranging marriages. The realm depended upon magnate dynasties and their economic, military and political resources. Hence, rather than an opposition between elite kinship groups and the polity (and its ruler) we see a continued interdependence. Successful rulers collaborated with nobles. Attempts to forcibly subdue them often resulted in civil war, deposition of the monarch and even more rights for the nobility. This teaches us that collaboration, rather than coercion, is a key to polity formation.

Chapter 5 analyses the early modern era in Europe (c. 1500–1800), a time that political scientists and historians generally consider to be the period when unitary, sovereign states came into being. Older scholarship on state formation has associated state growth with the obsolescence and defeat of the aristocracy. However, revisionist historians show that the nobility remained fundamental to the political system despite the establishment of bureaucracies and standing armies. Although the period saw rebellions by noblemen, kings and nobles continued to depend on each other. Far from being opposed to royal order the nobility complemented the rule of kings. This chapter shows how international politics was also dynastic politics. The internal wars of succession of the Middle Ages became international wars of succession and rulers thought as much in terms of dynastic interests as interests of state.

The process of formalizing the nobility gained strength through the creation of estate assemblies in all European countries. During the eighteenth century, the development of catalogues of the nobility and of state functionaries made the political and social system even more transparent. Although the nobility adapted to growing state structures, this period also strengthened the connection between formalization of elite families and the formalization of political institutions.

Chapter 6 concludes the European section of the book and analyses the long survival of aristocratic elite families in European polities during the nineteenth century. I show that aristocracy and monarchy survived and even prospered by adapting to modern politics until the beginning of World War One. Strong liberal, nationalist and socialist forces challenged hereditary power, but they were only successful in Britain, France and Scandinavia. The Central European, Ottoman and Russian monarchies and aristocracies were ousted only because of their defeat in World War One. The capacity of monarchies and aristocracies to survive even in the century of modernization means that the idea that kinship and political order are incompatible is weakened further. Rather we must conclude that it is possible to have modern states ruled by elite families and legitimated by hereditary rule. However, it is not possible to build democracies on such foundations.

Chapters 3 to 6 show us that (a) kinship groups were part of durable polities in Europe between 500 and 1800, (b) formalization of these groups was necessary to formalize polities and (c) successful rulers collaborated with the aristocracy. The next four chapters investigate if this was only a European phenomenon or if similar traits can be found in Middle Eastern history. The first in this part, Chapter 7, shows that the empires of the first centuries of Islam depended on kinship as a principle of legitimacy. Descent from the extended family of the Prophet Muhammad was necessary in order to become Caliph, the political and spiritual leader of the faithful. Consequently, the Umayyad and the Abbasid dynasties both legitimated their rule by reference to blood relations to the Prophet's family. Nevertheless, the Arab empires had an ambivalent attitude towards hereditary power and imperial rulers often tried to break the power of the hereditary elites instead of embedding them in a stable system. The result was that few elites trusted the political system and opted for exit rather than loyalty in times of crisis and war. It also destroyed the Arab Empires since rulers had to import foreign mercenaries.

Chapter 8 analyses empires created by Turkic and Mongol peoples in Western Eurasia between c.900 and c.1300: the Seljuks and the Mongols. Although vast in size, most Turkic polities were very short-lived. All empires were torn between the desire to centralize rule and the need to manage their multitude of different peoples. Generally, rulers that tried to impose a centralized, top-down order and break the power of local aristocratic orders soon saw their empires fail. Similarly to medieval Europe, successful rulers managed the multitude of sub-rulers and peoples by accepting a looser form of empire. Eventually, the Turkic polities disintegrated because of their lack of embedding institutions and because of their unclear rules of succession. These findings support my argument that kinship is not an immutable structure and that both hierarchical kinship patterns and institutions were necessary to build durable political orders. Also, successful polity formation seems to hinge on developing political forms based on negotiation and shared rule – a pattern visible in Europe but not in the Middle East.

Chapter 9 analyses the successor polity to the Seljuk Turks. Classically, the Ottoman Empire was considered as a polity that really broke with kinship as an organizing principle by raising armies and bureaucracies of slaves beholden only to the Sultan and an ideology both of equality and subjugation. In this interpretation, conflict between the state and kinship characterized the Empire. In fact, the Empire contained numerous kinship-based elites, both formally recognized and informal. Kinship groups permeated the administration at the centre and ruled in the provinces. Furthermore, the Empire's longevity and several of its main conflicts can be understood by studying the charismatic power and legitimacy of its most central kinship group: the Ottoman dynasty. However, kinship-based elites were (a) mostly informal, (b) kept isolated by the Imperial centre and (c) dealt with in an improvised ad hoc manner rather than through institutionalized procedures and organizations. Kinship elites were central to the Empire and to its legitimacy but they remained without a legitimizing framework. The most successful Western Islamic polity collaborated with its many kinship-based elites; the Sultans did so more than other Turkic and Arab polities but not as much and as publicly as European rulers. This explains the Empire's relative success in the Islamic world and its frailty compared to European powers.

In Chapter 10 the historical insights are brought to bear on the problems of political order and war in the modern Middle East. We learn that kinship groups like clans, dynasties and tribes can contribute to state stability in the modern Middle East. Similar to the dynamics found in the historical chapters we see that rulers who try to 'break' influential clans or use them to 'divide and rule' end up fracturing the polity and exacerbating civil war. This chapter analyses Saudi Arabia and Somalia in the twenty-first century. Both countries have strong kinship-based groups but different political orders. The former country is commanded by the large and sprawling al-Saud' dynasty which has created a deeply undemocratic but relatively efficient state. Somalia is characterized by political division and by a society strongly based on clans which many observers have concluded are intrinsically linked. However, the causal chains are unclear since dictatorial manipulation and civil war have strengthened, politicized and militarized the clans. Also, there are several relatively well-functioning local and regional polities (like Somaliland) that incorporate clan authorities in their nascent structures. The chapter concludes that a society where kinship is the basis of legitimacy and organization is incompatible with democracy but not with political order per se nor with flexible forms of sovereignty.

Chapter 11 summarizes the results from the empirical chapters and advances a synthetic theory on the development and maintenance of political orders. It argues that theories of political order in general and the state in particular have been one-sided in their emphasis on coercive power and the monopoly of violence. In light of the empirical results, coercion and violence must be complemented by consent, co-operation and integration as preconditions of stability in order to create more comprehensive social science theories of political order. Concerning modernity, the chapter argues that there was no single path to the secular and egalitarian societies that developed in the West during the twentieth century. Given that aristocratic and royal forms of inherited power were so long-lived we could have ended up with societies that were administratively and technically modern but not egalitarian and democratic. Thereby the book problematizes the idea that pre-modern and modern forms of political orders are the timeless concepts claimed by modernization theory.

By filling in a centuries-old gap in political science this book provides a new interpretation of European and Middle Eastern history that yields a new theory of how successful and stable states develop. As is further explained in Chapter 11, it presents a new idea of political order, of modernity and a synthesis of conflict and consent theories of societies.

2 HOW SOCIAL SCIENCE SEPARATED FAMILIES FROM POLITICAL ORDER

Introduction

Kinship in its various forms has had a strong place in macro-narratives of the development of political order but its presence has been that of the shadowy enemy of political organization. There is a tradition in the study of political order to argue explicitly or implicitly that kinship groups and kinship as an organizational principle are fundamentally opposed to states. This chapter deals with the development of this separation since the seventeenth century but also with its critics, upon whom I will base my subsequent analysis. Kinship and political order have been constructed as mutually exclusive in two intricate ways.

First, stage theories have been strong in ideas of political development since the seventeenth century. In such schemes, kinship-based and state forms of organization belong to different eras. Although powerful narratives, stage theories overemphasize the discontinuities of history and introduce an unwarranted teleology that has led scholars to overlook the role of kinship in political order (simply because of the assumption that it had faded away) and to denigrate kinship-based groups (because of the assumption that they ought to fade away).

Second, in part due to the influence of stage theories, kinship groups and states have often been defined as competing. In the history and sociology of Europe, this narrative follows the shape of an opposition between the nobility (which is based on descent and kinship) and the political order. This image has had political roots and political undertones, from the normative projects of early modern philosophers to modern Marxist and liberal historiography and sociology.

The trend is, however, not uniform. The early modern Aristotelian tradition saw families as integral to the state. Several later writers, like Walter Bagehot, recognized the decline of kinship and the aristocracy but acknowledged their functional importance. Nevertheless, it is only with recent scholarship that historians have begun to peel away previous interpretations and recognize their political background. Since stage theories and the narrative of antagonism have been intertwined, this chapter outlines how the two have interacted throughout the European history of ideas.

Scholarship on the Middle East, North Africa and Central Asia has cast kinship-based groups and political order in a similar way. Stage theories have not been as prominent. Instead scholarship has focused on the relation between 'tribal' formations and political orders, as two separate and distinct entities. Some researchers, often inspired by a reading of the works of Ibn Khaldûn (1332–1406), claim that tribes and states have generally clashed. Others, however, point to the interdependence of tribes and states. In debates and research on political development in political science and sociology, the conflict narrative tends to dominate. Regardless of which stance they take, researchers have focused on the relation between states and tribal groups that can be distinctly delineated on the basis of their lifestyle (nomadic) or location (arid hinterlands).

Although the idea of a separation between kinship and political order can be traced far back in history some distinctly modern traits have reinforced it. The disciplinary divide between anthropology on one side and sociology and political science on the other has left the study of kinship groups in the former discipline and political order in the latter two. As Bruno Latour demonstrates, modern knowledge production works by positing binary relations such as state-society and law-politics (Latour, 1993). Binary categories are purified of their opposite number in order to create strict either–or distinctions. Latour does not discuss the kinship-politics distinction, but it fits the scheme that he identifies. The idea of a clean and violent break with the past is also central to the self-description of modernity as a period – and of modernists as political protagonists. Thus, modernists and modern sociologists distinguish between 'traditional' and 'modern' traits. Indeed, this distinction was foundational to sociology. A result of the purification is that kinship groups have been defined as too primitive (segmentary and egalitarian) and the state as too modern too far back in time (Giddens, 1985:18).

The idea of kinship-based groups as an impediment to political organization, understood as state formation, often entails recommendations for political action. Since kinship-based groups such as the aristocracy and tribes are often considered problems, the state must reduce them either through political institutions or by military action. That idea is in turn connected to an understanding of the state as resting on coercion and a monopoly of the means of collective violence. If we instead recognize how political organization has been dependent on kinship-based elites and on notions of kinship as political legitimacy, then we arrive at an understanding of political order as also resting on collaboration and embedding.

A note on the relation between this chapter and subsequent ones is necessary before proceeding. Since ideas about politics are always part of a political context, some of the theories about the relation between kinship groups (and hereditary elites) and political order must be studied as part of their time. Hence, some of the political theories about an irreconcilable opposition between the nobility, the monarchy (as a kinship group) and the political order will be dealt with in the chapters on the early modern period (Chapter 5) and the nineteenth century (Chapter 6). The ideas of Adam Smith, Thomas Paine and John Steward Mill could have their place in this chapter – in order to illustrate how centuries of political opposition to hereditary power have accumulated in our time as a transhistorical 'given', however, these ideas also have their places in the aforementioned chapters below – as time-bound political projects. I will try to balance the two approaches by treating general traits of their works in this chapter and specific questions (such as Adam Smith's opposition to entail) in subsequent ones. This chapter also overlaps subsequent ones on the MENA societies. Chapter 7 will present a re-reading of the works of Ibn Khaldûn that stresses his emphasis on the interdependence between political order and monarchy (as a form of kinship). Chapter 10 touches upon the debates on the viability of Arab monarchies in the twentieth century.

This chapter has both a chronological and a thematic organization. It first deals with the separation between kinship and politics in early modern political theory and then moves on to modern anthropology and sociology. The final section is an overview of recent revisionist literature that moves away from the separation between kinship and politics. The chapter closes with a summary that unites the conceptual framework presented in Chapter 1 with the ideas of the critics and revisionists presented in this chapter. Together, they form the necessary toolkit for the empirical analysis.

Stages and Antagonisms in European Political Theory

The idea that mankind first lived in kinship-based societies and later moved on to living in states has old and deep roots (Carneiro, 1987). Plato was the first thinker to pit families against politics. He argued that the family had to be abolished if the good state was to flourish (Hirschmann, 2016). Aristotle sees families as integral to political order (Aristotle, 2013). Since the earliest stages of modern political philosophy, heavily influenced by natural law, families have been cast in opposition to the state. Many of the political philosophers who are now fundamental to modern political science were political adversaries of the nobility. However, their political agendas affected how they described their contemporary conditions.

Jean Bodin, who is sometimes credited with the first formulation of the sovereign state, regards, in Aristotelian fashion, a commonwealth as composed of many different families and indeed originated from the family. Still, it was critical that a sovereign was set to rule over them and intermediate political bodies with undivided authority (Bobbio, 1993). One of the most important debates in the sixteenth century concerned where sovereignty (*majestas*) resided (Eulau, 1941:649). Did it reside with the king or with other actors and corporations who often exercised rule over limited areas? As a means to supporting monarchical claims of sovereignty, Bodin argues that the sovereign prince had ceded the power of feudal lords to them (Bodin, 2010 [1576]:64).

The early modern republican tradition, which drew upon Aristotle, tended to view societies as ascending orders of corporations. Such corporations were nested in each other and ranged from families, over guilds and towns to kingdoms and beyond to the community of all mankind. Johannes Althusius argues in this tradition and claims that families are the original natural association and the relationship between the family is 'not one of opposition but rather of continuity, or development' (Bobbio, 1993:8). Thus, the state is the result of previous and lower forms of association but not its antithesis. In addition, the state is not an aggregation of individuals, but of families and can indeed be seen as a large family.

A century later, we find a very different stance in the thought of Thomas Hobbes. Hobbes' main works exhibit traits of both stage theories and of the idea that there is a principled antagonism between kinship-based groups and the political. The starting point of Hobbes' theory of the state is the contrast between the conditions people lived under in 'the state of nature' and how they lived when united in a political society, under the rule of a Leviathan. Hobbes regards the state of nature as a brutal condition of perpetual strife and want. But who inhabited the state of nature? Some interpreters have argued that individuals inhabited Hobbes' state of nature, but others have stressed the role of families in the state of nature (Schochet, 1967). In Chapter XVII of *Leviathan* Hobbes outlines an implicit stage theory *avant la lettre*: 'And in all places where men have lived in small families, to rob and spoil one another, it has been a trade, and so far from being reputed against the law of nature, that the greater spoils they gained, the greater was their honour ... ' (Hobbes, 2008:111). However, by subjugation through contract, to a common and absolute authority, this condition ceased.

Hobbes has been canonized as the first modern political philosopher (Strauss, 1952:xv; Skinner, 2002:368). This epithet is interesting since he began constructing the modern state as something divorced from and opposed to families; he was preoccupied with the idea of the family as a 'rival to the state' (Runciman, 2011:5–6) and claimed that the power of the state derived from individual subjects, a construction that bypassed families. In *Leviathan* he argues that although families have power, it must be subjected to and bound by the power of the state. Hobbes sees families, civil associations and the state as separate entities – not intertwined (Skinner, 2002:368). These three categories were not only ontologically distinct but also engaged in a struggle for the loyalty of individuals – a struggle that the state must win. This was an early statement of the idea of the autonomy of the state. Hobbes is agnostic as to the sources from which the ruler of the state derived his legitimacy, to him, a republican leader like Cromwell is just as legitimate as a monarch like James II (Haldén, 2012:280–303). Hobbes' understanding of the state is thus a direct attack on the idea that monarchs were invested with a particular kind of hereditary legitimacy.

The fundamental building blocks in Hobbes' political theory can be found in later works by writers as diverse as Spinoza, Locke, Pufendorff, Rousseau and Kant. All advance a natural law-informed rational theory of the state based on the idea of a state of nature (which can be peaceful or warlike), as the antithesis of natural man, the state as composed of individuals and the state as born through a social contract (Bobbio, 1993:1–4). By contrast the Aristotelian tradition, represented above by Bodin and Althusius, has a historical-sociological conception of the state based on the analysis of actual conditions. It regards the state as a complement of natural man, as social and organic and as founded on naturalistic relations, not contractual ones (Bobbio, 1993:9). In the Aristotelian tradition, the state does not stand free from other forms of associations but is intertwined with them and emanates from them.

Natural law theorists argued that domestic and political power do differ and ought to be kept distinct (Bobbio, 1993:15). Thus they severed the chain in which the family was the first link and the last was the state. Hobbes and Locke wanted to lay the foundations for a new kind of political legitimacy by arguing that political power is different from domestic power. By arguing that legitimate power is based on consent, expressed in contract, Hobbes, Locke and Rousseau claim that the power of family fathers (from monarchs down the social scale) is neither political nor legitimate. For Locke, a family is a temporary society but a political society is a permanent one (Bobbio, 1993:20). The following chapters will demonstrate how, in the case of monarchies, the royal family and the realm actually existed in symbiosis and nourished each other. It must be noted that the arguments of the natural law theorists were normative. They claimed that hereditary power ought not to be legitimate by saying that it is not. Since this political tradition has gone from a normative project to an analytical grid it is difficult for modern thinkers to recognize that orders where family power was or is political power are indeed political as well as legitimate. From within the natural law tradition, one must conclude that such orders – since they are not based on a separation of the kinds of power and the contract of free individuals – must be built on coercion alone. Hence undemocratic orders cannot be studied as orders of consent. This idea ignores the question that hierarchies can be supported by consent and that consent is necessary among the ruling elites in order to produce orders. We will return to both points in the empirical chapters.

The Separation Between Kinship and Politics in Anthropology

It was in the nineteenth century that stage theories of the origins of political order, often inspired by Darwin's theory of evolution, really flourished. Anthropology emerged as an independent discipline and ever since, kinship and lineage societies have been classical subjects. Several of the founding fathers of anthropology and sociology elaborated the idea of a principled and temporal division between kinship groups and states as distinct forms of sociopolitical organization – or, more distinctly put, of a pre-political and a political stage (Trautmann, 2008:217–30).

The most theoretically rigorous formulation came with Henry Sumner Maine's work *Ancient Law* (1861). Maine formulates what could be seen as an agenda for the study of kinship and thereby of the pre-history and history of political order. Maine's work attempts to trace the development of law and societies. His account expresses a number of ideas that would become very influential: the idea that kinship 'was more important to the working of simple societies than of complex ones, and that in the course of their development complex societies have substituted something else for kinship' (Trautmann, 2008:180). In other words, kinship belongs to pre-political societies, not to advanced political ones that had developed contract as the substitution for kinship and the foundation of law and politics.

Maine thus creates the basis for a conceptual distinction between kinship and states by positing a mutually exclusive and binary relation between 'status' and 'contract'. If a society operated on the basis of contracts among individuals, kinship was out of the equation and – conversely – if kinship was central to a society then it was not advanced. Like many nineteenth-century thinkers, Maine thinks that there is a movement through history where some societies were progressive and others were not, and that progression has a single definitive trajectory from an origin common to all societies and a single goal that was not everyone's to reach (Trautmann, 2008:180). As we shall see below, these ideas and teleological thinking more generally have profoundly affected the self-description of modernity and the study of the history of political organization.

Maine sees kinship as 'the central political fact of primitive society' (Mamdani, 2012:16). To Maine kinship is elastic and able to encompass other relations than blood relations. Ancient society was not a collection of individuals but of families and kinship was a kind of coupling mechanism that allowed new groups to be incorporated into society (Mamdani, 2012:16–18). These facts, claim Maine, held for ancient societies, but not for modern ones (Mamdani, 2012:22–3). Kinship was central to societies held together by status, not by contract. I will argue that in pointing to the central role of kinship in older societies, Maine is not far off the mark. He errs, however, in arguing that kinship served these functions only in very old or non-developed societies and that once contractual relations and more advanced forms of law were developed, kinship fell by the wayside. I will demonstrate that kinship was highly important in societies, or more precisely, political orders, until the nineteenth century. I will also show that it was overlaid by a number of formal and informal institutions, such as parliaments and the idea of a common polity as well as that, contrary to the claims of modernization theorists, the more institutions overlaid kinship relations and organizations, the stronger they became. Maine was right in his historiographical impulse but wrong in his views on social and political developments.

Maine was not without critics. Walter Bagehot argues that the early stages of social organization were in fact also political (Bagehot, 1875:24). Without using the terminology of modern sociology, Bagehot also expresses an understanding that embedding and integration, not simply coercion, were central to early forms of political life:

> [I]n early times the quantity of government is much more important than its quality. What you want is a comprehensive rule binding men together, making them do much the same things, telling them what to expect of each other – fashioning them alike, and keeping them so. What this rule is does not matter so much. A good rule is better than a bad one, but any rule is better than none. (Bagehot, 1875:25)

I will build upon this line of argumentation in the empirical chapters below. Finally, Bagehot also points to the key role of kings and nobility in early stages of polity formation: 'In the beginning of political life, as it were, kings were necessary and so were the "close oligarchy" as custodians of law and as the people who implemented it' (Bagehot, 1875:28, 30). As will become evident, their importance stretched far beyond the very beginnings.

In the nineteenth century the separation of kinship societies from state societies was reassuring since European societies, defined solely as states, were fitted with a suitably rational and modern certificate – which in turn provided modern nineteenth-century societies with a long and stable pedigree. This division rhymed well with notions of a fundamental division between primitive and civilized peoples that was steadily growing in importance in the nineteenth century. Mahmood Mamdani demonstrates that Henry Maine created a new form of colonial governmentality after the Great Rebellion in 1857. He did so through his theory of history and theory of law (Mamdani, 2012:6) that separated tribes from settlers, pre-modernity from modernity and kinship from politics. By drawing parallels between contemporary India and ancient Europe he imposes a modernist colonial perspective not only on the British colonies but also on Europe's past (Mamdani, 2012:14). The concept 'tribe' was created and shaped by the political project of the colonial state (Mamdani, 2012:45). Tribe was a way to designate all peoples that were deemed indigenous in origin in contrast to peoples designated as races who were deemed 'non-natives' (Mamdani, 2012:47, 74). 'Tribe' and races were governed under different codes of law.

Tribal people were not only seen as backwards but also as dangerous. The trope 'warlike peoples' was integral to the colonial projects in Africa, Asia and North America. The violent reactions to European intrusion caused anthropologists, missionaries and soldiers to brand resisting people as 'savages' (Bayly, 2004:436, 437ff). The more marginal and alien these were to settled Europeans, the more their savagery was emphasized. At the same time, the tribal label was coming more and more into vogue. Thus, in a conceptual perfect storm, resisters, tribes, savagery and bellicosity were lumped together. Tribal peoples were also seen as having their own distinctive type of war and for some Western thinkers this fact legitimated ignoring the laws of war when fighting tribesmen (Colby, 1927:283). Furthermore, it was believed that tribal peoples were not motivated rationally for war but psychologically, personally and socially. The idea of 'tribal warfare' proved to be long-lived. In the 1970s, Ada Bozeman claimed that 'traditional societies' had a positive view of warfare (Bozeman, 1976:18). In the 2000s Azar Gat and Francis Fukuyama both employed the construction of tribal warfare in their analyses of warfare and political order (Gat, 2006: Chapter 9; Fukuyama, 2012:74, 75). Military interventions and state-building in the Middle East and Central Asia have rekindled the question whether societies with pronounced kinship elements have specific way of war. Arguments that tribal peoples are essentially different in terms of military, political and social organization resurfaced in connection with the wars in Afghanistan, Iraq and Somalia (Shultz, 2009:4, 6, 262). Motifs like revenge, honour, blood feud, vendetta and vengeance have been commonly highlighted when discussing motivations for tribal violence (Kilcullen, 2009:227). However, substantial critique has been levelled against tribal warfare as a distinct category. Several authors claim that the warlike 'nature' of tribal peoples is actually a historical product of their warring with colonial intruders and shaped by the interaction of indigenous elements and exogenous factors (Ferguson and Whitehead, 1992:2–3; Kilcullen, 2009:232; Shultz, 2009:250). Porter describes the terms as a case of 'military orientalism' (Porter, 2013:68–71).

A distinction between kinship and politics continued in twentieth-century anthropology and is visible in the classic works of Evans-Pritchard, Fortes and Radcliffe-Brown (Kuper, 1982:86; Fortes and Evans-Pritchard, 1987; Barnard, 2000:62–3). In their studies of the Ashanti, Fortes and Evans-Pritchard note a tension in society between influences from a 'domestic' or private sphere, and a 'politico-jural' or public sphere (Fortes and Evans-Pritchard, 1987). The distinction was clearly influenced by the natural law theorists reviewed above. Evans-Pritchard's later claimed that the clan model of organization was the greatest impediment to political development. Kinship studies were swallowed up by lineage theory which became the mainstay of anthropological research which often essentialized lineage societies in the belief that their structures determined the thoughts and actions of individuals and groups. Handbooks of kinship studies taught students an elaborate grammar of kinship, replete with terminology for coding different kinds of relationship and techniques for drawing charts and diagrams. Today research stresses the fluid, multifaceted and malleable nature of kinship groups (Kuper, 1982:79; Peletz, 1995:343–72; Barnard, 2000:62–3; Sahlins, 2011a, 2011b). The tendency to use the terminology of kinship/lineage theory ahistorically and acontextually is also largely discredited. However, the view of kinship groups as obstacles to development continued to be deeply embedded in modern thought (Kuper, 1982:82). After 1945, 'development' of the Third World became a political programme across all Western societies as well as a scholarly field of its own. However, there were important continuities with earlier thought. Early political scientists viewed tribal societies as a problem and assumed that traditional and modern societies were incompatible (Inkeles, 1975:25; Al-Haj, 1995:311). However, around the mid-twentieth century modernist social scientists abandoned the claim that the tribal other was eternal and immutable. Instead they adopted a teleological view of the predetermined development of the modern state and of democracy. Consequently, the onset of modernization dissolved kinship groups and created modern, democratic nation states (Rostow, 1960; Collins, 2004:229).

This version of modernity built upon the ideas of natural law theorists like Hobbes, Locke and Rousseau who claim that individuals were the building blocks of society. A modern society was associated with free and rational individuals capable of exercising their own agency. The ideal type of the kinship group as a collective dominating the individual serves as a polar opposite of the ideal type of the rational individual (Wagner, 2001:43). Indeed the idea of the inflexible and fettering kin as a feature of traditional societies serves to underpin one of the chief postulates of modernization theory, that of a principled, binary distinction between traditional and modern societies. As Latour points out, traditional and modern societies are often subject to a process of conceptual purification that keeps them apart and distinct (Latour, 1993). One example is Max Weber's juxtaposition of traditional and rational-legal authority (Weber, 1978:215–41). As Wittrock demonstrates we see that this contention is highly problematic when we study contemporary societies outside the Western ambit as well as when we recognize the dynamic nature of societies in history (Wittrock, 2002:39). Other binary dichotomies have also played a part in the exclusion of kinship groups. One reason why kinship groups often fall outside the purview of political science investigations is that they seem to belong to 'society' that is juxtaposed to 'the state'. From another perspective, they seem to belong to the 'private' rather than to the 'public' sphere and are thus neither factually nor normatively part of the business of rule.

Classical modernization theory presupposed that societies would conform to a simple model as they entered into modernity. Indeed, modernity consisted of a single model of state-society relations, moulded on the United States. When a society entered into modernity it was assumed that traditional forms of power and social life would be broken and abandoned (Eisenstadt, 2002:5). Several scholars claim that the main postulates of 1950s functionalist modernization theory have largely been discredited (Bernstein, 1971; Glenn, 1997:45–63). However, the main ideas of modernization theory were resurrected in the early 1990s and became central to the intellectual and political projects of post-Cold War state-building and international social engineering (Gilman, 2003). Societies in which kinship plays a major organizing role once again came into focus for policymakers, policy advisors and scholars. In the widely read works of Robert Kaplan and Samuel Huntington kinship-based groups are portrayed as a threatening factor that explains war and state collapse (Huntington, 1996; Kaplan, 2000).[1] Thus, classical anthropology was based on a clear distinction between kinship and politics as ordering principles of society. Although the rigid models of previous kinship studies have been abandoned, kinship has still not been studied as a positive element in the formation of political order.

The Separation Between Kinship and Politics in Sociology

When sociology was established, the idea of a distinct kinship stage and a distinct political stage had set down strong roots. It can be found in the works of Marx, Durkheim and Weber. Marxist theory and historiography is centred on a stage theory of economic, political and social development from feudalism to capitalism to communism. That Marx and Engels were critics of the nobility and saw it as a force that held back the course of history is of course well known. It also became a standard idea in Marxist historical sociology (Anderson, 1974:43). A stage theory that explicitly singles out kinship is found in Friedrich Engels' *The Origins of the Family, Private Property and the State*, which laid the groundwork for much of Marxist theories on the family (Engels, 1985). Inspired by Morgan, Engels describes how a kinship-based order, which he calls a 'gentile constitution', first existed among the ancient Germans, Greeks and Romans. Gradually this mode of organization was initially partly replaced and 'then at last superseded entirely by real state authorities' in all three peoples (Engels, 1985:142).

Durkheim reinforces the idea of a fundamental distinction between lineage societies and states in *The Division of Labour*

---

[1] For a critique see Besteman, 2005.

(Durkheim, 1966). Although the clan organization is a politico-familiar form of organization, advanced societies based on a division of labour and organic solidarity rather than kinship and ancestry are fundamentally different to the 'preceding type' (Durkheim, 1966:128). In line with stage theory the earlier, kinship-based, mode must vanish in order for the more advanced one to develop (Durkheim, 1966:133). Drawing upon history, Durkheim claims that in the early Middle Ages in Europe, any kind of clan organization had disappeared.

An interest in analysing social evolution also characterizes Max Weber's historical sociology. Although stage-theoretical ideas are to be found in his writings, his conceptual vocabulary nevertheless provides the tools to transcend them. Weber recognizes the importance of hereditary rule as a category. He coined a term that is usually translated as 'clan state'. A more precise translation would, however, have been 'kindred state'.

> The term 'clan state' [*Geschlechterstaat*] will be applied when a political body is strictly and completely organized in terms of this principle of hereditary charisma. In such a case, all appropriation of governing powers, of fiefs, of benefices, and all sorts of economics advantages follow the same pattern. (Weber, 1978:250)

The term is not divorced from political order. However, by including the requirement that hereditary charisma is the only organizing principle Weber performs what could be called an act of purification that separated this form of rule from the state (Weber, 1978:226). Still, if this requirement is loosened we are provided with an interesting heuristic tool. The examples that he gives are the Indian caste system and China, Japan and Russia before the introduction of bureaucracy. However, Weber links the term to societies that are organized on the basis of hereditary privilege: 'Indeed, all hereditary social classes with established privileges belong in the same category' (Weber, 1978:250). This formulation opens up for comparative study of hereditary rule.

Weber saw history as a movement through time. He claims that the relation between 'the Chief' (*Der Herr*, the Lord) and his 'administrative staff' as central to all advanced forms of sociopolitical organization. This dynamic relation changes the whole sociopolitical configuration and, in Weber's neo-Hegelian phrase, 'drives history forward'. Of particular importance for this book is that he portrays the struggle between on the one hand the monarch and their staff and 'the feudal classes or other groups that enjoy appropriated power' as central to European history (Weber, 1978:264). Thereby, both the idea of a movement through history and the idea of the nobility as usurpers found their way into Weber's thought.

Many works on state formation theory have been influenced implicitly or explicitly by the ideas of modernization that have been deeply inscribed in the social sciences. The movement towards modernization (as classically conceived) has been projected backwards into history as state formation scholars from Weber onwards have tried to trace the particular elements of the classic configuration of modernity (an autonomous state, rationalization, etc.) (Møller, 2012). Historical-sociological theories of state formation have generally aligned themselves with the discourse of hereditary elites as a problem for the state. A common theme is a narrative whereby the princely state, often in alliance with the emerging bourgeoisie, breaks the particularistic influence of the aristocratic lineage groups in order to pave the way for consolidation and expansion of the state. Norbert Elias claims that state formation proceeded through the marginalization of the medieval nobility. One component was military conquests, as the French kings tore down the castles of the seigneurs and subjected them to royal control. When their military independence vanished, they were also spent as a political force (Elias, 2000). Elias' story ends with the nobility being reduced to social butterflies flitting about their Sun King in the playground of Versailles. As we shall see in Chapter 5 this was not the case.

In his discussion of pre-industrial societies (agro-literary societies) Ernest Gellner stresses that most elite groups have been hereditary. Agro-literate societies were dominated by elites 'whose chief distinguishing attributes are the management of violence, the maintenance of order, and the control of the official wisdom of the society, which is eventually enshrined in script' (Gellner, 2008:14). However, Gellner also argues that elites pose problems for the state because of their connections to particular and particularistic kinship groups. Hence the state has to break the kinship bond through 'gelding' hereditary elites This term includes methods that aim to transform members of elite groups (mostly men) into dependants of the state, such as the imposition of celibacy, the employment of eunuchs or of slaves. Gellner notes that 'gelding' was neither dominant nor complete anywhere. In fact, the Chinese bureaucracy was recruited from a hereditary gentry and the European nobility succeeded in making the principle of heredity and descent foundations of social order (and thus of social power). In contrast to the gelded elites, 'elites who are formally allowed to reproduce themselves socially, and to retain their positions for their offspring, are called *stallions*' (Gellner, 2008:16). These stallions were far more common than the geldings and it is their history that we need to explore. Andrew Cowell has argued that warrior aristocracies have been cast 'too often the last historical "other" before the birth of "modernity" . . .' (Cowell, 2007:174–5). The emphasis on controlling or breaking these aristocracies as a precondition of state formation in modern sociology certainly matches Cowell's argument. I will show below that they in fact were important forces in the formation of political order.

Charles Tilly, the most influential scholar of modern state formation theory, defines states as 'coercion-wielding authorities that are distinct from households and lineage groups and exercise clear priority in some respects over all other organizations within substantial territories' (Tilly, 1990:1). This definition rests upon an implicit stage theory that contains two components, lineage groups and states. If the state is a category applicable to all forms of rule existing between lineage societies without any other form of organization and the twentieth century, then it is far too broad and – to echo Giddens critique of Weber's definition of the state – projects the modern state too far back in time (Giddens, 1985:18). Conversely, divorcing lineage groups from states makes the latter far too primitive. Runciman separates states and kinship even more explicitly by claiming that a precondition of the state is 'emancipation from real or fictive kinship as the basis of relations between the occupants of governmental roles and those whom they govern' (Runciman, 1982:351). The one central component in the conceptual dichotomy is that kinship groups are egalitarian while states are hierarchical. Transcendence of the tribe has been pointed out as a crucial moment in the emergence of politics. Relating the shift from kinship-based societies consisting of tribes and clans to states is a fundamental part of the study of 'pristine state formation'. This field investigates when and how states first came into being in Egypt, China, Mesopotamia, Greece or in Europe of the Dark Ages (Mann, 1993:67–70, 196–7). Christian Meier and Per Jansson claim that politics emerged in ancient Athens when its elites began to see themselves as part of a greater polity that transcended their tribal particularities (Meier, 1980; Jansson, 1997). John A. Hall echoes this point by arguing that the weakness of kinship in Europe paved the way for a more cohesive, tight-knit state (Hall, 1986:132).

In Michael Mann's magisterial work we find combinations of the conceptual separation of kinship and states with traces of a stage theory of political development. An oft-cited scheme consists of four stages: bands (e.g., hunter-gatherers), tribes, chieftaincies and finally states (Mann, 1993:42–4, 61–2). Michael Mann outlines the image of an egalitarian pre-state past by beginning his inquiry with the question: 'How do the people lose control?' He further adds that 'Between rank and stratified societies, and between political authority and the coercive state, is an unexplained void' (Mann, 1986:62). Hence alongside the conceptual separation is the idea of a temporal separation between societies organized exclusively or mainly on the basis of kinship and those organized like states.

Since the nineteenth century, scholars, politicians and the general public have been very interested in why European societies, later redefined as 'Western', came to assume their distinctive form and why they came to achieve a position of global dominance. In the early twentieth century, this interest has been re-kindled. In some of the recent literature, we see the very old ideas of stage theories and in particular the separation of kinship from statehood resurfacing. Francis Fukuyama fuses stage-theories of classical anthropology and the state formation literature of historical sociology. A cornerstone in his account is how some societies left the kinship stage and developed hierarchical polities. Fukuyama aligns himself with this tradition of thought by stating that:

> Once the state comes into being, kinship becomes an obstacle to political development since it threatens to return political relationships to the small-scale, personal ties of tribal societies. It is therefore not enough merely to develop a state; the state must avoid retribalization or what I label repatrimonialization. (Fukuyama, 2012:81)

Following Elman Service, Fukuyama defines bands and tribes as structured on the basis of kinship and as egalitarian forms of organization. In contrast, chiefdoms and states 'are hierarchically organized, exert authority on a territorial rather than kinship basis' (Fukuyama, 2012:53). Furthermore, some of the current literature on tribes and

clans in relation to war and social development suffers from historical
and typological shortcomings. In much of the literature are examples of
prehistoric, medieval and contemporary tribes and clans often mixed
and generalized to support arguments of the authors (Keeley, 1997; Gat,
2006; Fukuyama, 2012). For example, Fukuyama argues that all people
originally organized themselves in tribal societies. He highlights that the
Celts, Romans, Teutons, Indians and Chinese were historically organized in tribal societies similar to the ones existing in contemporary
Afghanistan, central Iraq and Papua New Guinea (Fukuyama,
2012:15).

Relations between kinship groups, often understood as tribes,
and states have been the mainstay of studies of Middle Eastern and
Central Asian societies (Tapper, 1983; Lindholm, 1986; Khoury and
Kostiner, 1991). Contemporary scholarship on Middle Eastern polity
formation often takes a nuanced view of the interaction between tribes
and states. Patricia Crone argues that relations between states and tribes
in the Middle East have been one of a long period of co-existence and
mutual influence (Crone, 1993:366, 370). She also argues that the
'modern state intensifies the dichotomy between the tribe and the
state, however, by demanding actual integration where traditional
states were satisfied by mere submission' (Crone, 1993:372). Still,
Richard Tapper has criticized Crone's earlier understanding of tribes
(Crone, 1986). Tapper claims that 'tribe … is rather a state of mind,
a construction of reality, a model for organization and action' (Tapper,
1990:56). Consequently, a stable terminology that pinpoints a clear-cut
order of either segmentary or hierarchical systems is not possible to
create (Tapper, 1990:55). It is also not possible to ascribe to tribes and
states, like Crone did in a previous work, 'a purity of organization that is
never found' (Tapper, 1990:64). Tapper argues that the commonly
accepted notion that tribal groups in Afghanistan and Iran are incompatible with the state is incorrect. Before the twentieth century, tribal
groups had created and supported several dynasties (Tapper, 2011:4).
Similarly, Samira Haj argues that Western researchers have imposed an
artificial distinction between tribes and governments on Iraqi society
(Haj, 1991:46).

The three great traditions of political theory, anthropology
and sociology have, to various degrees, been strongly influenced by –
perhaps even based on – the idea of a separation and irreconcilable
difference between kinship and families from political orders. Each

tradition has wielded influence on its own but there are also traces of cross-fertilization between the traditions and of joint influence. As I noted in the introduction to this chapter, the trend is not uniform but the thinkers who have argued that families, kindreds and other forms of kinship groups are a part of political order are in the minority or represent largely forgotten alternatives. The influence of the idea of the separation of kinship from politics is not difficult to explain. Most of the canonical political philosophers, anthropologists and sociologists have in one form or the other signed up to it.

The historiographical, conceptual and typological separations between kinship – defined as certain groups, strata or as an organizing principle – and states are interdependent with central themes of classical theories of modernity. This interdependence takes the form of co-constitution: the separation of kinship and states depends on modernist themes and these modernist themes are nourished by the separation between kinship and states in the historiography of political organization. Indeed, kinship, monarchies, warrior aristocracies, tribes and clans – resting their claims on what Weber called 'hereditary charisma' – seem to function as 'others' of modernity. To study kinship and states as symbiotic and not opposed entities forces us to move beyond classical theories of modernity. This move is not only significant for the historical-empirical task that is central to this book but also more generally for social and political theory. Where and how does one start such a task? Fortunately, other scholars have recently embarked on similar projects.

The Revision: Aristocratic Orders as Political Orders

Recently, some state formation theorists have begun to recognize that political orders and kinship-based elites were in fact intertwined and that the latter contributed to the development of the former (Gorski and Sharma, 2017). In a series of works Francis Oakely has charted the history of kingship – the principal form of political kinship – in Europe, the near East and Asia. He argues, and demonstrates, that rule by sacred kindreds has been the norm, not the exception, throughout most of human history (Oakley, 2006, 2010, 2015). David Graeber and Marshal Sahlins argue that since kingship is close to a universal form of governance, 'any theory of political life' must take it into account (Graeber and Sahlins, 2017:1–2). They set out to formulate the basic elements of a theory of kingship as a central aspect of the cosmic polities into which human societies are organized. Their cases are mostly drawn from outside Europe, which means that they come close to but not entirely succeed in deconstructing the canonical material of (European) political thought and history.

David Sneath argues that contrary to widespread belief the societies of nomadic inner Asia were not based on segmentary or egalitarian kinship but on aristocratic rule (Sneath, 2007). Central and Inner Asian societies are usually described as clan or tribal societies. Sneath demonstrates that they are better understood as states with strong aristocratic elements. Mongolian and Turkic societies were stratified according to a division between nobles and non-nobles and Sneath shows that the terms used to describe European polities, such as state, prince and aristocracy, are fully applicable to Inner Asian societies. The latter were regulated by codes of law and controlled by powerful aristocracies. Sneath's critique of scholarship on Inner Asia suggests a general critique of both anthropological research on kinship groups and sociological research on the state and state formation. He shows that the image of tribes and clans as egalitarian, primitive and segmentary and the state as hierarchical is a myth. Instead, many societies that have been regularly branded with the 'tribal' level were in fact hierarchical and complex and were led by aristocratic families (Sneath, 2009:165).

Sneath argues that the state precedes kinship as a form of organization in several societies. Rather than seeing kinship as an apolitical and natural form of organization, he claims that organization according to kinship is a construction that has served as a way to exercise power and he proposes that we should consider aristocracy as the primary form of social organization and state as a secondary one. He develops the concept of 'aristocratic order' which he sees 'as an inclusive category . . . to indicate societies that are shaped in fundamental ways by the power relations of hereditary rule' (Sneath, 2007:202).

Over the past decades, research into African polity formation has advanced significantly beyond the narrow confines of the colonial conceptual vocabulary. For example, the work of Yusuf Bala Usman has deconstructed concepts like 'traditional societies' and instead devised conceptual frameworks to capture the specific characteristics of African polity formation. Abdullahi Smith has followed in his tracks and broken with the colonial theories of kinship handed down by Henry Maine. However, this new historiography has not so much abandoned kinship as redefined it as a political association that was 'porous and historical, rather than closed and unchanging' (Mamdani, 2012:104). The colonial conceptual vocabulary still remains in place in studies of polity formation in Europe and in the Middle East. It has meant that modernization theorists have directed a colonizing and denigrating gaze towards Europe's past. Traits that have been identified as alien to modernity's self-image have been ignored or portrayed as obstacles. Conversely, traits that in retrospect could be identified as modern have been elevated and praised. Inspired by the postcolonial reinterpretations of central Asian and African polity formation I will embark on a similar, perhaps also in a way postcolonial, reinterpretation of European polity formation over the next four chapters. That understanding will then help to produce a new understanding of polity formation in the Middle East and Central Asia over the subsequent four chapters.

There is plenty of equipment to choose from when assembling the necessary kit for the road ahead. Sneath's concept of aristocratic orders allows us to adapt Maine's suggestion of the importance of kinship in early orders and Weber's idea of a kindred state beyond the earliest phases of history well into recent history. Identifying the ideological intent behind the elements that form the canonical conception of modernity with the help of Bobbio's genealogy of natural law philosophy and Mamdani's and Latour's analyses reverses the process whereby these elements grew into a taken-for-granted analytical framework. Once dismantled, we can construct a historical narrative of political order from distant to recent times. In a way it resurrects the historical-sociological programme of Althusius and Montesquieu and reinforces it with the elements chiselled out in Chapter 1: the systems theory concept of political order and a constructivist understanding of kinship. Bagehot and Shils' 'soft functionalism' gels with the emphasis on embedding in modern systems theory. Thus equipped, the journey through time can now commence in Chapter 3 with the early Middle Ages in Europe.

3 FORMLESS KINSHIP IN FORMLESS POLITIES
Europe *c.*400–*c.*1000

Introduction

This chapter deals with the period between the beginning of the Germanic migrations and the year 1000. I will be asking if kinship in the shape of organized groups and legitimating principles was integral to the political order. I will also analyse the conflicts that took place between kinship-based elites and the central organizations of the political order.

During the early Middle Ages, polities were formed in Europe. Naturally, their form, content or purpose did not correspond to the ideal type of the state. There was no monopoly of violence, institutionalization was very rudimentary by modern standards and the self-description was very different. However, these polities were not the loose kinship structures suggested by state formation theories. Anthropologists use the term 'chiefdom' to describe a sedentary pre-state formation led by a chiefly lineage that organized the population into warriors and non-warriors (Malešević, 2010:255ff). Chiefs led the formation in war, decided alliances and distributed surplus and plunder. This term is appropriate for Germanic formations between, say, the second century BC and second century AD. However, contact with the Romans quickly changed these formations. From the fifth and sixth centuries more elaborate polities emerged in West and East Francia (the precursors of France and Germany) and in England. Susan Reynolds has coined the term 'regnal polities' or 'regnal communities' to describe this kind of political order (Reynolds, 1984). I choose to call them 'realms'; formations that had their own semantics of legitimacy, a personality separate from rulers and ruled, a form of publicness in the shape of assemblies, titles and offices and ways to define the public interest and duties (Haldén, 2017a). This chapter mainly deals with realms and how kinship structures permeated them.

The institution of kingship also integrated different elite formations into a common network. Kings were sacred figures who possessed a connection to the transcendent foundations of authority (Kalyvas, 2002) and aristocrats needed to be close to kings in order to share in their authority and charisma. Kings were patrons who distributed land and offices and thus necessary figures in the networks of power, but in order to fully grasp their significance for social integration and thus for political order we have to recognize their role in distributing authority in a metaphysical way. Finally, kingship rested on kinship. Even societies where kings were elected by notables or had to earn their standing by proving themselves in battle emphasized that kings should come from a king-like lineage in order to be 'eligible' for office (Mitteis, 1944). The idea that there is a conflict between groups organized as kindreds and the political order, or the king, is also incorrect for this period.

The attraction of a public sphere and of the worldly and transcendent power of kings does not mean that we can view early medieval politics as centralized or dominated by a centre. Instead, elite families possessed considerable influence and power, including military power, that kings depended upon. Without the support of powerful aristocratic families, even a strong ruler like Charlemagne could accomplish little. The rule of kings was mediated and negotiated power-projection, working best when it created consensus and win-win situations, thus neither kings nor nobilities could dominate or even function without the other.

Both kinship groups and polities were amorphous at this time; neither was formalized to the degree that they would be in later periods of European history. The relatively low degree of formalization applies to institutions as well as to semantics. The conception of the realm and the king was the first to begin to be formalized and aristocratic kinship structures followed soon after. However, the survival of the political order depended on the degree to which aristocrats were embedded into it and supported it. In turn, these aristocratic families depended upon the realm for their legitimacy. Thus, kinship organizations and principles were joined from the start in post-Roman Europe.

I will focus on kinship in the political order of the Franks and Saxons during the Merovingian and Carolingian periods, with occasional forays into the Anglo-Saxon and Lombard realms. The rest of the chapter is organized as follows: first, I discuss the kinship societies of the early Germanic peoples, then I analyse the Merovingian period, then the Carolingian followed by the post-Carolingian period (c.850–1000). Some themes criss-cross the chronological sections. Thereafter two thematic sections follow: one on the nature of kingship and then another on kinship and war, and a summary of the chapter.

The Migration Period

During the third century AD, Germanic peoples began migrating into the Roman Empire. The newcomers established new realms, some of which proved to be short-lived, others more robust. Regardless of longevity, during this time practices and ideas of political organization were established that would set the pattern for political interaction and for the position of powerful kinship groups within figurations of abstract rule. In Spain the Visigoths established a kingdom. In Italy first the Ostrogoths and then the Lombards created polities. In what are now Belgium, France, the Netherlands and Western Germany the Franks created a number of linked kingdoms. East of the Rhine a series of small polities were formed around the Bavarians, Allemanni and Thuringians. They were independent until the sixth century when the Franks conquered them. In England, the Anglo-Saxons founded six kingdoms – Northumbria, Mercia, East Anglia, Essex, Kent, Sussex and Wessex.

Kin was a primary factor of all early medieval societies. However, 'kin' was not a closed category and that the people to which one had to be loyal or generous was not a recognized 'unit'. The oldest Germanic heroic poem *The Lay of Hildebrand*, written in the eighth century but building on material from the fifth, offers a telling example. Two warriors, Hildebrand and Hadubrand, meet on a battlefield. 'Hildebrand, the older and more experienced man, spoke first, asking, with few words who his father was and from which family he came. "Tell me the one, young man, and I'll know the other, for I know all great people in this kingdom"'. They realize that they are father and son. Shocked, Hildebrand says: 'With Almighty God in Heaven for a witness, may you never go to battle against your next of kin' and tries to make peace with his son. However, Hadubrand spurns his father who deserted him when he was a boy, and seeing that his father is a great warrior he attacks. The end is unknown, but most interpreters agree that the father kills his son.[1]

The lay is highly telling: a man would introduce himself with his kinship group (*Folche*). Also, the idea of kinslaying was abhorrent to the society that produced the poem. Germanic lays were often tragic and so is this one, not only do father and son fight but by slaying his son, the father extinguishes his line. Although tragic and contrary to the ideals of the society, such events were known and probably resonated strongly with its audience. We see other motivations than kinship loyalty at work. A modern interpreter might stress the anger of the abandoned son but the medieval text emphasizes the handsome chain mail, wealth and great reputation of Hildebrand; all of which spur Hadubrand to fight in order to win fame and fortune. Thus ambitions could trump kinship loyalty (Gentry, 1975:11).

Kinship was central in law codes from this period. The law of the Salian Franks stated that an individual was unprotected if he did not belong to a recognized lineage. As among all Germanic peoples, a man needed the help of relatives to bring anyone who had offended against him to court and to act as his witnesses (Drew, 1988:2–3). If a man was killed half of his compensation money (*Weregild*) went to his children and the other half was divided between his father's and his mother's kin group (Drew, 1988:2–3). Kinship was a reciprocal relation of rights and duties. One was also obliged to help penniless kinsmen to pay their debts and compensation money. Kinsmen up to the sixth degree could be called upon to help with debt payments (Drew, 1988:3). According to the law codes, only blood relatives (not relatives by marriage) were obliged to aid kinsmen. This restriction was an important limitation in the creation of alliances and large kin groups. Still, kin groups could exclude transgressing members and include new ones. Women's property rights worked against the building of large, consolidated kinship groups. A woman owned her own dowry, consisting of gifts from her husband and her father, and her husband could not alienate it (Drew, 1988:5–6). Normally her children inherited her property upon her death, even if her husband was alive. Women could also inherit property and own this independently

---

[1] *The Lay of Hildebrand*, www.pitt.edu/~dash/hildebrand.html (accessed 7 January 2017).

of their husbands. The law code stated that females were banned from inheriting Salic land, in other words family land, not allodial land, which both men and women could inherit (Drew, 1991:44). Normally, family land was not alienable among Germanic peoples, instead it had to stay within the family. If there were no children that could inherit a piece of land, then it passed to the mother and father, failing that to brothers and sisters, next to the father's sisters, to the mother's sister's and finally to the father's relatives (to the sixth degree). The property and inheritance rights of women were strong among all Germanic peoples, but particularly among the Franks (Drew, 1991:42–3). However, we must be wary of interpreting the law codes as a direct picture of society. Alliances with the kinsmen of one's wife could be of great strategic use against one's own kinsmen.

Early Germanic tribes were once seen as solid units – or kinship-states (*Sippenstaaten*) – bound by a rock-solid constitutional feature to aid each other in times of feud, especially to avenge wrongdoings against members of the extended network. However, kinship groups during Germanic prehistory were fundamentally unstable and dynamic groups (Wenskus, 1961; Wolfram, 2006b:43–66). Despite the image of the clan as a tight-knit and robust unit of identity and action (a notion inherited from Greek and Roman ethnographers), Germanic kindreds tended to fragment, be absorbed into larger kindred groups or absorb other kindreds with considerable frequency and ease. The malleable and mutable nature of kinship-based groups may also explain the ability of Germanic and Celtic peoples to form large alliances that encompassed many different kinship groups or even what we today would call ethnic or linguistic communities. The names of several of the most important groups – which we in retrospect have categorized as tribes or even peoples, thus equating them with the two modern ideal types of tight-knit communities connected by mechanical solidarity or *Gemeinschaft*-ties, the clan and the nation – betray their origins as pragmatic unions: Franks meant 'the honest ones' and the Allemani, 'all men' (Geary, 1988:53). As Geary notes, 'throughout the tribal history of the Germanic peoples, these groups were more processes than stable structures, and ethnogenesis, or tribal formation was constant, although certain historical moments saw this process accelerated' (Geary, 1988:53). Bazelmans notes that Germanic tribes were corporate or regional groups 'which recruited their members on the basis of kinship and residence in the same geographical area' (Bazelmans, 1999:3ff). Its members were also members of cognatic kinship groups that were principally open in nature.

Although obligation to help kinsmen was central, the definition of the kin-group was elastic. In times of feud, when you needed as many allies as possible, protagonists usually tried to use as wide a definition of kinship as possible in order to mobilize people who were obliged to join the feud (Wickham, 2009). In matters of inheritance, however, kinship was often defined as the most immediate family (Fouracre, 2002:18). During this period we are looking at kinship systems in the sense that 'kin' was a mutually intelligible unit of communication and a category that created meaning. Kin-groups were also not strictly defined units. Instead, they were fluid and amorphous and so was the political order. As will be discussed, the most important institution was the annual assembly and royal elections which were rare. Thus kin-groups and the political order were both loosely formed and weakly institutionalized. Later, both parts of the equation would become more firmly defined and institutionalized.

Some social scientists portray the 'barbarian' societies of the migration period as lineage societies (e.g., Fukuyama, 2012). These were certainly societies in which kinship played a paramount role, but they were not egalitarian. Celtic, Germanic and Slav societies were stratified and they distinguished between free men and slaves and had proto-nobilities and a royal family at the social apex (Fleckenstein, 1979:12; James, 1988:83). The Roman author Tacitus claims that the Germanic peoples elected their kings but the eligible were drawn from a privileged stratum of society (Tacitus, 2005:31). Even among the dynamic, socially flexible and polyethnic Goths, the royal lineages such as the Amal clan played a crucial role (Wolfram, 2006a:51–2; Wolfram, 2006b:82). Archaeological findings from the early Middle Ages demonstrate stratified societies. Bodies found in elite tombs were richly decorated and equipped with costly status items such as weapons, drinking vessels and products from the Mediterranean area. The burial sites of Sutton Hoo in East Anglia and Vendel close to Uppsala in Sweden are perhaps the most famous examples (Carver, 1992; Ljungkvist, 2005; Klevnäs, 2015). The practice of building burial mounds for 'high status' individuals, is attested from the early fourth century (Hamerow, 2005:272). Later law codes also attest to social stratification, for example the compensation money (*Weregild*) depended on the social rank of a victim.

Although many innovations were created once the kingdoms of the Anglo-Saxons, Franks, Goths and Lombards were established, three traits from the migration period would remain important: (1) Roman models were central; (2) kinship was important but kinship groups elastic and open to interpretation; and (3) the societies were stratified and stratification built to a large extent on descent, but stratification was not institutionalized.

The Merovingian Period

The Frankish polity became the most important of the post-Roman kingdoms. In the eighth and ninth centuries it dominated what is now France, Western Germany, Italy and Catalonia and influenced Denmark, Southern England and the Czech lands. However, the history of united Francia begins with Clovis (481–511) who conquered the rival Frankish kingdoms, subdued non-Frankish warlords and conquered Aquitania, all of which united most of the former Roman province of Gaul. By the middle of the sixth century, Frankish rule was established in the Burgundian kingdom and the Bavarian as well as, in a looser form, in northern Italy and Thuringia in what is now central Germany (Wickham, 2009:113). The kingdom of the Franks consisted of three kingdoms: Austrasia, Neustria and Burgundy. The dynasty that Clovis founded was called the Merovingian and it ruled Gaul until 751 when a new dynasty, the Carolingians, seized power. The Carolingian dynasty in turn ruled until the mid-tenth century. The Carolingian era was characterized by foreign conquest, institution-building, and by moral reform. Three generations of Carolingian kings conquered Saxony, Lombard Italy and Bavaria.

Clovis' rise to power contains several details that illuminate the connections between kinship and rule. First, a crucial move was Clovis' conversion to Christianity that won him the support of the Church (whose administrative capabilities were invaluable), the Emperor in Constantinople (who was a great power in terms of legitimacy and military capabilities) and the support of the Gallo-Roman aristocracies of the country (Geary, 1988:86). It was crucial to gain the support of the dominant Frankish families and of the Roman ones that were the dominant landholders in command of local communities (Geary, 1988:93). Conversion thus enabled the Franks to 'tap' the Roman heritage of administration that had passed into the hands of the aristocracy and the Church. Religious unity enabled Clovis and his successors to create a synthesis of Frankish and Roman elements, or at least make them work in synergy to create stability and continuity over time. This possibility was an asset that Gothic and Hunnic conquerors did not possess, which made their polities unstable and eventually unable to survive (Wood, 1994:44). When Clovis, in alliance with the Byzantines, defeated the Visigoths the Emperor Anastasius appointed him honorary consul and symbolically adopted him into the imperial family; an act that strengthened his authority with the Gallo-Roman nobility. Thus we can conclude that the nobility was a crucial element for a ruler who wanted to establish a political order. But what did this nobility look like?

Early medieval societies did not have a formalized noble stratum. This is evident when we study the semantics of early medieval polities. Early medieval law codes do not mention an aristocracy as a fixed legal category. A common distinction was between completely free, partially free and completely unfree individuals. Law texts from the Merovingian period differ greatly as to whether they mention the nobility. The *Lex Salica* (*c.*507–11) did not. Other early medieval legal texts did. The *Law of the Burgundians* distinguished between unfree and free, who were further subdivided into *optimates* (*nobiles, procures*), *mediocre personae* and *minors* (*inferiors personae, leudes*) (Drew, 1972: 23–4, 85–6). Similarly, the categories of the Lombard laws were freemen, semi-free (*aldi*) and slaves (Drew, 1952:68). There was a lack of a distinct legal and social category of nobility but the laws of King Liutprand mentions groups of people referred to as *fideles, iudices* (magistrates), *optimates* or *nobiles*, who together with the king issued the laws (Drew, 1973:39, 131, 215) in what was clearly a loose noble stratum. The seventh century Law of the Alamannians had similar threefold divisions of free, half-free and unfree. The free were subject to a further tripartite division of *primi Alamanni, median* and *minofledi*. Similarly the law of the Bavarians from the early eighth century distinguished between *liber, frilaz* and *servus* (Hechberger, 2004:9). However, the laws of King Aethelberht of Kent in the early seventh century mention 'nobles (*eorlas*), freemen (*ceorls*), unfree peasants and slaves' as the subjects of the king (Hamerow, 2005:283). Hierarchy is manifested in the differences in compensation (*Weregild*) that had to be paid for committing crimes against different categories of people. In the Salic law the main categories are Franks and non-Franks, freemen and non-free, men and women (Fischer, 1991:45–9). Similarily, Lombard sources make obscure references to social distinction using adjectives like *devotus* and *magnificus* but it is clear that – as Wickham says – 'the precision of titles of the late Roman state and its various aristocratic hierarchies had now disappeared' (Wickham, 1981:132).

Nobility was not a closed category during the early and high Middle Ages. We cannot draw a clear line between aristocratic and non-aristocratic in Carolingian and Lombard polities (Wickham, 1981:115). The Lombards lacked a concept of the 'nobility of blood'. Instead, contemporary uses of *nobilitas*, for example in Paul the Deacon's eighth-century *History of the Lombards*, rather corresponds to our terms 'eminence' or 'notability' (Wickham, 1981:130). One of our major sources of social and political relations east of the Rhine, the Annals of Fulda, repeatedly mention terms like *optimates* and *principes*. Noble as they sound to our ears, they should be understood as corresponding to an expression like 'leading men' rather than 'nobles' or 'aristocrats'. Also, the term *fideles* should be shorn of any feudal associations that we might want to project retrospectively from the high Middle Ages and not be understood as 'vassals' but as 'faithful men'.[2]

What were the origins of this stratification and what were the power resources of families that were defined as noble? *Optimates* and their kin had several sources of power: land ownership; possession of *honores* (enmeshment in a system of contacts and prestige, recognition by other *optimates*); a military retinue – the most powerful kin groups and their retainers gradually monopolized military power and a network of kin contacts on the local, trans-local and realm levels (Wickham, 2009). Aristocracy in the Merovingian and Carolingian periods was based on a combination of birth, illustrious ancestry and, importantly, public service. Costambeys, Innes and MacLean outline military leadership, hunting, control of high offices and conspicuous consumption as four characteristics of the Carolingian leadership (Costambeys, Innes and MacLean, 2011:274). Merovingian Gaul was a hierarchical society based on kinship groups and the principle of descent. It combined a horizontal solidarity between elite groups with a vertical loyalty towards the royal centre of power and legitimacy. The Frankish elite as well as the monarchy was hereditary.

[2] Reuter, 1992:13. See also the entries of the years 852 (p. 32) and 855 (p. 37). See also Innes, 2000:90–1, 181, 187, 151–3.

The elite families were important to Frankish society but so were kingship and the conception of a kingdom. Both gave society a structure and a framework within which one could be a nobleman. The Frankish world was characterized by a strong focus on royal power, materially as well as symbolically, and by a strong sense of the kingdom as the framework for political action (Samuel, 1988; Kasten, 1997). On the level of ideas, the Frankish political system during the Merovingian and Carolingian dynasties was eminently centred on royal power. From the Merovingian times onwards, a consistent trait in Frankish Gaul was the legitimacy of a single ruling lineage. Every ruler who claimed the throne after 530 claimed that they belonged to the Merovingian lineage. We find a similar pattern among the small Anglo-Saxon, Welsh and Irish kingdoms but in the Gothic and Lombard kingdoms, the lifespan of a dynasty was rarely more than four generations (Wickham, 2009:113). All these societies attached great importance to the idea that a legitimate ruler had to descend from the right royal lineage.

Dynasticism was both a source of stability and tension. Wood tells us that many of the early Merovingian kings had many wives and thus also many children (Wood, 1994). This seems to have been a major source of instability in Frankish polities during Merovingian and also Carolingian times. The number of Carolingian claimants to the throne was far too big to be stable, which destroyed the polity in the end (Wickham, 2009:403; Costambeys, Innes and MacLean, 2011:37). In Merovingian times polygeny, the practice of having many wives, was the norm, even for kings. The sexual partners and thereby the reproductive partners of powerful men, even kings, were not limited to recognized wives but included mistresses and casual relations. All offspring of the sexual contacts of kings were considered to be of royal blood and hence eligible for succession to the throne which made the position of the early Merovingian kings unstable. The way to strengthen their position was by marriages with other royal and elite dynasties but by the end of the sixth century they had become strong enough to forego this strategy and instead have relations with concubines and lowborn wives since reproduction was more important to them than alliances (van Dam, 2006:228). In order to stabilize the polity, it is necessary to have stable rules of inheritance, most importantly with regard to who inherits the primary political authority. In other words, a widely recognized order of succession is necessary for kinship polities. It seems to me that the greater the degree of complexity among potential claimants to the throne – or to the leadership of any political family – the greater the scope for conflict. Consequently, stabilizing marriage and reducing the number of wives who could produce legitimate offspring (and laying down the rules for what constituted legitimate and non-legitimate offspring) is one of the most important pathways to political stability in societies where political power is hereditary. This is why the (re-)invention of marriage and primogeniture became important for polity-formation in the high Middle Ages.

The dominant view of charisma as the property of all the king's sons and the lack of institutions of inheritance created geopolitical tensions.[3] At the death of a Merovingian king the kingdom was often, but not always, divided among his sons (Wood, 1994:50). However, during long periods towards the end of the Merovingian period, royal authority lost control over several sub-kingdoms and Charles Martel had to wage war in order to bring Aquitaine and Burgundy back into the Frankish polity. A sign of the importance of the polity is that there were very few attempts by aristocrats to exit the Frankish realm, strike out alone and found completely new polities. The fact that political life was so focused on the king and his court did not mean that there were not any power struggles between powerful members of the aristocracy and the historical record provides us with ample examples of plots and coups by factions that often involved rival members of the royal family. Also, the orientation of politics towards the king did not entail automatic or unquestioned loyalty towards the currently reigning monarch. The purpose of many intrigues was to replace the king and to modern eyes, the evidence of fighting and scheming aristocrats is hard to reconcile with the image of a king-centred polity.

The relationship between the king and the elite families of Francia resembles a symbiosis rather than principled opposition. According to Wickham, the aristocracy did not have power in and of itself and did not strive to create autonomous local units (Wickham, 2009:126–7). Instead, aristocratic power strategies aimed at gaining offices, titles and land grants, which granted the owner power to command and coerce as well as collective power manifested in access to the circle of actors who could counsel the king and have influence on political decisions, material resources and authority. Most elite kinship groups seemed content with Merovingian supremacy, which could provide networks of patronage at best and at least symbolic authority during low points.

---

[3] Concerning royal marriage patterns, see Wemple, 1985:54–8.

Relations with the king were crucial to a high social standing (Hechberger, 2004:6). Conflicts between the elite families tended to take the form of attempts to gain influence in the royal palace (Fouracre, 2005:375). A manifestation of the importance of this proximity was that people who possessed royal offices and belonged to the 'company of the King' (*Antrustionat*) were protected by the fact that their *Weregild* was substantially higher than for other men (Hechberger, 2004:7). Only the king could bestow offices and titles, which meant that actors who aspired to power had to travel to the royal court and perform active service. One reason why the king and his court had such a central position was that the Roman conception of public sphere, public power and public service was still in existence and widely shared. However, a author from the fifth century, Lupicinus, emphasized that the realm of Chilperic was something qualitatively new. He saw the Frankish polity as a kind of kingship (*condicio regna*) rather than as the exercise of political power (*ius publicum*) so to contemporaries, Frankish rule did involve new elements that broke with the Roman past (Wood, 1994:16).

The origins of the European nobility have been debated since the eighteenth century. Early liberal scholars like Montesquieu argued that the French nobility originated with the conquering Franks (Montesquieu, 1989:619–722). In their eyes, the revolution of 1789 was the revenge of the descendants of the original population. In the nineteenth century, this notion was severely criticized by Fustel de Coulanges who could find no or little evidence of conquest or ethnic origins of the early modern social system in the sources (Wood, 2013:185). Still, ideas of an opposition between a nobility or proto-nobility and the political order, whether invested in the people or in the kings, have lived on. Since the early twentieth century the debate has been framed in a chicken-or-egg fashion, either the nobility created itself (Brunner, 1959) or it was created by kings (Bush, 1988). The first position argued that whatever their local variations, the privileges, powers and rights of the nobility originally belonged to the noble families and were later taken over by kings. The second position argues that noble privileges were originally regalian rights that were the king's to bestow and take away and that noble families usurped them when kings were weak (Bush 1983:6–13; Kaminsky and Van Horn, 1992:xiii–lxiii).

Framing the issue as a question of ultimate origins turns the debate by necessity into a zero-sum view of power between the two main poles of premodern politics. These two analytical moves reinforce a view of societies as being shaped by conflict rather than co-operation between rival centres of power, principles and elites. In contrast recent research on the ruling stratum and the political order during the early Middle Ages have focused on a symbiotic relation between proto-aristocratic groups and kings (Innes, 2000). Thus since historical analyses demonstrate that kings and noble strata arose almost simultaneously in post-Roman Europe and were tied into a symbiosis of mutual dependence from the very beginning then debates on polity formation and on the nature of social systems may be turned in a slightly different direction. On the most abstract level, this historical analysis lends support to the assertion that co-operation between the power elites are central to the existence and operation of a society; thus supporting Parsons' and Shils' more co-operative views of society rather than that of conflict theory or later state formation theorists that emphasize coercion as the main form of power. Of course, the dominant strata exercised plenty of coercion and violence towards the lower ones. Still, the business of coercion was based on a pact between the nobility and king and between hereditariness and political order.

The Carolingian Period

The Carolingian dynasty came to power when the Mayor of the Palace Pippin II overthrew the last Merovingian king in 751. The rule of the Carolingians was more extensive geographically than that of the Merovingian dynasty and it was more intense. With the Carolingian rise to power came a highly ambitious programme of reform, or *reformatio et correctio*. The Carolingians institutionalized a number of practices that cemented the relations between kings and aristocrats and served to create and uphold the sinews of government. These relate mainly to the network of offices, relations, monasteries and bishoprics. All kings have ruled through practices that we somehow or other may dub as patronage. The Carolingians made several important innovations in this respect. Charlemagne distributed lands as well as offices in the form of *honores* or in the form of temporary benefices (Wickham, 2009:381). The Carolingian kings also sent out representatives, *missi*, from the court to the provinces (Wickham, 2009:389–90). The programme of reform also had a strongly religious and moralizing side. Particularly the successors of Charlemagne employed a strongly religious discourse in describing and legitimating their rule. They also encouraged religious, even theological, awareness in the court and among leading aristocrats.

The Frankish realm consisted of several sub-kingdoms, Neustria, Austria, Aquitaine and Burgundy. Under both Merovingians and Carolingians, the Franks had a practice of giving members of the dynasty lordship over the different sub-kingdoms (Einhard, 2008:20). This was partly a means of administering the composite polity and partly as a means to manage the dynastic system/kinship system (the internal politics of the royal dynasty and its different branches). At times the sub-kingdoms were fairly coherent, at other times more independent and had to be reconquered. As a part of this tradition, the realm was divided into three parts in 843, West Francia (current France), East Francia (current Germany) and Lotharingia (the Italian parts and a long borderland running from Piedmonte to the Netherlands). Nothing indicates that the division was intended as a permanent measure, but it proved to be lasting. The treaty of Strassburg/Verdun in 843 was written in Old French and Old German in order to create trust with the magnates of East Francia who did not attend the assembly. All three kingdoms consisted of multiple small and big lordships. The boundary between the three kingdoms was porous for the good part of a century as kinship networks spanned the entire area and magnates and other lords moved easily across the boundaries.

One of the most important integrating elements in the Carolingian realms was the idea of a public sphere, which was ultimately an inheritance from Rome. It is essential to note that noble kinship groups always existed in a common context. They co-existed in a figuration together with an ideal of service, they were connected to the royal power (both through patronage and since elite status was connected to closeness to the king) and they existed in a context in which notions of public power, public duties and public enemies were discussed and formed a part of the system of concepts that gave meaning, direction and possibilities of action in the social world. Highlighting the existence of an encompassing sphere of community and public power also gives new meaning to the struggles between magnates and the king as well as among magnates; these were conflicts over public power and its distribution.

The Carolingian Empire also pioneered a number of institutions of government, some were regular and recurring practices, others were more formalized and permanent. An example of the former was the public assembly, which was the core of the Carolingian polity. The king regularly held assemblies which temporal magnates, church notables and others attended. Some assemblies were large, such as the public assembly usually held in springtime, which was often used to rally troops for the campaign season. Other assemblies were smaller, such as the more intimate assembly held in the wintertime (Ganz, 2008:xi; Roach, 2013:21). Royal patronage was the most important factor in structuring social hierarchy and a very important way of entering into the top echelons of society (Innes, 2000:89). Other important practices through which public power were exercised were the instruments of written communication that circulated, the most important being the *capitula* in which the king could issue commands, either of a specific nature or more generally.

Despite the ideational focus on the royal dynasty, the Frankish kingdom contained many powerful elite lineages (Innes, 2000; Bouchard, 2001). An important element in the Carolingian form of rule was the forty to fifty families of the so-called imperial aristocracy or *Reichsaristokratie* (Tellenbach, 1943; Schulze, 1978; Wickham, 2009:388). The Carolingian Empire was organized as a kinship network. At the centre was the *domus carolingica*, the royal line to which the kingdom was tied. Around it clustered a number of powerful magnate families from whom the Carolingian kings took their queens and whose leading individuals held public offices. Charlemagne's marriages are a case in point. His contemporary chronicler and friend Einhard tells us that he first married 'a daughter of Desiderius, the king of the Lombards', then Hildegard 'a very noble Swabian woman' and finally Fastrada of the eastern Franks (Einhard, 2008:31–2). In addition, Charlemagne also had numerous concubines. This network of kinship groups who counted kinship both in the male and female line (cognatic), was called the *stirps regia* (Le Jan, 2002:55).

Noble kinship groups were networks of high-status and low-status branches. Members of the high-status branch of a certain network were active at court, formed part of the *Reichsaristokratie* and held *honores*. These people moved around the empire during their careers in royal service. However, their mobility, power and usefulness to the King depended to a large extent on their family connections. More specifically, this meant their connections with lesser branches that were firmly established in the provinces to which the high-ranking aristocrats

were sent depending on their office (Airlie, 2006:431–50). Older literature claimed that the Merovingian and Carolingian elites were itinerant,
rootless and not – as they would become in the 900s – linked with
a particular territory or castle that formed the territorial powerbase
and fixed seat of the lineage (Duby, 1977). Aristocratic kinship groups
did have 'local' connections, that is, a relation to and standing in
a certain territorial area that was often mediated by the lower-ranking
branches that actually resided in this area. What is clear, however, is
that a kinship network was not necessarily confined to a single locality
but different families in the same network might have roots in several
different localities.

The power struggles and alliances during this period demonstrate that kinship was not an unequivocal identity or orientation and
we see kinsmen engaging in fierce rivalries and betrayals as well as
forming alliances with each other. We can also enumerate many examples of actors allying with non-kinsmen either vertically as in the search
for patrons or horizontally, as in the formation of sworn associations.
The multitude of ways that early medieval actors could relate to their
kin does not imply that kinship was not important. Rather it should
direct us towards an examination of what is the best way to conceptualize kinship. Certainly, kinship groups in this place and time were not
closed, disciplined units that obeyed commands from a designated
superior, rather they were fluid and they constantly re-formed. Since
people traced kinship bilaterally and married exogamously, kinship
groups were formed anew with each generation and inheritance practices meant that kin networks fluctuated from generation to generation.
Also, kinship was not uniform or automatic in its operation. Actors
were very flexible in how and when they used kinship ties (Innes,
2000:56, 68). Speaking schematically, it seems that kinship networks
resembled two concentric circles: an inner circle of 'practical kin with
whom a political and social strategy could be shared' and a wider group
of official kin with whom ties were much looser (Innes, 2000:53, 61, 68;
Crouch, 2005:115).The importance of kinship as a principle of descent
cannot be underestimated for stratification of society and the shape of
political order since it underpinned the proto-nobility's claim to rule.
However, kinship as a form of solidified practice or as a cohesive group
was weak and fluctuating. Interestingly, it seems that in kinship ties
(both real, and earlier fictive) blood relations were both important in the
sense of creating community and identity and weak in the sense of

guiding action. Innes notes that kin was frequently an arena for conflict, not just collaboration and Fleckenstein notes that although fictive consanguinity was central among the formations of the migration period, such alliances were fragile and short-lived and peace-keeping efforts within the group were seldom effective (Fleckenstein, 1979:8–9). Seeing kinship as a fluid system of action open to interpretation and improvisation by the actors within it also means that the considerable degree of improvisation with regard to heritage becomes understandable. We find over and over again evidence that the early medieval kinship structures were not unambiguously agnatic or cognatic, but actually flexible (Airlie, 2006:438–9). If descent on the mother's side could confer status then actors often chose to emphasize it rather than the father's side in their constructed genealogies. It seems that kinship was situational or relative to the activity that one wanted to pursue, '[f] or some purposes, then, the aristocratic family appears to have been a large kin; [for example if one wanted to mobilize in times of feud], for others, much smaller unit' (Airlie, 2006:440–1). The networks of aristocratic kinship groups constituted the veins of the Carolingian empire and the relation between dispersion and connectivity also illustrates the relations of mutual dependence and mutual enabling between royal and aristocratic power. As Airlie notes: 'Members of this [e.g., imperial] aristocracy may have passed from one region of the empire to another because of royal command, but while the kings provided a framework and opportunities for such movement, it was the family connections of the aristocracy that made it possible' (Airlie, 2006:435). Elite kinship groups were tied into the political order in a variety of ways. Receiving public offices, *honores*, was essential to the career and standing of nobles, they firmly anchored a family's status as part of the nobility (Costambeys, Innes and McLean, 2011:312–16). They were a combination of rewards, a formalized connection between the king and a noble and his lineage, and a way to exercise local power. A common office was that of a count (*comites*). As we saw above, the Carolingian Empire was a fundamentally kingship-centred polity. The royal court was a centre of political life and of political struggles. Powerful nobles tried to win offices that the king could bestow or the title of duke (Wickham, 2009:115). Royal patronage in the form of offices and estates was a powerful source of power and legitimacy for the Frankish nobility. Kinship structure and inheritance patterns also played a part in making *honores* valuable. During the eighth and ninth centuries inheritance was partible, meaning that all children inherited equally. This practice constituted an inherent weakness in the power base of the kinship group and as a result it was very difficult to sustain standing and resources over several generations. In order to counter this tendency to fragmentation, royal *honores* were a potential source of stability as regards power base, income and status (Airlie, 2006:446). The nobility had to seek the favour of the king in order to be confirmed as nobility and in order to partake of the resource networks that the king managed, if not controlled.

Although *honores* were granted by the king and could be revoked most became hereditary within the same family. The hereditary nature of offices and titles has often been interpreted as a sign that royal power was weakening. However, there was a tendency for positions to become hereditary over time and interestingly, they conferred certain stability on the relationships that constituted the kingdom of the Franks (Costambeys, Innes and MacLean, 2011). There has been considerable debate on the extent to which the Frankish nobility was a continuation or discontinuity with the Roman model of public service (Wood, 2013). The exact roots of the connection between nobility and public service do not have to be established here. However, there was a strong connection between kinship groups who possessed local legitimacy and power, the king, and the idea of a common polity and that connection was transmitted through public office.

In the Carolingian period the idea that the nobles of the realm constituted the people (*popolus*) was developed (Le Jan, 2002:54). This idea arose from the special relation between the nobility, and in particular of the magnate families to the polity, and an entitlement to rule and to partake in the rule not only of the territory firmly in the family's possession but also of the larger unit such as the kingdom of West France. This was a significant factor behind the formation and maintenance of large-scale political organization based on joint rule and collaboration, which was to remain a salient feature of the Western world for centuries. It also facilitated the 're-unification' of Francia under the Capetingians from the eleventh century onwards: 'In a system of representation characteristic of élites, the nobles participated in the common weal, that is, in a form of public service' (Le Jan, 2002:64). Regarding Lombard Italy, Paulo Delugo stresses that acting within the framework of the political order was a defining feature of what it means to be a noble, 'taking an active part in public military service was considered as the most complete and honourable form of freedom, whereby the free-born co-operated in maintaining both order and justice within the kingdom, and its independence or superiority with respect to other peoples' (Delogu, 2008:290). Elite families, or at least the magnates, sought not to escape public power but to be a part of it. As we shall see below, when they fought, noble factions did not fight the public power, they fought over it. But how was a connection between kinship-based elites and the political order achieved? The ideology of the Carolingians was based on an ideal of consensus of ruling groups. During the ninth century a rich vocabulary was developed to describe the kingdom as a polity, a collective that was greater than the rulers and ruled. During the reign of Charles the Bald (823–77) the idea of a *communis utilitas* became particularly articulated (Nelson, 2008b:426). The symbiotic relationship between royalty and nobility is seen in how the Franks described their own rule in the laws that they wrote for themselves as well as for subject peoples. The shorter prologue to the Salic Law, known under the Merovingians as the *Pactus Legis Salicae,* is one example. It tells us that: 'With God's help it pleased the Franks and their nobility, and they agreed that they ought to prohibit all escalations of quarrels for the preservation of enthusiasm for peace among themselves' (Wood, 1994:109). The formulation is significant because the Prologue ascribes the *pactus* to the nobility and to four possibly legendary lawgivers, not to a king. Nevertheless, many articles in the *Legis Salicae* are of royal origin. This is even more apparent in the Austrasian law code, the *Lex Ribvaria.* The Neustrian, Burgundian and Austrasian kingdoms had their own law codes (Drew, 1991). The epilogue to the *Lex Salica* points to a joint legislative responsibility for the king and the aristocracy[4]: 'The first king of the Franks established titles 1–62. After a little while he and his magnates added titles 63 (for 66) to 78 . . . ' (Wood, 1994:111). A similar relation can be found in the Law of the Bavarians, *Lex, Baiwariorum* which 'stated that the law was decreed before the king and his leading men (*principes*) and before all the Christian people who live in the Merovingian kingdom' (Wood, 1994:117). The war-leader (*dux*) in charge of the people should, according to the *Lex Baiwariorum,* always be of the gens of the Agilolfing family. The relationship between the Merovingians and the Bavarians was also defined in terms of relations between aristocratic families.

---

[4] It should be noted that the epilogue is included in fewer manuscripts than the prologue.

Certain notable families were to receive compensations or *Weregild* and we may see this list as a roll call of the pillars of that society. It clearly points out the role of five families (Huosi, Drazza, Fagana, Hahilinga and Anniona) who would always receive twofold compensation and the Agilolfings – including the dux – who would always receive fourfold compensation (Wood, 1994:117; Hechberger, 2004:11). Interestingly, these families had substantial staying power over the centuries (Wickham, 1981:131).

The two most important structural characteristics of elite kinship during this era were that it was flexible and unregulated. It is only in retrospect that historical studies of family networks have been able to reconstruct networks and historians have named this group 'the imperial aristocracy' (*Reichsaristokratie*), such catalogues were not available to contemporaries. We can assume that the members of the top magnate families were well aware of each other. However, this was not a standardized and formalized group. Over the course of the high Middle Ages (see Chapter 4) and the early modern period (see Chapter 5) the kinship-based elites gradually became more formalized, institutionalized and standardized. It was a very long process but it coincided with the equally long period of formalizing and institutionalizing the political order.

The Post-Carolingian Period: A Symbiosis of Nobles and Realms

Towards the end of the ninth century, the Carolingian realm crumbled. Frankish overlordship over Bavaria and Italy melted away and West Francia and East Francia were increasingly seen as separate entities – although there was considerable and possibly quite strategic ambiguity on the matter well into the next millennium. Inside the heartlands of the Frankish realm, power became increasingly local and small scale. In the historical literature this last process has gone by many names, 'feudalization' is possibly the most familiar but it has been highly controversial and is all but abandoned by medieval historians today. The fragmentation of central power was most extreme in West Francia. In Italy, England and East Francia, fragmentation was not as extreme and political development followed different pathways.

In the ninth century, offices became hereditary, a process that led to the establishment of principalities in France and duchies in

Germany and Italy. As magnate families founded dynasties they also established the idea of nobility as a status that was permanent, not only on loan from the king. Since it was established by blood, rooted in the past and transmitted by birth, it could not be revoked. The late ninth century has often been seen as a period when rule was 'privatized' by individual aristocratic lineages. However, the increase in conflicts among the aristocracy should be interpreted as an increasing conflict for royal patronage and *honores* as political rivalries increased at the royal level rather than as a zero-sum conflict between nobles and kings (Costambeys, Innes and MacLean, 2011:316, 320).

This newer interpretation of aristocratic power struggles in the early Middle Ages as involving stakes in the common polity rather than rebellions against it bears striking resemblances to the reinterpretation of aristocratic power struggles in the early modern era, almost 800 years later. As we shall see, more recent research sees the latter as indications that the aristocrats' stakes in the polity had increased rather than diminished (Zmora, 2001). Far from being the low point of government, characterized by centrifugal forces and 'feudal' fragmentation, the tenth century was actually a crucial period in the development of political order in Western Europe. At the beginning of the century, it was far from certain whether the West Frankish kingdom would fragment into its component realms (*regna*) or turn into a larger empire but at the end of the century, the West Frankish polity had been firmly established as an entity (Dunbabin, 1999; Nelson, 2008b). The tenth century was a time when the idea of the realm became stabilized. The cohesion of the realm was in no small measure thanks to the sentiment of commonality among the aristocracy and their interest in keeping the polity united under a single royal dynasty.

Not only did the idea of the realm became stabilized during the tenth century, but also the institution of kingship (Nelson, 2008b:100). Two elements can be mentioned in support of this view, the stabilization of rights of succession in patrilinear form and changed perceptions on violence within the royal family. Rebellion and murder within the royal family began to be considered lamentable and as a misfortune for the entire country. During Merovingian and Carolingian times, it was common to divide the kingdom upon the death of the king into smaller entities that were ruled by the sons of the king. This practice began to change and during the tenth century we see a distinct trend for realms to be regarded as indivisible and everywhere magnates played a decisive role in driving this development (Nelson, 2008b:103–5). In sum, during the tenth century three central components of the configuration of political order changed: the idea of the realm, the institution of kingship and the idea of lordship.

Lordship itself began to be more explicitly connected to and legitimated by being part of the realm. As a noble, to tie oneself to the king and to the realm was the best and most rational strategy for social survival as an individual or head of a family and for the survival of the realm itself. Interestingly, the two presupposed each other. The survival of the realm depended upon the active collaboration of the nobles who saw themselves as the 'collaborators, subordinates and surrogates' of kings (Nelson, 2008b:106). To some degree, nobles who wanted to survive had to invest in the kingdom and in the standing of the king since 'their exercise of lordship was in principle legitimated by being part of the realm'. Since there was no semantic that legitimated noble rule apart from the kingdom and the king, nobles had no choice in order to continue ruling. This tendency has been noted in Francia as well as in the Lombard kingdom in Italy. Paolo Delugo notes that in the latter 'the survival of the autonomous kingdom was essential for them to maintain their power and prestige' (Delugo, 2008:313). In the East Frankish kingdom successive Saxon dynasties came to power and abandoned several Frankish customs. The old custom of dividing the kingdom between the heirs of the king was abandoned in favour of a conception of the kingdom as indivisible. The basis of the kingdom was

> the community of aristocratic and ecclesiastical magnates [who might have come from the same kinship groups]. The Kingdom was conceived of as existing apart from the ruling family, and the royal office was contrasted with the person of the king. To preserve the unity of the kingdoms evidently corresponded to the interests and intentions of the new non-Carolingian dynasties as well as of the princes and the major churches. (Müllen-Mertens, 2000:243–4)

Thus, the loyalty of kinship-based elite groups towards the political order stabilized and saved it during a low point in the capacity of central institutions to enforce commands and issue regulations. An alternative strategy would have been to exit in order to try to set up an independent kingdom or simply dominate a locality without a legitimating framework. As we will see in Chapter 8, such strategies were common when Turkic polities crumbled but they did not occur in medieval Western Europe.

Kingship, Kinship and the Polity

Susan Reynolds has proposed the term 'regnal communities' as a name for early medieval political orders (Reynolds, 1983, 1984; Watts, 2009:141, 379). One of its merits is that it firmly places the focus on the institution of kingship. The political language of the time also emphasizes the role of kings: from the Latin *regnum* – as in *regnum francorum* (the Realm of the Franks) – to vernacular terms like *chunincriche* (king-realm). We now need to examine kingship, which at this time was evolving from a field of practices, customs and beliefs into something more institutionalized and standardized across Europe, although it was not tantamount to an institution in a modern state. I will focus on the beliefs and ideas that made kingship so powerful and indispensable; a conception of holiness that was transmitted in the bloodline.

The understanding of charisma in Weber's early works, as an institutionalized feature of a community, accounts for the formation of stable polities as well as of the conditions of stability (Kalyvas, 2002). The concept of 'institutionalization' captures the fact that many forms of rule continue to depend on the connection to something transcendental and divine. These forms, however, find ways of harnessing this connection and embedding it within the polity. Institutionalizing charisma – in the sense of maintaining but harnessing it in a framework of collective meaning – was an important element in the formation of more stable polities in European history. A classic example is the evolution of the institution of kingship. European kingship was always surrounded by a connection to divine powers and grace, either in pagan or Christian form, in other words it was charismatic. A central part of each coronation ritual was the unction, when a bishop anoints the head of the king with holy oil, thereby marking him as the Vicar of Christ (Isidorus of Seville, 2005:155). In the early Middle Ages charisma was capricious both in terms of whether a king possessed it and in terms of how it was passed on to his successor. A successful king was deemed to be favoured by the pagan gods, later by the Christian God. An unsuccessful one that was unable to rouse his supporters was deemed to have lost or never possessed grace. Hence, the charismatic community formed around such a king, consisting of his liegemen and their followers, was bound together by choice, not by institutionalized duty (Osiander, 2007; Wickham, 2009). Early medieval societies lacked rules for how charisma was passed on. All children that a king had sired were deemed to have the royal blood in them and hence the magical, charismatic quality. This was particularly marked in Norse societies. Because kings usually had many sexual partners, the number of potential legitimate claimants to the throne was often large (Jochens, 1987), meaning politics was often turbulent and polities rarely stable.

The factors that determined the structure and stability of early polities changed with the growing influence of the Catholic Church. By linking kingship to the rituals of the church, such as unction and coronation, the office of the king was strengthened by the institutionalization of charisma. The tight coupling of church and kingdom meant that routines and rules were established to make a person charismatic in the sense of having a connection to divine grace. The charismatic community centred upon the king changed accordingly and it became condensed around an office and it is at this stage that we can talk about 'charisma of an institution' (*Amtskarisma*). The community of barons, followers and subjects became stabilized and expanded. Devotion to the office, but not necessarily to the individual king, became a duty, not a choice (Eisenstadt, 1968:xvii–xix). From the tenth century onwards, the Church established that only children born within monogamous marriages were legitimate and that royal offspring succeeded to the throne in the order in which they were born. Both sets of routines harnessed and institutionalized charismatic authority.[5]

During the eighth and ninth centuries kings were embedded in kinship groups to which they belonged by descent and by marriage. Members of the royal dynasty were a constant threat to the king, most acutely so the king's own brothers. In struggles between the king and his brothers, the kin group of the queen could provide crucial allies (Nelson, 2008a:402). For the king, brothers and sons were often problems that had to be solved by providing them with a place within the ruling hierarchy and the polity. One way of doing so was to create sub-

[5] See Chapter 4.

kingdoms that the members of the royal family could rule, another was to appoint relatives as kings of conquered kingdoms like Lombardy.

One of the principal components of kingship was that it became linked to the conception of a people, a gens, 'and hence in the bonding of ruler and ruled' (Nelson, 2008a:423). In the Frankish case, the idea of a distinct people blended with the idea that the Franks had a divine mission, they were God's chosen people. The traditions of elective monarchy were a manifestation of the link between the people, often defined as the leading families, the realm and the king. The belief that the king had to be elected or at least approved by the elites probably has old roots. It was first mentioned in Tacitus' account of the Germanic peoples (Tacitus, 2005:33). Elective kingship existed in all of the post-Roman kingdoms. In no case was candidacy entirely free; in all cases there seems to have been a strong idea that a number of king-like lineages that were eligible for kingship existed in the realm (Mitteis, 1944:55; Tacitus, 2005:33). As Tacitus famously puts it: 'They choose their kings by birth, their war-leaders by merit' (Tacitus, 2005:33, my translation). Of course material resources also help explain why only certain lineages could be elected kings. In Anglo-Saxon England, the assembly, the *Witangemot*, usually elected kings, but other parties participated in some elections such as after the deaths of Ethelred and Canute. Although succession was not automatically hereditary, most royal elections followed the principle of succession in the male line. There were, however, notable exceptions when an illegitimate son was preferred over legitimate offspring or a King's brother over his sons (Turner, 1840:86–7).

Frankish kingship had both elective and hereditary elements. The Merovingian dynasty was considered holy, but its kings were still elected. When the Carolingian dynasty assumed power the elective element varied in importance. When Pippin deposed the last Merovingian king and took over the Frankish throne he was elected 'according to Frankish custom, anointed by the Bishop Bonifacius and elevated to the kingship in Soissons in 751' (Wormald, 2005:603).[6] However, at his death the sources tell us that the Franks 'elevated' his sons Carl and Carloman (Einhard, 2008:20). When Charlemagne died, Louis the Pious 'succeeded his father with the full consent and support of all the Franks'. According to the Carolingian historian Nithard, this

---

[6] See Royal Frankish Annals, year 751, in Scholz, 1972 [1970]:39.

was done by 'the chief men of the whole kingdom of the Franks in a solemn assembly'.[7] Louis obviously wanted to break with the elective tradition by appointing his son Lothar to emperor and his other sons to kings of the sub-kingdoms.[8]

In East Francia, the elective nature of kingship was increasingly strengthened. While Charles the Bald, son of Louis the Pious, had proclaimed that that kingship was hereditary, Arnulf was chosen king by all of the tribes of East Francia and was subsequently crowned in 887 (Fried, 1995:160; Airlie, 2002:27). Still, Arnulf's heritage was royal since he was the great-grandson of Charlemagne. Thus descent and the elective element was mixed in German kingship. In the same year the Carolingian dynasty was without a direct heir in Western Francia and the elective element of kingship came to the fore. The count of Paris, of the Capetian line, was elected (Spruyt, 1994:78–9). During the following century different dynasties would alternate on the throne of West Francia, which had become an elective kingdom under the leadership of its most powerful princes. In 987 the king Louis V died and a council of West Frankish princes elected Hugh Capet, who was acceptable to all but one of the major dynasties. His descendants would rule France until 1328. After his coronation he had his son Robert crowned joint king to secure the succession. All Capetian kings until the reign of Philip Augustus (1165–1223) followed this practice (Dunbabin, 1999:389–90). Elections at this time offered the magnates real choices between the pretenders from powerful dynasties and the king had to agree to conditions for his election (Dunbabin, 1999:393, 395). However, the ninth century elections were ad hoc affairs, and most of the princes were not present. A further example of the low degree of the institutionalization of kingship during the period was that the king and his princes rarely met. The elective element varied along a spectrum between two poles. The first was cases where the princes selected between two candidates, for example in choosing Hugh Capet over Charles of Lotharingia. The opposite pole is represented by cases where there was only one candidate and the election, acclamation or elevation was more a way of granting approval. Elections were public displays of the idea that early medieval kings could not rule without the

---

[7] Royal Frankish Annals, year 814, in Scholz, 1972 [1970]:97; Nithards *Historia*, §2, in Scholz, 1972 [1970]:130; Einhardt, 2008:39.

[8] Royal Frankish Annals, year 817, in Scholz, 1972 [1970]:102–3.

support of their magnates, the representatives of the leading kinship groups of the realm (Roach, 2013).

We must be careful not to use modern democracy as a yardstick to judge or evaluate medieval elective monarchies. However, the institutions and practices of elective monarchies did play important functions in the formation of political order. The polity had a focal point in the person of the king, but the elective element played an integrating role by ensuring participation and granting the leading men – and by extension their networks of family and followers – a say in the polity. In Hirschmann's terms, the elections granted voice, which in turn produced a modicum of loyalty and forestalled exit (Hirschmann, 2004). Jeffery Herbst's analysis of the problems of state formation in modern Africa highlights that unless the population of a country have a stake in the polity by contributing to its maintenance, it becomes very hard to build effective and permanent structures. Like many other state formation theorists, Herbst's argument centres on the role of taxation. However, the election of the king is another form of participation that gives the participants a stake in the realm (Herbst, 2000). Here we see cumulative dynamics at work: the more local power holders are drawn into the political order, the more can be achieved through collective action and, increasingly, the political order becomes more and more important. As it becomes more important, locally powerful actors become keener to engage in the business of co-rulership. Thus, the intensification of elective kingship was connected to the widening conception of the realm in the 900s, which included co-operation between the king and the magnate families. This development will be dealt with in detail at the end of this chapter.

Elections, whether at the 'true-choice' end or at the 'acclamation-approval' end of the spectrum, were not only about creating the possibility to muster greater material resources, they were also about the accumulation of symbolic capital and the mutual trading of authority (Haldén, 2014). On the one hand, the authority of the noble families came from the king but conversely, the authority of the king came from or at least was increased by the approval of the noble families. The way that kings and aristocrats supplied each other with crucial ideational 'goods' illustrates that they were not engaged in a zero-sum competition. Rather, they engaged in symbolic and material practices that constructed and intensified networks of collective power and interdependence. Since the institution of elective monarchy was elaborated and institutionalized in the high Middle Ages, Chapter 4 will deal in greater detail with this form of interplay between kings and nobles in the political order.

Kinship, War and Political Order

I have so far discussed the integrative functions of kinship principles and elites and the symbiosis between kinship elites and the political order. However, anyone who reads the chronicles and histories of this period will immediately notice how common and intense violence was between kin groups as well as within. Bishop Gregory of Tours (c.538–93) recounts many gruesome episodes such as King Lothar's murder of his two nephews, ages seven and ten, and how the woman Deuteria had her own daughter drowned lest the king should take a fancy to her.[9] Kinship was thus an infrastructure of power but not in the sense of permanent building blocks. This section discusses the ambiguity of kinship in relation to the organization for and waging of war and thus to political order (Crouch, 2005:142). As stated in Chapter 1, warfare and political order have been conceptually linked in historical sociology for a long time. Max Weber, Otto Hintze, Carl Schmitt and Charles Tilly regard them as mutually constitutive and as drivers of their mutual development. I will first discuss kinship as a factor in military mobilization and thus the phenomenon of fighting for one's kinsmen or for someone due to their prestigious descent. Second, I will discuss the phenomenon of intra-kinship group fighting.

Fighting for Kin and Realm

The concept of 'feud' or 'blood feud' is probably one of the most widespread ideas about fighting between kin groups in the Middle Ages. The idea that one had an obligation to join one's relatives to defend them or avenge a wrongdoing is attested in several legal sources (Wickham, 2009:191–4). However, it seems that long-term strategic violence was rare, except in Scandinavia (Halsall, 1999; Niles, 2015). One example of a prolonged war between elite kinship groups was the conflict between the Babenbergers and the Conradiners between 902

---

[9] Gregory of Tours, 1974:180–2 (III:18) and 185 (III:26), respectively.

and 906, one that also involved the Liutpoldings of Bavaria (Meynert, 1846:21–3; Fried, 1995:163). The feud as a phenomenon has been interpreted as evidence of autonomous, cohesive kin groups with considerable armed capabilities that operated according to a justice system of their own. If interpreted in this way it could lend support to the idea of a contradiction between elite and non-elite kin groups and the monarchy. Alternatively, they could be seen as indicative of a conflict between the principle of the 'tribe' and the 'state'. However, historical evidence contradicts this interpretation. First, kin-group loyalty was not automatic and kin groups were not cohesive (Crouch, 2005:142). Second, the vengeance was not unregulated or decided by the parties concerned. Several kings made sure that they or their officials preserved the right to decide what kind of vengeance was legitimate. A declaration of *faida* called the matter to the attention of royal officials and hence the conflict was embedded in the political order. We find such examples from the sixth century to the ninth (Halsall, 1999). We can expect a degree of discrepancy between actual behaviour and the law but the idea of the autonomously feuding society seems overstated, at least in Francia.

While the feud and kin-vengeance are the most evident ways in which kinship structured military force and fighting, there were two other forms in which kinship and descent structured military organization and thus the political order: military nobility and warrior kings. A substantial change since the Roman era was the militarization of the nobility. Kings and warriors shared a warrior culture not only among the Franks but in England, among the Lombards and among the Visigoths. The magnates of the Carolingian era were military commanders that wore the *cigulum militare* (military belt) as a sign of their authority (Le Jan, 2002:64). As Régine Le Jan notes, both kingship and the nobility were strongly based on their identity and capacity as warriors (Le Jan, 2002; Costambeys, Innes and Maclean, 2011:278–82). Warrior identity was a crucial source of honour and both were central elements in noble status and self-understanding. Military and political organization also coincided. The major events of the Carolingian political year, except for religious feasts, were the two annual assemblies. The larger assembly, usually held in the summer, was in essence a preparation for that year's campaigns (Ganz, 2008:xi).

Warfare was a dominant concern of early medieval elites and it was so frequent that chronicles mentioned the absence of war as a noteworthy event.[10] Still, we know little of the details of how armies were actually raised and composed (Reuter, 1999:27–8). The major armies of this period were heterogeneous, but a major component would be contingents raised by magnates and royal household troops. The people who made up a nobleman's armed retinue would not all be biologically related to him, some would be relations, but other retainers would be followers, *antrustiones*. Another part of the armies would be levies of commoners who owed military service to a lord and in the more urban areas of the south, towns could provide militias (Bachrach, 1972). In several cases, both lords and kings recruited mercenaries. Kings in England and Francia were relatively powerless against external enemies like Vikings and Hungarians without the support of troops raised by aristocrats and churchmen (Nelson, 2008b:123–4). Magnates were military leaders and probably important for the cohesion of the forces. Their ability to attract warriors and to command obedience was a matter of 'charisma, military reputation, and the ability to reward service' (Reuter, 1999:27–8).

Max Weber argues that charisma could be both a strictly personal attribute and a relation established because of the leader's connection to the symbolic foundations of the world view of the society (Kalyvas, 2002). In some cases belonging to an ancient line, particularly if it was royal, would confer some degree of the latter type of charisma. The symbolic and ideational component was the warrior ideal that was central to kingship. In contrast to the civilian culture of the Romans, in the post-Roman kingdoms and among their elites, both aristocracy and kingship were defined in terms of a warrior ideal. Prowess in war was intimately tied to the (charismatic) foundations of royal authority. However, charisma – in the sense of connection to the supernatural – that could command deference and service was also linked to performance in war. Conversely, military failures might reduce royal charisma (Weber, 1978:263). Wartime success had two components, one material and one symbolic: the material component was the need to continuously gain material resources in the form of lands, plunder and people that could be distributed to followers. This element remained important even in the Carolingian world of the ninth century. Charlemagne was a successful ruler largely because of his military victories over neighbouring peoples, which allowed him to sustain an

[10] See *The Annals of Fulda* year 847 in Reuter, 1992:26.

economy of patronage (Nelson, 2008a:392–3). The similarities to Inner Asian Khans were considerable in this respect as their rule also rested on their ability to distribute patronage in the form of plunder and treasure to their retinue (Kradin, 2002). When the conquests ended in the later ninth century, tendencies for looser royal control and increased autonomy soon appeared (Wickham, 2009).

Can the armies of the aristocracy be interpreted as a sign of their autonomous power and thus as confirmation of the thesis of the contradiction between the nobility and the political order? Considering the extent to which they were connected to the political order, such an interpretation seems exaggerated. The king bestowed offices, which were military in nature. Even if the leaders of powerful families are likely to have gathered armed followers anyway, the offices gave them legitimacy and authority and it seems like the nobility internalized this need for royal sanction. The militarized character of the nobility meant that their military forces and their identity and political function as military leaders were not independent from the polity as a whole (Le Jan, 2002:61, 65).

The warrior ethos was not antisocial but had a social and a patriotic component. Central to the idea of an honourable warrior was the status of a protector of the lower orders, of the Christian faith and of the fatherland. Moreover, Janet Nelson argues that 'military obligation was fundamental, failure to perform it [was] a most serious breach of the ruler's authority. All were involved when external enemies attacked' (Nelson, 2008a:422). In Merovingian times, kings organized local levies and garrisons on the basis of Roman models and institutions of service that continued to be in use (Bachrach, 1972:125). From the Carolingian era, many capitularies survive that outline landowners' obligation to render military service. One example is the *Capitulare missorum de exercitu promovendo* from 808 that stipulated obligations according wealth (Boretivs, 1883:136). Another is the *Capitulare Aquisgranense* that gave instructions how counts, bishops and abbeys should prepare their forces. In Anglo-Saxon England royal diplomas were regularly issued detailing the military obligations of subjects from the rank of ceorl upwards as well as the penalties for non-compliance (Brooks, 1971:69–84). Charles the Bald's (r.843–77) imposition of the death penalty for those who failed to rally to the support of the fatherland when it was attacked demonstrated both the centrality of the norm to the new conception of the polity as a collective undertaking and the fact that this command was not always and automatically obeyed (Nelson, 2008a:422). Carolingian kings could declare certain actors public enemies. Failure to attack them led not only to loss of honour but of status. *The Capitulary of Boulogne* from October 811 outlines military duties and clearly states that 'If someone from among those holding a benefice of the prince should fail his comrade-in-arms when he is going on campaign against public enemies and refuse to go or stay with him, he is to lose his honour and benefice' (King, 1987).

Do these facts lend support to the interpretation that nobles were subject to royal authority, or at least owed their positions to the king? That would also seem to be an exaggeration since Anglo-Saxon, Frankish and Lombard kings were entirely dependent on magnate armies and on successful negotiations and rituals of bonding with them in order to retain their support, both for military campaigns and for their reign. Typical ritual occasions were funerals, coronations, mass, hunting and assemblies as well as feasts during which gifts were exchanged and kings and magnates bonded by eating and drinking together (Roach, 2013:174–93). Thus, even in this area we see that the old zero-sum interpretations are problematic and that the political order was conceived through a symbiosis with kinship groups and inherited charisma.

Fighting Against Kin

Having powerful kin to turn to for help or descending from a materially or symbolically powerful line could be considerable assets. However, powerful kin could also be a liability or even a threat. Descending from a long line that might make you powerful could be life-threatening since it would mark you as a target to your enemies. I will now survey some examples from Merovingian and Carolingian history.

In the reign of Clovis (r.466–511), the first king of all the Franks, kinship was ambiguous. While symbolic kinship with the Emperor was important to his standing, to Frankish kingship and to the project of creating a cohesive Frankish-Gallic-Roman polity, Clovis' relations to his real kinsmen were quite different. An important step in the consolidation of the monarchy was to murder other Frankish chieftains and their families, most of who were his kinsmen (Geary, 1988:87–8). This campaign tells us that kinship ties were not a form of automatic solidarity and relatives did not always form natural alliances, however, kinship was important. Clovis' campaign can of course be understood as directed against the most powerful actors in Gaul, many of whom happened to be related to him. Marriage was an important technique in creating alliances among Frankish and Gallo-Roman elite groups as well as between the Burgundian, Gothic and Frankish polities (Wood, 1994:42). However, relation by blood meant that inheritance could be claimed and because of the prevalent belief that royal blood conveyed legitimacy and charisma, everyone who shared blood ties was a potential rival beyond 'mere' geopolitical strength since they could claim legitimacy. Fifth and sixth-century politics were family-centred. The ruling dynasties of Europe were connected in a web of matrimonial alliances, a practice that could be used in an attempt to create stability, trust and co-ordination (like Theodoric the Ostrogoth did) or uncertainty that could be strategically exploited (like Clovis did) (Wood, 1994:42).

Belonging to a prestigious family could be dangerous. When Clovis died, the realm was divided between his four sons. However, their positions were not secure. Childebert and Chlothar were troubled by the affection that their mother showed the sons of Chlodomer, their brother. Fearing for their thrones, they began to plot. They saw two alternatives: either to cut the boys' hair short and deprive them of their royal charisma (long hair was the property of the Merovingians) or to kill them. According to Gregory of Tours, the boys' grandmother could not bear to see them shorn of their hair and standing so their uncle Chlothar killed them. When powerful kinsmen were out to remove someone from the line of succession, spectacular and credible abdication was the only salvation if one could not fight. Chlodovald, Chlodomer's third son, cut off his own hair, thus renouncing his heritage, and became a priest.[11]

Bloody struggles between members of the sprawling Merovingian kinship network characterized the sixth century. The death of a king often resulted in political crisis and fraternal conflicts were frequent. In 613 Theuderic, the king of Burgundy, attacked his brother Theudeberg but died just before he could attack Chlothar who was king of Neustria. Thus, Chlothar conquered Burgundy and tortured Theuderic's grandmother to death. By taking over Burgundy he was now king of all Francia, which was a lucky occurrence since his own

---

[11] Gregory of Tours, 1974:182.

nephews had plotted his downfall only a few years previously (Fouracre, 2005:373).

The enabling factors of these conflicts were the absence of fixed and accepted rules of succession, a clear hierarchy in the royal network and the fact that Merovingian kings had many sons with many different wives (Wood, 1994:92). The shape of kinship, descent and succession during this time constituted the shape of violence; in particular the prevalence of fighting within large kinship networks. During this time the kin group was amorphous, the family had yet to become central and legitimate descent was not agnatic in a straight line so all descendants had an equal share in the charisma of the lineage. As Gregory of Tours said: 'all boys born of kings are called king's sons' (Wood, 1994:58). Kinship groups only became hierarchical dynasties on the other side of the year 1000, which is dealt with in Chapter 4. Succession was not regulated in law in the way that it was later. Existing laws expressed themselves rather vaguely on royal succession and on the position of the king in the realm: it was central but as yet unregulated and laws were not as firm and formal as later. Hence this was a period of strong practices but weak systems. Descent granted power since charisma was transmitted by blood but since kinship systems were not firm, formalized and hierarchical there were considerable structural incentives to fight one's relatives. In addition, the magnates with their own armed forces needed royal patrons. Thus magnates 'unsure of their position at court, those who had already fallen from royal favour, and those whose royal patron had been killed' would always be on the lookout for a new or more reliable patron (Wood, 1994:99). Even though magnate opinion shifted between individual Merovingians, no one questioned the sanctity and right of the dynasty itself (Wood, 1994:99) and while the bewildering record of these conflicts gives a chaotic impression, Ian Wood argues that 'the struggles between members of the Merovingian family actually held the kingdom together by providing a focus around which other conflicts could cluster' (Wood, 1994:100). Below I will return to the question of how wars that seem disruptive in fact confirm the importance of the political order and embed its antagonists further in it.

Fights over political power within kinship networks did not only take place during the Merovingian period, they also characterized the ninth century after the introduction of a more institutionalized conception of kingship and governmental procedures. After the death of Louis the Pious in 840, Charles the Bald and Louis the German joined forces against their brother Lothar and Pippin II of Aquitaine. Neither side, however, could gain a definitive advantage, and the war ended in 843 with the settlement of Verdun that divided the Empire into three parts. Division of the Empire was nothing new, having been a well-established practice since Merovingian times and evidence suggests that it was not intended as a permanent settlement and it was re-drawn several times in the century. Later in the ninth century the dynamics of competition changed. Previously rivalries tended to be between fathers and sons but now conflicts began to 'cut horizontally and diagonally across the family tree' (Costambeys, Innes and MacLean, 2011:386). Despite attempts at reconciliation and regular consultation between the different Carolingian kings, Louis the German invaded Western Francia in 858 (Innes, Costambeys and MacLean, 2011:395). This war was followed by another period of reconciliation during which all three kings manoeuvred, not without difficulty, to prevent revolts by their respective sons (Innes, Costambeys and MacLean, 2011:401–7).

The effect of a king siring many sons was ambiguous: it provided the dynasty with a reservoir of legitimate heirs but also a recipe for fraternal strife. Merovingian and Carolingian conflicts resemble intra-dynastic wars in the early Ottoman Empire. Both polities had unclear rules of succession, and all sons born of the King or Sultan shared equally in the royal charisma, and thus fraternal war was common. No changes in formal institutions or in the distribution of military power could alter this situation of recurring wars. Its origins were dynastic and it was only with the changes in dynasty structures in the eleventh century that the form of war would change (Innes, Costambeys and MacLean, 2011:424) to one where European wars mainly took place between royal dynasties, backed by the resources of their kingdoms.

Social theorists who share a Hobbesian understanding of political society as necessarily pacified under a single 'Leviathan' are likely to regard the frequency of violence between and within kin groups as evidence of the negative effects of a strong element of kinship on political society. Based on such a theoretical understanding one could even claim that the frequency of violence shows that there was no durable political order during this time and that periods of stability were too infrequent, even ad hoc, to talk about a stable 'order'. However, not all social theorists agree that conflict is incompatible with social integration or even with society itself. Indeed conflict takes place because two or more groups are integrated with each other in an institutional arrangement and 'quarrel with each other over their respective roles, positions and shares within them' (Shils, 1982:28). Georg Simmel pointed out that antagonists are opposed to each other only with regard to the particular actions, intentions and ends but that competing for the same prize unites them (Shils, 1982:43–4). War is, indeed, a means to manage conflicts, rather than the conflict itself, it is not necessarily the breakdown of society into 'anarchy' or an anti-social stage as Hobbes and his latter-day adherents would tell us. Conflict can be seen 'as a sign of cohesion rather than collapse in a relation' (White, 1986:257–63; Angstrom and Widén, 2015). Such abstract propositions may seem difficult to reconcile with the gruesome examples given above but they nevertheless provide the key for a new interpretation of kinship-based struggles and the formation of political order.

During the early Middle Ages much organized violence took place within kinship groups or kinship-based networks. People within the *stirps regia* mobilized their followers and allies, who in turn recruited warriors through their networks of kin, friends and dependants in order to wage bloody and unrelenting wars – many times against people to whom they were related. Kinship and descent were the very basis of these fights and wars. Descent transmitted legitimacy and could be invoked to command loyalty and thus military, political and economic resources meaning that every actor's worst rivals would be those that possessed similar symbolic capital through their noble or royal descent. It was precisely because actors during this period knew that kinship and descent could mobilize resources that relatives became dangerous. Since a rival with the right kind of descent could, by force of his 'blood', be equally or more legitimate they had to be killed, blinded, or sent off to a monastery for life if there was a conflict over succession. Thus, the numerous kinship-based conflicts demonstrate the strength rather than the weakness of descent as a symbolic capital.

To continue with the metaphor, this capital would be useless unless there was an institutional arrangement of which it was part. That framework was the realm. Once at the centre of it, after winning a successful fight, one could claim resources, command obedience and distribute patronage. At a lower level of society, say a county, or a sub-kingdom, once in possession of the centre – that is, the legitimate title – one could successfully claim offices, honours and resources from the centre of the realm and demand obedience from below. Because the political order existed and because it could render such great rewards, people chose to fight and to do so hard and remorselessly. In more primitive situations where no such order exists a rational strategy in case of a conflict over resources or succession is to migrate into an uninhabited area (Herbst, 2000: 39–40). Another contrasting example can be offered from tribal societies in North Africa and the Middle East. There, as Gellner shows, conflict between tribes was common but these conflicts were seldom fought to annihilate the opponent, gain supremacy or to survive. Instead, tribes may actually choose to dissolve themselves rather than be forced to yield to superior force (Tapper, 1990:66–7; Gellner, 1998:145–6). One reason why fighting is restrained (albeit frequent) is that there is no great prize to fight for since the political society that encompassed different kinship groups is very weak. Defeating a rival does not propel one into such a momentous position as medieval European kingship where fighting for the crown or to put one's patron on the throne confirmed the importance of the kingdom (Wood, 1994:100).

These findings go against the grain of some conventional wisdom about conflict and the severity of conflict. It is often assumed that antagonists will fight very hard against an opponent that they do not recognize or consider illegitimate. Accordingly, an opponent who can be constructed as an 'other' to one's 'self' and whose right to exist is not recognized will be subject to harsher military violence than an opponent whom one recognizes and with whom there is a degree of likeness. While the first is an enemy, the other is merely a rival in a more civilized competition (Schmitt, 2007:27–9). Numerous historical examples are often invoked, the Greeks and the Persians, the Conquistadors and the Aztecs, and the perpetrators and victims of genocidal atrocities (Wendt, 1999:261ff, 279ff). I do not deny that 'dehumanizing' and the creation of a foe as radically different can lead to horrific violence. However, the conflicts of the early Middle Ages demonstrate that mutual recognition, similarity of identity and the realization of another person's legitimate role can provide a structural incentive to fight determinedly against them and, upon winning, wipe that person out. The frequency and intensity of inter- and intra-kinship groups fighting demonstrates that kinship could be a source of co-operation as well as conflict, that kinship as well as the political order mattered greatly and that they jointly provided the structural incentives for conflict. Kinship thus resembled an entry ticket into a contest for power that was fought with violence and through marriage alliances. Beyond that, kinship was agnostic in relation to war and peace. It could mean that someone was a valuable ally, potentially or actually, or a fearsome rival.

Finally we must ask: Was there a tension between loyalty to one's king and loyalty to one's lord? Chris Wickham argues that there was no opposition between loyalty to kin and loyalty to lords. Indeed, far from being the two ends of a spectrum between which society oscillated, from the Merovingian period onwards, 'both kin loyalty and lordship became tighter and more articulated' (Wickham, 2009:193, 508–29). Furthermore, Janet Nelson argues that lordship trumped kinship during this period (Nelson, 2008a:406). Strikingly, this is a development – in somewhat varying form and language – that is attested to for many periods in time, from the sixth century to the nineteenth. Thus it seems that the solidification of groups and of political order went hand in hand. Sabean and Teutscher have made a similar connection between kin-formation and state formation in the early modern era (see Chapter 5). Historians of different epochs now seem to converge on an image not only of symbiosis but of co-evolution of formal kinship groups and formal political structures in different times in European history. If this is a general connection then we must conclude, in opposition to previous theories of political development, that formal elite kinship groups have been an asset to polity formation, not a liability.

Conclusions: Kinship and Political Order

This chapter has demonstrated a symbiosis between political order and kinship in early medieval formations. Kinship in the sense of kinship-based elite formations and in the sense of principles of legitimacy was central to the political orders found in early medieval realms. One might ask if this symbiosis resulted from the central power, for example, the king's, need to adapt to and compromise with well-entrenched proto-noble elite kindreds. Such a question is flawed since elite kinship groups, kings and realms never existed autonomously from each other; certainly not as far as the sources tell us for the more advanced post-Roman kingdoms. Conditions in Scandinavia, Ireland and Eastern Europe may be a different matter, but they lie outside the scope of this study. Descent and the idea that power, legitimacy and a quasi-sacred aura were transferable by blood was never questioned during this period. They were a foundation of the social order, not a negotiable variable. Also, kings and magnates were functionally similar to each other; both were leaders of dynasties whose legitimacy rested on descent and whose power rested on patronage, kinsmen and followers. Finally, royal and magnate dynasties were too intertwined to be logically separated in any kind of political programme. However, if one were to apply a functionalist perspective on this period, then it is clear that the proto-nobility was an asset, not just a necessary evil.

This chapter has stressed the importance of co-operation between king, proto-nobility and the abstract idea of the realm (or political order). Still, it must be said that formations during this era were also characterized by a lot of coercion, often violent, against the lower orders of society. Chapter 11 deals with the question of how the interplay between collaboration and coercion as two forms of power can be united in a theory of polity formations. Also, on a theoretical note, this chapter has demonstrated that kinship did not imply automatic solidarity or exist as a fixed structure. Conflicts within kin networks were as common as those between them. Rather, kinship functioned more as a language than as a structure.

Chapter 2 surveyed two assumptions in social theory: first, the idea that kinship-based organization and political organization (often equated with states) occurred in two different stages. This chapter has demonstrated that there were no 'pure' forms of lineage or kinship organizations. On the other hand, kinship-based organizations were the basis of the polity and one of the main ways of legitimating political authority. Second, I discussed the idea that kinship had to be transcended or broken for political orders to develop. I have shown that this assertion is not valid. Theoretically it rests on an unrealistic construction of a lineage society in which only one principle of differentiation is operating. Such an order did not exist during the period. Instead, ideas of the political order always permeated these societies. Empirically, the idea of transcending kinship in state formation theory rests on a neglect of the early Middle Ages. Kinship-based formation and ideas of kinship and descent as the basis of legitimacy were preconditions of the political order. It was perfectly possible to have a political order in a society in which kin and descent were important. However, both kin and political order were rather amorphous during this period and both had to be formalized and solidified for a major change to take place. That is the theme of Chapter 4.

4 CONSOLIDATING DYNASTIES AND REALMS
Europe *c.*1000–*c.*1500

Introduction

Over the centuries that this chapter covers, European polities grew increasingly solid, stable and regular in their operations. The organizational, symbolic and ideas-based aspects of elite kinship were also becoming more regular and regulated. This chapter does not deal with the history of kingship and nobility in its entirely during the high and late Middle Ages. Rather, my aim is to show ways in which kinship was an inalienable part of the political order. Indeed, both kinship-based organizations and ideas of kinship as a legitimating principle were symbiotic with the political order. Kinship is defined as the symbolic and institutional aspects of kingship and nobility.

Monarchy was the principal form of the political order, the legitimacy of which rested on the transmission of charisma through generations. Since it was family based, it generated dynamics of its own. Through inheritance and marriage, conglomerate realms could be created. I will also analyse ways in which members of the nobility and the nobility as a collective group were active and indeed necessary in its symbolic and institutional functions. This took place through elective monarchies, the rituals of monarchy, the ideology of consent and counsel, the institution of the Council (*curia*), the embedding of magnate armies in the royal hosts, and royal influence and control over noble marriages. I will examine conflicts among nobles and conflicts between nobles and kings and argue that neither type threatened the political order. I will also look at how the nobility was created as a collective category, a social stratum. This took place through legal innovations such as codifications of the nobility, conceptual innovations such as the stabilization of concepts, and cultural innovations in the shape of chivalry, heroic poetry and heraldry.

First I discuss two debates in medieval history, whether conflict or co-operation characterized the political order and the nature of changes in family structure. Second, I analyse the political order in the shape of European realms and composite monarchies. Third, I analyse the role and position of noble families in the political order. Fourth, I analyse what I call the 'soul' of the medieval political order by looking at chivalry, heraldry and the kinship elements in medieval Christianity. Fifth, I analyse medieval polities as 'families of families' by studying royal attempts to control aristocratic marriages. The last section confronts possible objections that I have painted a too harmonious picture. My way of doing so is to analyse wars and rebellions and see if they can undermine my argument of a symbiotic relation between kinship organizations and principles, on the one hand, and the political order, on the other. My conclusion is that they cannot.

Conflict or Co-operation in the Middle Ages? The Stakes for Social Theory

How the condition and nature of political order between the tenth and thirteenth century has been understood has had significant consequences for how the development of political order has been understood – and for interpretations of the relation between kinship groups and political order. As we shall see, the stakes are high.

Since the Enlightenment, the idea of a medieval 'anarchy' has been floating around in European historical, political and social thought. Its origins can be traced to Montesquieu who described the end of the Carolingian era in France as one when the centralized power of the kings fell into the hands of a predatory aristocracy. As it did, the realm of France crumbled and 'lost its domain' (Montesquieu, 1989:716; Crouch, 2005:192, 262). This idea has proven very long-lived as a standard narrative of the Middle Ages. For Montesquieu the turning point comes with the re-conquest of France by the Capetian dynasty in the late twelfth century.[1] Norbert Elias used the image of feudal anarchy in France as the starting point and tabula rasa in his narrative of state formation. Inspired by Marc Bloch, Georges Duby launched the thesis of the 'feudal mutation'. According to him, the feudal mutation was that power passed from the weak Carolingian kings into the hands of the counts of the realm. Soon the counts too lost exclusive control and their immediate vassals gained both the rights and the means to exercise it. Eventually, control over this, the most central kind of power, passed into the hands of the even lower levels of sub-vassals. Duby called this process the 'descent of the ban' and singled it out as the basic mechanism of fragmentation of structures of power and authority and as such the root cause of the medieval or feudal 'anarchy' (Duby, 1977).[2] Since a multitude of actors, uncontrolled by any higher authority, exercised the means of violence, the result was endemic violence. Among later writers, Hendrick Spruyt places great emphasis on the Capetian dynasty in France as the starting point of the model of the sovereign state after the feudal anarchy (Spruyt, 1994; Ertmann, 1997:48, 55–9). Today, however, medievalists question the feudal mutation thesis. Dominique Barthélemy has argued that it is largely based on nineteenth-century notions of the difference between public and private power (Barthélemy, 2009). Instead of interpreting the agency in war and peace of actors who were not monarchs simply as the fragmentation of public power – even of the realm itself – we ought to see it as a new way of upholding order. Thomas Bisson has defended the mutationist theory by pointing at increased levels of violence among lords and between lords and peasants (Bisson, 1994, 2015). Stephen D. White argues that the image of increased violence after 1000 is both overstated and misinterpreted. Medieval actors used violence instrumentally, just as they used peace agreements to settle affairs of political order (Crouch, 2005:195–8). Otto Brunner's reconstruction of the feud in the German lands as a rational practice that served to uphold order, predictability and trust also provides a very important counterpoint to the idea of a feudal anarchy (Brunner, 1959). More recently Timothy

[1] It should, however, be noted that Montesquieu regarded the co-rule and co-dependence of the nobility and the monarchy as a pillar of strength and justice in medieval and *ancien régime* France (Montesquieu, 1989:18; Ward, 2007:566–8; Goldoni, 2013:24).
[2] For a nuanced discussion of the ban and the thesis of a 'descent of the ban' see Flori, 2004:148–84.

Reuter has argued that the image of evaporating political order in post-Carolingian Europe is overstated (Reuter, 1997).

The stakes in this historiographical debate are high and they extent far into political science and sociology. The feudal mutation theory is a link in a chain of historical narrative that portrays the absence of a centralized authority as chaos. According to F. L. Cheyette, Duby's view of society was decidedly Hobbesian (Cheyette, 2002:309, 313). Although he largely concurs with Bisson that a significant political and social change took place between 800 and 1150, Chris Wickham notes that the narrative of the anti-political aristocrats is heavily indebted to 'the nineteenth and twentieth-Century Grand Narrative of the triumph of the state' (Wickham, 1997:197). The construction of the feudal rule of the lord (*seigneur*) as a state of nature requires the antithetical construction of a royal proto-state that comes to the rescue by imposing order, coercively. The historical narrative of the descent of the ban portrays the kinship-based noble groups as anti-political forces and their reign during 'feudalism' as an apolitical stage before the establishment (or re-establishment) of political order. Some scholars are more unequivocal in their judgements. Poly and Bournazel regard 'feudal society' as the antithesis of the state and Bisson calls it 'unpolitical' (Barthélemy and White, 1996:201). We also see the term state used as shorthand for political order by advocates of the 'descent of the ban' thesis, which means that other forms are rendered unpolitical: '[a]nd since for Duby, as for Bloch, the state could be only royal ... their feudal centuries are devoid of the smaller polities' (Evergates, 1997:648). By creating an image of a feudal anarchy, this narrative resets the clock to a pre-political stage dominated by nobles. In this imaginary, the reforms of the Capetian dynasty re-established political order through state formation.

What is at stake is whether political science, sociology and war studies have to choose between order imposed from above, by a proto-state Leviathan, and anarchical chaos or if we can discern other forms of order. In the first Hobbesian interpretation, order has to be imposed through the threat or use of coercion. Thus, the Middle Ages can be used (and has been used) as a foil for a philosophy of politics, society and war that regards the state as resting on coercion. As we shall see, the strong collaborative elements of political orders during the high Middle Ages point to another interpretation, namely that political order depends on elite co-operation and on the embedding of elite kinship groups in an institutional and conceptual framework.

Family Change

Medievalists have debated the nature of kinship around the year 1000 since the early twentieth century when Gerd Tellenbach, Georges Duby and Karl Schmidt argue that in the early Middle Ages, families had been sprawling, diffuse networks. Families were sprawling since kinship was counted both on the maternal and paternal side (Bartlett, 1994:49). Inspired by German research, Duby argues that before the year 900, although kin was a central aspect of society, it was not organized as a lineage that connected past forefathers with the present. Nobles would have seen themselves as operating in a series of horizontal relations in the present. The most important people to have relations with were individuals connected to sources of power and patronage such as a king, a duke, or a local leader (Duby, 1977:147). However, Duby claims that family structures changed between 900 and 1000: families became smaller as only descent through the paternal line, or agnatic kinship, came to dominate. According to 'the Duby thesis', primogeniture (passing the inheritance undivided to the eldest son) was introduced as a means of preserving family property and territory. Individuals began regarding themselves as a family group with vertical connections backwards and forwards in time. Duby's work was influenced by structural anthropologists, such as Claude Lévi-Strauss. Like Lévi-Strauss, Duby saw kinship as a rigorously defined structure (Cheyette, 2002:315). We now know, from European and non-European evidence, that kinship can be important and flexible.

Subsequent research on medieval kinship in France and Germany tends to refute the idea of an abrupt transformation around the tenth century. The current consensus is that this shift took place only towards the end of the Middle Ages (Le Jan, 1995; Sabean and Teuscher, 2007). Changes were gradual rather than abrupt. In twelfth and thirteenth century Germany, Lyons identifies several 'lineages' in the high nobility such as the Staufen, the Welfs and the Wettins. They did not practice primogeniture but partible inheritance and siblings often co-operated (Lyon, 2012). In Germany we see families that in the space of a few generations moved between several main seats and titles as their inheritance fortunes propelled them to increasingly prestigious and valuable holdings (Arnold, 1991:135–51). Although some traits are distinctly German, such as the absence of primogeniture and inheritance through the female line, the situation was similar in Flanders and France. In sum, the aristocratic family is now classified anthropologically as a 'bilateral kindred rather than a patrilineage' (Evergates, 1997:650). Noble families, who were fundamentally cognatic, employed a range of strategies to enhance their standing and were not restricted to patrilineage and primogeniture (Le Jan, 2002:59–60; McHaffie, 2015).

However, the rules of marriage changed. Previously polygamy had been widespread among those that were able to afford to keep many wives. At the turn of the millennium, the Church began to advocate and enforce monogamy much more resolutely as the only legitimate and legal form of marriage (Duby, 1993; Howell, 2009) as well as tightening the rules on who could marry whom. Early Germanic laws had forbidden the marriage of close kin, such as cousins, aunts, or the wife of one's brother. But in the eleventh century, the Church prohibited marriage up to the seventh level of relation.[3] These changes prevented the creation of isolated kinship units that reinforced their bonds and delimitation against outsiders by generations of cousin marriage. On the contrary, nobles had to marry outside their circle of relations, which over time forced them to search even further afar for marriage partners. The ban on endogamy prevented elites from entrenching themselves in only local communities, which would have created intense local ties and prevented inter-regional integration. Instead the opposite occurred, the integration of elites across comparatively large distances and the creation of wide networks. In sum, it is wrong to claim that kindreds only contracted into lineages at this time. In fact, we can see both a contraction into tighter groups and an expansion into a wider network of connections. However, this was not a shift between two structures or strictly defined legal systems. Medieval nobility was flexible, dynamic and mobile.

There is, however, one area where a trend towards primogeniture and stabilization of succession is visible: the royal dynasties. Kokkonen and Sundell argue that the changes in the order of succession were crucial to the increased stability in European political orders.

---

[3] Papal Letter 56 (K.h. 2:621 n:o 22) in Liljegren, 1829. The Pope also exhorted the archbishop in Lund to investigate whether a burgher, Strange, in Lund had married a woman to whom he was related to the fourth degree without papal dispensation. Papal Letter 142, 7 November 1211 (K. m. 2:560 An. 14. Ep.121) in Liljegren, 1829:165.

Before the year 1000 most kingdoms lacked clear rules on succession; in many cases, all of the king's sons were considered to be of royal blood and thus legitimate. As Chapter 3 demonstrated, a common practice among the Franks was to divide the kingdom among the sons of the king at the time of his death. A generation later a strong ruler of a sub-kingdom usually reunited the patrimony by conquest. Other kinds of succession were election, usually in the form of magnates giving their approval to the candidate from the royal family, and horizontal inheritance (Kokkonen and Sundell, 2012:10–11) which often took the form of the oldest brother of the king inheriting the throne, which then passed through the line of brothers in the same generation. The youngest brother in the generation was then supposed to pass the crown on to his eldest brother's son, upon which the cycle started afresh. This system tended to produce many potential claimants, which made it complicated and prone to coups. The introduction of primogeniture changed all this and introduced internal stability. Primogeniture means that the oldest son of the king inherits the crown, which he in turn passes down to his oldest son. This practice was first introduced in the Christian kingdoms in the Iberian Peninsula (Aragon, 1035; Barcelona, 1017; Navarre, 1004) and had gradually spread to the majority of kingdoms in Europe by the fourteenth century (Kokkonen and Sundell, 2012:9).

Political Order

Almost all European polities were kingdoms. In the high Middle Ages the office of kingship began to take on a sacred character of its own, distinct from the sacred person of the king. The sacralization of the office of kingship started a process to make the realm an abstract entity separate from rulers and the ruled. The development of ideas of nationhood and national communities in the Middle Ages often centred on the idea of the royal dynasty (Reynolds, 1984:261), being royal subjects was highly important to national identity. In England the 'symbiosis of king and people ... came to define in practice what it meant to be English' (Davies, 1995:13). Another example is the common occurrence that royal saints became national saints and thus joined dynasty with nation (Scales, 2012:63–4).

Because a king was holy the kingdom that he ruled took on a particular quality that set it above other forms of political organization. However, a king was still mortal. A major problem was to

construct a notion of kingship that had greater longevity than individual kings. By elaboration of ideas that supported the notion of
dynasty, the realm was 'raise[d] beyond its purely physical existence
and ... transcendentalize[d]' (Kantorowicz, 1997:208). The idea that
a people and a realm could have perpetual existence was found in
legal writings of all European countries from the late Middle Ages
(Bartelson, 1995:97–100; Kantorowicz, 1997:295, 298, 301, 304, 311).
English jurisprudence began to conceptualize 'the Crown' as the
abstraction of the institution of the monarchy, separate from the king
himself. In the fourteenth century, Baldus argued that a realm had an
existence separate from those of its kings (Kantorowicz, 1997:299;
Haldén, 2017a).

Kinship was part of what Ruggie calls the 'generative grammar'
of this world of realms in the sense that dynastic unions were both a tool
and a constitutive feature of politics between realms (Ruggie, 1982).
A key structural feature was female inheritance and property rights.
Daughters of royal, ducal, comital and baronial families were often
given territories as dowries. These dowries and their titles were added
to the domains of her husband's family if the marriage lasted or – as in
the case of Eleonore of Aquitaine – sundered from them when the
marriage was annulled. The composite nature of many polities and
cognatic family structures meant that territories could be contested by
heirs and relatives who could lay more or less legitimate claims through
maternal or paternal inheritance if their ruling dynasty died out without
any direct heirs. Because of the ban on endogamous marriages and
because marriage was a way to advance the interests of families, elite
families (particularly at royal and ducal levels) became increasingly
intertwined with each other and by the fourteenth century genealogies
were excruciatingly complex. This complexity, both in the same generation and over generations, meant that record-keeping became important. It also introduced an element of flux as the extirpation of a line
could result in sudden and unexpected claims coming to the fore.

The examples of families coming to power through marriage are
too numerous for me to list them all. Although running the risk of
interpreting history retrospectively we can distinguish between two
types of composite monarchies: one in which the parts retained sufficient integrity to engage in war against each other and thus broke up and
another in which the parts remained distinct but nevertheless combined
into a durable polity. Not all dynastic unions resulted in durable

polities, but the practice of dynastic union had a strong systemic impact in the sense that it generated wars over succession and the inheritance.

Some polities were very durable. The marriage of Ferdinand of Aragon and Isabelle of Castile in 1469 united the two most powerful kingdoms of the Iberian Peninsula. Although Aragon remained distinct, with its own laws and representative institutions, the dynastic union generated a relatively cohesive fusion of realms. The Kingdom of Poland and the Grand Duchy of Lithuania were linked successively over four centuries through the marriage strategies of first the Piast dynasty and then the Jagiellonian (Davies, 1981:95–7, 102, 115–16). When King Casimir died in 1370 without a male issue, his nephew King Louis of Hungary was crowned king of Poland, briefly joining Hungary, Poland and Sicily. When Louis died, his daughter Jadwiga was married to the Lithuanian Prince Jogalia in 1386. This marriage came about after an intense process that illustrates how important dynastic links were for politics. Louis' other daughter, Maria, was married to Sigismund of Luxemburg who was Holy Roman Emperor. Jadwiga was, however, originally betrothed to a Habsburg prince. Since the Polish barons were afraid of being dominated by the Western dynasties they chose to ally with Lithuania (Davies, 1981:115–18). The union between the two countries was successively strengthened until they were finally merged through the Union of Lublin in 1596.

Other unions were more unstable. The Scandinavian realms, Denmark, Norway and Sweden, were joined in the Union of Calmar between 1397 and 1523. The crowns were united under a single monarch but in practice the relations between Danish and Swedish nobles were tense and erupted in war on several occasions. Its dramatic history demonstrates that the respective realms had solidified as entities to which its elites were loyal. Some of its kings were Danes or Swedes, but others were brought in from northern Germany, Eric of Pommerania was one of the latter. He was deposed both by the Danish and Swedish councils in 1439 (Carlsson, Cornell and Grenholm, 1966:190). Teschke has argued that between the fourteenth and seventeenth centuries, European kingship was 'proprietary' in nature (Teschke, 2002:9). However, I believe that the Danish-Swedish wars and the deposition of Eric demonstrates that kingship in composite monarchies was far from proprietary in this period. Kings could not dispose of realms as their property but had to negotiate its politics with elite groups.

The so-called Angevine Empire of the thirteenth century was also unstable. Although England and Normandy had been associated since the Conquest in 1066, through the marriage between King Henry II and Eleonore of Aquitaine large parts of Western France entered into a union with the Anglo-Norman realm (Hollister and Keefe, 1973). The connection and intertwinement of England and France continued for another two centuries; a period that bridged the off and on fighting of the Hundred Years' War. The entanglement of England and France represents a type of union where the two kingdoms were intact enough to mobilize support for an armed struggle. The fact that royal marriages did not always produce stable compounds and that kings did not own their realms further weakens the idea that polity formation in this era – or indeed in any – era was primarily dependent on coercive power. What produced stability was rather the successful use of collaborative power.

The chequered history of Burgundy also illustrates how marriages could create as well as unravel composite polities. Burgundy has been a name attached to many different polities between the sixth and fifteenth centuries. It is now a region of France but in the high Middle Ages it was a polity situated between what is today France, Germany and Italy. In 1032 the ruling Rudolfine dynasty died out. Since it was connected to the Ottonian dynasty that ruled Germany, the kingdom of Burgundy became an Ottonid possession. The German king-emperors never paid Burgundy much attention which meant that its constituent parts exercised considerable independence. In 1127 the heiress of Provence, a part of Burgundy, gave away her rights to her husband, the Count of Barcelona. More than a century later, in 1246, the Count of Anjou, the youngest son of the French king, married the last Catalan countess of Barcelona and Provence passed into the patrimony of the French royal family. The country-palatinate of Burgundy had passed from dynasty to dynasty with almost cyclical regularity, in 1156 the Hohenstaufen acquired it, in 1208, the Bavarian House of Andechs and in 1315, the Royal House of France (Davies, 2011:127). If fragmentation had characterized the twelfth and thirteenth centuries, then spectacular growth characterized the fourteenth and fifteenth. The 'mechanisms' were the same in both epochs, marriage and inheritance. The duchy and the county were united in the same ducal dynasty, which managed to exercise considerable independence as well as influence within France. The polity grew with the marriage of Philippe Le Hardi to Marguerite de Dampierre who brought today's Belgium and the Netherlands into Burgundy (Davies, 2011:131–2). Although prosperous and sophisticated, the Burgundian polity was unstable. Duke Charles the Bold (r.1467–77) plunged into war with all his neighbours and after his death in 1477 the states of Burgundy fell apart. The French occupied the duchy and the county-palatinate reverted to the empire. The Burgundian possessions in the Low Countries came into Habsburg possession after the marriage of Charles' daughter Mary to Maximillian von Habsburg (Mann, 1986:438–40; Davies, 2011:138–9).

Burgundy was perhaps a special case of rapid accumulation and swift disintegration, but it can tell us something about more general traits of the relation between kinship and political order in its time. First, it must be said that had it not been for the misfortunes of war, the states of Burgundy might have survived for longer. However, the fact that it was not a recognized kingdom or even a composite of kingdoms meant that it was vulnerable. Other polities that were kingdoms with more established institutions, deeper embedding of elites and thus able to command greater loyalty remained intact in periods of weakened central power. Examples include Francia (France) in the tenth century and Sweden in the fifteenth century where noblemen rallied to support the polity, indeed claimed to represent it (Haldén, 2014:137).

The Realm and Noble Families

It was not possible to separate the idea of the realm from royal and noble lineages, in fact, by acting as something that one could represent it served as a way to embed and unite powerful men, who often came from powerful lineages. The great men of England, France and Germany were in principle 'supposed to be bound together by the affective bonds of mutual loyalty' (Reynolds, 2004:105). These findings directly contradict the two arguments of the 'mutationist theory': first that left to their own devices, nobles engaged in an anarchic state of endemic warfare akin to a Hobbesian state of nature, and second, that it took the evolution of an overwhelming military capacity to end this condition. Even in times of materially weak kingship, magnates (the nobility with the highest status and most powerful resources) were used to 'attending meetings to discuss and decide disputes and polity and then to serving in armies to carry it out' (Reynolds,

2004:105–6). The idea of the realm was also a factor that mobilized the magnates to fight in foreign wars such as the crusades. Moreover, it seems that group solidarity preceded formal political institutions (Reynolds, 2004:111). Records show that not only nobles but also knights and towns partook of this realm-centred patriotism and felt a responsibility in times of crisis to defend it from foreign invasion and to show loyalty. Were the nobility and in particular the magnates, the most powerful nobles with the highest status, anything special in this regard?

Despite their strong standing, kings were not, and could not be alone in a realm. One aspect is the need to draw on the resources and managerial capacity of others. Considering that magnates were important landholders and could draw on large networks of patronage, and thus of manpower, they were indispensable. Another aspect is symbolic and pertains to what Edward Shils terms 'central values'. There is plenty of support for an argument that the nobility as a whole and the magnates in particular had a special position in the political order. First, the medieval idea of community was encompassing in a way that is difficult to understand through the lense of modern political theory. It included strong elements of inequality and hierarchy and different orders, nobles and peasants (*rustici*) alike, 'belonged together because each needed the others. Whatever the conflicts of interests between rulers and subjects, great and small, rich and power, they all acted within a dominant system of values that assumed that interests could be harmonised if only sin could be restrained' (Reynolds, 2004:111).

The idea of co-rule and harmony of the orders was strong in all European countries. Walter Ullmann argued that in England the political order was decidedly bilateral. The king did not stand outside the community, he was a part of it (Ullman, 2010:97). The collaboration between the king and his barons was pronounced in England and co-rule was a strong tradition in England and, as we shall see below, in Germany. Several medieval writers spoke of a *pactum*, a contract between the king and his subjects (Ullman, 2010:98). The English jurist Bracton (*c.*1210–68) tried to unite the theocratic aspects of the king with the embedded aspects by saying that the king is the true sovereign as the Vicar of Christ. However, the king was under the law and could not make laws without the agreement of the barons (Ullman, 2010:115). The community, *comunitas regni*, consisted of the baronage and the 'Crown' – the abstraction of the monarchy – united, according to Bishop

Grandisson of Exeter in 1337, the king as head and the peerage as members, hence neither could do without the other (Ullman, 2010:-117–18). An image of this relation, common in France, was that of a marriage between the king and his kingdom (Ullman, 2010:120); part of what Shils called 'central values' of medieval politics were the ideas of hierarchy and of co-operation.

The identification of the political order with its chief kinship-based elements, kingship and nobility, was not just an English phenomenon. A seminal work in the mirror-of-princes genre was *de regimine principum* (the government of kings and princes), written by Giles of Rome for Philip the Fair in *c*.1280. Giles is careful to instruct the prince to take advice from the wisest of his realm and the wisest of them all will come from members of his nobility (Briggs, 1999:4, 61, 71). Furthermore, for Giles kinship was central to the well-ruled kingdom (or city). He advocated hereditary succession since that was more peaceful than elective and, importantly, it was more likely to guarantee rulers interested in the welfare of the realm (Briggs, 1999:72). Giles was deeply steeped in the Aristotelian tradition of political thought (Briggs, 1999:11). His work was divided into three parts, the king's government of himself, the king's government of his family and household and finally of the realm (Romanus, 1997). Chapter 2 presented Norberto Bobbio's juxtaposition of the Aristotelian tradition and the natural law tradition. The former saw families as central to the political order, but the latter cast them out of it. The natural law tradition was an invention of the early modern period, but in the Middle Ages, Aristotelianism was more dominant and hence families were more natural in the political order.

In Chapter 1, I argued that there is a connection between the social science tradition of defining families as outside of the political order and the dominant view of state formation, and the state, as resting upon coercion and forged through warfare. These views would have been alien to medieval intellectuals. Sir John Fortescue (1394–1479) was one of the most important political theorists of the late Middle Ages. His works on the laws and government of England are those of a highly informed inside expert and a normative political writer. The idea of the *communitas regni*, the realm as a political community, gained currency in the thirteenth and fourteenth centuries, and Fortescue further elaborated on the idea and ontology of the realm. The relation of the king to the realm and its inhabitants was central to contemporary political theory. For Fortescue the king is not separate from the realm that he ruled; for example, the fourth clause in the coronation oath required the king to abide by the laws 'chosen by him and the people': 'The government of the realm is "political" because it is ruled by the administration of many ... and "royal" because subjects cannot make laws without "the authority of the king ... " and because "the realm is possessed by kings and their heirs successively in hereditary right"' (Lockwood, 1997:xxiii). The two central strands in Fortescue's political theory are the notions of a polity-centred kingship and of England as a *dominium politicum et regale* – a realm that is ruled politically since many are involved in the making of its laws and ruled regally since the king is the ultimate guarantor of the legitimacy of laws and rule (Fortescue, 1997a:83–90). The king is indispensable since his authority is necessary to make laws (Fortescue, 1997b:133–6; Lockwood, 1997:xxiii). In Fortescue's political theory then, the just polity is constituted by collaboration between its main actors, not by the capacity to coerce its subjects.

The kingdom was an abstract corpus standing above the king and surviving beyond the span of the king and of his subjects. Still, the kingdom needs a king in order not only to be ruled but to be ruled justly. Thus, the king who is a hereditary ruler, is indispensable to a political order that is true to its central values. Fortescue likens the realm to a minor that is under the protection and stewardship of the king, a metaphor that has associations of reciprocity and legality: just like a minor, the realm has rights that the guardian cannot overstep; laws govern the relationship. The polity that Fortescue describes owes a considerable debt to ideas of *res publica*, the realm is a public thing that all inhabitants have a part in and a responsibility towards (Lockwood, 1997:xxxvi).

Fortescue discusses not only the ontological nature of the realm but also the necessary institutions. Laws and the legal profession are one prerequisite; parliament as the legislative body in which the realm is embodied is another; a third is that of good councillors. In connection with the last point Fortescue discusses the nobility, more precisely the magnates. Like many contemporaries and predecessors, he argues that the high nobility has a natural place in the councils of the realm (Fortescue, 1997a:114–17). However, he differs from them in saying that they should not be the only councillors (Lockwood, 1997:xxxvi). In sum, England is a land governed by law and consent, not by force

(Ullman, 2010:127) but Fortescue was writing of England as it ought to be, not as it was. In reality, kings did exercise force from time to time. Still, he was reflecting norms of co-rule that in England were quite old, so the realm existed as an abstract, yet powerful figure. It assembled support and enabled action in a way that corresponded to Shils' idea of central values. But what do we know of concrete practices and institutions in which kings, magnates and nobles were embedded in a political order (and which rested on the idea of hereditary legitimacy)?

The role of parliaments in creating a political order and generating material resources has been studied frequently. Less well-researched is the development of the council. In most countries the papal curia served as the model for the intimate circles of government (Arnold, 1991:35). In England the Norman kings established the King's Council (*Curia Regis*) in the eleventh century. It was divided into the Great Council (*Magnum Concilium*) and the Small Council. The Great Council was summoned by the king at irregular intervals and its members were the magnates and their servants. It eventually developed into the House of Lords while the small council remained a more intimate and central instrument of government (Hintze, 1962a:126). The development of small councils took place all over Western Europe in the thirteenth century, in England, in France, in the German principalities and in the Iberian states. The council was the King's body, he summoned it and he chose his councillors (Quillet, 1988:547).

There was a consensus among political theorists of the high and the late Middle Ages that the king needed to surround himself with councillors to help him govern. One of their principal tasks was to make sure that the king managed the art of governing by consultation and dialogue and did not act as a tyrant (Rigaudière, 2008:33). Political thinkers stressed that counsel that was given to the king in the royal council was a relationship based on the reciprocal relation of duty. Attendance in a council was not a right, but a duty, one of the obligations that a vassal had to his lord was to provide him with counsel and help, *concilium et auxilium* (Flori, 2004:12). The 'great men' who were the advisors of the king were not only expected to assist their king, they expected to be entitled to do so (Althoff, 2000:11). Conversely, according to Jean Gerson and Nicole Oresme who represented mainstream views in fourteenth century France, the king had an obligation to consult his subjects, or members of the three estates, or at least men that were considered prudent and wise (Quillet, 1988:549).

During the early modern era, the council seems to have become more of a noble preserve but in the Middle Ages this point was under debate. Several political commentators argued that councillors should not only be chosen from the noble estate or even from the magnate class. We have already encountered Fortescue's views on the situation in England. In France, Jean Gerson (1363–1429) believed that voices from all ranks of the kingdom should be heard, not because it was their right to voice concerns but because the fullness of information would be more beneficial to the king (Quillet, 1988:548). The views of Fortescue and Gerson are interesting not only as polemicists but because they imply what the norm was: the high nobility counselled the king.

Representation and the Political Order

A long tradition in social thought identifies medieval representative institutions as the origins of modern parliaments and modern representation (Hintze, 1962a; Hegel, 1966:96; Koenigsberger, 1971; Downing, 1989; Blickle, 1997). Late-medieval representative institutions have been studied as elements of state formation. The standard account is that local and national assemblies enabled a more effective taxation system that yielded revenue to the state, gave rulers control over their subjects and gave taxpayers a stake in the state (Downing, 1988; Tilly, 1990; Rokkan et al., 1999).

This functionalist interest in representation is a result of the influence of the 'warfare thesis' of state formation that argues that the primary driver of state-formation was the systemic pressure to defend the (proto-)state from external and internal enemies (Kaspersen, Strandsbjerg and Teschke, 2017). The connection between representative institutions, taxation and state formation is important, but representation played an earlier, more fundamental, role in creating political order through a political community of trust mainly between kings and magnates. Chapter 4 covered the subject of electoral monarchies among the Anglo-Saxons and the Franks. I will now deal with this topic in the Central and Northern European polities of the high Middle Ages as a form of representation and argue that it accounted for a particularly important form of interdependence between kings, nobles and the political order. Electoral monarchies existed in Denmark, Sweden, Bohemia (Barudio, 1998:137–44), Hungary (Duchhardt, 2003:116, 139, 184), Poland and the Holy Roman Empire (Haldén, 2014) and to some extent in France in the later Middle Ages and early modern period (Jackson, 1972). Electoral monarchy lasted until 1544 in Sweden, in Bohemia until 1620, in Hungary until 1687, in Denmark until 1620, in Poland-Lithuania until 1792 and in the Holy Roman Empire until 1806.

The electoral nature of the German monarchy goes back to post-Carolingian times. The only real attempt to transform it into a hereditary monarchy was made during the Staufen dynasty but this failed (Schmidt, 1987:264). Not just anyone could stand for election, instead there was a strong idea that a number of king-like lineages that were eligible for kingship existed in the realm (Mitteis, 1944:55). Before the twelfth century, candidates seem to have used the authority that derived from royal descent to pressure nobles (princes) to vote for them. Some early elections were open competitions between candidates from the different peoples of the German kingdom, such as the Bavarians, Franks, Saxons, Suabians and Thuringians. In the twelfth century the political system shifted in a more aristocratic direction that meant that the principle of free elections was established. The condition for being elected king was that an agreement could be reached with the noble electorate. Royal descent does not feature as a condition for election in the sources and no candidate raised kinship with the preceding king as an argument for why he should be elected (Schmidt, 1987). However, material resources partly explain why only certain lineages could be elected kings. The office had no independent resource base, which meant that the elected king-emperor had to finance 'public' expenses from the revenues from his own lands. This explains why the Habsburgs, the richest and most powerful lineage, dominated the office for so long.

An important part of the institution of kingship is its connection to divinity. In this respect the electoral monarchy of the German lands differed from the hereditary ones of France and England. In the empire, the sacredness of the emperor was a direct function of the fact that he was elected (Schubert, 1977:260ff). German scholarship calls this *Wahlheiligkeit* (holiness through election) while in France this connection was contained in the connection of a certain dynasty to the divine. This difference was expressed in the greater importance attributed to the ritual of anointment in France, whereby the king was sanctioned by and connected to God (Schubert, 1977:264). In the empire, as we have seen, the most important ritual was the election. The tradition of the emperor's holiness through election found echoes in political theory. In his defence of the empire Dante claimed that the German princes that elected the emperor in fact were mouthpieces of God (Shaw, 2007: xxix–xxx). During the late Middle Ages, Nicholas of Cusa illustrates the ambiguity of where the emperor's authority comes from. In *De concordantia catholica* from 1483 he states that the might of the emperor rests on the will of the population of the empire. However, the office of the emperor is derived from God and as *Vicarus Christi* he stands above all princes and peoples (Nicolas of Cusa, 1991:228–34). Although other sources of authority were necessary in order to become a king, authority transferred through election was necessary in order to become a king. In order to interpret what this meant for the German realm and other electoral monarchies we must first analyse who elected the king.

According to the most important German source of law in the thirteenth century, the *Sachsenspeigel* ('mirror of the Saxons'), all princely members of the nobility had the right to elect the king. Gradually this right was transferred to seven electoral princes (*Kurfürsten*) – the bishops of Trier, Mainz and Cologne, the Count Palatinate of the Rhine, the Duke of Saxony, the Margrave of Brandenburg and the king of Bohemia (Eckhardt, 1955) . Later, the king of Bohemia did not take part in the elections. The Golden Bull of 1356 formalized the exclusive right of election by the seven major princes and the principle of majority in the elections of the emperor (Müller, 1964:31–5). In contrast the *Sachsenspiegel* states that all princes had the right to elect the emperor and even after the electors had been given the exclusive right to elect the emperor, the other princes remained important as a 'public' whose acceptance of the candidate was considered essential (Schubert, 1977:266, 269).

The interplay between authorization and accountability is central to representation (Pitkin, 1967). In electoral monarchies it was exercised through an institution called 'electoral capitulations', the promises that the candidate had to give to the electorate in order to get elected. In many European realms the monarch had to swear an oath upon his coronation that usually contained promises to respect the liberties and privileges of the nobility, uphold the laws and defend the realm. Coronation oaths also existed in countries whose monarchs were elected but the electoral capitulations varied from monarch to monarch and they were negotiated with the electors.

The first formal electoral capitulation was that of Charles V in 1519, but important predecessors exist. In 1400 the election of Ruprecht was accompanied by a document that can be seen as a capitulation (Schubert, 1977:319). Another important predecessor was the agreement between the emperor-to-be and the electors in 1348. Schubert sees this document as an expression of common responsibility for the entire realm (Schubert, 1977:321). The oath taken by Sigismund in Aachen in 1414 was already of a distinct political kind: 'This oath shows that it was dissimilar to the coronation oath ... but that it was rather a special obligation/commitment to the electorate' (Schubert 1977:322, my translation). After this obliging promise had been spoken, the original coronation oath was sworn. These oaths, as well as their formalized successors, the electoral capitulations, were intended to bind the elected to the will of his electors, or in modern language the representative to the represented (Schubert, 1977:326).

The electors, who dictated the capitulations, acted as representatives or speakers for the other princes who set the boundaries for how an emperor could act (Stollberg-Rilinger, 2007:26–7). Before drawing up each capitulation the electors looked back upon the reign of the previous emperor and tried, by means of the capitulation, to rectify or avoid a repetition of the mistakes (from their point of view) of the predecessor (Gotthard, 2005:10–11). Thus, the electors exercised a certain kind of accountability, although with the delay of one generation. In cases where the reigning emperor tried to have his successor appointed while he was still alive in order to secure the succession, the terms agreed on in the capitulation had the character of settling an account with the reigning monarch. The early capitulations were preceded by agreements between the candidate and individual electors. However, in the late Middle Ages and early modern period the capitulations were negotiated with the electors as a collective (Schubert, 1977:319; Fehrenbach, 1984:451–2; Stollberg-Rillinger, 2007:26–7). The Golden Bull of 1356 considered the election as a common action of all the electors and the character of the electors as members and representatives of the polity, as an entity larger than the sum of individual components, was more pronounced than in the earlier period (Schubert, 1977:319).

Sweden also had an elected monarchy, as stated in the code of laws for the entire realm from 1350. Like in Germany before the twelfth century, candidacy was not free. The Land law stated that the king should be a man born in Sweden and 'preferably the son of a king' (Holmbäck and Wessén, 1962:19–20). However, it is unclear whether this was always adhered to in practice. The king was to be elected by grandees, the so-called men of the law, as well as twelve other representatives from the core lands of Uppland, Westmanland, Dalecarlia, East Gothia and West Gothia. Royal elections were often a two-step process: a first informal de facto election made by the lords and a second formal but in fact confirmative one by the representatives of the non-nobles (Schück, Bengtsson and Stjernquist, 1992:32). The election of Karl Knutson Bonde as king in 1448 took place in this way. First an assembly of sixty to seventy noble 'men of the realm' elected him. Only after this internal decision was made did the men of the lands perform the election. The Swedish lords created their authority by making two claims of representation. On the one hand they claimed to represent the realm by calling themselves 'men of Sweden' (*svenske men*), on the other they stated that they spoke on behalf of 'the Men of the Realm in Sweden'. The two expressions referred to two different facets of representation: making something abstract present, embodying, and acting in the place of another, standing in. They could be seen as strategies to claim authority but also as strategies to enable collaboration with other groups by linking up with them.

As in Germany, the king-to-be had to give two kinds of promises: the first was the general coronation oath to safeguard traditional liberties and the right to political participation of the estates (Schlyter and Collin, 1869:12ff). The second was the more specific electoral capitulations (*handfästningar*) (Nordström, 1839:84–5). Similarly, there were also two sets of promises in the Polish-Lithuanian Commonwealth. The first, *Articui Henriciani*, was general and 'specified the powers of the King, the privileges of the nobility, and the basic rules of the system of administration'. The second, *pacta conventa*, was specific and changed from election to election (Lerski, Wróbel and Kozicki, 1996:416). The requirement to give *handfästningar* that guaranteed the traditional liberties of the estates lived on even after Gustav Vasa made the Swedish crown hereditary. His son, John III, had to give *handfästningar* at his coronation in 1569, so did Charles IX in 1609 and Gustavus Adolphus in 1611(Nordström, 1839:86–7). Electoral capitulations also existed in neighbouring Denmark until the seventeenth century (Geijer and Lundvall, 1836:379–81). The longevity of this practice testifies to the enduring importance of the estates at royal elections.

Of central importance to this book is the fact that the royal elections not only expressed but in fact constituted a condition of mutual dependence. An actor had to be elected and/or appointed in order to become king – despite the fact that the candidate had so many and such strong resources of power at his disposal, the king needed the approval of the electors for his authority, which in turn means that we have to interpret the electors as having authority that they could bestow. Conversely, the electors and the other princes and nobles had to have a king not only to unify the realm but they needed him also in a more fundamental sense since he was the fountainhead of their authority. Without a king there could be no nobility and as Montesquieu later argued, there could be no king without a nobility (Montesquieu, 1989:18; Krieger, 1992:106). This leads us to the interesting conclusion that the king and electors (as well as the other princes) were the sources of each other's authority. A contemporary expression of this bond can be found the concepts of *Wahlheiligkeit* – the king's holiness as dependent upon his electoral status – and *Königsnähe* – the nobles' need to be close to the king in order to have authority. The two concepts complemented each other, not only by creating a relation of mutual dependence but in fact in the sense that the two co-constituted each other.

Nobles did represent the kingdom not only in institutions and practices of election but also in the many rituals of monarchy. Although the king was the central person at his coronation and funeral, he was not alone. These were eminently political events because they (re-)created the king and the kingdom. They were also magical rituals in the sense that certain actions had to be performed and certain words had to be said in order to start the machinery of power, there were many rituals at which the representatives of the realm had to be present in order for the realm to be conjured into existence. Royal coronations, marriages and funerals were among the most important. In the following I will concentrate on coronations and funerals in France.

Some nobles attended these ceremonies as witnesses, making up the audience that guaranteed that the ritual really took place and did so in the right context. Others acted as functionaries. A French coronation proceeded in several stages: preparation of the church and the king, the combat with a victory over impurity, the request made to the king and his oath, sacred vesture, unction, communion, investiture with the regalia, and the acknowledgement through a procession and celebration (Lafages, 1992:19). The most important functionary in many of these stages was the archbishop but the peers of France, who were the leading nobles of the land, were indispensable at medieval royal coronations (Jackson, 1971:27–46). The peers brought the king from the palace to the church for the coronation and afterwards presented him to the people (Lafages, 1992:32–4). During the coronation, they performed important ritual acts. First, the Senechal of France held the king's sword when the latter received unction, that is holy oil on his head, stomach, back, shoulders, under the arms and on the palms. When the king received the regalia, the spiritual and temporal peers held up the crown and conducted the king to his throne. Later, the barons did the same for the queen (Jackson, 1971:29; Lafages, 1992:25). The peers also fitted the shoes, spurs and sword onto the king. These were part of a knight's attire and armaments and thus symbolically indispensable to the king's role as a warrior and protector of the realm (Lafages, 1992:26, 38–9). The fact that peers of the realm equipped the king for this role demonstrates not only their allegiance to him but also his dependence on them. This ritual is similar in form to the way that kings and nobles equipped each other with authority in royal elections; strengthening their bonds and demonstrating their symbiosis. Finally, the peers bestow the kiss of peace upon the king and swear an oath of loyalty to him (Lafages, 1992:32–4). As a whole the ritual is one of mutual dependence, the peers place their 'might and substance' at the service of the king but the king cannot do without them, neither during the ritual (which must be performed), nor in governing the country (which the ritual demonstrates). I believe that it is important not only to interpret the actions of the peers of France during the coronations of their kings as signs of submission or servitude. In a way they were but they were also indispensable to the set of ritual actions that made a king a king and the transferred kingship from the dead to the living king.

How should one interpret representation, what is it as a social phenomenon and what did it do to the configuration of kings and nobles that were united by its institutions and ideas? A key is, I believe, to focus on its relational character, actors in a social system depend on each other and have to co-operate. It is likely that different groups will have access to different resources of power which in turn may create mutual dependence since group A may need the resources that group B possesses and vice versa. In discussions of power, resources are often conceived of in material terms or as control over institutions. I will focus on another resource: possession of political authority. Some resources are mutually exclusive and hence subject to zero-sum competition. Authority, however, can be cumulative, shared and transferred if one decides to confer it on another party. Moreover, it is a resource that can rarely be conquered by arms alone. The more authority a group or person has either on their own or as part of an authority-sharing coalition, the more that group or coalition can do. Since representation involves the transfer of authority, it can be seen as a means to create collaboration and enable a division of authority and power between different groups. Hence, representation connects societal groups with each other and creates larger formations. The arrangements that we usually study as representation are authority-sharing arrangements that result from deals as well as from power struggles. Thus, representation is a regulating force in social systems involving the distribution, allocation, legitimating and control over authority, and prescribes the relations between actors of the in terms of ties and duties. However, it is important to emphasize that the relations between representative and represented can be described not only in terms of connections, ties or bonds, but also of tension and conflict (Pitkin, 1967:114).

Because of the uncertainty when one party grants authority and power to another, representation necessarily involves trust. I see trust as a contingent social category existing in various degrees in different social systems (Luhmann, 1968, 1998; Giddens, 1990). Although trust is contingent, it is nevertheless fundamental since it 'makes the formation of systems possible' (Luhmann, 1995:129). All individuals or groups that interact face uncertainty that they can transform into trust or distrust. Trust is a more profitable strategy but because it widens the scope and potential for action (Luhmann, 1995:128) it entails more possibilities of rational action. In a social system this means that the more trusting relations there are the more alternatives are available in the system (Luhmann, 1998). Thus trust-increasing rituals allow the construction of social systems; in our case the political order.

Furthermore, recent developments in political theory have stressed the constitutive effects of representation which allows us to ask research questions focused on 'what representation does, rather than what it is' (Nasstrom, 2011:506). In this interpretation, representation is not a process of transmission between two pre-existing entities but a performative act constructing both the represented and the representatives. There is no 'people' that pre-exists the representative or the act of representation (Nasstrom, 2011:506–7). A similar move away from formal-legal perspectives has taken place in the history discipline (Schmidt, 1987:5–34). Stollberg-Rillinger argues that a paramount aspect of pre-modern representation was that symbolic and ritual practices were constitutive of political communities (Stollberg-Rilinger, 2008).

This constitutive element was strongly present in the royal elections. To summarize, representation creates not only trust but also social groups, their relations, and the social whole that we in analytical terms can call 'the polity' but which was usually called 'the realm' (*regnum*) in the European Middle Ages.

To understand the formation of social and political systems we must also note the unintended effects of the act of claiming to represent. Claiming to represent something, in our case 'the realm', may be effective in order to get authority but it also increases your dependence on the thing or group you claim to represent. This 'move' to get authority will bind an actor through the claims he makes. In order to get authority your claim has to be credible, you have to assume some obligations towards the people or the abstraction you claim to represent. Obligations towards an abstraction like a 'realm' can take the form of having to remain loyal in times of internal or external war or assuming responsibility by performing administrative duties. I certainly do not mean to argue that such obligations were or are always automatic and I do not mean to idealize pre-modern societies. History is too riddled with stories of hypocrisy and exploitation for that. Also, political arguments did not bind medieval actors in the exact same way as they might bind modern actors since they did not take place in cultures with written records and mass media. My argument is rather to highlight the processes of embedding and self-binding that resulted as unintended consequences of strategies to attain authority and power.

The lords of Sweden claimed to have authority by virtue of representing the realm as an abstract figure and as a collection of other groups. Similar discourses existed in the empire. In one of them electoral princes claimed to be 'pillars of the Realm' (*solide bases imperii et columpne immobiles*) (Cohn, 2006; Heinig, 2009). In another, the empire was spoken of as a realm with 'head and members' (*Haupt und Glieder*), the 'head' being the emperor and the princes and estates 'the members' (Schmidt, 1999:42). My point is that that these discourses, symbols and arguments meant that the realm was constructed as belonging to this group of actors but it also worked the other way round, they belonged to and were inseparable from the realm; they could not constitute themselves as wholly autonomous centres of power. The fact that other actors were indispensable parts of the political (although not material) power base of each actor was a powerful inoculation against disintegration. It also may explain why attempts to declare independence as an autonomous unit were so very rare in premodern Europe, despite frequent, bloody and crippling civil wars. Most rebellions were directed against specific policies or kings, not the realm itself. In other words, they took place within the realm not against it. If we do not take the integrity of European realms for granted but instead we assume that disintegration would be a constant possibility then integrity must be explained. I believe that the political interdependence created by representation goes a long way in explaining it. Material factors alone cannot explain this. There were frequent civil wars during the long period when neither kings nor states as organizations had a monopoly of violence, were strong enough to enforce stability or could coerce would-be separatists. Despite this, most realms held together, and the answer must be sought in political factors.

In sum, through the political and intersubjective institutions of representation principal social actors and groups were constituted as existing in binding relations to each other. This created durable relations and commitments that over time coalesced into routinized and stable polities. This argument implies that general theories and accounts of state formation in history as well as today must pay more attention to politics, understood as the intersubjective and meaningful relations between important actors conveyed, contained and created through arguments, claims, narratives and rituals.

Noble Privileges

During the twelfth and thirteenth centuries a number of polities took the first steps of codifying what it meant to be noble. Or, rather, what it meant for a kin group to be part of the noble category. Classifications of what kin groups belonged to the noble category came a couple of centuries later. These codifications of rights and duties of a particular category of actors were also codifications of the polity itself. The social categorization was also a categorization of the political community and the rights and duties that defined it and the relations of its members to each other, to the centre of the polity (the monarch) and to some extent to outsiders. Privileges were central to the definition of nobility and were either seigneurial or noble. Seigneurial rights granted the holder powers to administer justice and govern locally. Noble privileges included tax exemption and rights of political participation, reserved military and civilian offices, trading concessions and the right to be tried in a separate legal system (Bush, 1988:2–3).

European nobilities varied substantially from country to country and from region to region. So did their privileges but the existence of privileges was, together with 'a reverence for lineage and an acceptance of the noble ethic', what united the nobilities of Europe (Bush, 1988:1). Privileges had different origins, some developed incrementally and varied from individual to individual, others were corporate and granted to whole categories of nobles. Examples of formal codification of liberties and rights through charters are the English Magna Carta (1215), the Golden Bull of Hungary (1222), Alnsö Stadga in Sweden (1280) and the Golden Bull of Charles IV in Germany (1358) (Näf, 1951). Other privileges were included in more general law texts such as the German law collections *Sachsenspiegel* (*c.*1220) (Eicke von Repgow and Eckhardt, 1955–66). The example of Hungary illustrates the link between noble privilege and polity formation. The country had one of the most numerous and politically strongest nobilities of Europe during the Middle Ages and the early modern era. The Golden Bull confirmed the nobility's freedom from taxes and granted them a right to resistance if these and other rights were violated. The document led to the growth of the idea of a political community of the realm (*communitas regni*) and the establishment of an estates-based parliamentarism from 1277 onwards. The country became a full-blown state of the estates with yearly diets in the 1450s (Konter, 2002:77, 116).

Not only legal documents outline obligation as the counterpart to privilege. We also find this theme represented in contemporary chivalric literature. Noble birth was not sufficient, one had to prove one's worth by performing deeds. Geoffroi de Charny, one of the leading authorities on chivalry (1352), chides and shames those who, although born into high social standing, have done nothing to win honour and fame for themselves through deeds (de Charny, 2005:62–3). De Charny also legitimates the high standing of 'Emperors, Kings and Princes of Lands' with their outstanding performances, courage, physical hardiness, virtues and by taking care of the population (de Charny,

2005:139–45). In other words, extraordinary and hence charismatic in its claims to legitimate domination, hereditary birth had to be matched by extraordinary feats. Of particular importance to our present subject is the focus of these deeds: the service of the realm and/or of the king.

Performing great deeds was not an expression of altruism. The value of the individual was, however, connected to deeds that benefitted the community or were told in front of it. However, the orientation towards the common in the script of roles and actions impacted on polity-formation. This is reflected in aristocratic literature of the middle ages. Brian Murdoch argues that the heroic epic of Germanic cultures from the sixth to the fifteenth century was a 'largely political' form of literature (Murdoch, 1996:3). The term Germanic includes Old English, Middle High German, Old Norse, Latin and Old French sources. Hence, the category of literary heroes and political role models includes an Anglo-Saxon figure like Beowulf, a Frank such as Roland from the *Chanson de Rolande* and a high medieval German such as Heinrich von Kempten. Such figures share several traits such as 'the value of [their] *res gestae* ... acts of fame, are given meaning only within a political construct' (Murdoch, 1996:4). This political context defines the Germanic heroic epic. Charles Fornara defines the genre as a 'direct concern with the description of the *res gestae*, man's actions in politics, diplomacy and war, in the far and near past' (Fornara, 1983:3). Epic poems like the Germanic *Heldenlieder* and the *Chansons de Gestes* were read aloud by professional minstrels and *Minnesänger* in a public context, for example, to an aristocratic audience or at princely or royal courts (Härd, 1993:24–5). They were normative and prescriptive texts intended to express and instil the values and world views of a medieval aristocracy. The deeds valued in this culture were performed on behalf of the king or the polity and, in order to be worth something, they had to be registered by an audience consisting of the main political actors. The heroic literature and the culture it reflected and reproduced thus oriented actions and values towards the centre, towards the political order.

Finally, we should not underestimate the constant stream of normative connections between heroism and deeds and the appreciation of women that is encountered in the chivalric literature. Medieval authors often tell their readers that a reward for great deeds will be the love of beautiful and noble ladies. Or, indeed, telling ladies that they should love and attach themselves to men capable of great deeds (de Charny, 2005:66). The idealized image of courtly love and the idea that such notions led to considerable improvement of a lot of women has been rightly criticised (Paravicini, 1994). However, we should not underestimate the normative-cultural linkage between performing deeds, either for one's own glory alone or for collective purposes, and gaining 'access' to love and reproduction (the latter being very important in a society focused on lineage and having heirs).

Embedding Through War

The nobility was a part of the political order not only in parliaments and processions but also through its military role. War, then as now, was a central aspect of the political order and it was central to the identity of the nobility. The organization for war provides us with insights into the shape of the political order and the symbiotic position of aristocrats in it. When the king wanted to raise an army, he would first call upon members of the higher aristocracy both for recruiting and for leading the army. Not only did they have the means of performing both tasks, they were considered as natural war leaders and the 'natural counsellors' of the king in major political decisions (de Charny, 2005:60ff; Davies, 2009:116, 119, 129). Rees Davies argued that raising an army and fighting with it was a natural and central, even foundational, part of lordship (Davies, 2009:122, 134). Although speaking of the British Isles his conclusions have a general validity. He describes military expeditions as joint-stock enterprises between the king and his magnates that bound the two parties closer together (Davies, 2009:124–5). 'Successful war was one of the best ways of forging an effective relationship between crown and magnates; nowhere did the interests of both parties more closely coincide' (Davies, 2009:127, 129). By the late Middle Ages the noble's ambition for honour and prowess and his obligation for public service amalgamated in the practice of war. In England fighting wars was the king's prerogative albeit with magnate armies but in Scotland and Ireland, military power and practice were more decentralized (Davies, 2009:134–5).

Any army of a more substantial size would be a composite of different forces, recruited by different leaders, serving under different commanders – only indirectly connected to what we would call a 'supreme commander' – and participating in the war under different terms and, often, for different motives (Nicholson, 2003:39–40, 47–9, 50–1). The various elements of the armed force would be connected to their commander by means of kinship, lordship and fellowship. There were four principal ways of creating military power in the high Middle Ages: a) mercenaries, foreign and domestic; b) magnate contingents; c) royal household troops and d) levies: *fyrds* in England and *arrière-ban* in France (Kaeuper, 1988). However, the core of an armed force, whether it was a small warband or a large royal army would be the household troops of the lord. These, in turn, would – speaking in terms of ideal types – consist of different groups of men: the unfree dependents of the *familia*, some of whom were peasants that could be drafted, others would be military specialists like the *ministeriales* (Althoff, 2004:103, 111). *Ministeriales* were a particular German phenomenon; a kind of knight that was legally unfree but in practice often important. Ties of lordship to their commander would bind such men. However, there would also be young warriors drawn to the lord's court by his reputation for prowess in war, hoping to gain fame and fortune for themselves, or older men attracted by the lord's generosity. A great lord in the late Middle Ages would have a network of military supporters, retainers, which he would be able to summon for wartime duty.

Autonomous magnate contingents played a considerable role in the royal armies of the thirteenth and fourteenth centuries (Kaeuper, 1988:27). During the fourteenth and fifteenth centuries the polymorphous armies of the early and high Middle Ages changed. In the late medieval period kings and princes began to assert tighter legal control over the organization of warfare and over arms-bearing actors. By the mid-fourteenth century the English government had begun to use paid contractors to recruit soldiers (Nicholson, 2003:48–9). In Germany, princes as well as emperors began to use *ministeriales* and mercenary troops to pursue dynastic politics of aggrandizement. In France and Burgundy a series of monarchs introduced institutional innovations that created the emergence of an autonomous royal army and in 1439 King Charles VII of France issued an ordinance that aimed to regulate the rights to bear arms and to raise forces. The king selected a number of captains and gave them and only them the right to bear the title of captain and raise companies. No one else, on the pain of death, was allowed to organize armed forces. Lords who possessed fortifications and garrisons were forbidden to raise taxes to support their troops, if they wanted to keep their troops, they had to do so at their own expense (Zmora, 2001:37). Hence the king claimed not only a monopoly on organizing troops or waging war but he also claimed the authority to designate legitimate possession. A problem of the medieval armies was that they were not standing armies but raised afresh for each campaign. In 1445, Charles VII introduced an early form of permanent army by appointing royal captains to command the best troops from the mercenary companies. In a series of subsequent ordinances he set up companies. The royal army would be financed through the *taille*, a direct tax on non-nobles. Still, nobles were a majority of those serving in standing companies, something contemporaries saw as natural (Keen, 2005:152).

Kings remained dependent upon the noble families as military entrepreneurs and commanders for a long time. War and diplomacy were the reserved domains of the aristocracy. As Strayer writes: 'Certainly the prelates, princes of the blood and great nobles, who were the dominant elements in the Council in most states, felt that these were areas in which they had special responsibility and competence. They were indispensable as heads of diplomatic missions, governors of frontier regions and commanders of armies ... ' (Strayer, 2005:86). Thus nobles were central by virtue of their connections and their descent that made them appear natural for these tasks. These ideas rather than autonomous power resources in the shape of delimited groups with which they shared real or fictitious kinship were the real foundations of noble power and their centrality in the political figuration.

There is a long tradition in sociology and political science to argue that the organization for and waging of war were important drivers of state formation (e.g., Hintze, 1962b; Tilly, 1990). State theorists often focus on the material and organizational aspects of the polities that they have studied (Gorski, 2003:22). However, Gorski argues that through this material focus, state theorists, with the exceptions of Norbert Elias, Michel Foucault, Gerhard Oestrich and Max Weber, have ignored the 'soul' of the polities that they have studied (Gorski, 2003:22). Arguments about the link between warfare and state growth are no exception to this rule as they often emphasize the growth in taxation, armies and organizations. However, the ideational or even idealistic aspects have been overlooked. The ideal and obligation of fighting together with other units from the same polity also had a unifying effect. Modern theories of political representation no longer claim that representatives represent a pre-existing polity. Rather, through the very act of representation, that polity is created. A similar line of argument may be applied to fighting, which is also a form of political representation although most of it takes place in camps, during marches and on the battlefields. By putting such considerable emphasis on fighting, together and for one's king and realm, in the noble spirit that very realm was conjured into existence, again and again.

The Soul of the Polity

Chivalry

A search for the soul of the medieval polity will quickly come across chivalry, the cultural expression of the habitus of the mounted, kinship-organized warrior elites of Europe (Keen, 2005). Chivalry, a set of values, practices and norms that created a knightly and later a noble identity, contributed to polity formation in Europe. To the extent that chivalry has at all featured in discussions of state formation it has been discussed primarily in the light of containing or preventing noble violence. For example, Kaeuper argues that chivalry did not only stem or restrain violence but actually produced it by promoting the quest for martial honour and the cult of prowess (Kaeuper, 1999). But the formation of political order is not merely about the absence or organization of violence. It is also about the formation of social systems. Limiting historical inquiry to whether chivalry prevented violence and by extension whether chivalry foreshadowed the internal pacification, a monopoly of violence and a modern state, runs close to teleology. Instead, we can ask how chivalry contributed to the formation of a social system that underpinned the political order and create symbioses between the collective reality and kinship groups. I claim that it gave elite culture a cohesion around a set of what Shils calls 'central values', oriented it towards the political order and increased the public character of the nobility (Shils, 1982).

Chivalry developed as set of values, prescribed practices and norms – in short a self-conscious identity and a culture in which this identity was reinforced and enacted. The reach of this culture was pan-European. It enabled nobles to recognize each other as members of a community, regardless of whether they called their code *chevalerie*, *chyualry* or *cauayleria* (Contamine, 1998:95). Participation in and conformity to this culture, or at least aspects of it, was mandatory for anyone who wished to be recognized as noble and to play a role in the higher circles of society. This does not mean that we should attempt to read contemporary treaties on chivalry or romances as descriptions of actual behaviour. Ideals of offering protection to the poor and defence-less, such as paupers and women, were often ignored or violated. Likewise, aspirations to lead a cultured lifestyle in many cases remained on the level of aspiration. What matters more to the questions raised in this book is that a strongly normative and prescriptive code emerged that demanded conformity at least in parts and could justify sanctions against transgressors. The value system of chivalry gravitated around a few key concepts: loyalty, generosity, military process, and courtly style and manners (Stacey, 1999:14). A related set of ideas was that of 'courtliness', *curialitas* or *cortezia* – the values and behaviour associated with life at court. These rules of composure centred on qualities like *disciplina* (discipline), *elegantia morum* (elegant ways), *hilaritas* (jolli-ness), *temperantia* (temperance), *generositas* (generosity) and loyalty (*triuwe*) and honour (Paravicini, 1994). *Triuwe* was a central trope in courtly literature of the high Middle Ages. The medieval concept had several meanings and connotations such as loyalty, engagement, duty and promise but also more emotional ones like well-wishing, sincerity, trustworthiness and armistice (Kirschstein and Schnulze, 2010:1771–2; Lexer, 1992:231, 454). We find it in the works of Wolfram von Eschenbach (*Parzifal*) and 'The Nibelungenlied', as well as in many other lesser-known romances (Poag, 1962, 1965; Frankki, 1990). In the culture of *prudomie* and *chevalerie*, it was central for retainers to show loyalty to their lords. Chrétien de Troyes (*c.*1130–90), one of the most important authors of romances and court poet linked chivalry not only to excellence in warlike activities but also with public duties of the aristocracy. The importance of following the duties of chivalry over the pursuit of personal happiness is echoed in works like *Erec* and *Perceval* (Maddox and Sturm-Maddox, 2005; Szkilnik, 2005). This central norm of chivalry comes to us repeatedly in the sources of the high Middle Ages, in romance, in didactic writing and in historical works (Crouch, 2005:56–62).

The social type associated with the chivalric habitus was the knight, a figure central to any discussion of medieval society, culture and identity. The origins of knighthood lay with the warriors, *milites*, who served in the retinues of noble lords and in particular of those of the castle-keepers, the castellans. Originally the term signified mounted warriors as well as foot soldiers, but in the eleventh century the term referred only to those who fought on horseback, with the by-meaning of being the true warriors (Flori, 2004:149). Knights were first distinct from nobles but towards the end of the twelfth century the concepts merged (Nicolson, 2004:53ff). Not every knight would be noble but almost all nobles were knights as nobility had adopted the culture and the rituals of knighthood as part of its identity. In most countries knights, many of who came from the upper stratum of the peasant class, formed a lower stratum of the nobility. Ambitious men could enter the knightly estate through service and royal or lordly favour. However, the original nobility, who defined themselves in terms of descent, heritage and office-holding, preserved their exclusive status (Flori, 2004:163). As Crouch puts it: '[t] he nobility was defined above all by birth. It was a matter of blood, of parentage; one was born noble and the Carolingian ancestry of the medieval nobility is hardly in doubt' (Crouch, 2005:129–35). Chivalry reinforced a community of the elite of the military professionals. The communal aspects and symbiotic effects were strengthened by the adoption of chivalric values by the nobility and even by kings. Chivalry created a fusion of knights and nobles was created on a social and a cultural level. This development was crowned with the development of royal orders of knighthood such as the Order of the Garter or the Order of the Golden Fleece (Allman, 1998:838; Keen, 2000). When kings adopted the values and organizations of the knights, to the point of becoming knights themselves, it by no means signalled social levelling but rather a linkage across the social hierarchy. By the twelfth century, however, knighthood became more restricted to the nobility. Numerous orders by kings and knightly orders state that only those who can trace noble descent, sometimes up to four generations, were eligible for knighthood (Keen, 2005:143–6, 159). This development went hand in hand with growing emphasis on the hereditary status of the elite. In practice, however, individuals and thus their descendants could be granted nobility for service, marriage or acquisition of wealth.

Chivalry was important because it initially integrated different social groups with each other. It also reinforced the orientation of elite groups towards the centre, understood as 'central values', the political sphere and the king. The fusion of noble identity and ideals of loyalty and the tropes that deeds must be done for the king exemplify this. Chivalrous literature made use of good and bad exempla such as the contrast between the virtuous and loyal knight and the fallen, traitorous one (Crouch, 2005). An example is the contrast between Roland and Ganelon in the *Chanson de Roland*. Another the contrast between Sigfried and Hagen in the *Lay of the Nibelungs*. The prime marker of the aristocracy was chivalry – practices, attitudes and abilities exercised in a public context, and for the public. Elite kindreds could not be closed and self-referential in their values and ambitions for recognition and honour – both of which were main drivers of action (Lebow, 2008). Chivalry may also have increased trust among elite groups. Since knowledge of and at least periodical conformity with the codes and tropes of chivalry were mandatory for aspiring and established elites, a broad cultural similarity was created. The norms of chivalry prescribed greater leniency in combat between members of the ruling elite. We can infer that nobles and knights trusted each other more to be treated more sparingly in combat and war (Grewe, 2000:114). The rich evidence suggesting that inter-noble encounters often aimed an ritualistic enactment of combat rather than optimal lethality testifies that this was not only an ideal (Bartélemy, 2009). Trust is central to the formation of any social system, and the larger a system is in terms of its membership and territorial reach, the more important systemic trust becomes (Luhmann, 1998). Naturally, there is no need to romanticize chivalry, the prototypical romantic subject, and presume that they were always loyal to their lord once they read or heard the *Chanson de Roland* or *Romance de la Rose*. However, the fact that the chief cultural product of the noble and knightly elite strongly emphasized loyalty, a public orientation for action and honour, and contributed to interpersonal and systemic trust attests to a movement towards embedding and publicness.

Heralds and heraldry are two other medieval cultural phenomena that theorists of political development have largely overlooked. Their importance to the topic of this book is that heraldry was a way of signalling and registering different elite kinship groups. Thus, it created a system that allowed important groups to be catalogued and registered. This system was public in two respects. It was a visual way of appearing in public and it made the groups that mattered part of a public sphere. The heraldic system was constructed between 1120 and 1150. Nobles acquired hereditary family names and signalled their existence through images and symbols. A coat of arms is a picture or a complex of pictures that signify a family. The main part is an image of, for example, a mountain, a mythological beast or an animal. Later, arms developed into composite pictures where the arms of several families were included, but in different fields, in ever more intricate ways. The purpose was to signal the lineage of a person or of a family from several different lineages. Heraldry strengthened the collective awareness of an abstract collective category that a person and a family could belong to. Heraldry made the nobility more public and transparent. Armorial bearings were displayed in public arenas where the elite gathered and enacted its community such as parades, hunts, battles and the tournament. Stollberg-Rillinger convincingly shows that medieval and early modern cultures were 'cultures of presence' where the personal presence of the ruler and co-rulers were crucial (Stollberg-Rillinger, 2007, 2008). Furthermore, the symbols and the families that they symbolized could be written down and thus registered, in books, in miniatures, in paintings, on graves, church windows, church walls and so on.

Bartolus de Saxoferrato is perhaps best known as a theorist of sovereignty but his work *De insignis et armis* (c.1355) was widely circulated treaty on heraldry. De Saxoferrato states that anyone could adopt a coat of arms but one that is granted by a prince is 'advantageous' because it has higher status than others. Also, a coat of arms is hereditary and the right to bear it is transmitted in the male line (de Saxoferrato, 1883:2, 11–12). During the late Middle Ages, lists of armorial bearings were written down in manuals and registers (Paravicini, 1994). Codification of membership in the noble class allowed a fixation of membership and status. Over time rules were developed for how a shield should and could be designed, what it could and should signal – in other words a symbolic language that referred to abstract categories and sub-categories had been created. Visual imagery, social categories, a new social structure and new possibilities of action flow together in the creation of heraldry. Heraldry not only created a catalogue but also a mode of observation and so both a subject that could be observed and observe itself and a position of observation. Phil Gorski argues that observation and self-observation were important parts of the disciplinary revolution of the Reformation (Gorski, 2003). In a similar way, heraldry enabled a perhaps analogous 'disciplinary revolution' that allowed a firmer kind of social system than the figuration that preceded it.

Of course, nobles observed each other but from the very beginning heraldry demanded a neutral observer, cataloguer and arbiter. This was the task of the herald, a historical type that has been researched very little (Paravicini, 1994). However, I believe heralds played an important role in the formation of the grid through which polity-formation was achieved. The chief task of the herald was to keep track of the noble families not only of a single region or even realm but preferably his knowledge and documentation of these sinews of power should extend, at least in some measure, to the European level. One of the tasks of the herald was to survey the battlefields after the fighting had ended to identify and count the noble dead. Another was to record deeds and write chronicles of events; thereby they served as an institutional memory of the noble societies. Heralds were indispensable as repositories of knowledge of the population of the noble system and of the values, norms and prescribed patterns of practice of chivalry. According to Maurice Keen heralds became the 'lay priesthood' of chivalry (Keen, 2005:142). Originally, this observer-figure was neutral and did not belong to a single lord. Heralds signalled their neutrality and impartiality with silver shields. However, gradually heralds became more and more attached to great lords and to the king as their representatives. At the end of the Middle Ages, only the king had heralds, the position of the observer of the nobility had thus been firmly appropriated by royal authority. The herald was not the only observer of heraldry and thus the observer of the nobility, soon the legal system also observed heraldry. In the fifteenth century authorities were established to register and overlook the system of heraldry and thus the system of nobility. The French King Charles VI created a corporation of French heralds in 1406 and Richard III founded a similar body in England, the College of Heralds (later the College of Arms) in 1483/84 (Noble, 1804:54). In sum, during the thirteenth and fourteenth centuries a self-observing, self-aware and self-designating social system of nobility and thus of noble families was created. By contrast, the ninth-century Carolingian nobility was not a system. Historians have only retrospectively been able to construct this social formation as a system of units. Such a classification is, however, an anachronistic imposition on an unsystematic and dynamic reality. The Frankish nobility was a 'system' only in a loose sense of the word, but it was not self-reflective in the way that high medieval nobility was. In contrast, we encounter the nobility of the high Middle Ages as a self-created system with a conceptual framework used by contemporaries.

The cosmological frameworks of medieval politics were also infused with the ideas and images of kinship. When the conversion of the European continent to Christianity was completed, a template for order that made intimate use of semantics of kinship had been introduced. As Marshall Sahlins and David Graeber point out, human societies are embedded in cosmic orders (Graeber and Sahlins, 2017), hence we cannot separate the supernatural from the study of political orders. Cosmic orders – which are usually called 'religious' in modern terms – are also political ones. They give a framework for the exercise of power on earth by laying down the law and stating the authorities that must be obeyed. With the conversion of Europe to Christianity, its populations were embedded in a cosmos whose ultimate authority emanated from God, the Father. The stand-in for mankind in this order was the Son of God, Jesus Christ, who had taken on human form. Finally, the most important religious figure for many people in medieval Europe was Mary, the Holy Virgin, the Mother of the Son of God. Thus, the semantics of order gravitated around a divine family.

In the high Middle Ages, the papacy emerged as a stronger power than ever before (Haldén, 2017b). The Church was a political order in two ways: in itself, in the papal territories and church lands all over Europe and as a structure that embedded other political orders (e.g., the *regna*). Its lands, its wealth, its administrative and military power but above all its intellectual resources and its claims to embody and interpret the central values of Christendom and thus of the supreme political order made it a considerable force. It was also strongly tied to kinship, organizationally and on the level of ideas. Organizationally, the kinship ties of the noble families that dominated the higher echelons of the church hierarchy criss-crossed its structures and institutions, from dioceses and archbishoprics to abbeys and nunneries. On the level of ideas, images of kinship permeated the Church. Not only did it represent the Father and the Son in Heaven but its leader, the Bishop of Rome, was the Holy Father – *papa* of course meaning father in Latin. Addressing the leader of the Church as the father was mirrored by the custom of addressing all priests as fathers, particularly in the sacrament of confession. Monks and nuns addressed each other, and were addressed by the lay population as 'brothers' and 'sisters'. Because of its enforced celibacy, the (Catholic) Church might be the last place where one would look for evidence of kinship-based political order. However, if one considers the anthropological foundations of political and cosmic order one sees that the Western (European) vision of spiritual and thus political authority was fundamentally expressed in kinship terms for over a millennium.

Medieval Polities as Families of Families

Elite lineages were also embedded in the political order through marriage. In medieval Europe it was, together with friendship and lordship, one of the principal ways to create alliances and thus one of the keys to domestic and international success. Because of the importance of kinship connections and since land and titles were the major sources of wealth and both commodities were inheritable, marriage and the production of heirs were the principal routes to career advancement. The fortunes of families rose and fell with royal favour, wars, and with successful and unsuccessful marriages. Marriages were a central issue for noble dynasties since they linked kinship groups and fortunes in the present and over coming generations. Since they affected power relations and had influence over common matters (by organizing the ruling elites) marriages were also political matters.

Ernst Gellner claims that the rulers of agro-literate polities tried to control some of their elites by preventing them from reproducing; turning them into 'geldlings'. European elites were in Gellner's phrase, stallions 'elites who are formally allowed to reproduce themselves socially, and to retain their positions for their offspring' (Gellner, 2008:16). Still, rulers tried to control their 'stallions' through the marriage market by influencing how they reproduced and concluded family alliances. In this respect, royal consent was an important instrument of control. As R. R. Davies writes: 'royal consent, even direct royal intervention, were essential pre-requisites for success in major marriage stakes' (Davies, 2009:143). Policies, as well as personal tastes, dictated royal control over marriages (Davies, 2009:151). In some cases, royal power of consent was codified, for example, section VIII of the Magna Carta stated that widows who held lands of the King were required to seek his consent before remarrying (Magna Carta, 2015:41).

In France, King Philip II Augustus (r.1180–1223) asserted the right to control the marriages of his major vassals, by subjecting them to royal consent (Baldwin, 1991:271). Philip Augustus is known as the great French medieval state-builder but so far, historical-sociological accounts have primarily focused on his wartime success and legal-administrative innovations (Spruyt, 1994:102, 160, 163; Ertman, 1997:60, 166). An equally important aspect was controlling the marriages of aristocratic power holders and thus their possibilities of creating alliances and strengthening their fortunes. He even pursued active policies of ordering their marriages down to the baronial level. Marriage strategies were also important innovations and steps towards knitting the French domains and actors into a more cohesive polity. The fact that his predecessor, Louis VII (r.1137–80), was unable to prevent his erstwhile wife, Eleanor of Aquitaine, from marrying the English king Henry Plantagenet (r.1154–89) in 1152 when their marriage had been annulled demonstrates the need to control marriage markets. Eleanor's marriage to Henry had disastrous consequences for the French crown since her inheritance meant that the English king controlled more French land than the French king (Ertman, 1997:60). It also created the Angevin Empire and the preconditions of the Hundred Years' War (1337–1453). Royal control over the marriage market did not mean that political development had locked on to a trajectory towards the modern unitary state and certainly not that it had arrived in the thirteenth century. It was also not the triumph of 'the state' over the autonomous power of the aristocrats (i.e., kinship groups). Rather, it was an organized symbiosis of political power and kinship networks. With this instrument, kings had something to work with in organizing the components of political order.

Because marriages were so important to the fortunes of an aristocratic family, they were subject to intense negotiations of the parties and considerable amounts of energy were devoted to creating advantageous strategies (Davies, 2009:152). Marriages were unpredictable – which created considerable turbulence in the careers of individual families and in the figuration as a whole. Would the marriage generate children, and thus heirs? Or would it be barren, leading to the extinction of an entire house or only a single line? In the latter case thus in turn leading to a realignment of the cadet and main branches in the next generation as the remaining branches would stand to gain from the extirpation of their relatives? Other risks were if the woman and/or husband would not survive the dangers of disease, childbirth and war. If they did not, then new realignments would follow, in the form of a new marriage or lifelong widowhood with the risk of properties reverting to the crown. The unpredictability of a marriage and thus of inheritance stretched over generations. The sections on wars of succession in Chapter 5 will explore this subject further. Sons and daughters were assets to a family's strategy in the politics of reproduction (Davies, 2009:155), which was controlled either by directing them into advantageous marriages or by preventing them from marrying and reproducing, at least in a legally sanctioned form. The latter tactic involved sending some children into the church, either to pursue careers advantageous to the family, to be kept in reserve in case something happened to their older siblings or indefinitely in a monastery or nunnery.

Jean Flori mentions the prevalence of the idea of society 'as one great *familia* of which the king was the *senior* and the kingdom a connected series of feudal tenures' (Flori, 2004:161). If we centre our understanding of the medieval kinship polity upon royal control and relations to the royal dynasty, then the connections rather than formal distinctions and categories appear central. In this interpretation, a king appears as a *pater familias* who pursued biopolitics towards the royal dynasty and its different branches. He was also a *pater familias* over other noble families, primarily those of the higher echelons that fell within his field of vision, figuratively and literally. Seen as a network of family networks, the European realms had a pyramid-like structure. The royal dynasty, centred on the family of the king with its cognate branches, is at the top of the pyramid. Below it we can group the magnate families, often bearing the titles of princes (in Germany), dukes or counts. Further below we find the baronial nobility and then the untitled nobility. We must not make the mistake of understanding this hierarchy too much only in formal-legal terms. Instead, we ought to picture a dynamic and moving network of families that could rise and fall in accordance with the fortunes of war, reproduction, inheritance and royal favour. Kings were not isolated from this network of networks. Royal dynasties had numerous marriage ties with aristocratic families.

A European king, ideal-typically, appears as the chief of many lineages that were connected in a macro-kinship system. This system was not static or rigid but highly dynamic, almost constantly in flux and renewal. It was also not a closed system but open vis-à-vis other European kinship systems. Nor were the 'units' of the system, such as kinship networks, closed and self-reproducing – which is the case in endogamous societies. They were principally open systems; networks that were embedded in a hierarchical system.

It is perhaps in this light that we ought to understand the infamous *affaire de tour de la neslé*. The French King Philip IV – the Fair (r.1285–1314) – had married his three sons to advantageous parties: Marguerite, daughter of the duke of Burgundy, and Jeanne and Blanche, daughters of the count of Burgundy (Adams, 2012:166). The marriages were important since they brought both the country and duchy of Burgundy closer to France. However, it turned out that the matches were less successful on a personal level. In 1314 it was discovered that two of the king's daughters-in-law, Marguerite and Blanche, were having affairs with two Norman knights, Philippe and Gauthier d'Aunay. Philip the Fair promptly reacted by arresting the two men, thus making the scandal public. He charged them, interestingly, with the crime of *lèse majesté*. They were found guilty and castrated, flayed alive and broken on the wheel before being hanged. Marguerite and Blanche were imprisoned.

There has been some speculation whether the allegations were true and if there was a political interest behind them. This is not the place to determine those questions, rather I will focus on interpretations of the consequences of the affair. Cuckolding two Princes of the Blood was considered a political crime of the highest magnitude. The threat of siring a bastard in the royal family and the very real injury to the honour of the princes and the royal family itself resulted in a vicious punishment because it struck at the heart of the political order. Moreover, it damaged the king as a *pater familias* as well as the realm on a symbolic plane. It was not unusual that queens were disposed of, cast into convents or even executed if they failed to produce heirs and adultery or incest was a convenient charge. However, the conduct of royal women had deeper implications for the stability of the realm. Geneviève Bührer-Thierry argues that there was a widespread opinion that there was a connection (*solidarité*) between order in the royal family and order in the kingdom (Bührer-Thierry, 1992). Bührer-Thierry analyses materials from the ninth century but the idea that the royal court and family represents a great cosmic ideal of order is attested from later periods too (Harste, 2013), Thus, adulterous or otherwise sinful princesses and queens cast doubts on the king's authority and on the cosmic order of the realm. Given the perils that adulterous women posed to the realm since they acted as a bridge between micro- and macro-orders, order had to be restored. Another interpretation focuses on the fact that a baronial revolt was taking place at the same time as the *affaire* and the princesses and their lovers were used as scapegoats, sacrificial victims almost, that allowed the king to restore macro-order by restoring micro-order (Adams, 2012:175). The three interpretations need not rule each other out. What they show, individually and collectively, was that kingship/ queenship, kinship and reproduction were central to the political order.

A Too Harmonious Picture?

One might want to raise objections at this point. Surely the picture that I have painted so far is too harmonious? An objection to my interpretation of medieval political orders might take its starting point in medieval warfare. Speaking in broad types, there were many instances of war between nobles and direct war between coalitions of nobles and their kings. To an observer that equates political order with some form of statehood based on Max Weber's criterion of a monopoly on legitimate violence or with the idea of internal peace under top-down imposed laws (as in Hobbes' vision) these two phenomena might appear as the most glaring demonstrations of the incompatibility of the armed hereditary groups and political order. At the beginning of this chapter I discussed the long tradition of branding the unrestrained nobility as violent and un- or anti-political. So far, I have dealt with the 'descent of the ban' thesis by pointing to the strong traditions of embedding and interdependence in medieval politics. Now the time has come to deal with organized violence head on. I will begin with violence between noble armies.

There are many examples of noblemen who used their armies to advance their own interests, by making war on other nobles or even on their monarchs. Some violence, such as the campaigns of Fulk of Navarra (1043–1109), count of Anjou, were part of a power-struggle with his neighbours (Bates, 2000:407–8). Even such interest-driven campaigns frequently had a ritualistic character where fighting was interspersed with negotiations (Barthélemy, 2009). Another kind of violence, the feud, was litigious in character. It has often been used to portray feuding noblemen as anti-political elements but as a form of action it has often been misinterpreted. Otto Brunner first calls attention to the fact that large-scale organized violence between nobles or other groups often had the character of litigation and thus upheld rather than threatened the political order. His findings have subsequently been reinforced by the anthropologically inspired writings of Stephen D. White and Dominique Barthélemy.

Initially, no principal distinction existed between armed conflicts fought by nobles and those fought by kings. Conflicts between monarchs and between non-monarchs were legally subsumed under the same category, feud (*Fehde* or *Faidha*) (Brunner, 1959; Poulsen and Netterstrøm, 2007; Whetham, 2009:76). Both kinds of actors used identical declarations of war (Grewe, 2000:69–74), and warfare in the sense of feuding was not understood as breaking the law but rather as litigation. One example is how Emperor Henry II (r.1002–24) in 1012 managed to successfully negotiate with the Count Balderich and Count Wichmann to get them to cancel their feud (Whetham, 2009:71–113).[4] In order to be recognized as a litigator one had to have just claim (Whetham, 2009:83), this was true even if the debtor was the emperor or the king. Feuding in cases concerning money, credibility and reputation ensured that others could be relied upon to coerce debtors and other lawbreakers not to renege on their word. Feuds could in some cases serve the purpose of systemic stability. Zmora notes that the importance of the traditional self-image of princes in Germany of as the keepers of law and order was 'central to their legitimacy and self-understanding' (Zmora, 1997:75). However, not only nobles engaged in feuds, so too did organized groups of townspeople, towns and peasant associations (Reinle, 2003).

There was, however, a tension between two legal and political principles: the right of nobles to resist and the right of the king to demand obedience. This conflict was particularly sharp in the Holy Roman Empire. A series of successive emperors tried to quell feuding and to establish the right of the king to decide over matters of war and peace and the king's role in protecting the peace. They did so by issuing proclamations promulgating the peace of the land (*Landesfrieden*). Sometimes they were valid only for parts of the empire but some were issued that aimed to declare peace over the entire empire,[5] such as Frederick I's proclamation in 1158.[6]

Proclamations could also be made only for a limited period of time, such as the five-year peace that Henry II proclaimed for Saxony in 1012.[7] Not only the emperor could proclaim a peace of the land, so too did individual noblemen, such as Balduin count of Flanders in 1200, or

---

[4] For the original source see RI II,4 n. 1760m, in Regesta Imperii Online, www.regesta-imperii.de/id/1012-00-00_1_0_2_4_1_497_1760m (accessed 24 March 2014).

[5] For proclamations of the peace of the land that were aimed at and valid for only parts of the empire see for example Henry II's proclamation on 17 June 1004 of a general peace for Schwaben. RI II,4 n. 1570a, in Regesta Imperii Online, www.regesta-imperii.de/id/1004-06-17_1_0_2_4_1_207_1570a (accessed 24 March 2014).

[6] For the original source see RI IV,2,2 n. 620, in Regesta Imperii Online, www.regesta-imperii.de/id/1158-11-00_4_0_4_2_2_62_620 (accessed 24 March 2014).

[7] For the original source see RI II,4 n. 1754a, in Regesta Imperii Online, www.regesta-imperii.de/id/1012-01-00_1_0_2_4_1_473_1754a (accessed 24 March 2014).

a collective of noblemen, such as the princes of the empire in 1135.[8] Another example is the ten-year peace that the princes of the empire pledged to uphold in front of Lothar III in 1135 (this peace was not proclaimed unilaterally by the king but agreed upon by the princes).[9] 'Private war' was finally interdicted by the proclamation of the 'Perpetual Peace of the Land' by Emperor Maximilian I (r.1486–1519) at the Diet in Worms in 1495 (Grewe, 2000: 115).[10] Feuding in Germany, where it had been strongest and most institutionalized, took another half-century to fade away (Zmora, 1997:122–46).

In England and France feuding ceased much earlier than in the German lands. In both countries kinsmen were expected to avenge their own and we find several examples in the eleventh and early twelfth centuries of kin groups that mustered considerable resources in feuds of vengeance and indeed acted as political groups (Crouch, 2005:139–44). However, by the twelfth century the blood feud had become a rare anomaly in England. The king and the system of royal justice was stronger there than elsewhere, which meant that self-help of kinship groups became prohibited, unnecessary and even normatively frowned upon (Crouch, 2005:144). It is, however, possible to find examples of truly disruptive forms of violence aimed directly at the nobility. One example is the so-called Jacquerie, a peasant uprising in 1358 that took place within the framework of the disruptive Hundred Years' War and turned into an assault on the nobility. Mobs ravaged the French countryside, killing and raping noble families and looting their property. According to contemporary sources, the revolt was quickly and savagely put down by a concerted effort of French and Flemish noblemen and their retinues (Froissart and Brereton, 1978:151–5; Hilton, 2003:229). Although long and terrifying to its targets, the Jacquerie had no comprehensive political programme and faded after military defeat.

A more serious and better organized challenge against royal authority, lordship and the structure of government came in England in the summer of 1381. The multiple risings in London and many other parts of England used to be called 'the Peasant's War' but it is now more

---

[8] For the original source see RI V,2,4 n. 10642, in Regesta Imperii Online, www.regesta-imperii.de/id/1200-07-28_1_0_5_2_4_24_10642 (accessed 24 March 2014).

[9] For the original source see RI IV,1,1 n. 440, in Regesta Imperii Online, www.regesta-imperii.de/id/1135-05-26_1_0_4_1_1_440_440 (accessed 24 March 2014).

[10] For the original source see RI XIV,1 n. 2251, in Regesta Imperii Online, www.regesta-imperii.de/id/1495-08-07_4_0_14_1_0_2255_2251 (accessed 24 March 2014).

often referred to as the 'English Rising' (Eiden, 1998:10) since labourers, craftsmen and clerics also took part (Ormrod, 1990:16; Hilton, 2003:219). The rebels murdered government officials both in London and the shires. Moreover, they attacked manors, abbeys and governments buildings, not only to plunder them but with the express aim of destroying records and archives (Ormrod, 1990:5). The rebellion reached considerable proportions and posed a serious threat to the stability of government. Its leaders in London, John Ball and Wat Tyler, even managed to parlay with the king, Richard II, outside of London before they were killed (Froissart and Brereton, 1978:226–7). Although the rebellion was large, it quickly dissipated when the royal government launched a political and military counter-attack (Ormrod, 1990:20).

How significant was the English Rising as an expression of opposition against the monarchical-aristocratic political order? On the one hand, the rebels had very far-reaching aims. There is a consensus that the revolt had clearly identifiable causes: harsh labour laws, altered town-countryside relations, the rural land market, the military failures in the Hundred Years' War, high taxes and a widespread feeling that the king's ministers and agents were abusing the law (Ormrod, 1990:1; Eiden, 1998:7). Rather than being a 'conservative' revolt that sought to address specific ills, but by and large accepting the general social structure, the leaders of the rising rejected it altogether. Although they seemed to envision retaining some kind of monarchy, it is clear that the rebels (or at least their leaders) wanted to eliminate lordship and the class of landowning nobles altogether (Hilton, 2003:223, 227). According to contemporary chronicles, both Tyler and Ball wanted to execute lawyers, justices and jurors and everyone else with knowledge of the law, so as to eradicate it completely (Hilton, 2003:221, 224–5). The strategy of targeting records is also a sign that they aimed to destroy the authority of lords and of the royal government. The aims of the London rebels were also echoed by insurgents in Essex who wanted to destroy lordship *tout court* (Eiden, 1998:11).

On the other hand, although it was both well-organized and extensive, it was, as noted, short-lived. Moreover, it was a singular event in the English Middle Ages, no other rebellion was as large or as ambitious. From this, we can conclude that there was certainly, at least in 1381, an opinion that was opposed to aristocratic government and privilege and perhaps to even to royal government. However, it was too conceptually, militarily and organizationally weak to provide a sustained challenge (Hilton, 2003:227, 233). England would not see a similar challenge to the monarchical-aristocratic political order for another 260 years.

Intellectual discussions about war centred on how wars can be justified and this concern had a direct impact on the shape of the political order. Over time, debates on just war shifted from the question 'what gives a right to war?' to the question 'who has a right to war?' (Janssen, 1982:571). A solution was to argue that only those actors who had no superior had the right to wage war (Kantorowicz, 1997:247–8; Whetham, 2009:81). Increasingly intellectuals began distinguishing between private and public violence. Violence exercised in public service was considered just, but private violence was not. Authorized killing, according to the law, may be carried out by a holder of public office (Hehl, 2004:220–1); when he stated that 'The discharging of an office implies no guilt, if there is no sin in the conscience', Bishop Gerald of Cambrai (c.1050) was giving absolution to those who did military service to the king (Hehl, 2004:189). Gerald as well as Ivo of Chartres (c.1040–1117) bestowed the duties and absolution of kings upon warriors (Hehl, 2004:193, 205).

The idea of the just war became increasingly centred on defending the common good, one's king, for the laws, the established order, and not just for individual gain or fame (Hehl, 2004:219). Canonists argued since the 1100s that war was just if it was fought for the defence of the fatherland, the faith and the Church (Kantorowicz, 1997:236). Ivo of Chartres distinguished between private killing, which was considered forbidden, and public killing, which was considered permissible, wars to defend one's country and its order were considered just. Intellectuals increasingly juxtaposed the king's just wars with unjust baronial feuds (Hehl, 2004:215). Conceptually, feuds began to be seen as different from wars during the later Middle Ages (Whetham, 2009:87), for example on 22 June 1495, Emperor Maximilian I distinguished between war and feud when he stated that in his absence the imperial courts should attempt to settle both kinds of conflicts between the larger members of the empire.[11] Finally, real war became conceptually and legally limited to kings and by extension to the realm (Whetham, 2009:87).

---

[11] For the original source, see RI XIV,1 n. 1966, in Regesta Imperii Online, www.regesta-imperii.de/id/1495-06-22_1_0_14_1_0_1970_1966 (accessed 24 March 2014).

Even if war between nobles largely had a system-sustaining character of litigation, then surely war against the king must be seen as violence against the political order? First, such a charge requires a one-sided identification of the political order with the king. As this chapter has demonstrated, such a view is hardly tenable given that magnates and other nobles were thoroughly enmeshed in the political order. But instead of restating my arguments, I will examine a couple of the most serious rebellions or wars in some detail. Naturally, I cannot deal with all wars between magnates and kings here. However, some general traits can be noted. Many of the major wars concerned the degree of centralization of the polity. For example, a culture of colla-boration and consent existed among the Saxon nobility in the tenth century and eleventh century (Althoff, 2000:277). This culture was sometimes expressed in sworn associations, *coniurationes*, that were often directed against the king. *Coniurationes* strengthened the collec-tive bonds, cohesion and links between the members, links that were often inherited from father to son, which gave certain permanence over time to the Saxon polity. Under the Ottonian dynasty, feuds against the king frequently ended in mediation and the rebels re-entering into the king's grace. The next royal dynasty, the Salian, was not as interested in or informed of the collaborative Saxon culture. Instead, they attempted to assert their claims to overlordship and obedience. As a consequence, Saxon rebellions became more serious and damaging to the Salian kings during the so-called Investiture Controversy (1077–1122) (Haldén, 2017b). The long-term result of the royal challenge to the collaborative and polycentric political culture of the Saxon nobility was that the two tendencies were accelerated in Germany. Thomas Ertman calls this development 'failed state-building' and perhaps he is right (Ertman, 1997:231–7), but failed state-building does not mean the failure of political order. There is a long tradition in historiography of decrying the alternatives to the sovereign state, but more recent research has re-evaluated them as alternative political orders.

In part, the English thirteenth-century rebellions confirm the pat-tern that kings that strive to expand their authority and rule without consent tend to provoke uprisings, a pattern that directly contradicts the idea that successful state-building exclusively rests on military superiority of the central power. The reign of King John (r.1199–1216) was marked by failures abroad, such as the loss of Normandy, and at home. His unprece-dented high levels of taxation and refusal to give the magnates a role in government alienated them, and they eventually rebelled against him (Crouch, 2010:80–3). In 1215 King John signed the Magna Carta, and the provisions of the Great Charter were repeatedly confirmed during the minority of his son, Henry III (r.1216–72) (Carpenter, 1999:314–57). The Magna Carta and the heritage of co-rule that it sparked demonstrates the perils of kings trying to rule without consent (Carpenter, 1999:357). The next big rebellion took place in 1258 and that was a more serious challenge to kingship. Its leader, Simon de Montfort, and his followers seized power and ruled the country in the king's name, but without the king for a brief period, 14 May 1264 to 4 August 1265 (Carpenter, 1999:340). The Montfortian experiment failed since it did not manage to secure lasting support from the magnates against the king, something that was highly unlikely (Carpenter, 1999:342). The two English rebellions each in their own ways demonstrate the importance of the magnate families and their commitment to the realm and to working with the kingship.

In Hungary, fighting between the king and the magnates characterized the years between 1310 and 1325. Towards the end of the thirteenth century a small number of barons had appropriated control over their own provinces (Engel, 2001:124ff). When Andrew III, the last king of the Árpád dynasty, died in 1301, Charles I of Anjou succeeded him to the throne. Many magnates had no intention of granting him the authority that he expected and a long war followed between 1310 and 1325 (Michaud, 2000:735–7). Charles' victory over the magnates gave him the opportunity to consolidate royal control over Hungary. These foundations enabled him and his son, Louis the Great (r.1342–82) to embark on very ambitious campaigns in Central and Southern Europe. Ultimately, these ventures were unsuccessful and generated discontent among the nobility, who were necessary for military campaigns (Michaud, 2000:739–40), and as a result Louis had to summon a diet and issue the decree of 1351 that reinforced the Golden Bull of 1222. It granted the same privileges to all nobles, confirmed their right to rebellion and strengthened the inheritance of noble property. The magnate stratum of the nobility continued to thrive despite the military success of Charles of Anjou. New magnates, whose social and political positions were even stronger than their predecessors, replaced the ones he had defeated. Thus in a longer perspective, the civil war of the 1310s and 1320s proved to be an episodic breakdown in collaborative relations between monarch and magnates. Attempts to impose stronger centralization forced a counter-reaction to which the king was forced to yield.

The Saxon, English and Hungarian examples prove not a principled opposition between kings (and, by extension, states or proto-states) and the nobility (as the reactionary and anti-political). They rather prove the strength of the norms of co-rule, consensus and consultation. When kings tried to break established practice and the ideal that the realm was a symbiosis of its most powerful groups (organized as kindreds), rebellion ensued. Or, if you will, kings that tried to create 'revolutions in government' sooner or later met with a counter-revolution, reactionary in the literal sense of the word, that not only established the customary order but reinforced, formalized and codified it further.

Conclusions

This chapter began by looking at the idea of the high Middle Ages as characterized by perennially feuding nobles that usurped the rights, powers and authority that rightfully belonged to kings. In narratives building on this idea, kings eventually managed to subdue the self-interested, proud and greedy nobles and thus set their countries onto the path of state formation. Building on recent advances in medieval historiography that question this idea I set out to describe a pattern of political order during the high Middle Ages of which kinship elites (e.g., the nobility and monarchy) and ideas of kinship were fundamental and inalienable parts. Observed from the vantage point of synthetic macro-history that tries to discern large patterns and drawing on examples from England, France, Germany, Hungary and Scandinavia I concluded that an acceptance of hierarchy and the ideal of co-rule and consultation amounted to what Edward Shils called the 'central values' of political order during this period. The prevailing emphasis on co-rule means that we have to further nuance the precise role that war played in the formation and coalescing of political order. Wars did not only have a functional importance in the sense that they concentrated resources, in the form of treasure and armed men, or centralized command (which is more efficient than decentralized) or as a tool of subjugation. They also generated cohesion among the ruling elites, drew them closer into the political order, organizationally and on the level of ideas. Wars allowed them to represent their realm, their monarchs and their political roles, something that strengthened these entities. A point for further research would be to deepen analyses of how warfare and organization for war create meaning for their participants. To paraphrase Phil Gorski's expression that I used earlier in this chapter, we need to understand the 'soul' of wars and warriors.

Naturally, there were nuances and differences between countries and periods, but as a general pattern, co-operation and co-rule were formulae for success and, conversely, policies that aimed at subjugation through coercion and royal autocracy resulted in large-scale rebellions intending to restore the old balance. The analyses in this chapter of political ideas demonstrated that the Aristotelian tradition of viewing families as central to the political order was highly influential, perhaps dominant, in this period. This means that views of the political that derive from or are indebted to the natural law tradition that was discussed in Chapter 2 must be seen as normative expressions of a particular period, rather than as starting points for empirical analysis.

I stated in the first section of this chapter that high stakes were involved in our conception of the Middle Ages. I said so not just because it is a long period of human history but because it was an important period in the formation of political order since it was the era when polities began to stabilize. It is also vital because the views that we hold of the medieval period are important for the kind of narratives that we can construct of political development in the long run. If this period is portrayed as one of conflict between kinship-based groups and the proto-state (or political order) then it sets the stage for a story of state formation as enforced from above and buttressed by the subjugation of kinship-based groups. If, however, portrayals of this period rather – or, at least, also – include the emphasis on co-rule and co-operation between elite groups and the various institutional and cultural ways that they were embedded in a political order then another long-term narrative becomes possible – or perhaps even necessary. That narrative stresses that kinship was central to political organization for a very long time and that kinship-organizations and ideas were vital to keep polities together during a period when the capacity of central institutions to regulate and direct people's lives was weak. It also casts serious doubts about the importance and centrality of coercion in the business of rule.

A reasonable objection to this argument would be that I am focusing on the elite of these polities and that most European populations experienced plenty of coercion and subjugation. To some extent, I would concede that point but that is not the focus of this book – which is elite relations. I still claim that the latter are fundamental to the formation of political orders. Naturally, a comprehensive account would take in large segments of the population. That, however, would be another and quite different book.

5 STRONG ARISTOCRACIES IN STRONG STATES
Europe *c.*1500–*c.*1800

Introduction

The period 1500 to 1800 is usually seen as the era of state formation par excellence. I will demonstrate that kinship, as a principle of legitimacy, was still a central part of the political order in Europe. Also, kinship-based elites, in other words the aristocracy, continued to dominate political life. Thus the idea of a principled incompatibility or a conflict between kinship and political order is untenable. Instead, co-operation and collaboration between aristocratic elites and kings continued to be a formula for success and stability. Also, the degree of institutional embeddedness increased during this period, which supported the position of kinship-based groups in the political order.

During this period a number of techniques and institutions were created that deeply affected the political order and societies in all of Europe: governmentality, new sciences of statecraft and administration, increases in the capacity of the bureaucracy to register and regulate, the increased capacity of the state to tax its subjects and enforce its laws and increased surveillance capacities as well as the expansion of the purview of the state and the extent of its ambitions. State formation affected or even transformed the nobility deeply. However, the effect did not amount to the changes presumed in the conventional narrative: that the power of the nobility and of kinship as an organizational principle waned and the impersonal, modern, machine-like state emerged triumphant. Instead due to the changes to the political order during the sixteenth, seventeenth and eighteenth centuries the nobility became more powerful and embedded into the state.

The changes that strengthened many noble families and especially the aristocratic elite as well as the system of the nobility are those that we today identify as quite modern such as cameralism, registers, registration, governmentality, and a broader and more effective state. This insight means that we cannot equate modern techniques of government and modes of organization and a certain form of society. The whole idea underlying the label 'early modern' for the period 1500 to 1800 is that we witness a proto-version of our own society during this period (Duindam, 2010). That in turn suggests that the social and political developments during this period put European societies on a trajectory towards the conditions that prevailed during the twentieth century. However, these innovations produced a society that in terms of techniques of government but not in terms of stratification, legitimacy or raison d'être correspond to our current understanding of modernity. Thus the condition during this period amounts to a form of hierarchical modernity underpinned by quasi-sacred references to the legitimacy of bloodlines. In other words, it was another modernity than the egalitarian, individual-centred one that has monopolized all other meanings of the concept (Göksel, 2016). As for trajectories, the major trends during much of this period do not point towards egalitarianism or any abolition of the hierarchy of kinship that characterized European societies. Previous research in the multiple modernities paradigm has demonstrated that an equation between modern techniques and organizational forms and a liberal, egalitarian, individual-centred (e.g., Western) society is untenable with regard to societies outside of Europe (Eisenstadt, 2002). This chapter demonstrates that the idea of multiple modernities is equally valid with regard to the European past.

The argument of this chapter is pursued in the following way. First I outline how historical sociology, political science and international relations (IR) have treated the period 1500 to 1800. Second, I discuss the major innovations in the art of governing and organizing during this era. Third, I outline how these innovations changed the political order and the nobility as well as strengthened the latter. Fourth, I analyse how kinship acted as a constitutive influence upon the European order of this period. I end with a summary of the chapter.

The Absolutism Thesis: State Formation as a Disruption of the Past

Most historians, political scientists and sociologists focus on the period 1500 to 1800 when they talk about the formation of the state. For example, although Tilly's book *Capital, Coercion and European States* claims to deal with the period 900 to 1900, its emphasis lies on the period 1450–1900 (Tilly, 1990). This was when the capacities of European states to penetrate, bureaucratically, coercively and ideologically into the lives of their subjects expanded strongly. Hence, many narratives about the genesis of the modern state and its specific characteristics focus on this period. Two major intertwined themes unite historiography and social science: the demise of the nobility in a struggle against the monarch and his state and the idea of the absolutist state.

The demise of the aristocracy (an elite group organized on the basis of kinship) is prevalent in many works of historical sociology. Norbert Elias explicitly bases his theory of state formation on the idea that kings destroyed the warrior aristocracy and turned them into harmless courtiers (Elias, 2000), meaning they lost their power as a political force that could field autonomous armies and rule extensive provinces. In Ernst Gellner's terminology, the nobility was turned from 'stallions' into 'geldings' that were dependent upon the monarch and his state for their status and wealth (Gellner, 2008). Joseph Schumpeter describes the processes after the wars of religion as 'the prince tore the sharp weapon, "the state" out of the hands of the estates which had begun to forge it' (Schumpeter, 1991:108). Max Weber claims that European countries went through a transition from one basic form of state to another. In the first rulers own their own means of administration 'money, buildings, the materials of war, vehicle pools, horses ...' (Weber, 2004:36). In the second the administrative staff is separated from the tools of administration. Weber goes on to explain that 'in a society based on "Estates" (*Stände*) the lord governs with the assistance of an autonomous "aristocracy" [an order based on charismatic hereditary rule], that is to say, he shares the rule with them'. However, the 'modern state begins to develop wherever the monarch sets in train the process of dispossessing the autonomous "private" agents of administrative power who exist in parallel to him, that is to say, all the independent owners of the materials of war and the administration, financial resources, and politically useful goods of every kind' (Weber,

2004:37). More recently, Francis Fukuyama portrays the story of political development in Europe from the fifteenth century as the story of a struggle between 'centralizing states and the social groups resisting them'. Moreover the nobility and the gentry are portrayed as being 'outside the state' and generally trying to resist it (Fukuyama, 2012:332–3). This, as we shall see, does not correspond to seventeenth- or eighteenth-century realities.

To emphasize the decline or even the demise of the aristocracy from the political order during the period when the modern state supposedly emerged further strengthens the trope of a fundamental opposition between kinship and statehood and that hereditary elites must be broken for a modern state to emerge. The theme of an opposition between on the one hand the monarch and his expanding state with non-noble bureaucrats and on the other the aristocracy is an old one in historiography (Dewald, 1996:1–15; Scott and Storrs, 2007:3). Such narratives stress the conflicts between kings and nobles during the sixteenth and early seventeenth centuries. Indeed, peasant rebellions and noble uprisings formed part of what historians call the 'general crisis of the mid-seventeenth century' that engulfed many countries in Europe (Parker and Smith, 1997). The first and second French Frondes (1648, 1650–3) were some of the most serious conflicts between royal authority and a noble alliance (Ranum, 1993; Sonnino, 2003). Another challenge was the English civil war (1642–51), which resulted in the execution of King Charles I and the proclamation of a short-lived republic. A classic theme in Swedish history is the oscillation between supposedly absolute monarchs like Charles XI (r.1660–97) and Charles XII (r.1697–1718) and aristocratic oligarchy (the so-called age of liberty (1718–72) before the return of an 'enlightened' absolute ruler, Gustavus III (r.1771–92). Other conflicts were the attempts of the Great Elector of Brandenburg to reduce the privileges of his nobility (Clark, 2007:53–61) or the confiscation of noble estates in Sweden under Charles XI (Villstrand, 2011). The image of a struggle between a reactionary and selfish aristocracy and a progressive monarchy with a modernizing state is evocative and provides a neat pedagogical device (Ostrowski, 2002). More recent research has, however, demonstrated that these conflicts were exceptions rather than the rule and thus the macro-historical image must be revised.

Uprisings that were aimed directly against the noble-monarch symbiosis did indeed take place during this period (Mousnier, 1972;

Blickle, 2004). Between 1524 and 1526 the southern parts of the Holy Roman Empire were shaken by a series of peasant rebellions. In contrast to late medieval peasant uprisings Peter Blickle describes the 'peasant war' of 1524–6 as revolutionary in its ambitions. Still, the rebellions were completely defeated by armies of the South German princes. They shared this fate with other would-be contenders to the established order in this period, such as the rebellions of the Swiss peasants (1653), Stenka Razin (1670–1) or Pugachev (1773–5). In short, with the exception of the English Civil War, the armed challenges to the noble-monarchical synthesis were too weak to pose any serious long-term challenge. More dangerous were struggles within the ruling order, which pitted coalitions of aristocrats against the crown or wars of succession. Similar to noble rebellions in the Middle Ages, early modern struggles were often reactions to earlier breakdowns in the collaborative and consensual form of rule. This pattern is quite similar to medieval noble rebellions such as the Barons' War in England or the insurrections against the Salian dynasty in Germany discussed in Chapter 4.

The conflicts between nobles and the crown are now seen not as a general tendency of the era but as exceptional breakdowns in the norm of a functioning collaborative rule. There is also an element of timing to several of the revolts and conflicts between kings and nobles. Nicholas Henshall argues that most eruptions happened in the mid-seventeenth century. After this period of conflict, there was a century of peace and reconciliation between the nobility and monarchs between 1650 and 1750. This rapprochement happened because both sides recognized how dangerous conflicts were to them. There were no social revolutions during this era, in fact in the period 1650 to 1750 monarchs did not touch noble privileges. It was only later with rulers like Joseph II of Austria in the 1780s that noble privileges began to succumb to a centralizing and uniform state (Henshall, 2010:5).

A macro-historical emphasis on conflicts between the nobility and the monarch is intimately connected with the concept 'absolute monarchy'. This concept entails the unchallenged rule of the monarchy and by extension his state, over older forms of particular powers, such as the aristocracy and estates, and as such is a forerunner of the modern state. The adherents to this concept tend to emphasize the establishment of standing armies (as opposed to temporarily raised hosts), the implementation of regular taxation, the creation of a bureaucracy and the supremacy of royal courts. In political science and sociology the concept of an absolutist state has gained a strong foothold and in several narratives and theories of state formation it has become taken for granted. It provides a strong 'type' or 'form' that can effectively be contrasted against earlier types to form a typology of forms of rule or state (e.g., Poggi, 1978). A prevalent trait in state formation research has been attempts to find trajectories to different forms of rule such as parliamentarism or absolutism and to identify the causal factors driving respective developments (Anderson, 1974; Ertman, 1997; Rokkan, 1999). Theorists as different as Perry Anderson, Benno Teschke, Christian Reus-Smit and Anthony Giddens all include some form of the 'canonical' absolutist state in their works as a stage on the path to modernity (Giddens, 1985:83–120; Tilly, 1990; Ertman, 1997; Reus-Smit, 1999; Teschke, 2003; Hui, 2005).

While the idea or 'entity' of the absolute state is taken as unproblematic in political science/IR and (historical) sociology, it has been completely re-evaluated in historical scholarship since the early 1990s (Henshall, 1992; Collins, 2009). Historians now recognize that local power-holders, estates and the aristocracy as a whole – what early modern political theorists called 'intermediate bodies' – were more powerful and important than the models of absolute rule have led us to believe (Zmora, 2001). Indeed, Zmora argues that nobility became the constitutive feature of early modern politics. The institutional edifice of the early modern state, with its tax authorities, standing armies, legislative monopoly, national debt, etc., seemed to point to similar developments during the nineteenth century (Duchhardt, 2007). On closer examination, the attributes taken as evidence of a new era of political organization seem to have been over-exaggerated. Today, the older image of the absolutist state with its associated tropes of a retrograde aristocratic elite, and increasingly modernizing state apparatus, has been almost completely demolished. The political order of the seventeenth and eighteenth centuries appears increasingly like a compromise or hybrid if you will, between the monarch and the rooted estate-based and kinship-based elements (Kunisch, 1986).

The re-evaluation of the concept of the 'absolutist state' creates serious problems for macro-narratives, theories of state formation, typologies of state and, eventually, theories of the state/political order and power in political science and history. In long-term historical trajectories the ideal type of the absolutist state forms a step between medieval forms of rule and the modern state. In such a trajectory, the modern state is first established through coercion and control and is later liberalized and democratized through a struggle between the forces of 'progress' and 'reaction'. However, since the assertion that the modern state was established through centralized control and coercion of both recalcitrant elites and the general population is deficient then we are left in the dark as concerning three questions: (a) what did the intermediate step look like? (b) what were the forces and institutions of social cohesion? – if coercion did not ensure cohesion, then what did? and (c) what were the continuities and discontinuities with earlier epochs?

In the rest of the chapter I will describe what the early modern political order looked like; a description that emphasizes collaboration between kinship-based elite groups. I will also outline the most important institutions and practices of embedding and integration of elite groups in the political order.

Changes in the European Nobilities

Elite kinship groups (i.e., noble families) and the kinship system as such (i.e., nobility) were formalized from the late Middle Ages onwards. Formalization proceeded from the state, that is, from the royal court, and the more advanced states had the most formalized kinship systems. Formalization enabled transparency and greater possibilities to organize the system. Another important aspect of the formalization of European kinship systems was the formation of the nobility as a collective, as an estate, vis-à-vis other social groups that enabled greater cohesion and collaboration among noble families. Because of the need of the state to organize systems in its environment we see the co-evolution of ever more self-organizing states and increasingly organized kinship groups in many places in world history. The formation of the European nobility is but one example of this phenomenon. Although powerful noble lineages had existed for centuries, it was only in the sixteenth century that they were organized into estates and more carefully delineated into distinct groups (Scott and Storrs, 2007:8, 18, 22, 35–52). The driver of this wave of organization was the increasingly cohesive and powerful state. By forming more cohesive groups it was easier for the princely states to assemble the noble estates in order to levy taxes and organize their military service.

During the early modern period we see the creation of stable kinship groups that are centred around almost state-like territories (Sabean, Teuscher and Mathieu, 2007). This development was initiated as much by non-noble administrators of noble estates whose fortunes were tied to the noble kinship groups that they served and hence it was rational for them to desire as much cohesion and stability in these groups as possible. The empirical findings of Sabean, Teutscher and their associates support the image that kinship groups become more important, stronger, and more cohesive as political structures are strengthened and routinized – the development that is usually labelled as state formation. Indeed, '[t]he traditional story is that emerging state institutions had to compete with older, kin-based forms of social organization. However, some recent studies have demonstrated that state organization systematically had recourse to normative concepts of kinship and reinforced their significance' (Sabean and Teutscher, 2007:9). Sabean and Teuscher conclude that 'state formation and the realignment among kin and family appear as strongly interrelated developments at the passage from the Middle Ages to the early modern period' (Sabean and Teuscher, 2007:15). However empirically significant these findings are, this argument can be taken much further. The empirical findings destabilize not only the traditional story about the development of kinship relations but they also render thinking about political order only in terms of the state and state formation problematic. In the light of the new discoveries about kinship and family structures, in particular the growing power, cohesion and rootedness of aristocratic and royal kinship groups the concepts 'the state' and 'state formation' cannot remain unchanged, particularly not as macro-categories of political order. I will now proceed to investigate the enmeshment of kinship-based elites in the political order.

Innovations Strengthened the Nobility by Embedding It in the State

Historians of the European nobilities carefully point out the differences between countries with regard to factors such as family structure, inheritance rules, legal status and political positions. In the following I will outline general traits. During the period 1500 to 1800 there were significant continuities with earlier eras, such as the tendency to subjugate the interests of individuals to that of the family. This was achieved through various strategies and it is with regard to these strategies that we find certain innovations.

One strategy to advance the standing of a family was to ensure that its sons made careers in the state and church. As the next section will demonstrate, the qualitative and quantitative expansion of the state made new avenues possible. Family strategies were not only careerist but also biopolitical in character. Another strategy was to secure advantageous marriages for both sons and daughters. The converse of this strategy was the increasing tendency to restrict marriage and thus the number of eligible heirs to the family property (Scott and Storrs, 2007:13, 26) that was a part of a larger tendency towards more unified families. In the seventeenth and eighteenth centuries most noble families made internal inheritance arrangements whereby one son would inherit the estates but the other sons would be provided for with smaller inheritances (Scott and Storrs, 2007:31) and such arrangements can be found even in countries without formal primogeniture. With respect to formal primogeniture, England stands out as a European exception since only the eldest son formally received noble status with its many legally codified privileges. This did not mean that his siblings of the same generation fell out of the top stratum of society but rather a decoupling between legal and social criteria for membership. The European norm, however, was that nobility descended in the male line (Scott and Storrs, 2007:13). The tendency towards more unified houses with clearer rules of succession favouring the oldest male was not restricted to the nobility, it also characterized the royal families of Europe during this time. In the section on the European order below I shall explore this tendency and its consequences further.

Biopolitics were combined with legal means to produce more unified houses than previously. One such instrument was entail, which regulated succession and usually banned the current proprietor from selling the estates (Scott and Storrs, 2007:33). Entail preserved a family's property over time and constructed a relationship in which the current head of a family did not own the property but only managed it for future generations. In other words, it was one of the clearest ways of subjugating the individual to the family, across time. It also enabled a distinctly new way of consolidating the power, wealth and influence of a noble family and the nobility as a whole during this period. Entail provides us with a way of understanding whether there was a structural conflict between kinship groups and the political order. The monarchs and their increasingly muscular states backed entail as a legal instrument (Scott and Storrs, 2007:32-4), in fact, monarchs encouraged the consolidation of landed noble power; both across time through entail and across space by promoting the creation of more unified estates.

Even Russian rulers tended to encourage the growth of large contiguous estates after Peter I abolished partible inheritance and introduced unigeniture in 1714 (de Madariaga, 2007:345). The argument that the conflict between kings and nobles accelerated through the formation of abstract states from the sixteenth century onwards is undermined by the development of entail, how monarchs actually promoted the nobility as well as by the fact that entail was guaranteed by the more effective and accountable legal systems developed as a part of state formation.

The consolidation of large family domains through entail in combination with rising agricultural prices was beneficial to the economies of the higher nobilities in all European countries. Ownership of land was always the basis of noble wealth and power but also of status and prestige. Wealth is a power resource in itself but not all nobles were rich (Bush, 1988). There was an enormous difference between the super-wealthy and powerful magnate segment and sometimes impoverished lower nobility. While the former moved in the circle of the king and had privileged access to patronage and privilege as well as to political power, the latter was confined to local and obscure existences. Although there were bankers and merchants that were far richer than many nobles, they lacked a resource that was crucial in *ancien régime* Europe: status. Non-nobles could not compete with nobles for social status (Osiander, 2007:482–3). This very fact, and the importance of achieving status in *ancien régime* societies, had an integrative effect: Many people aspired to noble status, which led them into an orientation towards the central institutions (since nobility was granted by the king) and towards the 'central values' of the polity (Shils, 1982). Since nobility served as a single focus for the most socially desirable goods it connected what would otherwise have been many sub-systems into a single system of honour and status. It was not a society in the sense of a modern national society, but it served as the basis, the building block of what later could become one. One's own small kinship group did not decide status, honour and wealth but belonging to an officially and politically sanctioned system of elite kinship groups did.

Stratification of the Nobility

The nobility became more hierarchical and formally stratified during this period. Rulers tended to promote the most powerful families and enrich them further by bestowing more patronage upon them (Scott and Storrs, 2007:22–3). Titles were increasingly used to distinguish different strata within the nobility and the immensely rich and powerful aristocratic elite from the mass (relatively speaking) of lower or even untitled nobility. In all European countries a system of rank was established over the course of the seventeenth and eighteenth centuries, beginning in France and gradually spreading to Central, Eastern and Northern Europe. In yet another expression of the expansion of royal/ state authorities that acted to shape a society that fed into the political order, categories of nobles were now legally formalized in laws the governed the nobility (Upton, 2007:19–20).[1] As a consequence it became illegal to claim noble titles, which of course people had always done; paying good money for fraudulent documents proving their pedigrees. However, fraud was now easier to police and punish.

State service was one way to ennoblement, either in the military or in the civilian bureaucracy. In France two categories of nobility began to emerge in the seventeenth century, the old military nobility, the *noblesse de l'épée* and the newly ennobled bureaucracy, the *noblesse de robe*. An older generation of historians used to assert that the older military houses were replaced by the increasing bureaucratic nobility. This idea fits in with the narrative of a conflict between the nobility and the state where the *robe* is seen as the tools of the monarch and his state. However, the idea that the *noblesse de l'épée* was replaced or even threatened by the *noblesse de robe* is now held to be mistaken. Instead, there is a growing consensus that the old military houses retained their significance. Although tension between the two noble groups was much discussed in its day it rather seems that they crafted pragmatic alliances in ruling the provinces (Mettam, 2007:127–9).

The monarch and his administration were the drivers of this development. Titles had been a way of conferring not only offices and privileges but also status since Carolingian times, but now the practice became more established. Not only were titles used more frequently, they and the distinctions between different categories were more formalized, creating a sharper hierarchy than before. Scott and Storrs write that 'there was an element of social engineering' to the creation of titles

---

[1] For example the Swedish King Gustavus Adolphus issued a series of laws that regulated the nobility. He issued laws concerning noble privileges in 1613, 1617 and 1622. He issued a law regulating the noble estate (*Riddarhusordning*) in 1626. These laws are available at https://sok.riksarkivet.se/?Sokord=Gustav+I&AvanceradSok=False&FacettLimits=%2FNjGwA%3Ao&page=10&FacettFilter=arkis_ark_typ_facet%24Volym%3A&postid=Arkis+030DC846-5084-4A26-B58F-A60250876EFF&tab=post (accessed 26 July 2018).

as 'rulers like Louis XIV were motivated in part by a desire to create a more stratified hierarchy both within the élite and within the nobility as a whole' (Scott and Storrs, 2007:23). The creation of titles and a corresponding system of rank bound elite families more tightly to the political order than before. Since it became an official way of allotting status and with status came appointments, patronage and marriage opportunities noble families desired titles and the monarchy was their only source for these. Moreover, the official system ensured that status and rank were no longer arbitrary and disputed, on the basis of multilateral agreement on the basis of deeds and reputation. A single unified system that was actively run and managed by a central co-ordinating body (with the monarch as the head) meant there could no longer be separate provincial or local systems of rank that could compete with that of the centre. Of course, a family cut off from royal patronage could still turn to its home province to cultivate a local base of patronage and standing (Mettam, 2007:136), however, the provincial order of rank was clearly not autonomous from the centre to which it was inferior. In the terms used by Hirschmann, the unification of the order of rank and turning it into a system cut off the possibility of an 'exit' from the polity into local, alternative sources of rank and resources (Hirschman, 2004), instead, it clearly produced loyalty (Mettam, 2007).

Cataloguing

The system of rank utilized many of the new techniques of government and of course the increased efficiency and reach of the state. The idea of producing systematic 'catalogues' of phenomena in the natural as well as in the social worlds and ordering them into 'systems' was a particular innovation of sixteenth to eighteenth century Europe. The most famous examples are Diderot and D'Alembert's ambitious project of the *Encyclopedie* and Linneus' system of vegetable and animal lifeforms. The new ideologies of government advocated that all the assets and characteristics of a country should be registered and catalogues and their techniques made it possible. Categories of titles and people with different titles were recorded by state officials, which meant that the elite was more visible to the state than before. They were also more visible to each other through the publication of calendars or *Almanachs* that listed the elite families, their titles and offices. Genealogy was an important tool for kings that aspired to greater control, for example, the ambitiously centralizing Swedish king Gustav Vasa (r.1523–60) instructed his scribe Rasmuss Ludvigsson to draw up family trees of the most powerful and richest families in the realm. This project made them, their assets and connections visible to the king and also to each other (Rosman, 1897:5–6, 19, 21, 22).

These procedures recall another technique that social theorists argue is a highly modern one: surveillance (Gorski, 2003). This in turn enables management of offices and patronage relations not only in the present but also over time. Not only were families recorded and ordered, so were the offices of the state. Both were also made public through the printing and dissemination of publications (another highly modern technique). The first initiatives were private, such as *Siebmachers Wappen-Buch* first printed in 1605 but reprinted and brought up to date in multiple new editions during the seventeenth and eighteenth centuries (Siebmacher, 1772–95). Siebmacher's work covered the nobility of the Holy Roman Empire. A later and more famous example is the *Almanach de Gotha*, which was first published in 1763 but issued annually from 1785. This was a catalogue of the European ruling families, the higher echelons of the states of Europe and statistics of European countries. Later, in the nineteenth century, genealogical publications such as *Burke's Peerage* (United Kingdom) and *Adels och Ridderskapskalendern* (Sweden) proliferated.

In several countries, the state took up the task of publishing registers of the highest offices of the state and who held them. The French *Almenach Royal* was first published in 1683 and then annually between 1700 and 1792. It was a catalogue of the ruling dynasty, the princes of the blood, and the major offices of the state and who held them.[2] Making catalogues of the state and its offices became a European phenomenon. Early examples include the 'calendar of names of the united Netherlands' (1700), the 'Prussian-Brandenburgian calendar of State' (from 1704) and the 'Calendar of Electoral Saxony' (from 1728). In the Holy Roman Empire a 'complete Genealogical and Schematic Calendar' was published from 1743 onwards. In 1748 its name was significantly changed to the *New Genealogical-Schematic Imperial and*

---

[2] These calendars are available through the National Library of France. For the years 1700–91 see https://gallica.bnf.fr/ark:/12148/cb34454105m/date.r=almanach+royal.langFR (accessed 26 July 2018). To name one example in the 1732 edition the princes of the blood are enumerated on pages 74–6. Then the Marshals and Colonels and Lieutenant Colonels follow.

State Handbook – thus signalling the symbiosis between families and the state(s).[3] In the Habsburg lands, a calendar was published annually from 1702.[4] In Sweden, a calendar of state was published from 1730 onwards with the aspiring title *The Flourishing Sweden* (Henel, 1730).

Calendars of state and publications like *Burke's Peerage* now seem quaint but they played an important role in the development of political order and in embedding kinship elites within it. They were a continuation of the traditions of registration and visibility from heraldry and its offices covered in Chapter 4. After they had begun to be recorded and publicised, powerful kinship groups could not exist in isolation from the public order or from the ordering power of the state. They were no longer invisible or, potentially or actually, forming a parallel society or structure of power – as is the case with many kinship groups in the Middle East of the twenty-first century. The visibility of positions in registers but also at court ensured a kind of mutual surveillance, and the catalogue of state was also an important innovation because it listed the public assets (in the form of offices) and primary networks (in the form of family members and relatives) of elite kinship groups. This meant European societies could avoid a situation of deep distrust like the one that has dominated modern Somalia, where everybody knows that clan and family membership was important for political influence but it remains uncertain what influence different clans, sub-clans and families have. This is further analysed in Chapter 10. Of course, publicness did not do away with intrigue, jockeying for position and intense rivalry – but it altered the preconditions.

Osiander claims that a defining feature of *ancien régime* Europe was that it was based on privileges rather than on general laws (Osiander, 2007:482). Privilege was an element that joined the nobility and the monarchy in a bond that no side could break without endangering itself. Royal prerogatives that formed the basis of monarchical power were but a kind of privilege. 'Any attempt to tamper with privileges as the basis of *ancien régime* society endangered – indeed would soon bring down – the crown, and with it that entire society

---

[3] Neues Genealogisch-Schematisches Reichs- und Staats-Handbuch 1766–97.

[4] Kayserlicher Und Königlicher Wie auch Ertz-Hertzoglicher Und Dero Residentz-Stadt Wien Staats- und Stands- Calender 1702–1806, http://alex.onb.ac.at/shb.htm (accessed 22 September 2016). This calendar was published until 1938, changing its name as the state whose register it was mutated from Habsburg possession to the Austrian Empire, to Austria Hungary and to the Austrian Republic.

itself' (Osiander, 2007:482). The privileges were what distinguished the European nobility from elites in other premodern societies as well as from modern elites. The European nobilities were quite heterogeneous in their composition; they varied between as well as within countries and thus their privileges varied. Noble privilege was a complex set of rights, liberties and duties that stemmed from different historical sources (Bush, 1983:6–13). Privilege was a way of expressing the social relations of many different kinds of actors, both individual and corporate during the Middle Ages and the early modern era; for example the clergy, universities (both individually and collectively), towns, mines, parliaments, monasteries, religious minorities and nationals abroad.

Increasing stratification within the nobility could have caused tensions but that seems not to have been the case. In seventeenth-century France alliances between families of the lower and higher nobilities were common. Such alliances took the shape of patron-client relations that created interdependence and loyalties over time. Similar patterns took place between the higher nobilities and the king. Integration across the ranks generally resulted in a pattern of upwards-directed loyalty. As Roger Mettam writes: 'effective use of royal patronage was vital to stability' (Mettam, 2007:135–7). Although patronage existed on all levels of society the king was the biggest patron and used the state with its offices, positions, etc. as means of patronage (Dewald, 1996:145–6; Lind, 2005:132, 140–2). The expansion of the state generated more resources and opportunities for enrichment as the number of offices grew and with them more opportunities for patronage and clientelism. Patronage networks also permeated the bureaucracy (Henshall, 2010:26) and were central to the wealth and standing of the aristocracy but also of the realm as a whole. The willingness on the part of kings to protect noble patronage networks was important in order to ensure their acceptance of the monarch's rule. William Beik has demonstrated that once Louis XIV proved he was willing to give such protection, the nobles who took part in the Fronde ceased their resistance (Beik, 1985; Ostrowski, 2002:541). The solution to the Fronde illustrates noble-monarch symbiosis in action: 'The strategy of protection provided a tradeoff by means of which the rulers gave the aristocrats the *authority* to keep their patronage networks intact and the aristocrats gave the ruler the *power* to act' (Ostrowski, 2002:541). This, then, was another instance of the symbiosis in which nobles and the king gave each other authority and power.

The Nobility in the State

Frederick II of Prussia ('the Great') placed great faith in the organizational powers of the state in peace and war. Sometimes he is regarded as one of the epigones of state formation, not least through his famous self-description as the 'first servant of the state' (Weber, 1978:957). However, Frederick viewed the role of the aristocracy in the state as managers of the land as very important. Like few other kings, he was a prolific writer and political thinker. One of his main works, the *Political Testament* from 1752 deals with every aspect of how Prussia ought to be run, from the economy to relations with other powers. A particular concern is the position of the nobility and he states that 'one of the subjects of the politics of the King of Prussia is the preservation [*Erhaltung*] of his nobility. Because, come what may, we will never have a braver or more loyal nobility' (Friedrich der Grosse, 1986:42). To preserve his nobility, the King of Prussia must make sure that noble estates never fall into bourgeois hands, if a nobleman must sell his estates, then they could only be bought by other noblemen. However, the verb form of *Erhaltung, erhalten,* denotes not only preservation but also receiving orders. Frederick goes on to say that the king must prevent the nobility seeking foreign service, moreover, they must be permeated by a patriotic spirit and consciousness of their estate (*Standesbewusstsein*). The noble officer corps stemmed from many different and disparate provinces but the king himself had taken care to instil the idea that they were all Prussians and belonged to a single state. Furthermore, it was appropriate that the nobility devote their service (*Dienst*) to their own Fatherland, hence, nobles going into foreign service should be harshly punished, while those that served the state should receive honours and privileges. However, King Frederick warned about the princes and princesses of the blood, in other words his own relatives; since their high status made them imperious, prone to intrigue and difficult to rule, it was imperative that they were robbed of independent power (Friedrich der Grosse, 1986:46, 52). The king advised that they should be showered with decorations and honours but kept far away from the exercise of state power and only given a military command when their personal character and talents made it safe to do so. These admonitions and Frederick's own policies in this regard were very different from high medieval conditions when the king's family members, the dukes, were important military commanders and advisors in most European realms.

Just like in the Middle Ages, the European nobility in the early modern era was characterized by a double-sided claim to social status and its exceptional position in regard to the political system. Not only birth but also personal performance was a necessary characteristic of nobility. According to the double-sided legitimation of birth/qualification it was not sufficient to be born into an aristocratic lineage, one had to prove one's worth by performing deeds. As Luhmann argues, the double criterion of birth/qualification enabled the prince to 'adjust' perceived or argued inconsistencies in the stratified society by rewarding qualification and compensating a low social position due to a person having been born into a 'false' social standing through ennoblement (Luhmann, 1997:941ff). The prince could also de-noble individuals and indeed entire families in cases of false conduct, such as pursuing the trade of a commoner, cowardice, or treason. Doubtlessly, ennoblement – grounded as it was in the double criterion of the charismatic claims of the aristocracy and the idea that nobility consisted in deeds and virtue as well as birth, was an invaluable instrument of power. The interplay between privilege and obligation in noble ideologies continued to be strong with respect to the relation between nobles and monarchs in the art of government. Most considered it a right and a duty to aid their monarch in ruling the country (Scott and Storrs, 2007:38).

The expansion of the state is one the most dominant themes in the political history of the seventeenth and eighteenth centuries. States expanded in terms of the number of people employed, the number of agencies and in terms of their capacity to control, influence and tax the population. Instead of being the death-knell of the nobility this expansion provided new opportunities. In all European countries the nobility dominated all levels of the state. In Britain the peerage exercised an almost total monopoly of high office in the army, national government and local government and its position in the House of Lords (Cannon, 2007:75). In France the *noblesse de l'épée* continued to dominate 'the officers corps of the army, the great offices of the Crown, posts in the royal household, senior positions in the Church and governorships of provinces' (Mettam, 2007:132). More sophisticated techniques of government required a higher degree of education. In the late Middle Ages, non-noble clerks and lawyers had threatened to replace the nobility as functionaries of the state. In the seventeenth century, this trend was countered by increasing levels of education of young noblemen who could take up qualified positions in government (Henshall, 2010:23).

Nobility and the Armed Forces

Because of the strong association between the capabilities for armed force and the kernel of political power in many theories of the state, state formation theorists have focused on the decline of noble armies in the early modern age. It has been inscribed into a macronarrative of the rise of the state and the increasing powerlessness of the nobility. Weber and later Hintze stress that who controls the means of violence is a key question in determining the shape of the state (Hintze, 1962b; Weber, 1978:54, 55). Tilly describes a development in which nobles go from being independent military actors, to entrepreneurs, to brokers and finally to being employees in the service of the state (Tilly, 1990). De Toqueville argues in the nineteenth century that the nobility lost their independent military power at the expense of the expanding state, while Norbert Elias argues that the nobility become neutralized as they regress from an autonomous centre of military and political power and are reduced to the powerless accoutrements of the royal court (Tilly, 1990; Elias, 2000; de Tocqueville, 2011).

However, recent historical research makes these models problematic since it has been demonstrated that the nobility retained a considerable military importance (Dewald, 1996:140–3). The nobility dominated the army – the nobility was not a power outside the princely state or court, but the political order was not autonomous of noble families and the nobility was indispensable in order to raise armies. In France, regiments were recruited in the provinces and led by a noble commander from the area. The positions of colonel of a regiment or captain of a company were proprietary, but unlike civilian offices, sons did not automatically inherit the posts of their fathers. Royal approval was necessary, but ownership as a rule passed to a successor pointed out by the officer or his family (Mettam, 2007:151). In the British army the commander-in-chief was always a peer and in the eighteenth century fourteen of twenty field marshals were peers (Cannon, 2007:75). Interestingly, as the size of armies expanded and the private armies of nobles disappeared, the proportion of noble officers increased dramatically from the seventeenth to the eighteenth centuries (Scott and Storrs, 2007:41–2). Brokerage was common in all European armies and it meant that the state did not own its armies (Henshall, 2010:24). The expansion of royal armies and perhaps states more generally were 'the result of the co-operation and consensus already negotiated between

rulers and elites and not the cause of it' (Henshall, 2010:16), and '[T]
here is little evidence that elites were coerced into partnership by military force' (Henshall, 2010:17). The noble ideology of the time supported this monopolization by arguing that leadership in war demanded
the qualities that were inherent in noble lineages.

Nobility in Government

Government took place on both the provincial and the central
level. On both we find the nobility playing important roles. Some discussions of the general trends of political development of the period
stress the fact that several central institutions of government where
nobles and kings had exercised co-rule were disbanded during this
period. One such example is the French Estates-General, which was
not convened between 1614 and 1789. Another is the Russian Zemsky
Sobor that also lay dormant. It is important not to make too much of the
dormancy of such central institutions because that ignores the importance of government on provincial levels. While the general assembly of
France was not convened, the parliaments of Paris and of great provincial cities flourished (Mettam, 2007:129); it was the local and regional
levels of the state that the majority of the population encountered and
thus where day-to-day power was concentrated (Scott and Storrs,
2007:37).

The institutions of the central level of government were the
council, the court, diets (e.g., representative institutions) and the central
bureaucracy. The central governing institution in all early modern
polities was the small group of intimate counsellors that surrounded
the king. Royal councils had been established in the late Middle Ages
and they were considered to represent the realm, rather than the interests of each individual member or serve as the instrument of the king.
During the Middle Ages such institutions often ruled together with the
king; effectively forming a 'diarchy' or in Otto von Gierke's words
a 'dualism' (Poggi, 1978; Gierke, 1990; Ribalta, 2007:21). When councils became too large, several countries began to develop the institution
of the inner council, consisting only of a small group of members. These
groups were the real governments of their age, occupying themselves
with matters of state of the highest degree, including foreign policy and
questions of war and peace. In Germany this was called the Geheimer
Rat, in Denmark Geheimconseil, in France Conseil étroit, and in Spain

the Consejo de Estado. Descent and kinship – and thereby social position – determined membership in the small council. The upper or high nobility dominated these gatherings. In France membership of the inner council extended to the royal family and the princes of the blood. A similar situation prevailed in Spain, where members of the upper nobility were the only members of the Council of State. In other councils, individuals from the lower nobility or even people of bourgeois extraction could be called in as members but only if they had professional and specialized qualifications (Ribalta, 2007). In Sweden, of the forty-seven members of the council that were appointed from 1602 to 1632, thirty-four were related. The families Oxenstierna, Bonde, Brahe, De la Gardie, Bielke, Banér, Horn and Stenbock held a virtual monopoly on council seats and they profited handsomely from the wars (Englund, 2000:153–4). In Britain, the high nobility, the peers, dominated government throughout the eighteenth century (Lebow, 2018:254) and in eighteenth-century France ministerial dynasties and leading *robe* families monopolized the posts of royal ministers, the king's councils and intendants. The old military houses of the *noblesse de l'épée* monopolized the highest echelons of the military as well as of the Church (Swann, 2007:182–3). The royal court remained a prerogative of the aristocracy. Several of the highest offices at court served as ways to bind 'powerful clans, including the Bourbon-Condé, La Tour d'Auvergne and Rohan, to the king's person' (Swann, 2007:183).

In historical sociology, Russia is often considered an autocratic state where the tsar had crushed or subdued the nobility into service (Tilly, 1990:30, 139–43). In this view the country did not have many of the characteristics singled out as drivers of development such as representative institutions after the Zemsky Sobor was disbanded, a corporate nobility like Britain, Germany or France, and serfdom was practiced until 1861 (Bendix, 1976, 1984:65; Tilly, 1990:139–43; Downing, 1992:38ff). Monarchs like Ivan IV (the Terrible) who created his own police force to suppress recalcitrant parts of the population or Peter I (the Great) who reformed the Russian state, including the nobility, are often invoked to support this extreme version of a conflict narrative. In sum, Russia is habitually presented as the 'other' of Western Europe with a strong Mongol heritage of despotism being overlaid by enlightened despotism in the early modern era (Neumann, 1996).

Recent research is unravelling the absolutist, and thus coercion-heavy interpretation of Russia. As in Western European countries, the discourse of the near omnipotence of the tsars served to bolster domestic and international claims for recognition. Behind the discourse, we can observe frequent co-rule and intense co-dependency (Kivelson, 1999:83–105, 2005:21–2). Hereditary noble families exercised a considerable influence over the state and the tsars from the sixteenth to the eighteenth century (Ostrowski, 2002:539, 544, 548). The Council of State was a powerful aristocratic body that exercised oversight of the tsars and at times even deposed and elected new ones. Here as elsewhere successful rule depended upon negotiations and continuous consultations between the monarch and the nobility as well as the formation of a consensus among the ruling elite (Ostrowski, 2000:267–304, 2002:550, 558, 562–3). The reforms of Peter I included creating a new system of rank, the so-called Table of Ranks, which is sometimes interpreted as creating a break with the old boyar aristocracy and instituting a new service nobility, the *mestnichestvo* (Weber, 1978:985). However, several studies have demonstrated that old princely (*kniaz*) and aristocratic families whose lineages stretched from the Middle Ages survived the Petrine reforms and retained a leading position in the eighteenth and nineteenth centuries (Meehan-Waters, 1971:28–75; Hosking, 2000; Ostrowski, 2000:544–5). Powerful ruling families like the Dolgoruki provided continuity in a country that went through considerable turmoil and dynastic shifts (Ostrowski, 2000:553). On several occasions they assassinated tsars that broke the compound between aristocrats and tsars or through their erratic behaviour threatened the symbolic solidarity of the rulers. Finally, it was crucial to gain the consent of the circle of elite aristocratic families in order to go to war (Jones, 1993).

Russia matters greatly to the investigation of this book. In line with the absolutist interpretation of Russia, Charles Tilly describes it as a coercion-intensive form of rule (Tilly, 1990). However, since specialists are demonstrating that even in the country that earlier generations of sociologists and political scientists regarded as the epitome of a coercion-intensive state, co-rule and consensus were the keys to successful formation of a political order we can conclude that these are general elements in Eurasian polity formation. Naturally, there was plenty of coercion towards the lower orders, particularly serfs, in Russia, which means that the country as a whole cannot be described as being permeated by collaboration. But co-operation and consent within the aristocratic and princely elite were absolutely necessary to govern the country. Thus here we can observe a form of power at work that is rarely dealt with in state formation studies: the kind of power that springs from collaboration or in Hannah Arendt's words, from acting in concert (Arendt, 1972:143–55), it enabled coercive and ideas-based powers against other social strata but in this case, as in others, collaborative forms of power precede and are preconditions of externally oriented coercion. We also see in the Russian case an important contrast to the Arab and Turkic polities discussed in Chapters 7, 8 and 9: attempts to break the power of ingrained hereditary elites usually backfired but policies that accommodated them resulted in successful and durable polity formation.

Representative Bodies and Polity Creation

In the period 1500 to 1800 representative institutions developed fully all over Europe. Representative institutions have been considered important in state formation research primarily because they enabled a greater degree of material exploitation in the form of taxes (Downing, 1989; Tilly, 1990; Ertman, 1997; Rokkan, 1999). However, I will claim that their importance also lies in the way that they connected kinship elites as a part of the political order. Their significance lies on an even deeper level as representation created the political order and a political community and since people were organized into abstract categories, estates, they were constructed as parts of a political whole. The normal division was tripartite: the clergy, the nobility and the commoners made up the three estates. Sweden was an exception since the farmers made up a fourth estate. The parliament of early modern Britain was of course divided into the House of Commons and the House of Lords, both of which were dominated by the nobility (Lebow, 2018:253). Representation did not take place between pre-existing social groups but representation as a relational phenomenon creates social groups (Haldén, 2014). Positions in an estate-based assembly were hereditary, at least in the noble estate, where one represents a specific kinship group, not an electorate. Noble status served as an entry ticket to politics. However, not everyone who was of noble status had a seat in parliament; only the head of the family had a seat (Bush, 1983).

This form of rule is often called the 'state of the estates' (Myers, 1975; Poggi, 1978).[5] Due to a series of causes including 'the entry of the

---

[5] This form of rule bridges the periods of Chapter 4 and this one. Treating it in two chapters would entail unnecessary repetition so I deal with it here.

towns into politics, the shift in the balance of power between the territorial ruler and the feudatory princes in favour of the former, and ... [changes] in the terms and structures of the feudal element's participation in the wider system of rule' the state of the estates came into being (Koenigsberger, 1975; Poggi, 1978:42). Another aspect of the increasingly institutionalized nature of politics was the courts or Parlements (Poggi, 1978:44). Estates operated according to written rules that stated their competencies and procedures as well as relations to other institutions (Poggi, 1978:43).

Estate assemblies were either central or local; in the former case the assembly represented the entire realm, in the latter they represented parts of a province. Central assemblies existed all over Europe, as variations upon a common theme. In Poland it was called the Sejm, in Sweden the Riksdag (which supplanted the earlier noble assemblies, the Herredagar), in Denmark the Rigsdag, in Norway the Stændermøte, in the German lands the Landtage, in the Empire as a whole the Reichstag, in Aragon, Castile-León, Valencia and Catalonia the Cortes, in France the Parlements, in Hungary the Parlamentum Publicum and in England the Parliament. There were different kinds of estate-assemblies. In a classical essay, Otto Hintze outlines a model of estate-based polities that differentiated between two-chamber and three-curie systems (Hintze, 1962a, 1962c). In the former, the representative assembly was divided between the higher nobility (magnates) and the lower (gentry). In the latter the assembly was divided into clergy, nobility and the cities (burghers). In Sweden, the third estate was divided into two groups, the farmers and the burgers thus creating a quadripartite scheme (Hintze, 1962a). The king or the prince convoked representative institutions, they did not assemble themselves, and few representative institutions were permanent before the eighteenth century (Bulst, 2005). The estates came together in parliamentary assemblies for the whole realm that were convoked on an irregular basis. Eventually, in many countries the leaders of the representative assemblies asked their prince for the privilege to have their assembly made into a permanent institution. In turn, princes often granted this request since it tied nobles and other representatives closer to a centre that was both communicative and symbolic (Bendix, 1978).

Representative Institutions and Political Order

For centuries scholars have argued that representative institutions played a central role in European state formation. They have been seen as central stepping stones in both the formation of the state as such and in the formation of democratic forms of governance. A strong tradition in state formation theory stresses taxation as a crucial driver of the growth of state institutions over time making them more extensive (i.e., covering more and more areas of human activity) and intensive (i.e., making state penetration more effective and thorough). Taxation as the means of state growth is closely linked to the tradition that identifies systemic warfare in a competitive environment as a driver of state formation. In order to be able to survive in the competitive environment of medieval and early modern Europe states need to obtain military resources and, in turn, the means to do so was to obtain funds through taxing their subjects (Tilly, 1990; Glete, 2002). According to this story, the proto-form of parliaments, estates and diets, were in many cases originally convened by the state, that is, the king and his household, in order to increase taxation and to meet with taxpayers/ collectors and local administrators, that is, the nobility.

Michael Mann argues that it was not the pressing needs of warfare that prompted increases in taxation and thus the growth of the state but the pressing and panicked needs to stave off acute bankruptcy (Mann, 1986:433–4). According to this view the need to obtain means through taxation prompted the growth of representative institutions in which the king and his officials could interact with other social groups and demand their resources (Bulst, 2005). Hence it would have been difficult to raise funds and equally difficult to get acceptance both from elites and from non-elite segments of the population without representative institutions. In return for their participation, the former gained concessions from the king, a voice in how funds were spent or non-monetary resources (such as different armed forces) were used. The growth of taxation thus led to a greater involvement from the people in the affairs of the state, where the taxed demanded greater accountability from the state that was taxing them.

Hirschmann's typology of strategies that actors apply in both states and firms is once again useful: he defines the three main strategies as 'exit', 'voice' and 'loyalty' (Hirschmann, 1978:90–1, 1980, 2004). A defining trait of the state of the twenty-first century is that wholesale exit is no longer possible. In the polities of the late Middle Ages it was still possible to use a number of exit strategies. However, representative institutions stabilized relations since they granted elites, primarily noble but also burghers, gained both voice and loyalty and thus eschewed exit from the polity. However important, the role that representative institutions played in the formation of political order does not have to be reduced to a building-block in a functionalistic account of a political system in which resources accumulate, are circulated, and services and public goods are produced in an input-output fashion. A problem with materialist-functional interpretations of representative institutions and their actors is that they emphasize the separation and opposition of the two poles of the system, the monarch and the estates. Hardly surprising, works in this genre tend to stress the conflictual relation between kings and nobles and underemphasize their mutual dependence. Finally, seeing the monarch and the estates as two separate entities that came together and interacted in the representative institutions misses the point that the new form of organization constructed the two parties in a new fashion. Representative institutions were important because they contributed to the formation of political order by reinforcing notions of political communities that transcended rulers and ruled alike as well as, through the process of representation, constructing the two poles in the equation. As seen in Chapter 4, recent developments in political theory stress the constitutive effects of political representation. In this interpretation, representation is not a process between two pre-existing entities but a performative act that constructs both the represented and the representatives (Haldén, 2014:132).

Estate-assemblies strengthened the embedding and community creating tendencies of earlier 'public' institutions and practices like assemblies and participation in royal elections and coronations. This strengthening partly came about since estate assemblies were more regular and formalized but also because the elites (in the case of the noble estate, kinship-based) belonged to and represented abstract communities on two levels: first the noble estate and second the realm. Estates and realms co-constituted each other since, to paraphrase Tilly, the estates built the realm but the realm built the estates. The importance of the corporate forms of organization cannot be underemphasized in this respect. They meant a transcendence of personal and thereby partial interests to larger entities in order to perform the tasks of ruling. This transcendence was enacted in a two-step process in the estate assemblies (diets, parliaments) first, when a single estate, for example the nobility, was to agree on a position and second, when all estates were to vote and agree on it. The corporative element meant an aggregation of interests as well as of identities into larger entities.

A central question of this book is whether the relation between kinship groups (in whatever organizational form they may appear) and 'the state' can be described as a conflictual relation between two separate entities. Scholarship on the state of the estates stresses it should be seen as a symbiotic formation whose two poles were joined in the business of rule not by constituting one centre but precisely since they constituted a polarity. This aspect was expressed through a principle that Otto von Gierke called 'dualism' without which the Ständesstaat system of rule cannot be understood. This principle 'confronted the ruler with the ... Estates ... and associated the two elements in rule as distinct power centres' (Poggi, 1978:48).

Would this form of institution and the form of political life that the state of the estates embodied have been possible without specific traits of the European kinship structure and in particular the structure of the European nobility? We have seen that previous research has tried to ascertain when European noble kinship groups were organized into lineages, and when (and if) their historical development can be adequately described as a process of shrinkage and consolidation from a sprawling clan-like structure to a more narrow family unit. The classical investigations of this matter have used economic and social practices such as inheritances and wills as their preferred research method or – to use Niklas Luhmann's terms – mode of observation (Luhmann, 1995). To continue with Luhmann's vocabulary, if we instead use the political system as our mode of observation, we can gain new insights into the matter. Seen from the viewpoint of the political system, we see European (noble) kinship groups as hierarchical groupings. Membership in estate-based parliaments was individual but representative of a kinship group (e.g., family, dynasty, lineage); it was usually the highest-ranking individual who occupied the family seat. In such cases, the envoy was a representative of the head of the family. Stating that a hierarchical family structure was a prerequisite of parliaments might be stretching one's argument. However, without a clear hierarchy within a noble dynasty it is difficult to see how it would have been possible to create a structure with one representative from each dynasty. A more egalitarian kin structure is likely to have produced intra-family struggles over the right to sit in parliament as the representative of the dynasty. Would it have been possible with a kinship structure of the Middle Eastern kind – that is, less hierarchical, more sprawling and more closed?[6] To continue with our hypothetical case, it would be much harder to resolve such conflicts without clear notions of legitimacy. For example, before the introduction of primogeniture in Scandinavia all children sired by the king were deemed to be of his magical blood and thus have a legitimate claim to the throne. Although being of noble blood was an important part of the ideology that legitimated a special status for noble lineages (Jochens, 1987), by 1400 most noble families in Europe were hierarchically organized with main branches/cadet branches and with a hierarchical structure within the main branch that enabled the identification of a family head. We have seen that the European kinship society was an integrated part of and precondition of this form of political order. Hence we can postulate a connection between this particular form of kinship and the representative institutions of the late medieval and early modern period and hence of the political order.

Kinship and Political Order on a European Level

A common theme in research about state formation is that Europe has, since centuries, consisted of different powers that have interacted with each other, in less technical terms, a system of states. These interactions and relations have been the drivers for the creation and constant development for European polities. According to many scholars, the most fundamental driver for state formation has been the systemic threat and often reality of war (Tilly, 1990; Ertman, 1997, 2005:367–83; Hui, 2005). Stephen Hobden argues that several works in the state formation genre rely upon a 'Realist' view of international relations as a precondition for their arguments. More precisely, the idea that the international system is inherently competitive and works like a struggle for survival among sovereign units is borrowed in some part from Realist IR (Hobden, 1998:151, 152, 153, 160).

Social scientists usually talk about Europe as a system of states and indeed, for centuries, Europeans described their own relations in terms of a 'system' or even 'republic' of states. However, Daniel Nexon, Andreas Osiander and Benno Teschke argue that the main actors in *ancien régime* Europe were not states but monarchs and dynasties

[6] For details, see Chapter 7.

(Teschke, 2002; Osiander, 2007; Nexon, 2009). Consequently, the main constitutive factors of the system were the attributes of dynasties and their interests. Teschke argues that the fact that kings owned territories – a feature he calls 'proprietary kingship' – created a territorial logic unique to seventeenth- and eighteenth-century European geopolitics. Territory, he claims, 'was not constitutive of sovereignty, but a proprietary adjunct of the dynasty' (Teschke, 2002:22). Because of these structural factors we have to see this system as one of interlocking rival dynastic networks. A consequence of proprietary kingship was that rules of succession became part of the public international law of Europe, marriages were the main means to creating alliances and territories could be bartered and swapped like goods. Teschke is correct in emphasizing the importance of dynasties as actors and a dynasty-centred way of reasoning for politics between realms but his account relies on a concept of absolutism and royal power that historians now consider to be exaggerated. Monarchs were not as powerful and alone in determining the fate of their domains as was thought. Instead they shared this power with other elites in their domains, most importantly the ones that based their power, legitimacy and status on kinship: the high nobility. In sum, this means that kinship was far from obsolete in the political order constituted by Europe as a whole.

The following section analyses the role of kinship in creating the European order on an international or, to avoid anachronisms, inter-realm, level in the following ways: (1) the creation of political entities through marriage and inheritance – the so-called composite monarchy, (2) the international dimensions of transitions within and between dynasties and (3) wars of succession.

Actors

Several historical accounts of IR theory centre on the idea that the sovereign state became gradually more important during the period 1500–1800 and was finally established as the only legitimate actor in what had become international (or inter-state) politics. While it is true that other organizations, such as trade leagues and city-states waned during this period, it would be wrong to see the sovereign state as the sole winner. Rather, the sovereigns – that is, the ruling monarchs and their dynasties – were the beneficiaries. Realms gained predominance in so far as they were run by a royal dynasty who could claim to be more legitimate by referring to their inherited semi-divine or numinous power. Thus, kinship and inherited legitimacy lay at the foundations of the new post-medieval European order. The result in turn laid the foundations for a secular, modern, order based on popular sovereignty and abstract statehood that was developed later. However, as Osiander has pointed out what many IR theorists identify as a modern system in the seventeenth and eighteenth centuries was characterized by traits that do not fit easily into a current understanding of what 'modern' is (Osiander, 2001:119–45). Several of the new developments that are often interpreted as modern or early modern in the sense of pointing towards the future can be interpreted as signs of the continued or increased role of kinship as the basis of legitimacy – and thus as being products of late medieval developments rather than predecessors of modern ones.

Kings were sovereign, not states; peace treaties were concluded between monarchs, not between states. The Peace of Westphalia in 1648, once considered the starting point of modern international politics, was signed between the Queen of Sweden, King of France and the Emperor.[7] This practice persisted until the late eighteenth century, when we still find it in treaties like the Treaty of Paris in 1763 and in the peace between Britain and the United States in 1783.[8] I will in the following outline some illustrations of how the dynastic element affected the scope of possible, permissible and necessary action. Until the Treaty of Utrecht in 1713, European powers existed in a rank society. Clark notes the treaty established the notion of equality of states (Clark, 2005:76). Although this notion would be violated repeatedly over the centuries it was nevertheless a departure from an earlier system in which powers were ranked on the basis of the status of their dynasties (Randelzhofer, 1967:207). Realms ruled by royal dynasties were in a class apart, which led to continuous discrimination against, for example, those German powers ruled by princes of electoral status or that were associations of smaller territories and cities (Duchhardt, 1990:19). The definition of the

---

[7] Peace of Westphalia (Osnabrück) Preamble, www.pax-westphalica.de/ipmipo/index.html (accessed 14 October 2016) and Peace of Westphalia (Münster) www.pax-westphalica.de /ipmipo/index.html (accessed 14 October 2016).

[8] See for example: The Treaty of Paris 1763, http://avalon.law.yale.edu/18th_century/ paris763.asp (accessed 13 October 2016); The Definitive Treaty of Peace 1783, http://avalon .law.yale.edu/18th_century/paris.asp (accessed 13 October 2016).

European system as an order of monarchs led to a rush among the middle powers of the Holy Roman Empire to acquire royal status, by marriage such as the House of Hannover's ascension to the British throne, by electoral politics such as the Saxon elector's ascension to the Polish throne or by shrewd innovation, such as the creation of Prussia as a kingdom in 1701 which enabled the Hohenzollern dynasty of Brandenburg to be crowned 'kings *in* Prussia' (Clark, 2007:67–77).

The dominance of the European order by monarchs and indeed the definition of that order as an order of monarchs was something new. Earlier peace treaties could and did include other kinds of actors. The novelty of this redefinition supports my argument that political kinship became more important, not less so, in the so-called early modern era. The absence of the Pope and the Hanseatic League from the Peace of Westphalia in 1648 and shutting the doors on non-royal actors (like the Swabian League which had fought in the war of the Spanish Succession) at Utrecht in 1713 meant that monarchs, unlike other actors (electors, princes, doges, etc.) were the only legitimate actors (Haldén, 2011:84–7). The European system at this time was thus a system of monarchical solidarity, not a system based on a knock-out competition between monarchs (Gorski and Sharma, 2017:98–123). Thus the idea that the European system of states was a quasi-Darwinian battleground in which only the strongest states prevailed is highly problematic.

The legitimacy of a dynasty decided whether it, its country and its inhabitants would be accepted in the wider European order. Erik Ringmar's analysis of Sweden's entry into the Thirty Year's War (1618–48) demonstrates these connections. Between 1361 and 1521 Sweden was a part of the Union of Kalmar with Denmark and Norway; a union with a single king who most often came from Denmark. Although the component kingdoms were sometimes at war with each other, it was only in 1521 during the rebellion of Gustav Vasa that Sweden revoked the union and declared independence. Many of Europe's courts saw this move by an obscure nobleman in an obscure country as usurpation. The Vasa dynasty continued to be seen, intermittently, as a 'rogue dynasty' and by extension Sweden was a rogue realm for the rest of the century and up until its entry into the Thirty Years' War in 1631 (Ringmar, 2008). European doubts about the legitimacy of the Vasas meant that they found it difficult to gain alliances and credit. Lacking recognition of the dynasty was infectious as Swedish merchants also found business dealings difficult. Dynastic recognition preceded national or state recognition. As Ringmar shows, not only the ambition but also the necessity to be recognized was a main reason Sweden entered into the war (Ringmar, 2008).

Marriage between two dynasties created horizontal ties synchronically. A dynastic connection could mean the possibility of a future alliance – and hence be a kind of investment. It could also be intended to crown an alliance. An example is how the historical rapprochement between France and Austria 1763 was crowned by the marriage between Marie Antoinette and the French Dauphin Louis Auguste in 1770 (Schroeder, 1994). A marriage also created diachronic linkages, connections backwards and forwards in time, through inheritance and through the descendants that the liaison (hopefully) created. An heir to two dynasties could inherit titles, land, followers and symbolic capital; he might also inherit grievances and obligations to correct these. An inheritance would thus harbour causes of war since it was not always the case that all parties inside and outside a polity would accept the heir as legitimate. Connections backwards in time created by kinship constituted an opportunity for political and strategic action in the shape of raising claims to a throne or a territory, either at the time of the incumbent's death or, in some cases, before that event. Kinship and the degree to which it was considered provable was the basis of whether claims to a title would be considered legitimate by potential allies that one had to mobilize in times of war, by actors one had to persuade within the country one claimed, and by other rulers who would be affected by the changes in possession and rulership. As we will see below, it was not enough that an inheritance was correct or legitimate in formal-legal terms in order to get other rulers to accept an inheritance. If a new ruler would suddenly be able to combine the inheritance of two bloodlines into an overpowering polity, then the threat to its neighbours that it would pose might be enough to drive them to war, regardless of both legality and legitimacy.

Composite Monarchies

Chapter 4 discussed the phenomenon of the composite monarchy, the compound of two or more polities under the same dynasty and under varying degrees of co-ordinated rule (Koenigsberger, 1975; Elliott, 1992). This practice continued in the early modern era. I will now discuss several examples of composite monarchies.

The two branches of the House of Habsburg, the Austrian and the Spanish, created two composite monarchies at their respective ends of Europe. The Spanish possessions contained several polities, Aragon, Castille, Galicia, the Netherlands, the Duchy of Milan and the Kingdom of the Two Sicilies as well as the American viceroyalties. In Central Europe, the Habsburgs knitted together the kingdoms of Bohemia and Hungary and the hereditary lands of the Habsburgs (Krain, Kärnten, the March of Austria) in a conglomerate that lasted until 1918. Marriage strategies, biological luck and inheritance enabled the formation of the largest empire in post-Roman Europe. Under Charles V (r.1519–56) the Austrian and Spanish dominions were combined under one ruler, during whose reign, the Habsburg dominions expanded further as most of Southern and Central America were added to the European possessions (Reifenscheid, 2006:477–509). Marriage strategies involving the entire family were important to consolidate the European lands. Charles' brother, Archduke Ferdinand, had married Anne Jagellonia, the sister of King Louis II of Bohemia and Hungary. Louis, who lacked issue, was later killed in the battle of Mohács in 1526. Then Ferdinand ascended the throne in Bohemia, was elected as the king of Hungary and incorporated these territories into the Habsburg domains (Erbe, 2000:34–9). When Charles abdicated in 1556 the united crowns of his empire went to different heirs, with Ferdinand ascending the Imperial Throne, and Philip gaining the Netherlands, Burgundy, and the Spanish and Italian crowns, dividing the Habsburgs between the Spanish and Austrian lines (Wilson, 2009:50). Charles had, however, promised his younger brother Ferdinand that he would receive the hereditary Habsburg possessions in the Holy Roman Empire. Therefore Ferdinand was made Archduke of Austria and appointed as the head of the imperial government in the empire.

After the separation of the Spanish and Austrian Habsburgs, the two branches of the family began to intermarry in order to strengthen the dynastic ties between them. Over time the repeated marriages between cousins, later between spouses who were both first- and second-level cousins, and finally between uncles and nieces generated not only increasing facial similarity but also genetic and thus political disasters (Alvarez, Ceballos and Quinteiro, 2009; Ceballos and Álvarez, 2013). In 1700 the last of the Spanish Habsburgs, the excruciatingly inbred Charles II of Spain, died childless and heirless. His death sparked the War of the Spanish succession (1700–1713/14), which will be discussed in detail below.

The Habsburg polity might be almost an archetypal example of a composite monarchy, but most major polities were of a composite character. Brandenburg-Prussia was a conglomerate of the various possession of the Hohenzollern dynasty such as the Mark of Brandenburg and the Kingdom of Prussia but also the miniscule counties of Ansbach and Bayreuth towards the south and, in the west the united countries of Jülich-Kleve-Berg. After the Succession Crisis of 1609, the Hohenzollerns had to settle for Jülich, Kleve and Ravensburg. From 1603 the two powers of the British Isles, England and Scotland, were joined in a dynastic union that was turned into a political union in 1714. The House of Oldenburg, kings of Denmark, ruled over a northern composite monarchy that encompassed not only Denmark proper (along with possessions in Southern Sweden until 1658), but also Norway, Iceland and the two duchies of Schleswig-Holstein that were part of the Holy Roman Empire.

Royal marriages and the children that they produced, created complications for legitimacy that in turn could create a *causus belli* for centuries, as exemplified by the Vasa legacy. John III of Sweden married Catherine Jagellonica in 1562. Their son, Sigismund Vasa, became king of Poland and grand duke of Lithuania as well as king of Sweden between 1592 and 1599. His uncle, Charles IX of Sweden, deposed him with the help of the Swedish Diet. Thus the House of Vasa was divided into a Polish and a Swedish branch that both claimed the Swedish throne. Since the split, all subsequent Swedish kings were concerned with forcing the rulers of Poland to renounce all claims to the Swedish throne. After Sigismund's deposition four wars were fought where this particular dynastic interest was, together with economic and geopolitical interests, a driving cause. Finally, in the Peace of Oliva in 1660, the Polish king renounced all claims to the Swedish throne.[9] Interestingly, when we study the debates preceding the war of 1655–60, we see that King Charles X was strongly concerned with the dynastic aspect but his councillors – who all belonged to the high nobility – were rather concerned with the economic gains and losses that might result from war as well as the security of Sweden (Roberts, 1991:100–43; Sundberg, 1998). In the council debates, therefore, we see

---

[9] See Friedensvertrag von Oliva (Warschau) www.ieg-friedensvertraege.de/treaty/1660%20V%203%20Friedensvertrag%20von%20Oliva%20(Warschau)/t-1473-1-de.html?h=1 (accessed 17 October 2016).

that the absolutist view of seventeenth-century geopolitics given by
Teschke is somewhat misleading. Charles X could not make decisions
on war and peace only based upon a conception of dynastic reasoning
and he was not alone in his decisions. His councillors, who were necessary to secure political acceptance and in order to fight the coming war,
had to agree and they argued along other lines. Does this episode then fit
into the narrative that I have tried to disprove in this book, the idea of
a principled conflict between kinship as a political principle and the
political order? I believe that it does not, not only did dynastic, economic and security concerns come together in this case; but dynastic
claims provided the language in which to legitimate a war of aggression.
Furthermore, the elites that also participated the decision were based on
kinship in the sense of descent. In total the process of going to war and
the reasons for doing so demonstrates a complicated symbiosis and
intertwining of kinship-based elites (nobles and monarchs) and kinship-
based concerns with the political order.

The fact that territories sometimes followed the monarchs through
inheritance generated the three processes of dissolution (although few
realms were completely and permanently divided), conglomeration and
swapping. For example, in the 1780s, Emperor Joseph II tried to exchange
the Austrian Netherlands in return for Bavaria but did not succeed
(Bernard, 1965). Some of the reasons for this failure were pecuniary and
international but the plans alarmed several of the smaller imperial estates
for whom the very prospect of an exchange violated old constitutional
norms of the Holy Roman Empire and alarmed several smaller polities who
allied against with Prussia against Joseph II (Aretin, 1997b:299–315;
Blanning, 2015). The internal opposition to the exchange project was
symptomatic of the trend that other elite groups, often the aristocracy,
tried to rein in the monarchs' policies vis-à-vis their realms.

Since at least the late fourteenth century the idea that the realm
was inalienable was firmly established in most European realms; that parts
or the entirety could not be given away, sold or traded stood in the way of
schemes to exchange or swap territories. Included in this idea was that it
was the king's solemn duty not to lose parts of the realm and if that should
happen, he was obliged to win them back (Kantorowicz, 1954:499–501;
Saenger, 1977; Meron, 1995:3–5). The doctrine of the inalienability of the
realm thus counteracted the tendency to dissolution by limiting the extent
to which kings could treat realms as their properties. The integrity of
territories and the idea that they had an existence of their own as legal

persons, as corporate personalities, also limited the extent to which rulers of conglomerate states could integrate their possessions. Highly developed territories with their own 'national' identity, legal systems and political institutions – for example Aragon – could resist the attempts of their foreign monarchs to impose uniform rule by referring to the sanctity of their own traditions, thus the powers of Spanish kings in Aragon were always more limited than they were in Castile. In the former territory, they had to deal with a more powerful parliament, the Cortes, and were forced to concede limitations to their authority (Gil, 2002).

Actors drawn from the high nobility attempted, often successfully, to engage in boundary-drawing activities that marked off their country against the other territories of their monarch. In the eighteenth century, the English Parliament refused to acquiesce in the Hanoverian monarchs' yearnings to support their ancestral electorate. The idea of realm as a corporate personality thus served as a counterweight to the process of conglomeration (Duchhardt, 1997; Waurechen, 2013). Rather than a dyadic conflict between kinship-based elite groups and the king or between kinship-based principles and political ones, we see a complex triad within which politics was played out consisting of the nobility, the realm and the monarch. There was antagonism within this field but an antagonism that also masked interdependence. Nobility was intertwined with the monarchy through ties of patronage and their dependence on legitimacy bestowed upon them by the king. There was also a similarity and thus dependence between the nobility and monarchy since they were both based on privilege. References to the realm and the service that the nobility did to it as a basis of their legitimacy also underpinned the standing of the nobility. The monarchy was dependent upon the nobility to man institutions, support its policies, however fragmented, and rule its territories. The realm was not an actor but a concept or a semantic field that enabled actions. However, it was also tied up with both monarchy and nobility by being defined (in most cases) as a kingdom. Thus, again we see a dynamic field of interdependence and conflict at the core of the political order – not antagonism.

Wars of Succession

Europe was plagued by warfare during this period and elite kinship was a constitutive aspect of most of the conflicts. Wars were important to maintain or enlarge intertwined networks of patronage, both royal and aristocratic, thus kinship elites and their characteristics created a structural incentive to go to war. Furthermore, a defining trait of aristocratic-monarchic culture was the frequent references to honour and martial prowess, which further added incentives in the early modern status culture. All wars were of course not legitimated entirely by references to kinship as a political principle or dynastic concerns. As always, economic gains, glory and even the security of the realm were motives. However, a particular kind of war was common in these years: wars of succession.

Times of succession and regencies were often times of crisis and occasionally war. However, wars of succession were not a homogenous category. As we saw in Chapter 4 they could take the form of struggles between dynasties largely based in one realm as well as struggles over the throne that involved dynasties with powerbases elsewhere. There is a historical dimension to the differences between different types of war. At a certain point in time, foreign dynasties stopped being contenders for the throne and their involvement became limited to supporting different parties that we can identify as domestic. I will illustrate this difference by comparing five different wars: The conflicts that are usually called the French Wars of Religion (1559–98), the Russian Time of Troubles (1598–1613), the Thirty Years' War (1618–48), the War of the Spanish Succession (1701–13/14) and the Austrian War of Succession (1740–8). The names of these wars that have been handed down to us are sometimes misleading, all the wars involved kinship elements to some degree or another along with religious elements, concerns of glory, recognition and reputation, as well as strong material interests.

The French Wars of Religion combined dynastic, economic, religious and inter-regnal elements. On one level they were a struggle between the great aristocratic houses of France – Guise, Bourbon and Montmorency – for influence over the heirs of the reigning house of Valois and eventually for the throne itself. The economic element came into play since control over or possession of the throne of France entailed control over vast networks of patronage and the great houses commanded considerable military power through these networks. When the Valois king, Henry II, died in a tournament in 1559 his widow and later three of his sons succeeded him. The Bourbons were the champions of the French Protestants and the Guise monopolized control over the Gallican (Catholic) Church.

Kinship ties as well as religious affinity ensured that all sides could call upon allies from other countries. England and the Netherlands supported the Bourbon faction and Spain supported the Guise and their Catholic League (Philips, 2010:119, 121). When the last Valois king, Henry III, died in 1589 Henry of Navarre of the House of Bourbon became the King of France after having converted to Catholicism and promulgated the Edict of Nantes (1598) that granted tolerance to the Huguenots. Henry IV was related to both to the House of Valois (he was a cousin of Henry III) and to the old royal house of the Capetian dynasty as a direct descendant of King Louis IX (r.1226–70). Thus, according to Valois advocates he was a 'prince of the blood' and a legitimate successor in accordance with the rediscovered Salic Law from Frankish times (Taylor, 2001).

What is striking about the French Wars of Religion, which also could be dubbed the Wars of the Valois Succession is the nature of foreign involvement. Other European dynasties (such as the English Tudors and the Spanish Habsburgs) supported the main antagonists but none intervened to claim the throne for themselves. Thus kinship seems to have been more the cause of alliance than egotistical greed. We can see a certain family resemblance with other wars where external parties have intervened in order to place an actor based in the country on the throne as a proxy, for example the Swedish and Polish interventions in Russia during the 'times of troubles' (1598–1613). Another reason is that Henry of Bourbon had strong claims to the throne of France and that it might be futile to contest them. We can also interpret this fact as a sign that the kingdom as a framework for politics had grown stronger than it had been in similar conflicts in the high Middle Ages.

The time of royal succession sometimes provoked a crisis in the matters of state. This was especially true if there was no heir, or perhaps not even a royal dynasty, or if the heir to the throne was young or his or her status was disputed. Such occasions tended to serve as tantalizing invitations to other powers to intervene. In 1598 the ruling Rurik dynasty of Russia died out, sparking a war between dynastic factions. Eventually Boris Godunov emerged victorious and claimed the title of the tsar. However, his legitimacy was still questioned and the country was ravaged by famine and the economic and political breakdown. At this moment Poland-Lithuania and Sweden invaded Russia. While Sweden sought territorial and economic benefits, the Polish King Sigismund was more ambitious. Initially he wanted his son Wladeslaw recognized as the tsar of Russia. Some boyars (magnates) opposed to Tsar Alexis who had seized power agreed to the plan, however, it seems that they had no intention of becoming Polish puppets or allowing Tsar Wladeslaw (i.e., the Polish King) to own the country as the theory of proprietary kingship would suggest was possible (Teschke, 2002). Instead, they wanted to rule Russia in concert with Wladeslaw as a figurehead (Dunning, 2004:271–4). The selection of Wladeslaw as tsar by a minority of the boyars sparked a feverish patriotic resistance in many parts of Russia; a movement that was strengthened when Sigismund declared his intention to conquer Russia for himself. Such a switch was unacceptable to most boyars and the people. Meanwhile, the Swedish kings started to hatch dynastic ambitions of their own and Sigismund's cousin Karl IX as well as his son, Gustavus Adolphus, contemplated becoming tsars (Dunning, 2004:283). The boyars assembled a council of the realm, organized a highly effective military resistance to the Poles and Swedes and in 1613 the magnate factions agreed upon a suitable tsar from a Russian lineage and elected Mikhail Romanov. His dynasty was to rule Russia until 1917. From this first Russian Civil War, it can be concluded that boyar loyalty to the idea of a Russian realm was strong.

Like many wars of this era, the Thirty Year's War was a complex of different wars over different issues that furthermore changed over time (e.g., Wilson, 2009). A first issue was whether the Holy Roman Empire should retain its polycentric character or become more consolidated – a question that initially concerned German princes but gradually engaged Danish, French and Swedish dynasties and governments (Barudio, 1998). Like the French wars it involved religion, pitting Catholic and Protestant estates and powers against each other. Like all wars, material interests mattered, not least for a foreign power like Sweden that could enrich itself by controlling the Baltic ports. It was also about security since a more tightly integrated empire under the command of a Habsburg emperor might threaten neighbouring powers like France, the Dutch Republic and Sweden. In this respect, dynastic connections entered into the equation. As we saw above, the two branches of the House of Habsburg ruled two parts of Europe: one ruled Spain, parts of Italy and the Southern Netherlands and the other large territories in Central Europe and reigned as a semi-permanent emperor over even larger areas in Germany and Italy. Thus the fears of a universal Habsburg monarchy dominating Europe that had animated Europe in the days of Charles V (r.1520–56) were rekindled.

Furthermore, we can discern two separate, but at times linked, conflicts. Spanish war efforts were directed against the United Provinces of the Netherlands, aiming to bring the war that had raged off and on from 1568 to a favourable end. Although the Spanish Habsburgs did not intervene in the war in Germany, Emperor Ferdinand sent his troops to fight the Dutch in an act of dynastic and religious solidarity (Wilson, 2009:379). The Spanish and Austrian war efforts alarmed the French who declared war on both the Spanish and Austrian Habsburgs. The wars ended through a series of peace treaties. The treaties of Münster and Osnabrück, known as the Peace of Westphalia (1648) ended the French and Swedish wars with the emperor and his allies. The war had some important dynastic effects for the Habsburgs; the electoral capitulation (the conditions for election) of Leopold VI in 1658 stipulated that the he could not ally with his relatives in Spain (Haldén, 2011:73).

Dynasticism as a constitutive factor in the shape of foreign dynasties fighting to control another royal crown returned in the War of the Spanish Succession (1701–13). In the late seventeenth century it was evident that the Spanish King Charles II was not fit to produce any heirs due to his poor health, which raised the question of who would succeed to the Spanish crown, one of the most powerful empires in the world. Since the Spanish crown could be passed down through females, the first in line to inherit was Louis, dauphin (crown prince) of France, the son of Charles II's sister Maria Theresa, and King Louis XIV of France, himself a first-cousin of Charles. However, Emperor Leopold I of the Holy Roman Empire and first cousin of Charles II also claimed the throne. To further complicate matters the previous Spanish king, Philip IV, had left a will by which he left the crown of Spain to the descendants of his younger daughter, Margareta Theresa, who had married Emperor Leopold I. By this will Margareta Theresa's grandson, Joseph Ferdinand of Bavaria, son of Elector Maximilian II of Bavaria, was to inherit the throne (Aretin, 1997a).

The potential problems of the Spanish succession were long foreseen, and as early as 1668 Emperor Leopold and Louis XIV reached a secret treaty, by which the Spanish empire would be divided between France and Austria if Charles died without any heirs. However, during the thirty years that followed circumstances changed dramatically, and the secret treaty was made void. In 1698 a second partition treaty was agreed upon between France and the Maritime Powers (Great Britain and the Netherlands). According to this treaty Joseph Ferdinand of

Bavaria, who was not dynastically tied to either of the Great Powers, and who was the rightful heir by Philip IV's will, would inherit the Spanish crown and the colonies, while Naples, Sicily, Tuscany and some of the Basque provinces would be ceded to France, and the Duchy of Milan would be ceded to Austria. In January of 1699 Joseph Ferdinand of Bavaria died, making the partition-treaty void, and once again leaving only French and Austrian candidates for the throne. New negotiations were initiated, and after one year the French and the Maritime Powers agreed that Emperor Leopold's younger son, Charles, would succeed to the throne in Spain, while the French would receive the same lands as before, and the Duchy of Milan would pass to the Emperor's nephew, Charles of Lorraine. The emperor did not accept the treaty, and neither did the Spanish. Instead, the Spanish king drafted a will by which Philip, the son of Dauphin Louis, would be offered the throne, followed by his younger brother and thereafter Charles, son of Emperor Leopold. When Charles II of Spain died on 1 November 1700, Philip of Bourbon was crowned King of Spain (Hussey and Bromley, 1970:387–8, 392–7). His ascension sparked a war that lasted fourteen years and involved most of Western Europe. The end result was that although French power was humbled, the Bourbon dynasty remained on the Spanish throne.

Times of succession could still be dangerous in the mid-eighteenth century as the case of the War of the Austrian Succession (1740–8) demonstrates. When Charles VI ascended to the thrones of the Habsburg dominions and the Holy Roman Empire in 1711, he was the only remaining male of the Habsburg dynasty, which means that from his ascension onwards, the matter of succession was problematic. To create a solution, Charles declared that all his hereditary lands would pass undivided to male heirs 'of his body' in the first instance and to his legitimate daughters in the second – the so-called pragmatic sanction. In 1720 Charles realized that his daughter Maria Theresa would be his only heir. Thus, his labours began. First he managed to persuade the diets of his lands and kingdoms to accept the sanction, then he campaigned to secure recognition from the other powers of Europe, in which he was successful between 1732 and 1738. When Charles died in 1740, the declaration was almost immediately ignored. While the Bavarian Elector Charles Albert claimed the Habsburg inheritance for himself, the Prussian Frederick II invaded Silesia. France intervened to support Bavaria and Prussia and Britain supported Maria Theresa. Spain invaded Italy in order to control the Habsburg dominions there;

which the Bourbon dynasty claimed because of their relation to the extinct Spanish branch of the Habsburgs. Charles Albert was elected Holy Roman Emperor in 1742 but when he died in 1745 Maria Theresa managed to get her husband Francis I elected Emperor. The war ended in 1748 with the Peace of Aix-la-Chapelle. The old Habsburg dynasty was now extinct in the male line and a new dynasty, Habsburg-Lorraine, took its place and was accepted by the courts of Europe (Anderson, 1995; Kunisch, 2004:185–203).

Between 1500 and 1600 most European countries managed to internally stabilize and constitutionalize the order of succession. The ascension of new dynasties or sub-dynasties to the throne, often by the elevation of cadet branches and distant relatives, becomes a more regulated affair. Partly this is due to the increased solidity of state institutions and the greater institutionalization of politics as well as the greater involvement of other groups actors (often from the aristocracy) that, instead of seeking the throne for themselves, acted in concert with other actors to form regency governments, recruit new dynasties or to bring peripheral branches of the royal dynastic network into the centre and onto the throne. An example is the ascension of Charles X Gustavus to the Swedish throne in 1654 when his cousin, Queen Christina, abdicated. He was the grandchild of King Charles IX (his mother was Charles' daughter) (Englund, 2000). Another example is Adolf Fredrik who was brought to Sweden and elected king in 1743. His relation to the Swedish crown was tenuous; his mother was the daughter of the son of a daughter of the Swedish King Charles XI. The realm and its institutions were evidently more solid than they had been in the twelfth and thirteenth centuries when the country had been torn by civil war between aristocratic dynasties. An interpretation focused on the material side of military capabilities could argue that the concentration of the means of violence in most European realms meant that aristocratic dynasties could no longer field the kind of forces that were necessary. I think that another conclusion can be drawn: the realm had become more solid and leading magnates identified their interest with keeping it intact. One could add the element of warfare and claim that because of the expansion of armies all over Europe, a conflict over the throne between magnate dynasties would be too dangerous.[10] This may have played a part but I rather believe that the development surveyed above confirms my argument that

---

[10] Regarding the expansion of armies in the early modern age, see the contributions in Rogers, 1995.

the realm had become a more solid entity by the 1600s. This does not mean that dynastic interests and strategies had faded, rather that they were intertwined with the interests of the state, or interests in the state.

The solidification of the realm as a frame of reference and action allows us to draw some general conclusions for theory. First of all, during this period we are not looking only at networks of dynastic networks, but the realms have a certain integrity and thus we may speak of a more robust understanding of a bounded polity with a clear 'inside' and 'outside'. The composite polities were linked, both in the sense of the territories of the ruler, and with territories belonging to other rulers. In that sense they were more open than latter-day sovereign nation-states. Nevertheless, realms of this period were more closed than their medieval counterparts. This is exemplified by, for instance, the refusal of English magnates to allow a merger with Hanover after 1714. Certainly, we can talk of composite polities from, say, the 1000s to the 1700s but we must also sub-divide this category into different types – or, viewed diachronically, the era – into different periods. The composite polities of the 1700s was not the same as that of the 1300s.

The interplay or co-existence of dynasties and polities is seen in Louis XIV's work *Mémoires for the Instruction of the Dauphin* (Louis XIV, 1970) when he talks both about the importance of his house, his lineage and blood and about his rivals and allies as countries, for example, Spain, England, Sweden. Thus we see that there is not necessarily a contradiction between *raison d'état* and what could be called *raison de la dynastie*. As Sabean and Teutscher's work suggests, dynasty formation and state formation proceeded hand in hand. Although the recent focus on dynasties as actors and as a structural feature of European politics is an important insight, I believe that it is also important not to substitute one structural image (that of a system of states) with another (that of a network of dynasties). Both social systems existed side by side during this period and evidently so in the minds of its leading actors like King Louis XIV.

Conclusions

This chapter has dealt with the period that historical sociology has usually considered the most important period of state formation in European history. How we understand this era is central to how we understand political order in general as well as politics in other eras and in other cultures. The reason is that 'the state' has become the macro-concept for expressing politics in modern political science. Thus interpretations of the period 1500–1800 determine how we understand this norm of political rule. Based on new historical research, I have demonstrated that the old models of the absolutist state and of an early modern era that teleologically precedes our own are untenable. This means that not only historical sociology but also political science is faced with a problem. The model of absolutism builds to a large extent on the idea of a struggle between the king (which represents the embryonic state) and the nobility; view that both builds on and underpins an idea of politics as a zero-sum game of resources and power. In turn, this sustains the dominant conception of power as coercive, either overtly or tacitly. The absolutism model is also a variant of the idea that I argue against in this book: that kinship as a principle and kinship-based groups must be transcended or broken for the state to emerge.

When the historical record points in another direction historical sociology as well as social and political theory have to redesign their maps. First, political communities were founded earlier which means that the period 1500 to 1800 can no longer be seen as decisive. Second, we have seen that successful polity-making was not based on success in internal conflicts but on durable and dense co-operation, even symbiosis between kinship-based elite groups. When we compare the European societies during this era with the Arab, Turko-Mongol and Ottoman societies studied in Chapters 7, 8 and 9 we see that conflicts and direct attempts to break hereditary power groups have led to the breakdown of the polity. Third, kinship and kinship-based social formations remained central in the political order until the end of the eighteenth century, which means that stage models of political development and the equation of kinship principles of social organization and an absence of political order are both untenable.

6 THE REVIVAL AND SUDDEN DEATH OF POLITICAL KINSHIP
Europe *c.*1800–*c.*1918

Introduction

Previous chapters asked if there was a principled conflict between the political order and kinship-based legitimacy. Such conflicts certainly existed during the nineteenth century and thus this chapter asks slightly different questions: How serious were these conflicts? How strong was the position of the monarchy and the aristocracy in the political orders of this period? When and why did the resistance to the principle of descent and to elite kinship groups become so strong that they were expelled from political orders in the West?

This chapter demonstrates that political orders with a strong element of kinship and, in particular, the monarchical-aristocratic formation endured and was viable far longer into the modern era than conventional narratives of political development usually claim. Standard narratives of the nineteenth century tend to portray it through the lens of a liberal Whig history in which the triumph of the now current democratic political order over its reactionary opponents was inevitable (Reus-Smit, 2001; Oakley, 2006; Rush, 2007). This chapter argues that although monarchy and aristocracy were ultimately abolished as parts of the political order in most countries in Europe, they were compatible with certain modern forms of political order but not, ultimately, with the liberal democratic state.

Liberalism was the strongest rival to this formation and its spokesmen argued against institutionalized noble privilege and a political role for monarchy. Towards the end of the century, different versions of socialism joined liberalism as even more radical opponents of monarchy and aristocracy. Even though ideologies hostile to the monarchical-aristocratic synthesis gained ground during the century the latter was far from dead or doomed. It preserved itself through reform and through different ways of merging with democratic and conservative nationalism (Arendt, 2004). Nationalism could be both an enemy and an ally of monarchy; an enemy if it was used as a tool to justify democracy and an ally in its jingoistic and bellicose form since it treasured the reinvented monarchy as a figurehead of the nation and its association with warfare. However, in both guises, nationalism rested on ideas of kinship ties that united the population. Such ties were conceived of in either fictive or 'cultural' forms and in real, biological terms. The latter was particularly prevalent in movements where 'organic nationalism' prevailed (Smith and Smith, 2013:146ff).

Nevertheless, if the monarchical-aristocratic formation was still vital well into the nineteenth century, why did it fall in the beginning of the twentieth? There are two explanations of this shift. One argument stresses the gradual economic, political and social changes that European societies went through during the nineteenth century. This argument has been strong in the social sciences since it equates egalitarianism with modernity itself, often with undertones of teleology (Strath and Koskenniemi, 2014; Strath and Wagner, 2017). Another argument stresses that the contingent events around World War One broke the link between descent, kinship and the political order in Europe as a whole. That position entails that monarchy and aristocracy did not die out as elements of the political order out of necessity and that thus it is possible to envision a hierarchical kind of modernity. My position, fully elaborated below, is that the structural changes acted as permissive causes, but that the war acted as a proximate cause. As a consequence, it is necessary to consider modernity in the plural, as different 'modernities', to understand the relation with kinship-based political orders (Buzan and Lawson, 2015:7–8). It seems clear that an authoritarian modernity, with a bureaucratic state and advanced technology, was compatible with a monarchical-aristocratic political order. Examples are nineteenth-century Prussia and twenty-first-century Saudi Arabia. Democratic modernity, based on autonomous and sovereign individuals, however, is not. This was demonstrated already in the early American republic's hostility towards monarchy and dynasties.

This assertion entails asking, what are the components of modernity or rather what is the common denominator of different modernities? From the end of the eighteenth century, the idea of modernity was deeply connected to a new view of time and history. In this view, humanity was no longer seen as bound to the political and social forms of the past but could and indeed had to create new conditions for itself (Weber, 1978:36–8; Giddens, 1990:38; Bauman, 1991; Koselleck, 1992a; de Tocqueville, 2011:1). The human condition was thus increasingly seen as malleable. Furthermore, the idea that we must actively shape societies in order to reach desirable ideals became stronger and stronger. Reinhardt Koselleck traced this shift towards a modern paradigm of thought to changes in the concept of revolution. Earlier thinkers considered revolution to be a circular movement in time, for example, the Greek thinker Polybius claimed that political development proceeded in cycles, from monarchy to oligarchy to democracy and then starting over again. During the Enlightenment, revolution was increasingly seen as a linear movement in time, as a break with the past (Koselleck, 1992b). Late eighteenth century thinkers regarded their own time as one of changes in all areas of human activity. This figure of thought was further strengthened by the French Revolution's strong break with current institutions, ideas and world views. To the revolutionaries, these practices became 'the past', which the future would overcome. The wars and reforms of the Napoleonic era lent greater force to the idea, or in fact proved that new societies and times can be wilfully created. Throughout the nineteenth century, this figure of thought about the new times and both the possibility and imperative of change grew stronger and stronger. Eisenstadt even claims that the possibility and requirement of change in order to realize utopias that were previously seen as transcendent is what characterizes Western modernity as a unique civilization (Eisenstadt, 2003:493ff).

But here we need to pause the narrative. This story of modernity is also a self-description of a political project that came to dominate Western thinking, one that must be critically scrutinized. Since the early nineteenth century the discourse of progress as not only the desirable but also necessary break with the past has been strongly entrenched (Vierhaus, 1982). In this discourse, time itself has a movement towards a clear goal, a *telos*, although its advocates have debated if that goal was the utopia of liberalism or socialism. According to modernist discourse, those who have worked for those utopian goals have been in tune with time, those who have worked against them have wanted to stop time itself. This idea is deeply inscribed in our political concepts of 'progress' and 'conservatism'. It is also one of Marxism's explicit principles. Furthermore, the social and historical sciences have been profoundly coloured by the idea of a movement in time (Strath and Koskenniemi, 2014). Marc Bloch once claimed that history is 'the science of change' (Bloch, 1949). Still, all historical or historical sociological inquiries must question in what direction different social developments have been heading, not just take a certain direction for granted or even accept the idea of history in the singular. A task for this chapter is to identify moments that retrospectively could be seen as, to use Bo Strath's term, 'path-breaking' against the grand narrative of modernity, but were actually developments along another path of political development (Strath, 2009). In sum, modernity thus entails two aspects, a normative programme and a description of a specific epoch. Central to the latter aspect is the mentality that social life is malleable, that reforms can be made and indeed have to be made. However, the direction that such reforms take is not given. As we shall see, the distinctly modern idea of reform can be used to many different political ends – democratic, totalitarian or even monarchical-aristocratic.

The rest of the chapter is organized according to the following plan: first, I analyse the American and French Revolutions. Second, I analyse the Napoleonic counter-revolution. Third, I analyse how monarchy once again became a constitutive aspect of the international system and a strong influence on how and why military force was used. Fourth, I analyse the monarchical states of the nineteenth century and the continued role of the monarchy and aristocracy. Fifth, I analyse the end of this order around World War One.

The Resurgence of Monarchy and Aristocracy in Europe 1797–1914

The Revolutions of the Age

Towards the end of the eighteenth century a new development in the history of political order took place: the launch of a republican constitutional state (Osterhammel, 2010:819). Both in North America and in France revolution and war launched this kind of order and in both countries its adherents were hostile to the idea of hereditary power at the centre of political order. The North American revolutionaries set out to create a republic from the outset based on equality of all men (USA, 1776). Although equality was defined so as to exclude non-property holders, non-whites and women it was a remarkable break with the past. It was further underscored by section 9 of the first Article of the Constitution that declared that no titles of nobility should be granted in the republic. Also, no one holding office would be allowed, bar dispensation from Congress, to hold titles from any foreign power (USA, 1783, I:9). The creation of an American republic with its legacy of egalitarianism and constitutionalism is well-known and it forms part of a story of modernity as a progress away from historical forms of monarchy and aristocracy. The French as well as other European developments, however, are not so unambiguous.

The French Revolution was a distinct clash between the ideas and institutions of elite kinship and a redefinition of political order. Since it is one of the most researched and debated issues in historiography I cannot account in full for all its causes or events (Spang, 2003; Hanson, 2009), however, its main traits must be noted; it was the first attempt in Europe since the English Revolution in 1649 to abolish the monarchy and the nobility and to design a political order without kinship and descent (de Tocqueville, 2011:26). Its purpose was not just to change the government but the whole form of society (de Tocqueville, 2011:17). The French Revolution is often seen as the start of the modern political era and it is true that it brought forth many concepts that would dominate the twentieth century (Spang, 2003). Nevertheless, its abrogation by Napoleon begs the question whether modernity and individualistic egalitarianism really are as close bedfellows as claimed by teleological accounts.

The goals of the revolutionaries developed gradually, when the estates gathered in 1789 no one foresaw that the king and queen would be executed in 1793. The main targets of the revolution were the power of the Church and the political order in which monarchy and aristocracy were central. In May 1790 the Constituent Assembly removed the powers of making war and peace from the king and vested them in the nation (Schroeder, 1994:93). In August 1789 the Convention claimed to abolish feudalism but it took them until 1793 to abolish all seigneurial rights (Sutherland, 2002). Early on, a solution with a constitutional monarchy seemed possible, however, contingent events made a compromise more difficult. Public opinion turned against Louis XVI after national guardsmen intercepted his flight to Varennes (Sewell, 1996) and the threat of foreign intervention meant that he could be portrayed as a traitor to the nation. On 10 August 1792, radicals overthrew the monarchy and proclaimed a republic. A year later, in 1793, the King and Queen were executed, causing shock waves in France and Europe. Several highly consequential conceptual and institutional innovations took place during the Revolution: the creation of new government institutions and a more effective state, introduction of the concept of the nation and a unified legal code applicable to all citizens (Sewell, 1985:82; Hont, 1994; Osiander, 2007; de Tocqueville, 2011:18). Of these innovations, the latter two were direct threats to noble and monarchical privilege.

According to William Sewell, the decisive turning point of the Revolution was the night of 4 August 1789 when the National Assembly declared the abolition of the seigneurial system and the privileged corporate order (Sewell, 1985:69). Privileges were at the centre of the ideological system of the *ancien régime* and this meant that the old order came apart. Noble privileges were the most important ones, but towns and other corporate bodies were also defined by their privileges (Sewell, 1985:62), that in addition linked the monarchy to the aristocracy. The king upheld, regulated, adjudicated and sometimes removed privileges. When they were abolished the raison d'être of the monarchy disappeared (Sewell, 1985:64). After the abolition of corporations and privileges, only individuals and the universal applicability of reason and rights were left as the basis of politics.

After privilege, the revolution's second point of attack was religion and the Church. The Enlightenment undermined the political order of the *ancien régime* by defending a conception of the world that operated according to natural principles rather than Divine grace mediated by and manifested in the monarchy and the social order of privileges (Sewell, 1985:65). Eighteenth-century kings were no longer believed to be able to heal people by their touch but the foundations of their legitimacy remained quasi-sacerdotal (Bloch, 1924; Sewell, 1985:63). Thus, the anti-clerical and distinctly anti-Christian policies of the revolution were metaphysically based statements of a new political order. For example, the creation of a new calendar that measured time from the revolution and not from the birth of Christ was not a cultural epiphenomenon of the revolution but at the core of its politics.

Thus, the revolution illustrated the foundations and institutions of the older monarchical-aristocratic order.

The struggle between the revolutionary and the monarchical political orders was also played out on an inter-state level since the French Revolution immediately threatened the monarchical paradigm in Europe (de Tocqueville, 2011:11). The aims and actions of the revolutionaries led to a series of European wars, the doctrine of popular sovereignty being the factor that internationalized the French Revolution. Since the government of France claimed to represent the people, it could also claim any territory whose population proclaimed its allegiance to the revolution (Schroeder, 1994:72). France attacked first, defeating the Austrian and Prussian armies and sweeping into the Low Countries, Rhineland and Spain. Although the Revolutionary Wars (1792–7) largely conformed to traditional French ambitions for European hegemony, the revolutionary armies changed the political order in the conquered territories by establishing republican rule, for example in the Netherlands and in the Rhineland.

The Revolution was short-lived but extremely influential over the long term. Its legacy cannot be denied in terms of participatory politics, the concept of the citizen, the formation of political ideologies, the secularization of the political order and the expansion of political and social possibilities (Sewell, 1985:84). Two other results also stand out: the establishment of universal human rights as a norm and as an aspiration and the modern centralized state. However, despite these innovations and violent changes, monarchy and aristocracy survived.

Napoleonic Reform and Restoration 1797–1815

Despite the upheavals of the Revolution, monarchical rule was gradually restored during the 1790s. The establishment of the Directory between 1794 and 1799 halted the radicalism of the The Terror (1789–94). From 1799 the circle of rulers narrowed when Napoleon Bonaparte introduced a Consulate, a triumvirate, through a coup d'état. The Consulate lasted until 1804, when Napoleon completed the reintroduction of the monarchy by declaring himself hereditary emperor of the French. By doing so, he created a new imperial dynasty that ruled France, off and on, until 1871. Its members also ruled several European countries until 1815. Other European dynasties readily accepted the Bonaparte dynasty by recognizing it diplomatically and by marrying into it.

Between 1797 and 1812 Napoleon dominated Europe through a series of conquests, client states and allies. Stunning military successes and coercive occupation were not sufficient to maintain the new order, however, they had to be coupled with institutional and dynastic innovations. French hegemony was expressed through the creation of entirely new states or the modification of old ones by the introduction of new legal codes or constitutions. The purpose of these constitutions and reforms was to strengthen Napoleonic monarchy in the conquered territories (Sellin, 2014b:101). This process was supported by the reconstruction of Europe through manipulation of its dynasties, by placing either members of the Bonaparte family or Napoleon's followers on the thrones of conquered, created or modified polities. Napoleon's elder brother, Joseph, was made first king of Naples (1806–8) and then king of Spain as José I (1808–13). His youngest brother, Jérôme de Bonaparte, was made king of Westphalia. The career of Joachim Murat illustrates Napoleon's simultaneous renewal and innovation of aristocratic and monarchic orders as components of political order: he was made Prince of France in 1805, Duke of Cleve and Berg in 1806 and king of Naples in 1808. As king he was given Napoleon's youngest sister, Caroline, as queen (Scott, 2007:384–5, 391). Thus, for the greatest attempt to change the European order since Charlemagne, there was no real alternative to using new dynasties as components.

Napoleonic reforms contributed decisively to the creation of the modern state, albeit on the basis of eighteenth-century innovations. Napoleon made the French state more centralized and effective and the *Code Civile* established a single legal system based on equality and confirmed the abolition of the seigneurial system (Grab, 2003:46–7, 48–51; Hanson, 2009:143, 153). But was this form of political order really contrary to inherited inequality and family ties as the basis of political legitimacy? Undoubtedly, Napoleon continued to dismantle the old nobility but as he did so, he also created a new one (Grab, 2003:xii, 20, 22, 23, 41, 42–3, 93; Blaufarb, 2008). The new elite of the empire was enriched with land grants in the conquered territories (Grab, 2003:28–9) and his military officers were rewarded with hereditary fiefs in Italy, the Grand Duchy of Warsaw and in the German States (Grab, 2003:41). In 1808, Napoleon created an imperial nobility consisting of princes, dukes, counts, barons and knights. At the apex of this hierarchy stood Napoleon's relatives and his marshals (Grab, 2003:44–5). With the return of a privileged nobility, the rehabilitation of monarchy was complete (Scott, 2007:384–5, 391). Circulation of elites, that is, recruitment of new families to the imperial nobility, was not a unique or novel thing, nor was the idea that nobility was based on merit and not just descent. Thorough reforms of a country's system of nobility had also been made earlier, for example by Peter I of Russia. Napoleon's rule in France and Europe was so short-lived that we do not know how the new system of nobility would have developed after a few generations. However, everything suggests that Napoleon planned for the survival of at least his own dynasty. Whether the marshals and counts of the Empire would have become a new and durable nobility is impossible to know.

Nevertheless, the Napoleonic Empire demonstrated clear prospects of survival until the invasion of Russia in 1812. The failure of the invasion and the military disaster that followed enabled the creation of a durable coalition that defeated Napoleon. Prior to the invasion all countries of Europe, except Britain, had shown themselves willing to compromise and make peace with Napoleon, despite his notoriety for breaking treaties. If France had not made a desperate gamble to invade Russia, the country might have kept its dynasty and position, therefore, it was war and its highly unforeseeable consequences that dealt the Napoleonic state, empire, and dynasty project its death blow, not any principled incompatibility between the modernity of that period and principles of legitimacy through descent.

Monarchy as a Constitutive Influence on European Politics and War 1815–1848

After Napoleon's final defeat at Waterloo in 1815, representatives from all European powers gathered in Vienna to draw up not only a peace treaty but also a blueprint for a new European order. The most important goal was to re-establish the order that had existed in Europe prior to the Revolutionary and Napoleonic wars. Numerous territorial disputes were settled in the Final Act of the Congress, but two issues stand out. First, the Bourbon dynasty was reinstated on the throne of France. Second, the 'monarchical principle' was established as the dominant script for legitimate political order in Europe. The Great Powers recognized that war and revolution were the two major threats to political order. Revolution and systemic war were seen as interlinked:

war had a revolutionary quality and might spark social upheaval. Revolution in one country was seen as an attempt to overthrow the monarchy not only in that country but potentially in all (Schroeder, 2004a:54, 59). Maintaining peace would be the source from which dynastic rule drew its legitimacy (Sellin, 1996:355), thus, the Congress of Vienna was an expression of solidarity between monarchies. To contain the two risks of systemic war and revolutions, a system was adopted where the Great Powers would meet in congresses to solve conflicts that might arise between them.

Monarchical solidarity in order to contain revolution was central to the re-design of Central Europe. The German Confederation, which united the thirty-nine German polities, was created to stabilize central Europe. One of its purposes was to prevent any changes to the character of the member states. This meant that its members were obliged to suppress liberal and nationalist movements that called the monarchical principle and the disunity of the German lands into question (Haldén, 2013a). If a single member was unable to do so, then the other members (of which Austria and Prussia were the most powerful) could intervene. Nationalist agitation led to powerful countermeasures in the form of the 'Karlsbad degrees' that limited the freedom of press and allowed authorities to pursue 'rebellious movements' (Haldén, 2013a). These strengthened the monarchical principle and undercut the power of parliaments.

The establishment of a constitutional principle in the post-Napoleonic order had a constitutive influence on how military force was used between the 1820s and 1840s. The desire to preserve individual monarchies and monarchical sovereignty as a principle of legitimate political order prompted military interventions to prevent changes to the legitimate status quo (Finnemore, 2003:117–24). The Great Powers intervened in Naples (1821), Piedmont (1821), Spain (1823), Modena (1831), Parma (1831), the Papal States (1831–2), Hungary (1848), Saxony (1849), Tuscany (1849), Bavaria (1849) and Baden (1849) to suppress liberalism or restore monarchies (Finnemore, 2003: 122–3). Monarchy had a constitutive impact on war and peace through the practice of restorative interventions; in this period dynasties did not fight against each other but for each other. While monarchy had been an unquestioned political principle, different dynasties could afford to undermine each other, but once a principled opposition had surfaced in the shape of revolutionary ideas solidarity was called for. Alongside the congress system, Austria, Prussia and Russia had formed the Holy Alliance for mutual aid (Schroeder, 2004b:199–201). The three powers would work to preserve each other against revolution, and revolutions came. In 1830 revolts broke out in France, the French-speaking parts of the United Netherlands and in Poland. A far more serious challenge came in 1848 when revolutions broke out in Austria, France, the German states (including Prussia), Hungary and the Italian states. Momentary concessions were made in all cases, only to be withdrawn after heavy-handed military victories gave monarchies the upper hand (Rapport, 2009; Weyland, 2009).

Besides interventions, monarchy still exercised a constitutive influence upon the causes and effects of war. In past centuries, monarchs and councils had been the principal military decision-making centres. That was much less the case in the post-Napoleonic era but there were, however, exceptions: Austria, Prussia, Russia and France under Emperor Napoleon III (r.1852–70), and particularly in the case of Russia, individual tsars decided foreign policy. Alexander I (r.1802–25) was personally involved in many of the great decisions of his reign and he alone decided to pursue a more restrained foreign policy in connection with the Napoleonic Wars (Schroeder, 2004c). Under Nikolai I (r.1825–55) Russian policy became more aggressive in the pursuit of national interests in Europe and Asia. The last tsar, Nikolai II (r.1894–1917), was an inefficient ruler, more interested in removing and blocking effective ministers than in taking action himself. However, this essentially destructive pattern of intrigue had a tremendous influence on Russia, crippling its decision-making capacity (Clark, 2013).

There were fewer wars between states in the nineteenth than in the eighteenth century and hence fewer in which dynasties could play a role. However, one of the most consequential wars of the period illustrates the changed role of the monarchy and that dynastic ties could still play a role. Both Prussia and France had prepared and readied themselves for war since 1866, yet no one expected war in 1870 (Howard, 1969:48). The spark that lit the Franco-Prussian War of 1870–1 was the vacant throne of Spain. In 1868 the Spanish Queen Isabella of the Bourbon dynasty was deposed and Marshal Prim was appointed regent. However, popular opinion in Spain rejected the idea of a republic and a foreign prince had to be found to take the throne. The offer went to Prince Leopold of Hohenzollern-Sigmaringen, a cousin of the Prussian king. Neither the prince, his father Charles Anthony nor even King Wilhelm of Prussia was keen on the idea. However, the Prussian Chancellor Bismarck was. He believed that a Hohenzollern on the throne of Spain could bring commercial and military advantages to Prussia and prevent a candidate with dynastic ties to a hostile power. These perceived advantages were yet another sign that dynastic links were still considered important. Thus, behind Wilhelm's back, Bismarck urged Charles Anthony to accept the throne for his son (Howard, 1969:49).

When the news broke, the French government and public opinion was enraged. Placing a German prince and relative of the ruling Prussian dynasty on the Spanish throne in this way was considered a break with diplomatic form. But, as the French Foreign minister the Duc de Gramont, stated it was also a disadvantage to France and placed 'in peril the interests and the honor of France' (Howard, 1969:51). De Gramont stated publicly that the candidature gave France a *causus belli* (Kolkey, 1995:130). Both Leopold and Charles Anthony were prepared to withdraw but Wilhelm maintained that he could not persuade them in his capacity as king of Prussia and indeed as such had nothing to do with it. Napoleon III and his government forbad Leopold to accept and wanted Wilhelm I to publicly demand that he withdraw his candidature (Fuller, 2011:236). Leopold and Charles Anthony did withdraw the candidature, but the French government pressed the issue and demanded that Wilhelm should forbid his relatives to renew their candidature. Bismarck skilfully exploited the occasion by condensing the French demands into formulations that made them seem more aggressive than they in fact were and then leaking them to the press. German public opinion was incensed at this smear on national and dynastic honour, and as the chancellor had calculated, French public opinion was even more enraged and demanded war.

As a last-ditch attempt to stave off the confrontation and similar *causus belli* from arising in the future the Duc de Gramont proposed a pan-European conference at which the reigning families of Europe would declare that they would abstain from allowing members of their families to accept the thrones of foreign countries (Fuller, 2011:237). Had it been accepted, each dynasty would have become exclusively national; the conference never materialized but the fact that dynastic containment was seriously proposed as a way to increase the chances of peace in Europe at the end of the nineteenth century demonstrates that family ties of kinship were still perceived as important for alliances, states-unions, and thus for matters of war and peace.

Nevertheless, the fact that national containment of leading dynasties was considered possible and pragmatic indicates a substantial change in the dominant patterns of international politics compared to the previous century. More importantly, the decisions were no longer made at court but by ministers appointed by kings. Thus at this time monarchy was important but only as providing the semantics of legitimacy, and to some extent for their capacity to spark geopolitical concerns, but monarchs were no longer the main actors. As we shall see, however, the semantics of monarchy and monarchies as organizations remained important up until the outbreak of World War One in 1914.

State-Building and Monarchy

That monarchy still provided legitimacy to a political order can be illustrated by how new states were created. In the nineteenth century, all European states, bar Switzerland, were monarchies of one kind or another (Osterhammel, 2010). All countries that were created in Europe between 1815 and 1914 became monarchies, Greece (1830), Belgium and Holland (1830), Italy (1861), the German Empire (1871), Montenegro, Serbia and Romania (1878), Norway (1905) and Albania (1913). Thus, the old ways of legitimating political order lived on. An important difference with previous centuries was that the concert of the Great Powers created new royal houses by importing members of minor dynasties to old states.

The importance of monarchic legitimation was evident in the most consequential state-building project of the century: the creation of a unified German *Reich* in 1871. Once France had been defeated, the support of the South German princes and above all the Bavarian king was crucial for the project to succeed. Its king, from the medieval house of Wittelsbach, was next in rank to the Hohenzollern king of Prussia and represented a far older dynasty. An empire only based on popular support would not be recognized as legitimate; certainly not in elite and court circles. Hence, imperial authority and the title of German Emperor had to be given to the Prussian king by the other reigning German princes. Curiously, in the modern age supposedly dominated by rationalism and formal-legal authority, this process mirrored much older forms of creating authority and legitimacy in electoral monarchies where aristocrats and kings gave each other authority through recipro-cal bestowal of office (Haldén, 2014). After substantial Prussian bribes King Louis of Bavaria signed the so-called Imperial letter (*Kaiserbrief*). Bismarck had written the letter but it gave the Hohenzollern king a princely permission to proclaim himself Emperor of the German Empire (Rumschöttel, 2011).

Still, new states did not come into being because of dynastic reasons but because of the growing strength of nationalism and the willingness of Great Powers, either collectively or individually, to support nationalist movements. Cases such as the British, French and Russian interventions in the Greek War of Independence or the Russian interventions in the Danubian Principalities were driven by a combination of national interests, domestic pressures to intervene and genuine sympathy with the insurgents. Particularly to liberal leaders such as the British Prime Minister Gladstone, nationalist senti-ment was a factor that created a legitimate political order (Haldén, 2013b).

This historical record leaves us with the problem of how to interpret the role of monarchy during the nineteenth century. Kings, courts and councils were by no means the only powerful players of the international scene. Nor was monarchy alone a legitimating element for political order. The growing tendency of ruling houses to embrace a national identity and character throughout the century testifies to this point (Oakley, 2006). Monarchy was simultaneously portrayed as an age-old and venerable institution and at the same time quite malle-able in a very modern fashion to suit current events. Thus, a conclusion could be that the semantics of monarchy and aristocracy were retained and perhaps gained in importance during the century but that monar-chies waned as organizations (Bayly, 2004).

Monarchical Forms of State 1815–1900

In the nineteenth century, the political order in all European countries went through a number of radical changes in the justice system, constitutions, administration, parliamentary rule and the advent of mass politics and mass media. The fact that changes took place is unequivocal but what they entailed is not. I will now examine whether the innovations in political institutions really introduced a fundamental split between the legitimate political order and kinship-based forms of rule. I will argue that many changes to the state represent a form of adaptation of traditional elites, not their extinction.

A major shift in the nature of domestic law was the introduction of a single legal sphere that emanated from the state. This unitary sphere, based on positive law, replaced the multiplicity of different corporations that created law and exercised governance with reference to particular rights (Poggi, 1978:102). It meant that many nobles lost their privileges and their roles as local lords. According to Poggi, the political system was no longer based on dualism, but it was a single sphere, as estate-based parliaments were abolished during the nineteenth century, the earlier interplay, opposition and co-operation between the estates (of which the nobility was the most important) and the king and his court-state were lost (Poggi, 1978:94–5). The abolition of the early modern form of organization did not mean the end of aristocratic dominance but rather that the latter changed into a new organizational form.

As estate-based diets were abolished across Europe, parliaments were created in their stead. Parliaments were often two-chamber systems with an upper and a lower house, however, the two houses always had different kinds of authority. In some cases such as the British House of Lords and the Prussian Herrenhaus seats were reserved for the aristocracy (Rush, 2007:44–6). There were parliaments in the constitutional monarchies that existed in the German states, and later in the German Reich. The relation and the tension between the parliament and the monarch as two poles of government characterized this form of rule. The parliament had legislative powers (that grew as the century wore on) but the monarch's exclusive sphere was the executive sphere and the administration. The status of the government demonstrated this split between the monarch and the parliament and the limitations of the latter: it was the king's government composed of ministers that were appointed by him and acted as his confidants and advisors. However, the ministers had to answer to the parliament. The trump card of the parliament was its right to determine the budget. Universal suffrage was rare, in some cases the lower house was directly elected, in others only the wealthiest could vote for members of the upper house.

In Britain the parliament had more power vis-à-vis the monarchy and courts circles than in Central Europe or Russia. However, even British parliamentary rule and the expansion of suffrage does not conform easily to a teleological interpretation of history. The strong

position of the British parliament vis-à-vis the crown must not, however, be interpreted retrospectively through the lens of modern, democratic parliamentarianism. Britain was a democracy with the rule of law
but it can also be described as an aristocratic oligarchy in which a few
families dominated politics by controlling the House of Lords
(Eisenstadt, 2002:10; Bayly, 2004). The British Reform Acts of 1832,
1867 and 1884 used to be interpreted as the progressive unfolding of
suffrage and democracy. More recently, they have been reinterpreted as
reforms from above that were made in order to stem the tide of discontent and to integrate the middle classes into the 'aristocratic constitution' (Kushal Merkins, 2014:354). Socially and politically a synthesis
was formed between aristocratic and industrialist families and interests.
However, over the last decades of the nineteenth century liberal opposition to the aristocracy generated a succession of reforms of the political
system. After 1867, the aristocratic House of Lords lost their co-equal
powers of legislation, but they retained veto powers until 1911 when the
Parliament Act limited the right of the House of Lords to veto legislation
and introduced provisions that allowed the House of Commons to pass
legislation without its approval. After 1911, the House of Lords could
only delay legislation, not stop it. As David Cannadine has demonstrated the pace of change in Britain was staggering, in the 1870s its
aristocracy was the richest and strongest in Europe, but only a few
decades later it was gradually being forced out of the political order
(Cannadine, 1990).

Constitutions were another legal innovation of the nineteenth
century. Once considered as the spearhead of democratization and
popular sovereignty, constitutions and constitutional rule are now
being reconsidered. Volker Sellin argues that different kinds of constitutionalism existed. The most well known is democratic constitutionalism, which took power from kings and gave it to the sovereign people,
a principle embodied by the United States of America and revolutionary
France. All revolts of the nineteenth century had democratic constitutionalism on their agendas. The successful French revolution of 1830
resulted in a national constitution, something that the failed German
revolutionaries of 1848 also attempted. A more common type, however,
was monarchical constitutionalism that imposed constitutions from
above. The French constitution of 1814, the subsequent German constitutions, the Prussian one of 1848 and the Russian of 1906 were all of
this type. In these cases, the king granted his subjects a constitution out

of his free will and did not give away his sovereignty, merely delegated its exercise (Sellin, 2014b). Thus, constitutions imposed from above strengthened the monarchy by modernizing it through reforms that included and co-opted some, but not all, revolutionary developments and embedded them in a monarchical context.

The constitutional monarchy was a distinct nineteenth-century form of rule, an attempt to design a political order that would contain kinship-based elements and the modern administrative and legal techniques. Constitutional scholars distinguish between monarchical constitutionalism and parliamentary constitutionalism. In a constitutional monarchy, the monarch precedes the constitution and, standing outside it, is not bound by it. In a parliamentary democracy, the constitution is prior, and the king only has the powers given him by the constitution. Where the monarchical constitution differed most from the parliamentary was that in the former, the parliament could not force a minister to resign by a vote of no confidence; a practice that is central to the latter (Böckenförde, 2006:285). In constitutional monarchies, the army was the king's army, not the parliament's (Böckenförde, 2006:287ff). In general, thus, high politics remained a monarchical preserve.

The Aristocracy in Politics and Society 1850–1914

During the nineteenth century societies changed fundamentally regarding the organization of work, the industrialization of production, the re-organization of society into classes, accelerating urbanization and the creation of mass media and mass politics. With industrialization, wealth and production became increasingly divorced from the ownership of land – the traditional milieu and power resource of the nobility. An agrarian and proto-capitalist society was giving way to an industrial and decidedly capitalist one. As a consequence, the textbook narrative goes, traditional family-based elites were threatened by the rising industrialist bourgeoisie and by the urban workers. These changes caused a flurry of self-reflection and analysis that, among other things, created the modern social sciences. A main intellectual and political problem was how to maintain stability in times of rapid changes; changes that came to be understood as 'social' (Owens, 2016; Stråth, 2016). The creation of urban working classes living under precarious circumstances contained the potential for upheavals. Established politicians recognized the revolutionary potential of social change and responded with the construction of rudimentary welfare states in order to lessen their need and to pacify them politically. Shifting economic, social and technological conditions caused a shift in political analysis and advocacy. This shift spurred liberal and socialist ideas and agitation – particularly in Britain (Taylor, 2004). Both of the new traditions were intensely opposed to the nobility and, especially the latter, to the monarchy.

Since the late eighteenth century, liberal thinkers had developed a powerful repertoire of arguments against the aristocracy and inherited wealth, status and power. Adam Smith, writing in *The Wealth of Nations* (1776) had lambasted entail and its power to transmit power over generations: 'Entails ... in the present state of Europe ... are founded upon the most absurd of all suppositions, the supposition that every successive generation of men have not an equal right to the earth ... ' (Smith, 1977:510). The consequences of entail were not only immoral but weakened the national economy by leading to sloth and unproductivity. An even fiercer critic, Thomas Paine, writing in *The Rights of Man* (1791), held that aristocracy was 'a law against every law of nature and Nature herself calls for its destruction' (Paine, 1998:133). Moreover, Paine thought that aristocracy and monarchy were doomed to disappear under the advance of reason, the principle underlying republics everywhere (Paine, 1998:190, 206). Thus, by the mid-nineteenth century arguments that monarchy and aristocracy had no place in the political order were already old and available. But by the mid-nineteenth century an even more powerful adversary to aristocracy and indeed to the rule of families was emerging: the emphasis on the individual, not only as a politically sovereign entity but as an autonomous moral authority. In *On Liberty* (1859), John Stuart Mill posited the autonomy of the individual human being. The end of the liberty of the individual was to develop himself: 'each is the proper guardian of his own health, whether bodily, or mental or spiritual' (Mill, 2003:83). Mill echoed approvingly Wilhelm von Humboldt who in 1792 had argued that the development of the individuality is the highest end of man (Mill, 2003:123). 'Custom' was an enemy of individualism and thus of human advancement (Mill, 2003:134). Many more people eventually shared this conception than luminaries like von Humboldt and Mill and in the twentieth century it became a foundational assumption of ascendant liberalism and indeed of the liberal model of modernity that conceived itself as universal (Strang and Meyer, 1993). The idea of the autonomous individual had even more far-reaching consequences than the older arguments that inherited power had no place in the political order. For those who shared it, collective political action by families and kin-based networks, where individual interests are subjected to those of the family, became more difficult. The workers movements became a powerful force in all European countries, from Britain to France and Germany and even in Russia, where it could stage powerful protests. Surely, this well-known and powerful assembly of economic, intellectual, political and social changes brought down the old regime? In fact, was it not predestined to do so?

This historical narrative, painfully but necessarily condensed in the preceding paragraph, used to carry the overwhelming weight of persuasion. However, historians now are less sure, and it is time for social science and its theories to adjust to these re-interpretations. The monarchical restoration started by Napoleon means that it is questionable to write a unilineal history of the breakthrough of democracy and a steady expansion of the electorate from 1776 to 1789. The nineteenth century was far from a triumphant march towards individual rights and freedom, social hierarchies persisted during the nineteenth century however, they were not simply a continuation of the past. During this period of considerable change, they were re-formed and re-constituted with the aristocracy and the monarchy at the social apex (Bayly, 2004:399). The entrenchment of traditional elites in the political order was underpinned by social norms that stressed that hierarchies were legitimate and beneficial. Despite national variations, the common cultural model of the good society was hierarchical (Osterhammel, 2010:1062, 1064, 1065). Hierarchies in which different actors had different tasks, rights and duties, were a natural part of this identity-shaping pattern, and a precondition of political action (Mayall, 1990:33; Osterhammel, 2010:1080–1, 1085–6). A prevalent aspect of nineteenth-century European society was the idea that different strata and groups were defined by their duties to other strata and groups as well as to the commonly binding legitimate order. Each societal group had rights but also owed duties in accordance with its station. This cultural trope echoed in upper-and middle-class ideas of public service and obligation of leadership as well as in the ideals of deference and loyalty prescribed for lower orders (Osterhammel, 2010:1069).

Certain historians have argued that the monarchy and the aristocracy not only clung on to power but actually strengthened their position in the final decades of the nineteenth century. Christopher

Bayly shows late imperial Germany and Britain as monarchical-aristocratic status societies that grew more extreme and elaborate as the century wore on (Bayly, 2004:429). Beyond Europe, the colonial empires perpetuated the rule of traditional elites, both aristocratic and monarchic (Bayly, 2004). In 1858, American intervention forced Japan to open itself to foreign trade and to embark on a programme of rapid modernization. A part of this modernization was, however, the re-invention and re-articulation of traditional political forms. The office of the emperor was brought back from the centuries of torpor imposed by the Shogunate (Swale, 2009). As a part of modernization, a new nobility was also created that could staff the higher administrative, military and political echelons. Thus reforms took place but it was the reform of a traditional elite family-based system much like the earlier Napoleonic experiment in France (Lebra, 1993:28–61). Indeed, reform and adaptation were central to the survival strategies of monarchies everywhere such as the Prussian one (Berdahl, 1972). Volker Sellin and Dieter Langwiesche argue that the explanation for the survival of the European monarchy should be sought in its capacity to transform itself (Langewiesche, 2013; Sellin, 2014a). Similarly, Michael Mann points out that the German model of 'authoritarian monarchy' was not only thriving but actually modernizing until 1914 (Mann, 1987:346). Arno Mayer demonstrates that old hierarchies were largely intact by 1914 in Continental Europe and in Britain (Mayer, 2010; Strath, 2016:427), not only did they command the top positions in government but they successfully co-opted new power-groups like wealthy industrialists (Mayer, 2010:12, 127). Although parliamentary rule was increasingly becoming part of the model of a modern society, foreign policy tended to remain in the hands of traditional elites. Universal male suffrage, like the one introduced in Germany in 1871, was used to legitimate author-itarian rule (Strath, 2016:427).

Michael Mann and Christopher Bayly both argue that until the end of World War One, traditional elites, even court circles and royalty, dominated foreign policy (Mann, 1993:413–19, 744; Bayly, 2004:236). The bourgeoisie was a far weaker force than is commonly assumed, argues Mayer. In Austria-Hungary, Britain, Germany/Prussia and in Russia, new forces and groups were pressed into the mould of the *ancien régime* (Mayer, 2010: 119). The aristocracy continued to set the standards for social prestige and desirable life styles and ideals. At the unquestioned top of the social hierarchy stood the monarchy, who reinforced the social pyramid through their power to ennoble and to bestow orders (Mayer, 2010:95). Thus, as a response to the upheavals of 1848, the monarchy and the aristocracy reasserted themselves and tightened their grip on society. Mayer argues that the increased domination of old elites between 1905 and 1914, which was to a large extent a counter-reaction to what they perceived as a threat, exacerbated the tensions in European societies which actually produced the Great War (Mayer, 2010:15).

The Expulsion of Monarchy and Aristocracy from the Political Order 1890–1918

If monarchy and aristocracy were so firmly entrenched in the political orders of Europe during the nineteenth century, why were they so rapidly expulsed at the beginning of the twentieth? At the end of World War One, no countries in Europe were directly ruled by monarchs (of course, constitutional monarchies like Britain, Denmark, Norway, Spain and Sweden existed) or had formally privileged aristocracies as parts of their political orders. However, as David Cannadine puts it in his study of the British aristocracy, there was no single cause of death (Cannadine, 1990). The road to extinction also differed between different European countries. In Britain decline of the aristocracy was more gradual than in Central Europe and in Russia and was caused by a combination of social forces and ideas. David Cannadine argues that the economic power of the British aristocracy declined sharply from the 1880s onwards. The global fall in agricultural prices meant that land was no longer the basis of wealth and when the aristocracy lost its relative wealth, its status and political power soon followed. The bourgeoisie gradually eclipsed the aristocracy in the legislature and in government (Cannadine, 1990:26–7, 183–4). By the first decade of the twentieth century the pace of change was visible in Britain and all informed and influential observers among the British aristocracy recognized that their political order, if not way of life, was on the way out.

However, in continental Europe World War One played a more decisive role in removing the monarchy and aristocracy from the political order. Arno Mayer argues that the wars of the twentieth century toppled the old order, not the democratic, liberal and Marxist ideological movements. Michael Mann argues that had it not been for the war then 'authoritarian monarchy, could probably have survived into advanced, post-industrial society, providing a distinctive, corporately organized, arbitrary combination of partial civil, political and social citizenship' (Mann, 1987:348–9).

World War One ended with the fall of the monarchy in three European empires, Austria-Hungary, the German Reich and the Russian Empire of the Romanovs as well as the dissolution of the Ottoman Empire. All four powers were transformed into republics, albeit of somewhat different character. The lost war caused an immense loss of prestige for the German, Austro-Hungarian, Ottoman and Russian monarchies that paved the way for strategically oriented revolutionary movements. In all four cases, the nobility was disbanded and outlawed. In Russia its members were even liquidated or forced into exile during the revolution, the civil war and subsequent Bolshevik rule. Thereby the formally recognized groups of elite families disappeared from the political order forever and a millennium and a half of political order was abolished.

External forces played a considerable role in dismantling their rule. One of the major aims of America in World War One was to promote the creation of democratic nation-states in Europe and to dissolve the old empires. Although President Wilson's hope eventually fell apart as the new states of Central and Eastern Europe turned to authoritarianism or outright fascism instead of democratic pluralism, his antipathy to the Habsburg Empire aided nationalist movements and it was a driving force behind the punitive dissolution of the empire in 1919 (Thompson, 1985:341, 342).

Interestingly and perhaps ironically, monarchs and the ideal of monarchy mattered greatly in the outbreak of World War One. On 28 June 1914 Gavrilo Princip, a Serbian nationalist, murdered the Crown Prince of Austria-Hungary, Archduke Franz Ferdinand. The deed sent shockwaves through Europe and in particular its German-speaking powers (especially Austria-Hungary). It caused the decision makers of the Habsburg monarchy, among others, the Emperor-King Franz Joseph to abandon their customary caution. The highly aggressively demands on Serbia after the killing can be explained in part by the immense prestige of the victim and the damage the deed had caused to the dignity of the monarchy. The response, whose consequences would turn out to be suicidal, in turn demonstrates the importance of the monarchy. However, no European army was commanded by a monarch, which further underscores the argument made above that they were highly important as symbols but not as organizers (Sellin, 2011:130). For example, the Kaiser was formally the supreme commander of the German Army in wartime. In practice, however, his role was primarily symbolic. By 1917, if not earlier, even his direct orders were ignored by the Generals of the High Command (*Oberste Heeresleitung*) (Stone, 2015:138–9).

Focusing on the war provides a contrast to teleological arguments. Researchers in long-term political change distinguish between 'robust process explanations' and 'contingent explanations' (Sterelny, 2016:521–39). The first kind is change that is due to a number of different causes where the removal or alteration of one cause would not seriously affect the long-term outcome. The second kind of change is due to a single cause or a small number of causes, the removal of which would create an altogether different outcome. Regarding process explanations, counterfactual arguments, so beloved by fiction writers and so feared by professional historians, become invalid. Concerning contingent explanations, as Lebow has demonstrated, they become serious challenges to arguments of path dependency (Lebow, 2010). The question for this chapter is, if a robust process explanation can be formed for the decline and disappearance of monarchy and aristocracy as forms of political order or whether that change was too affected by individual choices, local conditions and circumstances. For the sake of simplicity, I will focus on the three countries that, in various guises, have been at the centre of the long historical analysis pursued in this book, France, Britain and Germany.

The French case can be interpreted as a combination of contingencies and population-dependent explanations. The decline of the nobility and monarchy of France was affected by the direction of the French Revolution, which in turn was caused by the ideals and social forces set in motion by the Enlightenment. The Enlightenment was a movement that was sufficiently broad to be termed a population-level factor. Perhaps the monarchy could have been able to survive in a reformed version if it had not been for the international situation in the 1790s and the failed escape of the king. In a second phase its prospects for survival were affected by the military defeat of Napoleon that led to the collapse of his reformed Imperial House and nobility. If the Napoleonic Empire had survived, then its monarchy and nobility might well have survived too. Of course, they would have been different ones than in the eighteenth century, but it would have survived.

The British case is more clearly explained by population-level factors. The decline of monarchy and aristocracy can be explained by a combination of ideas-based criticism and the strong industrialism that propelled other social groups to a position of power, which gave them the upper hand vis-à-vis the landed aristocracy. The gradual marginalization of the Upper House and the growth of party politics took place in the context of a vigorous parliamentary system that sustained the power of the aristocracy for a long time but also contained the possibility to break it. Although in the British case it would seem possible to construct a robust population-level explanation, we must note that the aristocracy remained in power for a relatively long time and its decline began suddenly, from the 1870s to the 1880s.

Concerning the German lands and later the unified German Reich more factors support the argument that we are dealing with a more contingent development. Certainly there were social protests, a strong urbanization and industrialization and its social democratic party was Europe's largest. Despite these factors Mayer argues that neither the working class nor the liberal bourgeoisie were significant threats to the existing order (Mayer, 2010). Instead, both had been co-opted into an authoritarian system in which the monarchy and the aristocracy monopolized high positions in the administration and the army and dominated politics. In this case, World War One was rather an epochal shift. The country's defeat in the war created a moment of opportunity for revolutionary forces, but these were defeated by the regular army and irregular *Freikorps* forces. Before this occurred the Emperor had abdicated and a republic had been introduced. Volker Sellin claims that even at the last stages of the war individual actions mattered. If Wilhelm II had abdicated earlier he could have saved both his throne and his dynasty, however, his intransigence meant that the demands for abdication changed from concerning him personally to concerning the entire monarchy (Sellin, 2011). Similar arguments about contingency apply to Austria-Hungary and to Russia.

The degree of contingency in explaining the downfall of the continental monarchies after World War One leads us to ask whether the war itself was inevitable or could have been avoided (Sterelny, 2016). A generation ago historians tended to point to structural factors that they claimed made it inevitable. Even if it had not taken place in the year 1914 a major European war would sooner or later have occurred, given the tensions and contradictions in the system. Older scholarship tended to see the war as pre-determined. Arno Meyer suggests that the 'atavistic' and bellicose mentality of the aristocracy was an important driver (Mayer, 2010). Paul Schroeder (1972) takes a middle ground by arguing that while World War One was not pre-determined, some kind of war between the Great Powers was likely (Schroeder, 1972).

Today, explanations that emphasize the contingence have gained more ground. Christopher Clark emphasizes that individual decisions and non-decisions, in some cases, by the European monarchs, led to the war (Clark, 2013). Richard Ned Lebow stresses that the conditions for an aggressively conducted major war were perfect in 1914 but if a similar incident or crisis had taken place later it is far from certain that the Great Powers would have gone to war (Lebow, 2010:69–102).

In this light, World War One seems like an anomalous occurrence rather than the convergence of many deterministic trajectories. Furthermore, the war was not doomed to become as long and thus as consequential as it eventually became. The fact that it did was, in the end, also due to the contingencies of war and combat. If the Germans had prevailed at the battle of the Marne in 1914 and entered Paris, the war would have been shorter and would not have caused the epochal disruption in the history of political order that it did.

Although Cannadine argues that the decline of the British aristocracy began earlier and was driven by other causes, he points to the destruction that World War One brought to the aristocracy. The war caused the greatest loss of life among the nobility since the Wars of the Roses (1455–85) and reduced its capacity to act as a coherent stratum as well as shattered their previous aura of inviolability. The mixing of classes and backgrounds in the trenches as well as among the dead also dealt a blow to deference and the perceived distance of the nobility from the rest of the population (Cannadine, 1990:71ff, 81–5). In part the effects of the war can be found in how it was fought. Unlike the kind of war that had dominated the nineteenth century, the mechanized warfare of the World War One did not discriminate according to class lines and hence had a greater effect. However, in Britain, World War One was but the culmination of the high degrees of tension between democracy and aristocracy between

1880 and 1918. The democratization of Britain was also in a sense a revolution from above since the Liberal Prime Minister Lloyd George was an ardent opponent of aristocracy (Cannadine, 1990:86–7).

Looking at the war itself, we can ask whether ideas, social forces or the actual use of military force expelled the monarchical-aristocratic formation from legitimate political order in all Western countries during the twentieth century. There was considerable and unmistakable opposition to monarchy and aristocracy during the nineteenth century. This opposition surfaced violently in the 1820s, the revolutions of 1830, 1848 and 1871, in the shape of violent anarchism of the 1890s and, of course, in the Bolshevik revolutions in Germany, Hungary and Russia in 1917/18. It was manifested politically in the liberal opposition to privilege in Britain and the growth of social democracy in Germany from the 1890s onwards.

The answer must be given in two parts. First, none of these factors can be isolated from each other. Fundamental transformations always have compound rather than monocausal explanations (Harrisson, 2006). Second, the different components of this triad of explanations have different weight in different European countries. Without considerable social discontent and first liberal, then communist ideas, the Russian revolution would never have taken place. But it is doubtful if they would have had the same degree of effect and shape if it had not been for the devastating loss in World War One. The same applies to Austria-Hungary and to Germany. Britain is a different case. The shift came later than in France but earlier than in the continental empires, thus it can be explained more by the power of ideas and by social movements than by the effects of war.

A central idea in social theory is that warfare and the organization of warfare have been principal drivers of state formation. According to this argument, they account for the demise of non-sovereign states and the prevalence of the bureaucratic national state. This chapter has demonstrated another way that warfare has shaped political order, namely by breaking a pattern of rule that was thousands of years old. The gradualist argument for the decline of hereditary power works relatively well for Britain although the aristocracy was politically well entrenched until the 1880s. However, I have argued that the gradualist arguments why monarchy and aristocracy ended are not persuasive on their own regarding all countries. World War One brought about the decisive end of both forms in Central Europe and Russia.

The effect of World War One was only possible because of changes in the nature of warfare as a political instrument. After the French Revolution, wars began to be fought with a normative goal in mind – intentionally changing the political order in the adversary country. With a twenty-first-century term, attempting to enforce or stop 'regime change' was present in the revolutionary wars, the Napoleonic wars (from both sides), the Vienna Order interventions, and World War One and Two. To use Philip Bobbitt's terminology, the long wars that change constitutional structures acquired a new dimension of intentionality after 1792 (Bobbitt, 2002). This shift meant that warfare in the modern era, because of its political character, affects political order differently than in pre-modern eras. The decisive role of warfare in causing shifts in political order also has consequences for how we view social development. Warfare, by its very nature, is highly uncertain and brings a large number of contingent effects into play (Clausewitz, 1976; Betts, 2000; Strachan, 2013). The political results of any war are a complex and non-linear combination of intentional causes and unintended effects (Beyerchen, 1992). Only a few of the actors entering World War One aimed to bring about a systemic shift in political order, to do so only became possible because of many contingent events.

The degree of contingency in explaining the end of political orders legitimated and dominated by elite families matters not only to understanding nineteenth-century politics but to understanding modernity and the twenty-first century. The degree of robust process explanation and contingency in the downfall of the monarchy and aristocracy matters for how we view family-based elites in the modern era. If we choose the former, we can regard democracies as the norm of modernity and monarchies, dynasties and clans as anomalies. If we choose the latter, democracies rather appear as an improbable and contingent norm within modernity.

Conclusions

It is clear that elite kinship groups were compatible with certain kinds of political order during the modern era. These forms of political order were not merely survivals but were themselves shaped by ideas that are considered core parts of modernity. An example is the idea that social and political relations can and indeed must be continually reshaped in order to be viable. However, elite kinship groups – such as monarchy and aristocracy – were not compatible with the form of secular, democratic and individualistic political order that came to dominate Europe after the World War One.

Modernity per se, or the modern state, is not incompatible with hereditary rule. The modern state is a distinct form of rule with specific techniques of governance, modes of formal organization, bureaucracy, etc. As such it can be ruled by elites that are elected and rotated or elites that are hereditary and come from a group of lineages or, again, by more democratically circulated rulers. It is instead a particular form of the modern state, namely the liberal democratic state, which is incompatible with hereditary rule. We can imagine hybrid forms in which the electorate may be limited, or the range of candidates may be limited, to a number of lineages. But, the ideal form of the liberal democratic state with free and fair elections, in which every individual can run for office and vote, and in which rule is mediated by parties, is incompatible with hereditary rule.

It was only during the late eighteenth century that the opposition to elite kinship groups as a central part of the political order gained power, first during the American, then during the French revolution. Liberal and later socialist movements laboured for the abolition of hereditary rule, but in most European countries except Britain and France, they represented minorities and their victory was far from certain. The causes of the shift from a political order where hereditary rule was seen as legitimate and natural to one that saw it as abhorrent varied from country to country.

Taking seriously the demise of the monarchical-aristocratic order as an unintended consequence of World War One results in certain theoretical consequences. Models and theories of political development that emphasize path-dependency, determinism or even linear developments become difficult to sustain whenever there are major wars during the period under study. Conversely, studying the character of war in conjunction with major shifts in political orders reveals that if we want to understand the political consequences of a war then two things are necessary: on the one hand one must study the political context in which the war takes place as well as the actors' intentions. On the other, one must study the conduct of war and how it changes the scope of political action. Ignoring this interplay and only focusing on capabilities or on force employment will not capture the political effects (Biddle, 2004). Conversely, leaving out a study of the conduct of war will render an incomplete understanding of politics. In other words, warfare and politics have to be understood in tandem.

To summarize, this chapter argues that 'the modern state' must be regarded as an ideal type and not as a set formula. Since the early nineteenth century there have been several scripts that have sometimes overlapped and sometimes rivalled each other. Furthermore, until the late decades of the nineteenth century, we cannot detect a clear-cut opposition between kinship as a political principle and the political order in the West. Certainly, movements that argued that such an opposition was normatively desirable grew during the nineteenth century, but their victory was far from certain until the end of World War One.

7 THE ARAB EMPIRES *C.*632–*C.*900

Introduction

The Islamic world in general and its Arab heartland in particular is classic territory for the study of the relations between states and kinship-based groups. Here too we find expressions of the idea that there is a contradiction between states, often represented by sedentary civilizations, and kinship-based groups, represented by nomadic 'tribal' peoples. A second angle on our theme is the argument that sedentary states and nomadic tribes have been interdependent, even symbiotic, in Middle Eastern formations (Khoury and Kostiner, 1991). However, to understand kinship as a constitutive factor in the formation of political order in the Middle East we must extend the category of kinship beyond nomadic tribal groups. We must also include notions of descent from the Prophet Muhammad, monarchical dynasties of Caliphs, sultans and kings; and 'noble' families that possess status, legitimacy and military power. All three categories commanded legitimacy on the basis of claims of inherited charismatic power connected to transcendental values.

Dynasties structured political orders, both ideationally and socially, by providing legitimacy and means of amassing connections and force. Kin relations and ideas of kinship also structured military and political conflicts. This chapter analyses several historical conflicts in which political and religious legitimacy derived from kinship played a decisive role: the civil wars (*fitna*) of the first century after

Muhammad are sometimes presented as doctrinaire struggles but they were also wars over succession that were fought between different factions of the extended kinship network of the Prophet as well as over which principles should determine the succession and leadership over the community of the faithful. As Madelung states, the succession after Muhammad has been given surprisingly little attention (Madelung, 1997:2–3). I do not want my argument to be read as reductionist. The major wars and other political struggles were not only about kinship or succession, other well-known motives such as group honour, greed, grievances and security dilemmas played their part. Still, the kinship elements were undeniable. It is from this period that the split that would become the conflict between Sunni and Shi'a Islam originates. Today, this is widely portrayed and perceived as a religious conflict. However, it was originally a conflict between two kinship groups and two rival principles of kinship as a means of determining the leadership over the Muslim world. Only later did it develop a theological dimension. Of course, at the time, our ways of distinguishing clearly between 'political' and religious' principles and conflicts did not exist.

This chapter considers the following: (1) A complex relation between kinship and the political order existed in the Umayyad and Abbasid periods, the political order as such was based on principles of kinship in the sense that descent from the Prophet was the main way to legitimate Caliphal status. However, other aristocratic dynasties were gradually excluded from the polity. (2) The Arab empires were established with extraordinary speed and revolutionary fervour which transformed the Middle East and North Africa and created a situation of 'permanent revolution'. The result was a long period of flux and instability that negatively affected the polity's capacity to integrate elite groups with each other and to bind them effectively to the centre. (3) An old trope in European social and political thought is to contrast the dynamic 'West' with the static 'East'. Surprisingly, this chapter demonstrates that the reverse was true. In comparison with the West, where change was more gradual and kinship elites slowly integrated into common frameworks that layered upon each other, the situation in the Middle East was extraordinarily dynamic, revolutionary and fluid: old institutions and ideas were cast aside by Islam and over its first centuries successive groups of proto-noble kinship elites were destroyed or marginalized. As we shall see in Chapters 8 and 9, the geopolitically exposed position of the Middle East exacerbated this situation of flux and change.

With some exceptions, Islamic countries have only featured marginally in the historical-sociological literature on state formation (Gellner, 1981; Hall, 1986). Most works within this genre have focused on Europe (Hintze, 1962a, 1962b; Tilly, 1990; Spruyt, 1994; Ertman, 1997; Teschke, 2003). In his works on the development of political order after antiquity, Perry Anderson included two minor comparative chapters on Islam, mostly focused on the Ottoman Empire (Anderson, 1974:361–94, 2013). Reinhard Bendix discussed the Caliphate as an instance of sacred kingship but did not include any Muslim polities among his major cases (Bendix, 1978). Islamic polity formation is better represented in works of classical sociology, but often as a contrast that brings out the specificity of Western civilization.[1] Max Weber invokes Islamic societies when discussing charismatic (e.g., prophetic) and traditional forms of authority – which he places in contrast to the bureaucratic-legal authority characteristic of the modern West (Weber, 1978). Weber's interpretations coloured subsequent generations of scholars' thinking and theorizing about the Islamic world. His ideal type of patrimonialism and its extreme form 'sultanism' – the latter clearly derived from a reading of the Ottoman Empire – was particularly influential (Weber, 1978:231).

Other works have systematically distinguished between Europe where wider groups of people were engaged in government and subject to the rule of law and cultural areas like China, the Middle East and Russia that were governed by various forms of 'oriental despotism' (Wittfogel, 1963). Some scholars juxtapose the dynamic West and the static 'others' such as the Islamic world, India and China and present the latter as civilizations incapable of development (Jones, 2003; Ferguson, 2011). The juxtaposition between a dynamic and free Europe and a static, but powerful and oppressed Orient that includes China and the Middle East languishing under an oriental despotism dates back to early modern writers like Montesquieu (Said, 2003; Rubiés, 2005). Some works of comparative history have stressed the similarities and parallels between European and Islamic civilizations. One point of entry in this regard is to stress that both inherited Judaic notions of the

---

[1] For an overview of comparative civilizational analysis in classical and modern sociology see Árnason, 2003.

transcendence of God, which profoundly shaped the construction of monarchy and – by extension – of the political order (Oakley, 2006). Another is to emphasize the position of Christian Europe and the Islamic Middle East as heirs to Greek and Roman traditions in political and social thought and organization (Wickham, 2009). It is among comparative historians that we find most comparisons of political developments in early medieval Europe and the Islamic world (Brubaker and Smith, 2004; Lewis, 2008; Drews, 2009; Hudson and López, 2014). In sum, European, Middle Eastern and Central European templates of political order have rarely been compared with the aim of producing a common model or theory of political order. This can only be done in this book regarding a single factor: the relation between forms of kinship and the political order.

The rest of the chapter is organized as follows. First, I discuss general traits of kinship systems in the Arab Middle East. Thereafter four chronological sections follow, beginning with an analysis of the rise of Islam as a religion and as a political formation. Then, I analyse the establishment of political order during the phase known as the 'rightly guided Caliphate' and its early civil wars. After that I analyse the Umayyad Caliphate in Damascus (661–750). Next, I analyse the golden age the Abbasid Caliphate in Baghdad that lasted in name between 750 and 1258, but the real power of the Caliphs began to fade in the tenth century. After the chronological sections I present a re-reading of the works of Ibn Khaldûn, who is often cited as an authority regarding the perennial conflicts between kinship groups (tribes) and political orders (sedentary civilization). The final section summarizes the argument and draws comparative conclusions.

Kinship Systems in the Arab World

The standard image of the Middle Eastern kinship system is that it is segmentary and non-hierarchical (Lindholm, 1986).[2] For instance, siblings are not ranked in terms of seniority and the system does not recognize primogeniture. The image that these writers give of Middle Eastern societies is that they are a 'system of systems' containing a multitude of egalitarian lineages. According to this view there is no

---

[2] For a comprehensive review of the many different forms of kinship in Arab societies and Islamic law, see Altorki, 1980.

ranking of lineage within a group and, on a social macro level, no ranking between lineage groups that would amount to the creation of an aristocratic segment (Lindholm, 1986:349). This trait has been invoked as a structural reason for the perennial feuding among tribal groups, their ability to mount widespread resistance against colonial takeover and the difficulties of durable large-scale state formation (Lindholm, 1986:344).

Within this society, contest and conflict is endemic within the units as well as between them. The tendency of kinsmen to fight each other is only tempered by their capacity to unite against an external foe and fight him with as much fervour as they fight each other. One reason for the constant competition is that rank is not 'seen as an inherent attribute of any individual or group' but it is an acquired attribute won in competition (Lindholm, 1986:345–6, 349). Furthermore, kinship is strictly patrilineal; although the networks made up of patrilineal descent vary in size and property can be restricted by family considerations. In theory, Middle Eastern kinship systems distinguish between paternal and maternal lines, however, kinship with the Prophet was also transmitted through the female line, through his daughter Fatima. Another general trait is the 'strong tendency towards patrilocality', namely that men are expected to settle close to the family's holdings, whether sedentary or nomad, urban or rural. The tendency to form geographical clusters is mirrored by the tendency to marry within the same kinship network in order to consolidate it: men are encouraged to marry their cousins, particularly the daughters of their paternal uncles. Hence there is no counterpart to the very extensive ban on cousin-marriage – which was branded as incest – that the Catholic Church instituted in early medieval Europe (Lindholm, 2013:298). The lack of ranking of siblings in terms of older and younger had significant political consequences for inheritance of political positions. The system of inheritance did not recognize primogeniture instead, a ruler was often succeeded by his brothers, not his sons. Kinship ties were ambiguous in relation to conflict and co-operation. On the one hand, kinsmen were expected to aid members of their bloodline in feuds with members of other lineages. On the other, we see recurrent patterns of rivalry between blood relatives. The tendency of the egalitarian tribal ethic to undermine hierarchies is sometimes given as an explanation for the dynamics of the rise and fall of dynasties and the shallow (and performance-based) legitimacy of any lineage. Charles Lindholm has claimed that: '[t]he family system of

Arabia, it seems, favored the rise of prophets, while that of Central Asia favored the coronation of kings' (Lindholm, 2013:299). This argument is problematic to sustain. As demonstrated in Chapter 2, substantial criticism has been levelled against the tendency to impute political structures from a structuralist, and thus static, conception of kinship. Kinship does not operate like a forcing structure but rather as a factor that enables several different and often contradictory patterns of action. I will now move on with a historical narrative that examines hierarchical and sacral forms of kinship formations that actors employed in order to create political order.

The Emergence of Islam

In the sixth century CE the Arabian Peninsula lacked major centralized polities. At this time it was a backwater in the shadow of the great empires and main trade routes. The relative lack of major political structures and institutions in the area should not mislead us into thinking that this was an undifferentiated society. There were cities like Mecca and Medina with urbane merchant elites and an arid, rugged hinterland dominated by pastoralists. It seems likely that tribal networks criss-crossed this socio-economic divide. Tribal society was not socially undifferentiated or egalitarian. Some tribes were more prominent, wealthy and powerful than others (Sharon, 1983:78). Each tribe was differentiated into sub-groups, typically referred to as 'clans', that differed with regard to power and status.

The most important tribe in Arab and Islamic history is the Quraysh. It was in this formation that the Prophet Muhammad was born and from which all subsequent caliphs until 1258 would come. Drews argues that this idea was particularly prevalent in theories of the caliphate that were developed during the high Middle Ages. Shi'a theology is particularly clear that its Imams must hail from the Quraysh (Drews, 2009:452). A caliph is the representative of the Prophet on earth and until the mid-ninth century the title of the temporal ruler of the Arab empire and the spiritual leader of Islam. After political power had passed into the hands of sultans, the caliph remained the formal leader of the community of Islam. Like all tribes, the Quraysh had sub-groups. The two most important ones were the Banu Hashim, to which the Prophet belonged, and the Banu Umayya (or Umayyads), a related but rival clan. The two shared a common ancestry: the legendary ancestor of the Quraysh, 'Abd Manaf, who probably lived in the fifth century had two sons. One son, Hashim, begat Muhammad's bloodline (Banu Hashim) and the other, 'Abd Shams, begat the Umayyad line. The two clans intermarried and on some occasions they were allies, and on others foes. The two clans contested the leadership of the Arab empire and of the Islamic community of believers over the centuries after Muhammad. Much of the early history of the Arab political order can be understood in terms of kinship as a principle of political organization, a point that is often recognized in writings on the pre-Islamic Arab society. I also believe that kinship is a powerful heuristic lens through which we can read the subsequent Islamic era. The forms of kinship that were significant for political order were not only tribal but also dynastic.

Scholarly knowledge of the early history of Islam is limited because sources are scarce and often unreliable. For the purposes of this book and this chapter only brief summary is necessary.[3] The Prophet Muhammad was born into the Banu Hashim clan of the Quraysh around 570 CE. Although it had once been powerful, at the time of the Prophet Muhammad's birth its standing and power had declined relative to other Quraysh clans. Around 610 CE the Prophet Muhammad began to experience visions of messages from God of a new religion of absolute monotheism.[4] The message included new cosmological and political order on earth. Gradually, the new faith attracted followers and powerful enemies. The aristocratic families of Mecca, among them other branches of the Quraysh, were among the latter. Increasing persecution in Mecca forced the Prophet Muhammad to seek converts and allies elsewhere. When the Kawraj and Aws tribes of Medina accepted him in 622, the Prophet fled. Between 622 and 630 periodic war raged between the increasingly Muslim city of Medina and the opposition in Mecca. In 630 Mecca surrendered and other Arab tribes joined the new faith and expanding empire. A preceding step to uniting the tribes of Arabia was reconciliation with the Quraysh and in particular with the Banu Umayya. According to Gerald Hawting the latter only joined the Islamic movement when they saw that its victory was inevitable (Hawting, 2000). At the time of Muhammad's death in 632

---

[3] The following is drawn from Lapidus, 2012:39–54.

[4] When discussing Islam I have chosen to use the English term 'God' instead of the Arabic 'Allah'. I will use Allah (which, incidentally, is also used by Arabic-speaking Christians) when a contradistinction needs to be made to the Christian God.

his followers had conquered the Western half of the Arabian Peninsula from the Hejaz in the north to Yemen in the south.

Islam had an ambiguous relation to kinship as a social and political phenomenon. First, the new religion claimed to make a break with the existing networks of tribes and the culture that legitimated these. The message of Islam was that the community of the faithful should supersede other human communities. Second, the construction of the community of the faithful, *umma*, was based on an analogy with kinship. As Patricia Crone puts it, the genius of Muhammad was to create a new community in the form of a 'supertribe' (Crone, 2005:19). Some suras, like number eight, Al-Tabawah (Repentence) do argue that biological kinsmen are to be abandoned if they are unbelievers (Koran, 2014:189).

However, in many more parts of the Koran we find strong emphasis on the importance of kin (Madelung, 1997:6–18). This is expressed both in terms of general admonitions to aid kinsmen and in exemplary stories from the lives of earlier prophets and biblical figures. Madelung demonstrates that all preceding prophets wanted their own close kin to succeed them (Madelung, 1997:8–12). In some suras of the Koran the prophets of mankind are presented as a single bloodline stretching all the way back to Abraham. The power-political implications of the image of prophetic succession that the Koran conveys will be apparent below: succession to the leadership of the faithful should fall within Muhammad's close kin. But the definition thereof proved contentious: Should the immediate kin (Banu Hashim) or tribe (Quraysh) succeed Muhammad as the leader of the Muslims and their Empire?

Modern political scientists and sociologists have been divided in their assessments of the relation between Islam and political order. Some scholars, like Patricia Crone and John A. Hall claim that Islam has an anti-political thrust. Ultimate authority and legitimacy belong to God alone and worldly rulers are always vulnerable to the charge that they have usurped authority. When the sacred law, the Shari'a, was finalized around 750 it had been given a distinctively unworldly and anti-political cast. Patricia Crone argues that it was even characterized by an 'opposition to settled states' and instead looked back to the nomadic and tribal history of the Arabs as the ideal model society (Crone, 1980:62–3). Kings and caliphs were not seen as sacred figures, incarnations of the Godhead, or the guarantors of a divine (or divinely sanctioned) order on earth. Instead, they were condemned as usurpers of the powers that belonged to God alone. The emphasis on purity and divine omnipotence in combination with the strictest monotheism in classical Islam meant a concentration of legitimate power in a single locus: God. Consequently, worldly power could always be denounced as illegitimate and an encroachment upon the Divine (Hall, 1986). Islam can thus been seen as harbouring a corrosive element that facilitates revolts and charismatic movements that seek to change or overthrow existing political orders with the aim of either returning to the legitimate primal state or ushering in the apocalyptic end times. The anti-political character of Islam could also be described by reference to what it is lacking. Unlike the Christian Church, Islam lacks a formal organization that could administer territories, produce codified knowledge, contain dissent and enter into binding arrangements with temporal rulers. All four characteristics of the medieval church were highly beneficial to the formation and maintenance of political order in Europe. In contrast to the negative interpretation of Islam as an element in the political order, some scholars have stressed its contributions. Ernst Gellner emphasizes that high Islam acted as a stabilizing factor on the decentralized tribal societies of the Middle East (Gellner, 1998).

By focusing on the way that ideas of kinship and Islam were intertwined in major issues of political legitimacy we inquire whether Islam was destructive or conducive to the creation of political order. Since Muhammad, according to Islam, received God's message he also gained holy charisma. This quality was spread to his followers and to members of his extended family network. Descent from the Prophet, his relatives or his close kin constituted the most valuable 'symbolic capital and came to constitute the basis for claims to rule legitimately over Muslim societies for many centuries' (Drews, 2009:440). The examples are many: the first (rightly guided) caliphs, the Umayyad and the Abbasid dynasties and all later Hashemite and Sharifal dynasties, such as the ruling families of Jordan and Morocco.

The Rightly Guided Caliphate 632–670

When the Prophet Muhammad died, the question of who would lead the community of Muslims became acute. Thus, polity formation and kinship were intertwined. Although each of the succeeding caliphs came to power through different formal procedures, such as by appointment and election, they were all related to the Prophet by membership in the Quraysh tribe, by direct blood relations and/or through marriage. In later Muslim scholarship the position of the Quraysh is ambivalent; they are either denounced as enemies of the faith (since some fought against the Prophet) or lauded as the champions of Islam (and of pre-Islamic monotheism). The conflicts over succession and the civil wars that rocked the unitary Islamic polity can thus be read as succession wars within the extensive Quraysh tribe (Hawting, 2000; Āghā, 2003).

Before proceeding to outline the sequence of events, the issues and resources that were at stake should be noted. The successor (and thus vice-regent, caliph) of Muhammad and his kin would command an empire and its peoples, and possess religious authority and considerable material wealth. Sura number eight (The Spoils) of the Koran says that a fifth of the booty (*ghanima*) as well as the property taken from infidels taken without combat (*fay'*) should be given to the kin of Muhammad (Madelung, 1997:13; Koran, 2014:181). The combination of command power, inheritable holiness and charisma and the provision of material wealth makes the close kin of Muhammad, Banu Hashim, a particular holy kindred in Islam. We must note that it was not a dynasty in the sense of a clear hierarchical line of descent with main and cadet branches after the fashion of later European dynasties, rather it was a network with a more undecided hierarchy.

When the Prophet Muhammed died, the dominant Arab tribes gathered in Medina to debate the issue of succession. Abu Bakr was elected the successor of the Messenger of God partly because he was Muhammed's close companion and he belonged to the Quraysh. Abu Bakr was also the father of Muhammad's second wife and hence his father-in-law (Shu'ayb, 2013:524). Before his death in 634, Abu Bakr appointed another member of the Prophet's extended kinship network, Umar ben al-Khattab as his successor. Umar was also Muhammad's father-in-law but through Muhammad's fourth wife. During Umar's reign the Arab armies conquered Egypt, Iraq and Syria.

In 640 Umar introduced a system in which two categories of hereditary elite groups were recognized by the imperial order: the Muhajirun, the families that fled from Mecca to Medina with Muhammad and the Ansar, the 'helpers' from Medina. Both kinds of actors and their descendants received a pension from the state coffers (the *diwan*). The *diwan* registry of recipients thus formed an early list of nobility. During this time the kinship-based elite was a fixed category with particular rights. Significantly, restricting the noble category to these origins closed it to non-Arabs and newly converted Muslims. This exclusivity made integration of previously existing and newly formed elite groups more difficult and caused tensions within the polity. A short-lived attempt to broaden the state-sponsored elite was made in the early eighth century by 'Umar II. Later in the century the policies of exclusion made non-Arabs more receptive to the propaganda of the Abbasids (Drews, 2009:205). Umar reigned until 644 when he was murdered. Before his death, he appointed a council of Meccan tribal leaders to elect his successor.

The council elected 'Uthman ben Affan as leader. 'Uthman was Muhammad's son-in-law twice over since he had married two of the Prophet's daughters, Ruqayya and Umm Kulthum (Hawting, 2000:26). In addition, he was also a descendant of Umayya. 'Uthman came to power as a counterweight to Ali ben Abi Talib, the leader of the Banu Hashim, Muhammad's clan and Muhammad's son-in-law through his marriage with Fatima. 'Uthman was a Meccan aristocrat of the Umayyad clan (Lapidus, 2012:81). During 'Uthman's tenure as caliph, he attempted to centralize the Arab empire and Islam. His consolidation of the conquests of the preceding years was made through networks of kinship. Some of these moves introduced a greater degree of stratification, for example appointing Umayyad kinsmen to governing positions and converting communal lands once held by provincial actors into estates of tribal sharifs that belonged to the Quraysh tribe (Anthony, 2013:584). Thus as a means to consolidate and administer a newly acquired empire, the caliph raised members of his own kinship group and tribal group (i.e., symbolic kin group) to positions of power; creating something approaching a descent-based aristocracy across the empire. Thus the principles of organization of the political order followed the principles of kinship organization. This applied both to the position of the ruler and the elites that administered it.

In 656 'Uthman was murdered by a son of Abu Bakr, Muhammad bin Abu Makr, after he refused to meet demands to step down (Wadad and Shahin, 2013:84). The Muslims of Medina selected 'Ali bin Ali Talib, a cousin of the Prophet Muhammad and his son-in-law through his marriage to Fatima, as 'Uthman's successor. He was one of the earliest followers of the Prophet and performed considerable military and diplomatic deeds during the Prophet Muhammad's lifetime. 'Ali came to power with the help of 'Uthman's assassins and without the approval of a council (*shura*). Despite his kinship credentials and his early military acumen, these circumstances compromised his legitimacy. As can be expected the Umayyad kin of 'Uthman were also out for revenge. and 'Ali's accession led to civil war, first against a faction of Meccan aristocrats headed by, among others, 'A'isha, who was the Prophet Muhammad's wife, and then against Mu'awiya (d.680) of the Umayyad clan; a sub-group within the Quraysh tribe (Hawting, 2000:21).

There were four major civil wars during the first centuries of Islam. For the purposes of this book, they can be conceptualized as wars of succession, taking place within an extended kinship network. A difference between the other wars of succession analysed in this book is that the stakes were higher. Not only was rulership of a newly acquired empire at stake but the rulership of a new religion. The First Fitna (656–61) led to the establishment of the Umayyad caliphate. In the Second Fitna (683–92) one branch of the Umayyad dynasty, the Marwanids, defeated another, the Sufyanids. In the Third Fitna (744–9) the Abbasid dynasty defeated the Umayyads and established a caliphate in Bagdhad. A Fourth Fitna was fought in 809–13 between Amin and Ma'mun, two sons of the great caliph Haroun al-Rashid (Robinson, 2013:99–101).

'Uthman's cousin Mu'awiya refused to give allegiance to 'Ali (Lapidus, 2012:82) and the two factions fought repeatedly and two attempts at arbitration failed. Eventually, Mu'awiya's side was stronger militarily and he also managed to gain support from a majority of Muslims. To make matters worse, some of 'Ali's followers, called the Kharijis (the secessionists) rebelled against him. Most of them were defeated in battle, a victory that only weakened 'Ali's side. In 661 a *khariji* murdered 'Ali and with his death the path was open to for Mu'awiya to assume the caliphate under his own dynasty, the Umayyads. He appointed his son Yazid as his successor, thus establishing hereditary rule in his own bloodline.

The succession conflict between the Hashemite lineage (direct descendants of the Prophet Muhammad) continued for a generation after the accession to the caliphate by Mu'awiya. Ali's son and grandson of the Prophet, Hasan b. Ali (624–70) was a natural candidate for leadership and potential rival of Mu'awiha. Although he declined to submit to Mu'awiya's leadership he maintained a policy of passive opposition from his base in Medina. Hasan b. Ali was, however, assassinated, perhaps at the order of Mu'awiya, in 670 (Anthony,

2013:216–17). On his death the loyalties of the Hashemite party shifted to Hasan's brother Husayn b. Ali (626–70). Husayn was the son of Muhammad's daughter Fatima and of Ali b. Abi Talib. When Hasan died, Husayn became the Hashemi patriarch. When Mu'awiya died in 680 Husayn refused to accept the leadership of Yazid and set out to gather his supporters in Iraq. However, Husayn and his followers were ambushed by Umayyad forces in Kerbala and massacred (Qutbuddin, 2013:227–8). Along with their father, 'Ali, Hasan and Husayn are considered as the first three imams of Shi'a Islam. The Umayyad's guilt in murdering Husayn would be a topos that legitimated political uprisings over the coming centuries. It featured as an argument for both the Fatimid and the Abbasid rebellions.

The two sides in the war of succession would form the basis of the long-lasting division between Sunni and Shi'a Islam. Muslims that accept the succession of Mu'awiya and the line of caliphs that followed him belong to the Sunni. The Shiites regard 'Ali as the righteous Caliph and, in addition, as the first imam – the divinely gifted spiritual leader and source of law. In fact, the term 'Shi'a' is an abbreviation of Shi'at Ali – 'the party of 'Ali'. They also believe that only the descendants of 'Ali can rightfully possess the title of imam and caliph. For the Shi'a the bloodline of 'Ali forms a holy dynasty in which physical descent and divine power and legitimacy are intertwined. Naturally, 'Ali's bloodline is also that of the Prophet Muhammad since they were related by blood. The Shi'a believe that the Prophet's family is divinely designated and endowed with the right to govern (Gleave, 2013:511). How the Prophet's descendants (*ahl al-bayt*) are to be defined has been a matter of considerable dispute. Most Shi'as have opted for a strict definition of the Prophet's lineage. Importantly, this definition excluded descendants of 'Abbas, the Prophet's uncle; descendants that founded the Abbasid caliphate in 750 (Crone, 1980:68). As a result, the network structure of the Prophet's kinship group enabled a cascading proliferation of parties and thus of potential conflicts over the leadership. This tendency towards winner-takes-all conflicts can be traced to the lack of a clear hierarchy. We saw parallels to this tendency in Chapter 3 that dealt with early medieval Europe. As Drews puts it, the debate over the legitimate genealogy of the Prophet Muhammad harboured considerable permissive as well as proximate causes of conflict (Drews, 2009:440).

In sum, the three main orientations of Islam, which all developed during the Umayyad period, can be distinguished on the basis of their position on the matter of succession and, in particular, over which definition of kinship should be included in the succession to leadership of the Muslim community. The Shi'ites argued that the caliph should belong to the family of Muhammad, and hence opted for a more narrow definition of the legitimate lineage. In contrast, the Sunni's believed that he should belong to the tribe of Muhammad, the Quraysh, and hence opted for a wider definition. Interestingly, the Kharijis rejected the idea that the Caliph had to be related to Muhammad at all and instead believe that he should be chosen on the basis of personal piety and religious excellence (Hawtin, 2000:3). This was not only a theological statement, but also a political one: the basis of leadership of the community should not be kinship but merit. The Kharijis represented an understanding of the principles of the political order that were distinct from kinship as a principle of legitimacy.

Although the first caliphs were either appointed or chosen by a council they still belonged to the kinship network centred on the Prophet Muhammad. This forms a parallel to early royal elections in European countries where only members of an already kingly line could be chosen by virtue of their inherited charisma (Mitteis, 1944:55). Mu'awiya later established a hereditary monarchy but it was also partly legitimated by its link with the Prophet Muhammad: its founder was the cousin of Uthman, Muhammad's son-in-law. The importance of the idea that the caliphate had to be held by a member of the Quraysh clan cannot be overstated. The central lineage that carried legitimacy could both unite a sprawling polity and focus conflicts.

The Umayyad Caliphate 661–750

Mu'awiya established hereditary succession within the Umayyad dynasty as the way leaders were made. Succession did not follow the rules of primogeniture, leadership could be passed from father to son, from brother to brother or between other relatives within the Umayyad dynasty. To legitimate their rule, the Umayyads emphasized their kinship with 'Utman b. 'Affan, one of the first four caliphs. Since he had been instructed by the Prophet, the lineage of the Umayyads were, by extension, also touched by the founder's charisma. They also portrayed themselves as the deputies of God (Landau-Tasseron, 2013). During the Umayyad period the titles of the caliphs changed and so did the emphasis on the basis of legitimacy of governments. The caliphs of the Umayyad and Abbasid dynasties called themselves God's deputy (*khalifat Allah*) instead of vice-regents of the Prophet (*Khalifat rasul Allah*) (Jackson, 2013:51). In the Umayyad period, as in the preceding and succeeding periods, religious and kinship-based legitimacy were combined and intertwined.

During the Umayyad caliphate, Islam was not initially defined as a universal religion but as an Arab religion that conquered people had no access to. Instead, Islam was 'regarded as the property of the conquering aristocracy' (Hawting, 2000:4). Some parts of the Koran, such as sura twenty-six ('The Poets') could be interpreted as indicating a divine sanction of the privileges of the Arabs (Koran, 2014:374). Since Muslims only payed tithes (*zakat*) and were exempt from taxes there was also an economic motive to maintain an exclusive community (Drews, 2009:206). Religion, social status and political rights were defined on the basis of belonging or not belonging to an Arab tribe, and descent and tribal affiliation continued to structure Islamic society after the period of conquest. In the Umayyad period people of Arab (tribal) descent ranked higher in status than converts, indeed they constituted the elite (Drews, 2009:205). Converts to Islam had to attach themselves as clients (*mawla*) to an Arab tribe (Hawting, 2000:4; Crone, 2003), in order to join Islam a convert had to become a kind of honorary but still subservient member of an Arab tribe. Later during the Umayyad period, Islam was redefined as a universal religion but the ambivalent attitude of the Arabic elite towards the conquered populations continued. Although large numbers converted to Islam the descendants of the conquerors were reluctant to share their power and religion. The reluctance of the early Arab elites to include converts as full members of the community only partly reflected theological concerns, power, prestige and wealth were also at stake. The unwillingness or incapacity to form an inclusive polity and integrate other elites into the Arabo-Islamic political order would be one of the main reasons for the downfall of the Umayyad dynasty.

Patricia Crone argues that the early Islamic state retained many important tribal characteristics. The Umayyads lacked formalized institutions of government and preferred to rule through personal connections with tribal chiefs, often buttressed by intermarriage (Crone, 1999:324–5). Crone also states that the preference for personal contacts over institutionalized government would prove to be a permanent feature of Islamic societies. The Umayyad caliphate consisted of a network of rule in which each node had to negotiate with actors below him in order to gain political or military resources. A central level in the system of rule was the provincial governor, the *amir*, below him we find the tribal leaders, the *ashraf*. Neither amir nor ashraf controlled the means of collective violence (Hawting, 2000:35–36), that lay in the hands of the tribesmen as a collective and in order to harness military capabilities political leaders had to bargain and negotiate. Positions on both administrative levels were strongly influenced by hereditary connections. The Umayyad often appointed amirs from prestigious tribes like the Quraysh and the Thaqif. Similarly, the ashraf tended to come from hereditary leading families (Hawting, 2000:36).

During this period, tribes were the central socio-political unit, not only in Arabia but also in the conquered territories like Iraq and Khurasan to which Arabic tribes had moved and reinforced themselves with newly acquired networks of clients (*mawla*) (Sharon, 1983:51–71). As a result of the migrations and the raised stakes of power after the conquests Arab tribes formed two large confederations, the 'southerners' (*Azd*) and the 'northerners' (*Mudar*). Membership in each group was determined more by genealogy than by geography (Hawting, 2000:53, 55). The formation of the two confederacies and their growing rivalry was of great importance to the politics of the Umayyad period. Tribal affiliation tended to be fairly stable despite the considerable movements of peoples and the dynamic political environment. For example, there were five tribal groups (*akhmas*) in Basra: Tanim, Azd, Bakr b. Wa'il, Abd-al Qays and Al al-Aliyah. These groups conquered and settled Khurasan, a key frontier province in what today is eastern Iran (Sharon, 1983:54). Despite being uprooted and despite intermingling with the local population to the extent of creating a new and distinct culture, the tribal groups remained the basis of politics. The tribes were rivals for power and influence; often attempting to promote their own members to political offices (Hawting, 2000:75). As in the rest of the Umayyad empire, tribes controlled the main resources of armed force. Consequently, their conflicts were sometimes violent but inter-tribal fighting often seems to have been of an almost ritual kind and not aimed at the annihilation of the enemy (Sharon, 1983:68–9).

The Second Fitna (683–92) took place between two branches of the Umayyad dynasty the Marwanids and the Sufyanids. The Marwanids instituted more direct government, the development of officialdom and a proto-standing army (Hawting, 2000:62). Factions in the army coincided often with tribal groups. The traditional tribal levies and their descent-based elites were sidestepped in favour of recruited and salaried regiments from Syria (Drews, 2009:204–5). This strategy represents a step away from integrating kinship-based principles with the principles of the political order by introducing a conflict between the two. As we shall see the 'Abbasid caliphate went further in this respect which weakened it. The unsettled nature of the order of succession continued to plague the Umayyad caliphate. Successions were disputed on several levels: within the Marwanid dynasty and between parties that advanced different branches of the Quraysh altogether. During this period the principles of succession and legitimate rule as well as major issues of religious doctrine were not settled. This two-fold uncertainty created problems for political stability and legitimacy: succession tended to be decided ad hoc as each incoming ruler usually wanted to place his own descendants on the throne, which clashed with the arrangements of the previous caliph.

We may contrast the situation in the Arab empire with that in Western Europe at the same time. Although the rules of succession had not settled upon a clear preference for primogeniture, some factors stabilized the European situation: Christian doctrine had been through several centuries of doctrinal development and during this time had developed a tradition of dealing with political order, first vis-à-vis the Roman Empire, second with the 'barbarian' kingdoms that succeeded it and third with attempts of the latter to reconnect to the former. In the Arabo-Islamic world of the eighth century, neither the religion nor the orders of succession had been fully formed. Instead, both remained in a formative stage and that contributed to instability. The civil wars were thus fought as conflicts over the framework of religion and politics rather than as conflicts within them, making them more destabilizing.

The undecided nature of the succession lay behind the Third Fitna fought in 744–9. It began as a struggle between parties within the Marwanid dynasty but soon expanded into a wider conflict as tribal groups from Khurasan rebelled (Hawtin, 2000:102). The combination of first intra-dynastic and then inter-dynastic conflict ended the Umayyad caliphate and began a new era: the Abbasid caliphate.

The Abbasid Caliphate 762–1258

Since the nineteenth century, scholars have debated the ultimate causes of the downfall of the Umayyads and how the Abbasids came to rule the caliphate. Recent analyses emphasizes that the revolt was driven by a secret movement, the Hashimiyya, and by native Iranian elites and not, as previously argued, by Arab immigrants to Khurasan (Āghā, 2003). The main tenant of the Hashimiyya was that a member of the Prophet's clan – the Banu Hashim – should rule the caliphate. The Abbasid family was not a driving force behind the revolt but usurped it once the rebellion had been successfully launched. The leader of the revolt was Abu Muslim al-Khurasani. He installed the obscure 'Abbasids as caliphs and intended to rule the eastern part of the Empire himself, but he was murdered by agents of the 'Abbasids (Al-Azmeh, 2004). The causes and course of the revolution are, however, not our main concern but how the new ruling dynasty was legitimate in terms of kinship.

Political and theological reasons combined to form a strong *causus belli* against the Umayyads. The Umayyad dynasty had never achieved a wide consensus concerning their claim that they as a branch of the Quraysh were the legitimate heirs of the Prophet and not families closer to his immediate bloodline. Their chief contenders in this respect were the 'Alids, the descendants of Ali ibn Talib, the cousin and son-in-law of Muhammad. 'Ali had become a pivotal figure in the religious tradition that would become Shi'a Islam. The Umayyads never managed to achieve closure in the matter of succession after Muhammad and many still considered the claims of the 'Alids legitimate. Although the 'Alids eventually failed to seize power, their existence as a political as well as a religious factor damaged the position of the Umayyads. Once in power, the Abbasids legitimated their rule in dynastic terms. As members of the Banu Hashim, they claimed that their dynasty was more legitimate than that of other branches of the Quraysh. Against other Hashimite claimants, most importantly the 'Alids, they claimed that their status as leaders of the revolution gave them additional authority (Crone, 1980:65). Their middle position between the pure Sunni/Quraysh and Shi'a/'Alid claims of legitimate descent remained problematic and the legitimacy of the dynasty dubious.

The Abbasid caliphate has been described as a charismatic theocracy that elevated the ruler to an unprecedented position of domination above their subjects (Drews, 2009:219). Abbasid power rested on two kinship-based formations: the royal family (who were often appointed as provincial governors) and the major families from Khurasan that had participated in the Abbasid revolution against the Umayyad dynasty in 750 but who came to settle in

Baghdad. Thus, the introduction of the Abbasid caliphate entailed a revolution in the sense that the dominant elites changed. Crone describes the families around the Abbasids as a 'system' of aristocratic families, often of Khurasani descent, that were arranged in concentric circles around the caliph. Some contemporary writers such as the Persian Ibn al-Muqaffa espoused a truly imperial vision of the Islamic state, centred on the caliph and his aristocratic public servants (Crone, 1980:69), a corporate nobility based on enrolment and service with a status that rested on descent. Its families possessed various honorific titles that linked it to the caliphal dynasty; ending with the *dawla* suffix (Crone, 1980:65–6). Another category was the kinsmen of the caliph, the *ahl-al-bayt*. This was a wide category that encompassed both real kinsmen, the princes who ruled as provincial governors, and honorary kinsmen bound to the royal dynasty by symbolic kinship. It is, however, important to note that the system of caliphal clientage was not a case of embedding or nesting existing networks of powerful actors with local power and legitimacy such as had been the case in the Frankish *Reichsaristokratie*. Rather the clients, the *Mahwali*, were of servile status without notable origins and bound to the caliph and his household (Crone, 1980:66–7).

Over time the leading families lost their Khurasani connection and were also relatively quickly demilitarized, Arab noble families of the Anshar and Muhagirun categories also soon lost their importance. The Arab nobility lost its power as lawyers and secretaries became more important and won power (Drews, 2009:225). An administrative elite was developed and we see how secretarial families formed vizir dynasties such as the Barmakids. The new elites gained their positions by virtue of their relation with the caliph not because of their local legitimacy or autonomous power (Drews, 2009:210, 216). Old noble families that were registered in the *diwan* no longer participated in the council of the caliph. Soon enough they also lost their guaranteed incomes from the state coffers (Drews, 2009:217). In this period, then, we can see a pattern that resembles the ideal type of a conflict between a political order and a nobility based on descent in which the former uses a meritocratic administration to outflank the latter.

Overall, both the Umayyad and the Abbasid caliphate were characterized by a failure to integrate different groups with each other and with a conception of society as a whole. The situation was characterized by a plurality of different and competing elites each with its own conception of legitimate rule (Drews, 2009:211). Recruiting slave soldiers was only one of several signs of the disconnect between the political order and local societies. Wealthy and locally powerful families could be found in all parts of the far-flung empire. In contrast to Europe, these were not privileged in the political order or even well represented in it. They were forces to be reckoned with but only in their particular localities. The fragmentation of society into a myriad of semi-closed areas and groups and the distinction between central and provincial elites meant that the former were not committed to upholding the political order. From their horizon, rulers came and went and as long as they ruled leniently, provincial elites neither resisted nor supported them with any greater enthusiasm (Wickham, 2009:334–6).

The Abbasid Caliphate began to crumble during the mid-eighth century. After a period of flourishing, the unitary polity of the caliphate disintegrated and gave way to a system or commonwealth of autonomous polities stretching from Spain to eastern Iran from the tenth century onwards (Robinson, 2010). The origin of the fragmentation and the creation of a new formation lies in the military sector and the emergence of what became a distinctly Islamic phenomenon: the slave army (Crone, 1980). With the growth of large-scale purchase and capture of slaves in order to raise armies the importance of princes and aristocracy as an institution waned. The shift in military power coincided with a loss in political power as the Arab tribes were no longer called up for their traditional levies. Instead, from the early ninth century caliphs began recruiting mercenaries and slave soldiers of Turkic, Iranian, Slavic and African origins (Drews, 2009:233–4). The first step in this development can be read as a strategy of the caliphate to rid itself of its reliance upon traditional, kinship-based elites in order to strengthen their rule. A means to do so was to strip kinship-based elites of their importance and instead recruit not only soldiers but also military commanders that would stand outside society. This strategy would prove counterproductive and in the long term accelerate the fragmentation of the larger social formation. Substituting endogenous elites with slave soldiers was a major shift in the political order as control over the means of armed force was subcontracted to an alien and isolated caste.

Slave soldiers were valuable to their commanders because initially they only owed their allegiance to him and since they had no other ties that could command loyalty or constitute alternative investments. They were cultural aliens in the societies in which they served which meant that they lacked a stake in the polity. Crone describes the contrast between the endogenous baronial elites of France and the Mamluk mercenaries of the Abbasid times: 'The barons were no aliens but members of their own polity who subscribed, with whatever cynicism, to its political values, whereas the *Mamluks* had to be born in Islam to acquire a comparable commitment to the political norms of Islam; and precisely for this reason home-born *mamluks* were eventually excluded from the army ... ' (Crone, 1980:78–9). This alien status made them a double-edged sword in relation to stability and the formation of political order. For a slave army to be beneficial to the cohesion of a polity, it is extremely dependent on the charisma and success of its commander. If this is lacking, it soon becomes a threat to the society in which it operates. Although the outsider status of slaves makes them amenable to command, it also constitutes an anti-integrative element in the social formation at large. It severs the military power from the political and distances other social groups from the central decisions and operations of government. In other words, it makes what we might call 'the state' like a thin layer on top of and cut off from society – much like the condition that Robert Jackson describes with regard to twentieth-century African polities (Jackson, 1990). The strategy of recruiting state soldiers contradicted what Edward Shils claims is a crucial condition for a functioning polity, that there is an orientation towards the central values of the political system.

   Some particularities of how civil war and rebellion had been viewed by Islamic jurisprudence must be noted. After the first five centuries of Islam, a strong opinion was formed against revolutionary struggles that would divide the community. Instead of rebelling against unjust or illegitimate rulers, large segments of society preferred to retreat into a private (or non-political) sphere of piety and local loyalties. This is a marked contrast to Europe, where religious and political struggles would mobilize large parts of all populations, elites and non-elites alike. Framed in Albert Hirschmann's terms, the choice of 'quietist' over 'activist' strategies would correspond to a kind of exit; not into another sphere of politics but from the political per se, rather in the form of an inner exile. In contrast the many wars European aristocrats fought over which dynasty should rule a country or the position of elite kinship groups in the polity should be seen as expressions of 'voice' and 'loyalty' – both of which are, in their own way, declarations of concern for the political order (Crone, 1980:87–8).

The capacity to integrate existing and incoming elite groups into the political order is a key resource for stability and durability. The combination of elites that are durable and with a legitimacy or charisma that is entrenched among people in a specific local context, or with a mobile group of people that constitute their followers, and an overarching framework that gives these groups a meaning through belonging to a collective transhistorical corporate entity means that elite power is harnessed instead of becoming autonomous or dissolved. A situation with wholly autonomous elites is dangerous since it leads to many different centres of power and to fragmentation. Dissolved elites are also dangerous since they can weaken the polity by leading to entropy and reducing its capacity to withstand external shocks.

Trans-cultural Comparisons: The Integration of Normans and Turks

An illustrative contrast may be drawn between how the Frankish monarchy handled the Normans in the tenth century and how the Umayyads and Abbasids handled the Turks at roughly the same point in time. During the ninth century Viking raiders frequently attacked the coasts of Francia and the Franks found themselves unable to defend their land. In order to handle the situation, Charles III, king of the Franks (r.898–922) co-opted the chieftain Hrolfr who had settled in Rouen in today's Normandy. The plan was to use Hrolfr and his followers in order to stop them from raiding and to make them defend the northern flank of Francia against other Viking raiders (Crouch, 2002:6–7). The Viking chief was converted to Christianity and baptized as Robert I in 911. The Northmen were relatively quickly embedded in the Frankish order and became 'Normans' (Crouch, 2002:10). The Duke of Normandy, his dynasty and followers became powerful actors within the French monarchy. There was, however, no substantial difference between them and their counterparts in, say, Picardy or Gascony. However, the Normans were transformed.

Granting land, status and religious-cultural assimilation through Christianization were not the only means of creating embedding. The leading family of the Normans was made into a ducal dynasty which made it compatible with other families, in the sense of socialization and matrimonial alliances. For example, marrying his daughter Giselda to the Viking chieftain was a part of Charles III's integration scheme for Hrolfr. Hrolfr's followers and their families were made into nobles. In the 930s, Hrolfs son, William, was titled *comes Rothomensis* – the Count of Rouen (Crouch, 2002:11). Thus, the Viking problem was solved by embedding the Normans into an existing cultural and organizational system whose pillars were shared central values and loyalty towards Francia and its kings. The conception of nobility, although not strictly formalized, was thus a resource that enabled the integration of powerful and potentially threatening elite groups. The nobility, even in this early stage, as a resource for politics of integration meant that the danger of wholly autonomous elites that could create polities of their own was averted. This achievement was even more remarkable given the weakness of the French monarchy at the time. In other words, the category of elite kinship groups stabilized the political order.

The successful co-optation of the Normans can be underlined by noting what did not happen after Hrolfr/Robert I had been granted his lands: (a) the Norman duke did not usurp the Frankish throne; (b) Normandy did not become an independent polity; (c) the creation of Normandy did not fragment Francia; and (d) Normandy did not fall apart. All four scenarios were theoretically possible and in fact took place in some form or another in the Middle East after the waning of the Abbasids and the introduction of Turkic peoples and their military elites. The failure of the Abbasid political order to integrate the incoming Turkic political and military elites stands in sharp contrast to the Frankish/Norman interaction. Ironically, the institution of slave soldiers was an attempt to prevent rival groups establishing dynasties. However, manumitted slave military commanders established dynasties anyway; from the mid-eighth century, elites were rapidly circulated and the Abbasid political order lacked a framework or stable system of elites into which newcomers could be integrated. Of course, old and new groups were not culturally isolated. Turkic newcomers were rapidly converted to Islam and there was plenty of cultural and ideational cross-fertilization between Arabic, Persian and Turkic traditions. However, the dynamic, even revolutionary, environment in combination with the Abbasid ambition of forestalling rival centres of power robbed the political order of stability and of embedding institutions. Hence, one may conclude that a 'recipe' for success is not to destroy hereditary elite groups but to make them loyal to and embedded in the political order.

A Re-reading of Ibn Khaldûn on Kinship and Political Order

The focus on tribe-state interactions in research on the development of polities in the Middle East can be attributed to the reception of the work of Ibn Khaldûn who wrote one of the classic treaties on the relation between nomads and sedentary peoples in the Islamic world and on the role of kinship ties and kinship-based institutions in human societies. Khaldûn is worth re-visiting not only because of his insights but also since several scholars that deal with kinship and politics in the Islamic World invoke his main work, the *Muqadimmah*, in order to support their interpretations (Gellner, 1981; Rosen, 2005; Alatas, 2006; Chapra, 2008). Ibn Khaldûn formulated a theory of the dynamics in human civilizations that was a synthesis of the historical experience in the Middle East. To him the division between nomadic and sedentary peoples is the fundamental typological difference among civilizations (Khaldûn, 2005:91). Nomads are the most basic group for Khaldûn. Nomads have several characteristics that set them apart from sedentary peoples: since they live in harsh terrain and under conditions of resource scarcity they are tough, wild, rapacious and skilled in the arts of war. They are connected through blood ties and therefore they possess *'asabiyyah* – a term roughly translated as 'group feeling' or 'tribal partisanship' – an egalitarian bond that creates unique cohesion. Their social organization is characterized by exceptionally pure lineages due to their lifestyle and geographical isolation. This purity accounts for the strength of their *'asabiyyah* (Halim et al., 2012). Arabs who have lived in more fertile areas have become more mixed with other blood lines, both Arab and non-Arab, which has contributed to their loss of *'asabiyyah*.

Khaldûn became famous for his dynamic philosophy of history that outlines a cyclical movement through time as new dynasties are created, fall into decadence and then are overthrown. Nomadic people are drawn towards sedentary civilization since they strive for more comfortable lives. Hence nomads at regular intervals will attack, and because of their more martial qualities defeat, sedentary urban civilizations. The conquering nomads will install themselves as a new dynasty in the cities but their reign will always be short since city life corrupts their toughness, dilutes their bloodlines and causes their group feeling to dissipate. Each dynasty is given a life span of about three generations (Khaldûn, 2005). During the course of settlement the rulers will depend less and less upon their original tribal group and its egalitarian group feeling and more and more upon servants, clients and underlings. Not only luxury is the cause of this decadence but the fundamental difference between nomad and city life with respect to rule and violence. The original habitat of the nomadic peoples is characterized by self-help and thus the need to be strong, tough and able to defend one's own kinship group – attributes that fortify the group feeling. In contrast city folk are ruled by laws, which weakens them militarily and spiritually. In Khaldûn's vision, the weakness of sedentary civilizations and the propensity of settled life to corrupt the martial abilities and communal life of new dynasties means that all polities in the Middle East are inherently unstable and that there will be a steady flow of newcomers from the arid badlands that conquer and establish themselves.

One could read Ibn Khaldûn's theory of Middle Eastern state formation as an expression of the thesis that this book argues against: that kinship organizations and states are fundamentally incompatible and, particularly in the Middle East, doomed to be at odds with each other. Khaldûn does emphasize a binary view of the relation between nomadic tribes and settled states but this does not exhaust his treatment of kinship-based organizations. I believe that this interpretation of parts of the normative ethos of tribalism and of Islam clashes with the record of imperial monarchies during the Umayyad and Abbasid periods. It also clashes with the prestige of the lineage of the Muhammad network and the longevity of certain of the royal dynasties that claim descent from the Prophet, such as the rulers of Morocco.

Khaldûn can actually be read as a strong supporter of monarchy. For as much as Khaldûn stresses the military and to some extent moral superiority of the Bedouins over settled peoples in some respects he also emphasizes their inferiority in others. The Bedouins and, one may presume, similar nomadic peoples elsewhere in the Islamic world are the ruin of civilization, says Khaldûn (Khaldûn, 2005:119). What is important to the argument of this book is the reasons that Khaldûn gives for his assertion. Far from simply stating an empirical fact about their propensity to plunder and pillage, the Bedouin violate a more general law of the social and cosmological order by their invasions and by their way of life. They are the destroyers of civilization since they bring anarchy and lawlessness that destroy mankind since royal power is the natural state of man and royal power alone guarantees mankind's continued existence and social organization (Khaldûn, 2005:119, 121,

151, 154). Thus, the nomadic invaders threaten not just the specific urban civilization of the Middle East but civilization in a more general and fundamental sense not because of their military actions but because of their social organization. Although they are superior in terms of 'asabiyyah and the purity of their lineages, it is only another kind of lineage-based institution that can support mankind in a social and cosmological sense: monarchy. In this reading, Khaldûn comes across not as the celebrant of nomadic barbarity and toughness but of the well-ordered polity that only kings and their kin-based hierarchy can create and sustain.

Although he considers nomadic peoples as the primeval form of human organization, for Khaldûn the rule of kings is 'a natural quality of man' and '[r]oyal authority is an institution that is natural to mankind' (Khaldûn, 2005:119, 151). Similar ideas are also found in the work Siyāsat-Namā written by the Great Vizir of the Seljuk Empire (see Chapter 8), Nizam al-Mulk (Ohlander, 2009:244). Thus kinship, in the wider sense of dynastic and royal kinship, is central to political order in Khaldûn's political theory. Royal authority 'implies a form of organization necessary to mankind' (Khaldûn, 2005:154, 256–7). This is so because 'human beings cannot live and exist except through social organization and co-operation for the purpose of obtaining their food and other necessities of life' (Khaldûn, 2005:151). However, since 'injustice and aggressiveness are in the animal nature' human societies need direction lest they fall into anarchy: 'People, thus, cannot persist in a state of anarchy and without a ruler who keeps them apart. Therefore, they need a person to restrain them. He is a ruler. As is required by human nature, he must be a forceful ruler, one who exercises authority' (Khaldûn, 2005:152). Ernst Gellner claims that Ibn Khaldûn's thinking about anarchy and social order as well as his idolization of the Bedouin makes him an antithesis of Thomas Hobbes who championed the unitary conception of sovereignty by arguing that all formations in a country should be subject to a single centre of authority (Gellner, 1998; Hobbes, 2008). However, Ibn Khaldûn can be read as quite the opposite: a philosopher of social order whose conception of true kingship is reminiscent of a European conception of sovereignty. Khaldûn distinguishes between real and defective royal authority. The former 'belongs only to those who dominate subjects, collect taxes, send out (military) expeditions, protect the frontier regions, and have no one over them who is stronger than they' (Khaldûn, 2005:152). It should be noted that the kind of kingship Khaldûn talks about is not one that shared power with his magnates like the kind of king envisioned by the English political theorist Sir John Fortescue (1395–1477). Rather, he is more of an absolute ruler.

Ibn Khaldûn was not unique. There are important similarities between the Muqaddimah and the Islamic mirror of princes and advice literature, nasīhat al-mulūk (Austin and Jansen, 1996:24; Marlow, 2009:526). Although I cannot deal in full with it here it must be noted that there is a strand in medieval Arabic tradition and thinking that emphasizes hierarchy and monarchical forms of rule, infused with sacral elements and charisma, against or perhaps in parallel to the egalitarian traditions. In this tradition, kings are natural parts of the divinely ordained cosmos (Ohlander, 2009:244–5).

Conclusions

The introduction of Islam fundamentally reshaped the conditions for the formation of political kinship groups and political order among the Arabs. A system of kinship groups had existed in pre-Islamic times and it was stratified in two respects: first, some tribes had more status than others and second, some clans had more status than others within the same tribe. However, we find little evidence of a strict ranking system or of a durable social hierarchy. Once Islam was introduced the system changed radically. As the last and definitive messenger (rasul) of God Muhammad has an unrivalled cosmological position in Islamic culture. Consequently, this bloodline and his tribe (Quraysh) gained a special position among the clans and tribes of Arabia. Since God's message and the new religion were transmitted through a member of the Quraysh tribe the Arabian tribal society became more hierarchical. The hierarchization of tribal society was strengthened by the tendency of the early caliphs to allow members of certain prestigious kinship groups to monopolize key offices (amir) in important provinces. The position of the Quraysh tribe and its clans (Hashemi, Umayyad) in Arabic tribal society remained contested for a long time. Indeed, it is possible to understand the many civil wars as a reaction to the trends towards making a formally egalitarian society of different bloodlines (or at least a system of bloodlines where hierarchies were not codified but flexible) into a hierarchical one. We can interpret it as a conflict between a centralized and codified political kinship system and an egalitarian and non-codified one.

Several scholars, like Patricia Crone, have argued that these traits and the conspicuous absence of state-like institutions explain its weakness and eventual downfall. Although there were fixed concepts and categories, the institutions that could have embedded the elite dynasties were too weak. There were strong kinship-based elites but only very weak political institutions and this caused the order to be fragile. The Abbasid caliphate seems to present us with the inverse structural situation, which might have been a historical counter-reaction to its predecessor: he different kinds of hereditary – and hence kinship-based – elites (Arab, Khurasani) were marginalized and eventually lost their place in the civilian as well as military administrations. In their stead we see pronounced tendencies towards meritocratic recruitment of both civilian and military personnel. There was an undeniable tendency of the Abbasid caliphs to elevate themselves to an exalted position above and beyond other powers in the order. The strategy of tying 'new men' into the administration and manning the military with mercenaries and slaves was consistent with a political strategy of eliminating other centres of power with autonomous legitimacy that might rival the position of the new regime. Still, the Abbasids did not establish durable political institutions.

Nevertheless, we can observe two successive regimes that were both unstable but each in its own way. On that basis we can conclude that hereditary elites, for example tribal and/or noble elites, are not in themselves sources of instability: when the Abbasids replaced the elites that had been a part of the Umayyad order they did not succeed in creating a durable polity; the political order was still unstable. However, we see that the absence of durable traditional elites, with a strong locally anchored legitimacy, and durable political institutions are causes of instability and weakness. European societies offer revealing comparisons: strong and durable hereditary elites as well as strong political institutions characterized these societies. Precisely this combination, buttressed by institutions and ideas that created a greater degree of embedding of elites in the political order, was conducive to stability and growth.

In this chapter, I have interpreted many of the key episodes in the first centuries of Arabo-Islamic rule in the Middle East as succession struggles and emphasized the (constructed) kinship dimension of many of its elites and rival factions. These are traits that the Islamic polities share with their European counterparts and adding the element of kinship, dynasticism and aristocratic orders provides extra heuristic mileage to understanding both the strong and the weak parts of the political orders in this place and period. In sum, this chapter seems to confirm the main argument of this book that a key part in any order is the capacity to integrate elite groups. The capacity to integrate new elites into an existing framework was a source of strength for the European and Ottoman political orders and a weakness of the early Arab empires. This consensual model of state formation stands in marked contrast to the more common conflictual models that emphasize that the state must defeat other centres of power rather than negotiate and work with them. The Umayyad resembled the latter model to some degree and the Abbasid did so to a very high degree.

8 SACRED YET SUPPLE
Kinship and Politics in Turkic-Mongol Empires c.990–c.1300

Introduction

This chapter deals with two of the Turkic-Mongol polities that existed in the Eurasian steppe between roughly, 990 and 1300 AD: they were highly successful polities that were able to conquer substantial, by European standards even vast, territories. Traditionally, steppe societies were portrayed as consisting of tribes or clans, terms that were not only vague but also laden with associations of egalitarianism and lack of sophistication. However, modern specialists on the steppe people emphasize that they were governed by strong aristocratic and royal lineages. For that reason they offer an important comparison and contrast to the European, Arab and Ottoman polities studied in other chapters. Outside the field of specialist archaeologists, anthropologists, historians and linguists, steppe polities are rarely studied by political scientists or sociologists (Neumann and Wigen, 2013, 2018). Turkic-Mongol societies are worthy subjects of investigation in their own right within the scope of this book. The chapter asks the same questions as previous chapters did: what was the relation between elite families and the political order? Was there a symbiosis or a contradiction? The answer is that the political and social order of Turkic-Mongol peoples was intensely stratified and unequal, and hence their nobilities – in the sense of recognized durable elite families – were certainly part of the political order. To the extent that we define political order, the large polities created by Turkic and Mongol peoples' notions that connected kinship to legitimate rule certainly played a role in their expansion as well as in their fragmentation. The identification of a single family with legitimate rule explains their ability to build large coalitions of elite families and retainers that conquered and created empires (Lindholm, 1986). The idea that charisma and legitimacy was equally shared among all members of the royal house accounts – among other factors – for their fragmentation. However, as I have argued before, kinship cannot be studied in isolation but must always be regarded in combination with other factors. For example, contingency played a part as individuals of extraordinary capabilities created several of the largest empires, such as the unified Mongol Empire and the empire of Timur Lenk. Also, as we shall see below, kinship in this cultural sphere was at times a rather flexible phenomenon. However, it seems most Turkic polities until the establishment of the Ottoman, Safavid and Mughal empires towards the late Middle Ages lacked a conception of the abstract realm and the capacity to firmly embed other elite groups. This takes us into a second *raison d'être* of this chapter: its value lies in providing an additional point of comparison for both the European realms and the Arab and Ottoman Empires. Before commencing, some specific characteristics in the terrain that these polities inhabited must be noted. The socio-ecological habitat of the social groups living on the steppe was characterized by a high degree of mobility (Rogers, 2012). The horse was domesticated early which created the possibility for pastoral nomadism. Being dependent on large herds of horses and sheep both enabled and demanded mobility in the search for pasture. Empires struggled with controlling both pastoral and sedentary elements in their lands. Once settled people were conquered, the pastoral nomads that made up the original element had to be managed and placated, otherwise they too might splinter and turn into an enemy. This chapter treats a number of polities, both Turk and Mongol, that had similar cultures, institutions and political challenges.

This chapter is structured in the following way: first I analyse the empire of the Seljuk Turks, the first Turkic polity that conquered a substantial agricultural population (Findley, 2005:70). Because they had to manage both settled and nomadic peoples under their rule, they faced new and special challenges to their rule. Second, I analyse the Mongol empires between the twelfth and the fourteenth centuries. The third and final section summarizes the chapter and draws comparative conclusions both regarding the steppe polities and between steppe and settled ones. I have excluded several peoples from this chapter that could have been included, like the Kipchak, Karakitai, Kazakh and Uigur. This is because space would not allow a full treatment of their history and politics.

The Seljuk Empire

Around 990 the Seljuk dynasty broke away from the loose confederacy of the Oghuz Yabghu Turks that lived beyond the Oxus River (Amu Darja) in Central Asia (Golden, 2008:361ff). The dynasty converted to Islam and thus linked its destiny to the Muslim world. They came to power during a turbulent time in Western Central Asia as the Karakanids were fragmenting. The Seljuk formed a coalition that invaded Iran and defeated the Ghazanids and established an empire (Bosworth, 1975). The Seljuk established vassal relations with other polities such as the Kipchaks in Transoxania. The empire as a whole was a 'confederation of semi-independent kingdoms over which the sultan exercised nominal authority' (Lambton, 2007:218). Different branches of the Seljuk dynasty built two main polities: that of the Great Seljuks in Iran, Iraq and Syria and the smaller Sultanate of Rûm in Anatolia. Both controlled, sometimes with great difficulty, loose confederations of Oghuz Turkic nomads and attempted to establish sedentary and more institutionalized polities (Dale, 2010:38–42). The empire of the Great Seljuks held together for three generations under the rulers Toghul (1040–63), Alp Arslan (1063–72) and Malik Shah (1072–92) (Lambton, 2007). After the reign of Malik Shah, the empire began to fragment into a large number of small polities. In 1141, the Battle of Qatwan against the Karakhitai north of Samarkand broke the Seljuk rule in Central Asia.

When the empire of the Great Seljuks fragmented into smaller components, the Sultanate of Rûm was formed in Anatolia (Cahen, 2001; Leister, 2010). After the Seljuks and their allies conquered Anatolia after the battle of Manikert in 1071, the peninsula was divided among a large number of principalities (*beyliks*) (Dale, 2010:41ff). The Sultanate of Rûm was never a cohesive or effective political order. Anatolia in the twelfth century was characterized by considerable migration of peoples and populations and numerous ad hoc groupings which made polity formation difficult. Like the empire of the Great Seljuks, the Sultanate of Rûm was also torn between competing branches of the ruling dynasty as well as having to contend with other rival beyliks of Anatolia. In 1240 the Mongol invasion of the Middle East reached Anatolia and reduced all of its local powers to vassal status (Findley, 2005:72).

The empire of the Seljuk dynasty and its development display several traits that touch directly upon our central problem: how political order can be combined with strong kinship groups and principles of political legitimacy. The Seljuks also wrestled with factors that all other political orders in the region had to come to terms with such as large groups of nomadic peoples, Islam as a fundament of political order, a difficult geopolitical predicament, the tension between traditions of rule from the steppe and Islamo-Persian ideas of royal autocracy, and the idea that charisma was inherited by all members of the royal dynasty. The pendular swing between macro- and micro-polity characteristics of Turkic history also plagued the Seljuk Empire: a capacity to rapidly build a vast but loosely coupled polity that soon fragmented into a myriad components despite a flourishing cultural sphere (Findley, 2005:71).

We can identify several cases when Turkic peoples have formed large coalitions, invaded empires of settled peoples and tried to form durable structures of their own. In many of these cases, the political orders have been short-lived. The Karakhitai as well as the Seljuks found it difficult to create the institutions and routines necessary for a formation to become more integrated and permanent in its operations of rule. One or two generations after the grand conquest, their formations have fragmented into a multitude of units fighting each other for supremacy or seeing their base dissipate as the pastoralist groups on which they were established wanted to remain nomadic and not become annexed to a sedentary formation. Once the possibility of plunder is exhausted and its successful distribution to various chiefs has been completed as a reward for joining the coalition, several nomadic formations found it difficult to establish other forms of political-economic organizations that were not predatory (or as predatory) such as taxation-based systems.

Ideas also hindered permanent structures. The Seljuks had the Turkic custom of considering royal charisma and legitimacy to be equally distributed among the members of the royal family. This provided a structural precondition for wars of succession and the establishment of local polities (Findley, 2005:71; Dale, 2010:38). We will now look at some of the reasons for this development. In combination with a martial and heroic ethos that dictates that charisma and the right to rule are based on performance in war, this form of egalitarian legitimacy within a stratified society has been quite disruptive. In short, Turkic formations have been strong on mobilization but weak on rule. The combined effect of the difficulties of maintaining the support of nomadic auxiliaries while administering a sedentary empire was too much for the Seljuks despite the efforts of the great Vizir Nizam-al-Mulk to create stable Persian foundations for the empire (Simidchieva, 2002).

Still, the Seljuk Empire did have a formal organization. It was, in theory, hierarchically organized according to the *amir-a-yan* system. At the top sat the caliph, the spiritual overlord of all of Islam. During much of the Seljuk period, this was still the Abbasid caliph that resided in Baghdad. Below the caliph, we find the sultan who was, theoretically, the custodian of the power of the caliph but in reality the actual ruler. At this tier other autonomous rulers, often belonging to the Seljuk dynasty, were located. Below the sultanic level we find the amirs, military commanders. These men were often Mamluks, manumitted slaves (Lambton, 2007:223). In theory, a Mamluk only held property temporarily and at his death it reverted to the sultan. In practice, however, the descendants of the Mamluks often inherited his property (Lambton, 2007:225). Thus, what could be interpreted as a way to curtail the power of semi-aristocratic lineages in fact often became a way that such lineages were created. Gellner calls the former elites 'geldlings', and argues that gelded elites were a characteristic feature of the Ottoman Empire – in contradistinction to Western Europe (Gellner, 2008). As we will see, the picture was more complicated. Below the amirs, we find the *a'yan*, local notables from the indigenous population. Below these four levels of rulers the subject population lived their lives (Findley, 2005:69). Formally, the empire was not only arranged according to a stratified hierarchy but also divided into provinces like Khurasan, Fars and Azerbajan. A final kind of formal-legal organization was the patchwork of Iqtas into which the empire was divided. However, the workings of the empire also ran according to a number of tensions and relations that did not fit into the formal-legal grid. Many of these dimensions involved kinship as a form of organization.

The conception of a legitimate ruler in Islamic political theory facilitated the establishment of new regimes and, more importantly, did not hinder the overthrow of old ones. A ruler was considered legitimate if he upheld Islamic law, regardless of how he came to power (Fuess, 2010:334). This conception was a marked contrast to the European situation where the dynastic principle of legitimacy was stronger and domestic, international and religious opinion worked against usurpers. A second precondition of the formation of political order in Western Europe was that religious and worldly powers formed an alliance. There, the universal religion was enshrined in and led by an organization, the Church, whose head, the Pope, was in many ways a temporal prince. The Church managed early in its history to combine the universal with the particular elements of order by allying with and stabilizing the different realms of Europe as corporate entities. For example, the conversion of its Piast kings to Christianity and the subsequent establishment of a structure of dioceses in the 900s and 1000s was crucial to Poland's survival and development as an independent polity (Davies, 1981:52–61). By making sure that 'France', 'England', or 'Poland' were entities of their own, linked to the Church, another layer of stability and object of loyalty was inserted into the relation between ruling dynasty and other powerful dynasties. An important difference was the stronger conception of the realm as an independent body in the European case. This meant that the sub-units were considered parts of a greater whole, not wholly new territories that their rulers could freely dispose of. Sub-kingdoms of the Frankish realm, like Burgundy or Aquitaine, were corporate entities of their own which ensured a further degree of stability. The fact that they were permanent parts of the kingdom rather than newly acquired territories that fluctuated in their extent and that might come and go, also furthered stability. Hence, French sub-kings did not break away and establish new dynasties and polities. Divisions of the kingdom were frequent but they were not expected to be permanent. This element, a particular identity of the political order, was lacking in the Seljuk case, which might have facilitated the numerous defections and frequent establishment of autonomous principalities. In all Turko-Mongol societies, there were many noble families but only one of them – which we would be tempted to call 'royal' – commanded considerable charisma and legitimacy. The Seljuk family was not of an ancient lineage but its founder, Saljuk, had risen to power as the leader of a confederation of Oghuz Turks through his personal charisma and ability to attract followers (Golden, 2008:362ff). Once the empire was established, however, belonging to the Seljuk dynasty became a precondition of a legitimate ruler. Several of the most successful

Turko-Mongol empire builders, such as the Karakhitai, Seljuk and the Mongols, had problems making these empires last. To some extent, these problems can be traced back to their inability to establish stable orders of succession.

The cultural template of Turko-Mongol peoples not only allowed but actively promoted the establishment of a hierarchical order with a supreme khan or *Khagan* ruling over lesser rulers of the empire. However, in line with the martial ethos of Turkic and Mongol peoples, the brothers of the royal house were, in many cases, expected to prove that they were fit to rule by fighting each other over the right to succeed the Khagan – a normative prescription not found in the Frankish context – although the practical outcome might be similar: war and fratricide (Neumann and Wigen, 2018:46–7). Hence although blood of the royal lineage bestowed a degree of charisma that made an actor eligible to rule, there was a strong element of performance – more precisely success in war – in creating the normatively necessary aura of supreme leadership.

Turkic-Mongol empires belonged to the ruling family as a whole, which meant that, at the death of the khan, the empire was divided among his sons. This situation is similar to conditions in Germanic kingdoms, such as the Frankish or the Norse, before the invention of primogeniture in royal succession (Jochens, 1987). In Merovingian France, the parcellation of the kingdom into sub-regna ruled by the sons of the former king was a recurrent phenomenon. Later, these had to be tied together through military conquest by a strong ruler. However, certain ideational factors that had to do with the idea of political order and the history of settlement changed the context in which these superficially similar lineage societies operated.

The institution of *atabeg*, or regent-ruler, contributed to the tendencies to fragmentation (Findley, 2005:71; Bosworth, 2011:73). This was a particular way of governing by means of using one component of the *amir-a-yan* system to control another. Its literal meaning is 'father of the prince' and it consisted in appointing an amir as a guardian or regent of a prince of the Seljuk dynasty. Any prince set up as a provincial ruler would be tempted to rebel and seize power, either locally or make a bid to rule the entire empire. Naturally, since all members of the Seljuk dynasty possessed the necessary charisma to rule legitimately the prospects of success strengthened the temptation. Hence the sultan appointed an atabeg for a prince in order to control him. Thus, the notion of a collective charisma also enabled ambitious leaders to claim to rule legitimately in the name of a princeling. In some cases a prince could have a succession of different atabegs but we also know of amirs who served a succession of princes as their atabeg (Lambton, 2007: 239–40, 242). However, the institution tended to backfire as ambitious amirs sought the appointment as an atabeg in order not to serve the sultan but to become a de facto ruler of an autonomous principality in the name of the legitimate prince. Indeed, due to the idea of collective charisma it was important for ambitious strongmen to find a weak prince to control. Once an atabeg had established de facto independence he often managed to pass on power over the province to their heirs, effectively creating their own dynasties. This reminds us of how a succession of Carolingian (or Pippinid) major-domos controlled hapless Merovingian kings in whose name and with the help of whose hereditary charisma they ruled, as dealt with in Chapter 3.

The institution of atabeg and the way it was systematically abused gives us important insights into how kinship works as a form of political power. It rarely takes on the strong, even automatic, character that we associate with structures. Instead, it is a resource that can be used either by the person who by means of blood ties officially possesses dynastic legitimacy or by a usurper acting in the name of the legitimate heir. Obviously, the ruthless amirs who became atabegs for their own gain were not awed into submission by the charisma of the Seljuk dynasty but knew that it must be used instrumentally in order to rule legitimately. Furthermore, it is inconceivable that other powerful actors did not see past the façade of an atabeg ruling as a cuckoo in the stead of a *fainéant* Malik. Hence we may conclude that kinship, in the sense that a ruler had to be belong to a certain bloodline, in many cases provided a necessary language for legitimate rule but that this language could be used by other actors. In the case of the many smaller breakaway polities that were founded by opportunistic strongmen within the shell of the late Seljuk Empire the legitimacy of the original line was soon forgotten since many atabegs were able to set up their own dynasties. By contrast, although many historians have derided the later Merovingian kings as mere puppets, the fact that it took so long for the Carolingians to actually make their move and depose them (as well as the fact that they had to both turn to the Pope and secure aristocratic backing for the coup) testifies to a more entrenched reverence for the legitimacy and charisma of the actual ruling house in Frankish culture.

Like all conquest empires that were created by originally nomadic peoples, the Seljuk Empire depended on the support of several other groups. One important group consisted of previous ruling dynasties that administered their provinces on behalf of the Seljuk sultan. The Seljuks sought to control these dynasties by creating ties of marriage with them (Lambton, 2007:236ff). An even more important and more dangerous group consisted of the Türkmen and Ghuzz tribes. They had been crucial in the conquest phase of empire-building but even once the empire had been established tribes were of considerable military importance to the Seljuks. Because of their autonomy, they had to be treated well in order to avoid them defecting to the enemy (Lambton, 2007:229). Because of the military and political importance of the tribes to the stability of this loose edifice and due to the fact that blood ties connected them to the Seljuk dynasty, the Great Vizir Nizam-al-Mulk advised that tribal revolts must be treated leniently (Lambton, 2007:218). The Seljuks' role as Islamic sultans and their use of a slave army – just like the Umayyad and Abbasids – further estranged them from the tribal coalition that brought them to power (Findley, 2005:71; Golden, 2008:366).

The Seljuk Empire was a hybrid between two political traditions: the collective and co-operative culture of the steppe nomads and the Persian autocratic conception of monarchy. The Ghaznavid Empire was also characterized by this tension but opted enthusiastically for rule along the Persian-autocratic lines (Bosworth, 1975:180). This tension had a chronological dimension, originally steppe traditions had been dominant but the Persian ideas of an absolute ruler became increasingly important as time went by and the empire took on a more sedentary character. The tendency towards 'Iranization' of the empire increased tensions and made it more difficult to retain the support of the Türkmen and Ghuzz tribes on whose shoulders the Seljuks had come to power. Nizam-al-Mulk attempted to create stable institutions and a lasting political purpose to the empire by stressing the importance of kinship in the shape of the royal dynasty. He argued that rights to rule were acquired and rested on force – as did the kingship in itself – hence rulers demanded no authorization and that the administration was concentrated in the person of the ruler (Lambton, 2007:211). Interestingly,

Nizam-al-Mulk lamented that the Seljuks did not exploit the possibilities of autocratic rule enough, like the Ghazanids had (Bosworth, 1975).

The adoption of an absolutist conception of kingship led to tensions in the empire and this development in turn has general implications. Attempts to centralize rule in a polycentric society with many centres of power that are autonomous and enjoy autonomous legitimacy lead to conflict and often to the dissolution of an empire. Instead, successful polity formation seems to hinge on developing political forms based on negotiation and shared rule. In early phases of Western polity formation we saw that successful rulers aimed at, and achieved, mechanisms of co-rule with powerful kinship-based groups, for example, the aristocracy, rather than imposing centralized rule upon them. Granted, European rulers did not have to contend with and placate large groups of militarily capable and mobile nomads but any ruler of a polycentric realm that went too far in centralization soon faced a revolt of the barons, as happened on numerous occasions in European history. One could stretch the point further and say that a more negotiated and decentralized form of rule is a prudent form of consolidation of a polycentric empire and it is the way to create the conditions of survival, not of demise. Hence, successful political organizations adapt to the social circumstances in which they develop rather than attempt to break them.

The Mongol Empires

The Mongols created the largest empire in world history. At its zenith it stretched from Hungary in the West to northern China in the East. Under Chinggis Khan (Temüjin) and his successor, the Mongol empire ruled European, Iranian, Turkic, Chinese and Siberian peoples. The empire's rule over Eurasia has even been dubbed a *pax mongolica* (c.1280–1360) that allowed an unprecedented traffic in goods, people and ideas – among them Marco Polo and his brothers (Di Cosmo, 2010). Hardly surprising for a world-conquering organization, it possessed extraordinary military powers.[1] In comparison the European political orders dealt with in previous chapters were small, population-wise and in terms of diversity and geographical reach. Hence the case for

[1] For a Mongol description of military organization see *The Secret History of the Mongols*, 1982:161–3.

including the Mongol empires in a study of how successful political orders related to kinship seems clear. I will ask the same questions as in previous chapters: was there a contradiction between elite kinship – defined as families and as legitimating principles – and the political order? Or were the former intertwined in the latter and, conversely, the latter dependent on the former?

For a long time Mongols were portrayed as the archetype of the savage nomadic tribal people, sweeping across the bad lands to lay waste to settled communities and states, relying on their ferocity and rapacity to do so. In anthropological terms, their social organization was thought to be strictly segmentary, according to the ideal type of the pastoral nomadic/tribal pattern. In a recent work David Sneath has demonstrated that this image is erroneous. In fact, Mongolian society was highly stratified with a strict division between nobility (the 'white bones'), the commoners (the 'black bones') and slaves. It was this aristocratic order that allowed them to produce military power of a quantity and quality that overwhelmed their opponents in Persia, the Middle East, China, Russia and Europe (Sneath, 2007). Mongol society was highly stratified and organized around noble families. Indeed in the Middle Ages the very concept *monggol ulus* did not denote an ethnic group – as it does now – but rather a set of elite families with retainers, dependents and slaves (Sneath, 2007:168, 171, 172). In the Mongol Empire, numerous noble lineages dominated and they organized subservient parts of the population into groups, *ordo*, on the basis of fictive kinship (Sneath, 2007:183–4). Judging from *The Secret History of the Mongols*, the earliest written Mongolian account of the reign of Chinggis Khan, military organization of the Mongol Empire was based on noble families like the Bo'orcu, Muqali, Ilügei, Jürcedei and Alci and their followers.[2] According to the same source, Chinggis Khan chose, or at least wanted to claim, that he chose the commanders of the units from the respective families. Historical texts dealt extensively with the genealogies of noble dynasties, not with the history of the people in any broader sense (Sneath, 2007:103, 171). In sum, society was strongly stratified and noble families were intertwined into the political order.

---

[2] *Secret History of the Mongols*, Chapter IX:164. The list above is not exhaustive. It is only the families named at a certain point in time, for a certain campaign.

Chinggis Khan unified the different Mongolian tribes by being named '*qaghan*' (Chief Khan) in 1206 and began to conquer lands to the West and to the East (Lattimore, 1940; Saunders, 1971; Sneath, 2007). Still, the contemporary *Secret History of the Mongols* describes tough struggles between Chinggis Khan and other contenders.[3] The Mongols swept into Central Asia at a time of disunity and conquered most of Inner Eurasia in the space of a few decades (Golden, 2008:370). What is interesting for the purposes of this book is how hereditary power was organized. It was clear from the beginning that Chinggis Khan and his successors would aim at centralizing their empire, creating offices and military forces directly under the command of a central ruling apparatus. The inspiration came partly from Turkic and, perhaps partly, from Chinese predecessors. They had, however, to contain, harness and combat centrifugal tendencies in the shape of particularistic loyalties and dynastic divisions. The Mongol Empire consisted of a number of different formations, subject peoples, vassals, as well as the Mongol tribes that made up the core of the empire. The basis of Mongol state-craft was the idea that only descendants of Chinggis Khan could bear the title khan, the highest political office (Biran, 2004:358; Findley, 2005:87). The origin of unity of elite families with retainers and subject peoples that underlay the vast Mongol Empire was in part religious: the Mongols believed that the supreme sky god of the steppe, Tengri, was able to confer the right to rule the earth upon a single clan (Biran, 2004:340). Importantly, there was no primogeniture – all sons of the Khan shared charisma and the legitimate successor was the prince who emerged victorious from the succession struggles (Findley, 2005:81, 87). Findley lists features typical of the traditional steppe culture that also characterized Mongol rule: 'The ruler's heavenly mandate, the charismatic ruling clan, bloody succession struggles, dynastic law, the division of the territory among members of the family ... [and] the identification of sovereignty with control of sacred sites' (Findley, 2005:87).

Kinship was both highly important as a source of legitimacy and very flexible in its application. This double nature accounts for the complexity of Mongol succession struggles and for some of the instability of their polities. Among the Mongols three different and contradictory principles of succession existed.

---

[3] *The Secret History of the Mongols*, Chapter IV.

(1) Linear succession in which the title passes from father to son.
(2) Lateral succession in which the title passes between the brothers in a single generation. Only upon the death of the youngest brother does the title pass to the next generation, in which it is transferred from brother to brother within the most senior house (i.e., lineage of the oldest son).
(3) Ultimogeniture, according to which the youngest son inherits his father's estate – that is, the core of the empire that has not been given away as appanages (Barfield, 1989:207–8).

These rules set the parameters of competition for succession, but they did not determine who would win – not least because the principles contradicted each other. In addition, five other practical considerations determined who would become khan:

(1) Regency and the will of the regent.
(2) Who controlled the imperial military forces.
(3) Distance, contenders whose appanages were closer to the imperial centre were usually more interested and the contender who arrived first at the capital upon the death of the old khan usually had an advantage.
(4) Personal standing and reputation.
(5) A khan had to be confirmed by a great assembly, a *quriltai*. If enough nobles decided to withhold their confirmation, then the Khan's standing would be weakened (Barfield, 1989:208–9).

These considerations and the contradictory rules of succession almost guaranteed that civil wars would break out in connection with successions. It should also be noted that succession concerned the 'office' of the great khan, but not of the empire in undivided form. For example, all of Chinggis Khan's sons were given their own lands, or *ulus*.

Chinggis Khan had four sons by Börte, his principal wife: Jochi, Ögedei, Chaghadai and Tolui. While he was alive, the four sons acted as military commanders that fought separate campaigns in the often multi-front wars that the Mongols waged. As always the real challenge for any pre-modern social formation comes with the death of its supreme leader and the challenge is particularly acute if we are talking about a new formation recently unified by a charismatic warlord or prophet (Findley, 2005:79). Initially, the Mongols solved the issue of succession with considerable discipline. Chinggis Khan's four sons became the heads of the four branches, or houses, of the Chinggisid dynasty (Forbes Manz, 2010:135ff). One of them, Ögedei, was named chief khan – Qaghan. The vast empire was divided into four parts, or *ulus*, each ruled by one of the sons. Interestingly although it was Ögedei who conquered Russia, the region fell to his brother Jochi since the latter was the ruler of the North-West. As mentioned above, creating centralized rule was one of the goals of Chinggis and of subsequent Qaghans. This ambition had to be balanced against dynastic concerns and those of the tribal/ethnic confederation. The solution in the first generation was to have representatives of the four houses of the dynasty accompany the Qaghan's officials (Forbes Manz, 2010:136) and represented in the campaigning armies. Finally, the territorial division of the empire into four ulus was not exclusive since armies from the four houses would be stationed in each ulus. Representatives from the different houses were also present in the others' ulus (Forbes Manz, 2010:139).

The system of overlapping and co-habiting rule did not prevent conflict and rivalry, which soon broke out between different houses. Ögedei died in 1246 and after a brief regency his son, Güyüg, took the throne. During Güyüg's brief two-year reign he attempted to curb the powers of the other Chinggisid houses. When he died the struggle for succession became more complex. Jochi's son Batu, who was now the ruler of the Golden Horde in Russia, supported Möngke, one of the sons of Chinggis Khan's youngest son, Tolui (Barfield, 1989:210–17). Möngke attacked the houses of Chagatai and Ögödei (Chinggis Khan's middle sons). Search parties hunted down and killed hundreds of commanders and nobles (Christian, 2018:18). The empire attacked and conquered southern China, Persia and Mesopotamia. However, the Mongol Empire was strongly dependent on its leader. When Möngke Khan died in 1259, unified Mongol rule came to an end (Forbes Manz, 2010:144). From 1260, the unified empire broke up and a number of successor polities to the unified empire were established: the Golden Horde in today's Russia and the Ukraine; the Ilkhanate in Anatolia, the Middle East and Iran; the Chagatai khanate in Central Asia and the Mongol Empire in China – the Yuan dynasty.

The successor states fell apart in the space of a century. The Golden Horde was the most long-lived but it too fragmented in the middle of the fourteenth century. David Christian lists a number of explanations: Ottoman seizure of Gallipoli closed an important trade route by sea; the collapse of the Yuan Empire in 1368 reduced trade along the Silk Road and new trade routes bypassed the Golden Horde; Timur Lenk's campaigns ruined many of its cities; and finally in the 1350s, the Black Death struck (Christian, 2018:53). Just like the unified Mongol Empire, the Golden Horde fragmented into smaller polities, or ulus. Although the political order fragmented rapidly, the Chinggisid lineage retained its hold on legitimate rule. But legitimacy did not mean effective control or embedding in a political framework. In a parallel to the atabeg phenomenon, different strongmen seized power and claimed to rule as regents of a Chinggisid prince. Examples of this kind of strongman include Emir Mamaq and Timur Lenk himself. The latter never declared himself khan, because that title was reserved for Chinggisid descendants. Instead he ruled as emir, that is, military commander and kept Chinggisid figureheads (Findlay, 2005:101; Christian, 2018:53–9). Neither Mamaq nor Timur Lenk managed to build lasting empires or dynasties. Although Timur Lenk's career as an empire-builder was spectacular, at his death in 1405 the realm fell apart into smaller units that none of his successors managed to reunite.

The careers of Mamaq and Timur Lenk as well as the previously analysed atabegs invite world-historical comparisons. It is not a unique occurrence that strongmen seize power and rule in the name of a hallowed figurehead from another dynasty while effectively establishing their own. In Europe, the Pippinid (later called Carolingian) dynasty ruled as majordomos (masters of the palace) with the last Merovingian kings as puppets. Similarly, in Japan rule by shoguns (i.e., military commanders) that established their own dynasties but retained the powerless emperor as a figurehead was the norm between the twelfth and mid-nineteenth centuries. The imperial family of Japan retained a kind of monopoly of legitimation of power, but the Kamakura, Ashikaga and Tokugawa families – who established shogunates in succession – monopolized de facto power and retained loyalty with legitimacy, patronage and coercion (Totman, 1981). Particularly the last shogunate, the Tokugawa, was able to rule a peaceful and stable country without challengers. In other words, the shogunate dynasties resembled European dynasties with the exception that they nominally ruled on behalf of someone else. Now, the counterfactual question arises – why were central Asian rulers unable to establish durable 'shogunates'? Instead, factional strife often within the Chingissid family network, but also led by outsiders (like Mamaq and Timur Lenk), tore apart the hastily assembled polities. The descendants of Timur Lenk also claimed to possess hereditary charisma. Both Chinggisid khans and Timurid *mirzads* proliferated from the fifteenth century, with no clear precedence. As Findlay puts it, 'One khan's or amir's [i.e., descendant of Amir Timur] inherited claims to rule were as good as any other's' (Findlay, 2005:105). Thus, the pendulum swung from macro-polities to micro-polities; leading to a fragmentation of Inner Asia that lasted until the Russian and Chinese empires began to partition the steppe from the late seventeenth century onwards.

David Sneath notes that Chinggisid families were very long-lived indeed and its members ruled, in various constellations, Inner Asian polities until the nineteenth century (Sneath, 2007:167; McCheseney, 2011:239–65). So, we face something of a puzzle as Central and Inner Asian elite families were long-lived, but the polities were not. There are several economic, material and military explanations for this instability. The polities were in general tribute-taking empires that combined highly diverse settings, environments and economic systems (Christian, 2018). Most of them were initially vast and it is unrealistic to expect an empire of the size of even the successors to the unified Mongol empire to last very long. Their history also provides an interesting challenge to Charles Tilly's 'warfare thesis' that has been so influential in state formation studies as military competition in this part of the world seems to have been too intense to set off the alleged virtuous circle of war, taxation and institution building (Kaspersen, Strandsbjerg and Teschke, 2017). But perhaps the reasons for the development of political order actually lie elsewhere than in economic relations and military affairs, which most probably was the case in Europe? I argued in Chapter 6 that the contingent effects of war make long-term historical theorizing very difficult and that assessment naturally applies to this part of the world too. We do not know if the Seljuk sultanate of Rûm would have been able to survive if the Mongols had not conquered it in 1240. Therefore, any judgement on their institutions must be made with significant nuance. Still, some institutional traits and trajectories are visible both in the Seljuk and in the Mongol case. An easy way of explaining their fragmentation could be to point to the lack of institutions, for example in the shape of regular and formalized councils. However, irregular councils, *quriltai*, existed in the Mongol Empire and administrative institutions, like the *divan*, in the Seljuk Empire. But that explanation would carry more than a whiff of the *post hoc, propter hoc* fallacy and run the risk of projecting later European or Persian institutions on to a setting that did not exist.

Another, perhaps fairer, approach would be to scrutinize the institutions that did exist, namely the shape of royal kinship and ideas of rule. Doing so means an opportunity to engage in comparative analysis of Turkic-Mongol and European conditions. It is clear that the polities in question did not have the same firm conceptions of the abstract entity of the realm that supported European political orders and commanded the loyalty of their elites. A partial explanation may lie in their nature as hastily constructed conquest polities. Instead of effectively embedding elite families, 'exit' was a constant possibility, to use Hirschmann's terms (Hirschmann, 2004). Differences in land use between Europe and Inner Asia also mattered. In Europe, proprietary rights centred on land, while in Mongol areas they centred on peoples. In the former, lands were part of dowries, in the latter people were (Sneath, 2007:175). The nature of royal legitimacy influenced the course of events. The doctrine of collective sovereignty made challenges to the throne possible and legitimate to an extent that they were not after, say, the year 1000 in Europe. However, the fragmentation of Turkic-Mongol polities cannot be explained by mere reference to abstract kinship structures.

Instead, we must take a comparative look at the figuration of rulers, elite families and realms. The rigidity of kinship in theory and flexibility in practice enabled the Turkic institution of atabeg and the Mongol practice of ruling through Chinggisid puppets. In European history, there were many regency governments that ruled when kings were still children but very few regents seized actual power in the sense that Timur Lenk did. Not that there was any shortage of capable and ruthless strongmen in Europe. What seems to have existed in Europe but not in Inner Asia was genuine reverence for kings, that is, for kingship, and for royal dynasties, that is for the idea of royal dynasties. Furthermore, Inner Asia did not have the same kind of material and symbolic dependence of elite families on kings – and vice versa. Nor did Inner Asian aristocracies depend on the idea of a realm with its associations of public power in the same way that their European counterparts did. Perhaps the concept of dependence cannot account for loyalty. In Chapter 3, I argued that elite families seem to have held genuine loyalty to the idea of Francia and this loyalty – not merely dependence – enabled and obliged them to support the political order during the turbulent tenth century. It is impossible to draw causal, let alone measurable, inferences in this regard but perhaps the considerable degree of co-rule and involvement in the business of rule (however low the degree of regularity) that European elites evidently felt entitled to and exercised assisted in this embedding and greater degree of loyalty to the political order. In Europe, there was a strong norm against usurpation and *lèse-majesté*, which meant that rulers often, but not always, banded together in solidarity against illegitimate rulers. For example, Sweden's Vasa dynasty felt the brunt of the dislike of usurpers in the early seventeenth century, well after a century after coming to power. According to Erik Ringmar, the disregard they faced was even a reason for entering into the Thirty Years' War (Ringmar, 2008). The brief study of this chapter and the sources to which I have access have not been able to prove the lack of a norm against usurpation among Turkic-Mongol elites. Nevertheless, there was an evident tendency among the latter to break away from the larger entities, perhaps established a generation before, and go at it alone or as part of a new and opportunist coalition. In sum, when comparing the European and Turkic-Mongol polities, the characteristics of the former – in the field of how elite kinship 'worked' – clearly appear. This comparison also sets the old notion of a dynamic Europe versus a static Asia on its head. European polities, for all their infighting and turbulence, appear far more stable and conservative in their operations than the dynamic, fluid and inventive Inner Asia.

Conclusions

Despite their success in assembling large confederations of allied groups, the leaders of Turkic peoples often experienced difficulties in creating stable long-term rule. In part these problems can be traced to kinship-based formations. First, the royal dynasty was both the centre of the polity and a major source of instability. According to Turkic and Mongol tradition charisma and thereby the potential to claim legitimate rule was evenly distributed among the members of the ruling house. While this was an asset in the sense that the family network was not as susceptible to die out due to natural causes it proved time and again to be a liability in relation to the viability of the polities that they built. All members of the royal house had equal claims to the throne and most peoples had difficulties in finding stable orders of succession that would not divide the empire into rival principalities. Second, once they faced the task of consolidation into a sedentary empire, the polities that we have considered in this section all had difficulties in retaining the support of the nomadic and clan-based formations upon which their power rested. Third, despite the best efforts of statesmen such as Nizam al-Mulk there was little interest or capacity to create an institutional structure that could embed either the royal family or the clans that were crucial components of the conquest formation. Thus the very factors that were assets in rapidly assembling large but loose confederations, for example, the legitimacy of a royal line and the propensity of large and powerful groups to reconfigure and join a new leader that either promised legitimate leadership and/or the spoils of war, undermined the stability of the early Turkic empires. In comparison with our other cases Turko-Mongol royal lines were exceptionally strong and legitimate in themselves. In Europe, we see how the country, the realm, over which a dynasty ruled, became an entity in itself that transcended the existence of the royal house and was equally or more important in gathering the loyalty of social groups, including aristocratic dynasties.

Fourth, we must add geopolitics to these three endogenous factors. The Middle East and Central Asia were more unstable than Europe because these regions were more exposed to new invasions from the steppes, lacked defensible natural frontiers and because of the military supremacy of mobile nomadic formations until the invention of gunpowder weapons. Even in the military sphere, then, the socio-cultural factors that enabled rapid empire building and conquest worked against long-term stability. The tendency of several dynasties to employ armies of slave soldiers and to create vassal relations that, over time, alienated them from their erstwhile Inner Asian tribal base is also often cited as a reason why their rule fragmented within the space of several generations after conquest. However, the empires founded by steppe peoples did not disintegrate only because of the external pressure of new waves of migrations and conquerors. They also suffered from inherent structural weaknesses rooted in the cultural systems for the transmission of royal charisma and the egalitarian orders of succession as well as the lack of a conception of the political order as an abstract entity that could embed the elite families. There is, however, a highly successful exception to this line of development that forces us to refine the argument: the Ottoman Empire, which is dealt with in Chapter 9.

9 THE UBIQUITOUS AND OPAQUE ELITES OF THE OTTOMAN EMPIRE *C.*1300–*C.*1830

Introduction

The Ottoman Empire is the most long-lived Islamic polity in world history. It is of particular interest to understanding if kinship is incompatible with or in fact central to stable political order. A long tradition in Western political and social thought argues that the Ottoman Empire terminated hereditary elite groups and established an impersonal despotic state in which all subjects, from the most exulted vizir to the most humble Anatolian peasant, were slaves of the sultan. This is also the image given by Ottoman political theory. Since the Renaissance Western social and political thought has tended to cast the Ottoman Empire as the radical 'other' of European realms. The efficiency and seemingly absolute rule of the sultans were originally the envy of European observers. To them, the Ottoman Empire differed from Europe where hereditary lords were essential and without whose support kings were powerless (Machiavelli, 1993:30–1; Çirakman, 2002:62ff; Bisaha, 2004). Later, the image of the Ottomans shifted. In the nineteenth century the weakened Empire was often portrayed as the 'sick man of Europe'. The two images of strength and decline, respectively, are sometimes combined to create a narrative of two phases of Ottoman development, one of expansion and one of entrenchment and decline. Recently, Ottomanists have questioned this narrative and instead argue that the latter phase was one of imperial readjustment.

The question of what role aristocratic elites played in the Ottoman Empire has dogged European observers since the sixteenth century. 'Patrimonialism' is a standard lens through which the Ottoman Empire is described both by historical and sociological scholarship; sometimes the hybrid patrimonial-bureaucratic form is used (Dale, 2010; Blake, 2011). By contrasting patrimonialism/sultanism with estate-type domination as two kinds of legitimate domination, Max Weber made an implicit contrast between the Ottoman Empire and European societies. The idea of 'sultanism' has been influential in Ottoman studies. Hilal Inalcik adopted Weber's ideal type as a heuristic figure in many of his works (Toumarkine, 2014). On this basis the Ottoman Empire has often been described as a strong state ruling despotically over a weak civil society (Mardin, 1973; Toumarkine, 2014:45). This reading emphasizes that the Ottomans, like the Mamluks of Egypt, created non-hereditary elites that were slaves of the sultan – and in Gellner's evocative terminology, geldings – as well as the idea that a relatively meritocratic system prevailed (Gellner, 1981). Gellner argues that Ibn Khaldûn's analysis of the perennial conflict between tribes and states holds true also for the Ottoman Empire but that the Ottomans managed to solve the opposition by recruiting slave soldiers and slave elites (Gellner, 1981:73, 85). Thus the Ottoman Empire could be invoked as yet another example of the conflict between kinship as an organizational principle. Hence, the sophistication and longevity of the Ottoman Empire might suggest that curtailing kinship is a formula for successful polity formation. However, I will argue otherwise.

Ottomanists increasingly see the central system of political institutions and elite groups as more polycentric than the schematic descriptions of earlier generations of scholars and observers (e.g., Barkey, 2008). In fact, the empire would not have functioned without its numerous kinship-based elites. Astute handling of such elites was a crucial factor behind Ottoman success. In theory there were a number of groups who owed their position only to the sultan. However, kinship networks played a large part in the formation of such groups and their positions were often inherited in practice. During the phase of imperial expansion, c.1300 to c.1600, the Ottomans employed aristocratic kinship groups in the civil and military administration and married into princely families in order to control them. In the period of consolidation, *c.*1600 to *c.*1800, we see the emergence of important civil service aristocracies, the *ulama*.

Kinship was also a constitutive principle at the core of the empire: the Ottoman dynasty was the element of cohesion through six centuries and an important part of the empire's raison d'être. Important innovations regarding 'biopolitics' – the order of succession, reproduction and the politics of the dynasty – enabled the Ottomans to break with the oscillation between micro- and macro polity typical of the Turkic peoples and establish a stable political order. The centrality of the dynasty and its structure to the empire is also attested by the fact that its structural features were strongly constitutive of the form that internal conflicts took.

Analysing kinship-based elites gives us new perspective on the Empire's origins and survival. Classic research attempted to explain its emergence as a result of a band of 'holy warriors' (*ghazi*), or through its spectacular success and sophistication in war (Wittek, 1971; Lowry, 2003; Rahimi, 2004). Wittek's '*ghazi* thesis' remains influential but it has largely become discredited among Ottomanists (Lowy, 2003:1–3). Although the martial acumen of its early sultans and their considerable military organizational skills are undeniable, they are insufficient for explaining the formation and cohesion of the empire. Instead, I believe that an important part of the answer to the question why the Ottoman Empire, out of a group of similar principalities (beyliks), lasted for many centuries is the astute management of the many different kinds of elites, both hereditary and non-hereditary (Lowry, 2003; Barkey, 2008:28–66).

Instead of using the Ottoman Empire as a contrast, or an 'other', to European realms either to explain its strengths or to teleologically explain its 'inevitable' decline, I will emphasize similarities as well as differences and highlight that it represents a path to political stability of its own. A major contrast with European realms was the lack of integration and public arenas in which elites could meet and integrate. Because of this lack of institutions that could embed elites and of semantics that could legitimate the de facto existence of hereditary, aristocratic elites and their mutual dependence on the 'Sublime Porte', the Empire had an in-built weakness.[1] For centuries, the empire managed despite embedding institutions and legitimating semantics but when

---

[1] In the following, whenever I am discussing the central government of the Ottoman Empire, I will use Ottoman terminology and refer to it as the Sublime Porte or simply the Porte.

European powers began to pressure it in the nineteenth century it eventually deteriorated. In the context of this book, the Ottoman Empire stands between the Arab and Turkic formations that did not establish stable relations with hereditary elites and the European formations that managed to do so. However, the Ottoman Empire never managed, or perhaps intended, to create durable institutions.

This chapter asks two questions: (1) What role did kinship as a principle of order play in the political order? (2) Was the relation of kinship-based elites to the political order principally conflictual or co-operative? Having answered these questions, I will apply the conceptual apparatus presented in the introduction to the Ottoman case in order to allow a historical-sociological comparison. This apparatus deals with bio-political practices, institutions, semantics (categories), kinship types and the structure of the elite polity.

I will answer these questions more fully in the conclusions. Briefly put, it is plain that even in the Ottoman Empire, kinship was intertwined with the political order. This means that any stark dichotomy between polities based on kinship elites and those based on meritocratic ones needs to be called into question. However, many elites operated informally and they did not have uniform and legally regulated relations with the imperial centre. The conscious manipulation by many kinds of rulers of hereditary elites and their employment in the administration means that we cannot draw sharp lines between 'kinship societies' and 'states'. The chapter proceeds in the following way: first I provide a brief overview of the empire's history, then I discuss the sultanic dynasty, after that I analyse elites in the Ottoman central administration and military, then I analyse the provincial elites. Thereafter I compare the Ottoman and European political orders and finally I summarize the chapter. It is not the purpose of this chapter to analyse reasons for the Ottoman decline and its eventual dissolution in 1920. Rather it is to outline its features and history in relation to the topics of this book.

A Brief History of Empire

The implosion of the Seljuk Empire of Rûm in the early fourteenth century left Anatolia with a number of unstable and weak principalities. Nomadic raiders and entrepreneurial state-builders and castellans interacted and fought with each other, the Byzantine Empire and with the numerous Latin polities in today's Greece. The founder of the empire, Osman, deftly made alliances and outmanoeuvred his competitors. The Ottomans expanded into the Balkans, territories that were to become a springboard for the project of gradually dominating and then absorbing the Anatolian principalities. The fledgling empire was almost destroyed in the early fifteenth century by Timur Lenk. At the battle of Ankara in 1405 he reduced the Ottomans to vassals (Imber, 2009:16–17). Timur Lenk, however, did not establish a durable empire in Anatolia and in the coming decades the major threat to the House of Osman was internal as civil war raged between the brothers of the sultan. Eventually Sultan Mehmet I (r.1413–21) managed to defeat his brothers and to re-consolidate the possessions and re-centre networks of the dynasty (Imber, 2009:19). In 1453 the Ottomans captured Constantinople and extinguished the Byzantine Empire. This period saw a circulation of aristocracies as the Turkmen warrior aristocracies were suppressed and the Balkan (Christian) and Byzantine were promoted.

Territorial expansion characterized the fifteenth and sixteenth centuries. The Ottomans conquered the Balkans, including Hungary, but failed to take Vienna in 1526. The Balkans south of the Danube were organized into the Sanjak of Rumelia and ruled directly but north of the river (excepting Hungary) the Ottomans established vassal relations with the Christian principalities Moldavia and Wallachia (Stavrianos, 2000). The empire also expanded southwards. In 1510 the Ottomans conquered Syria, what is today Iraq, Egypt and Libya. Doing so caused changed cultural and political orientation of the empire. The conquest brought large numbers of Arabs into the empire, and the empire's identity changed from a syncretistic Turkish and Christian empire into an Islamic one (Barkey, 2005). The conquest of the Middle East brought large numbers of intellectuals and administrators educated in the classic Islamic tradition, the ulama, to the empire. These groups became important in the administration of the empire and were soon a considerable social and political force.

Conventionally, the eighteenth century was seen as heralding the empire's long decline. Although the Ottomans came close to conquering Vienna in 1683, it is true that after the age of Süleiman the Magnificent (r.1520–66) territorial expansion petered out. The Holy Alliance re-conquered Hungary between 1683 and 1699. Still, Ottomanists point to the continued military acumen of the

Ottomans, improvements in the quality of the civil service and to the fact that 'declinists' tend to project nineteenth-century conditions too far back in time (Barkey, 2008). Certainly from the seventeenth century the Sublime Porte devolved considerable authority to local rulers in the Middle East and embarked on a strategy of negotiation with other groups (Barkey, 2008), on that is now regarded as a re-organization of the empire. However, given that the Ottoman Empire was built as a series of networks of negotiated relations in which local actors had considerable and variable power it can be questioned whether the seventeenth-century reforms were such a clear break with the past.

During this time the empire became more decentralized. First, the relative weight of the central institutions shifted. The Janissary corps and the scholars, the ulama, became more powerful and were thus able to balance the power of the sultan. The Janissary corps intervened actively in politics. On several occasions they deposed incompetent sultans and once deposition turned into regicide as Osman II was executed. Second, the relations between the central government, the Sublime Porte, and the provinces changed. In previous centuries, the centre had ruled more directly, but now the relationship between pro-vincial notables and amirs assumed more of a negotiated character (Tezcan, 2009).

In the eighteenth century, the Porte began modernizing and centralizing the Empire. Thus: '[t]he long-lasting internal peace and social consensus achieved with the recognition of the socio-economic and political privileges of the provincial notables as well as the Janissary corps became a distant memory' (Tezcan, 2011:78). Centralization took place by eradicating or replacing the rival and balancing centres of power. First Sultan Mahmud II (r.1808–39) began to support the ulama to weaken the influence of the Janissaries. In 1826 he destroyed the Janissary Corps. The next stage was to rein in the power of the provincial notables in Anatolia and the Arab lands, in some cases by defeating them militarily. By doing so the Porte had not just defeated rival power centres but also destroyed the actors who enjoyed local legitimacy and who were able to act as intermediaries between the central power and the local societies. Centralization and modernization also proceeded through the creation of new institutions. In place of the Janissaries a Western-style army was created (Quataert, 2000:63).

In the 1820s the semi-independent ruler of Egypt and Greek nationalists revolted against Istanbul. After British, French and Russians intervention Greece was declared an independent state in 1830 (Dakin, 1973; Finnemore, 2003). The 1830s saw the beginning of a comprehensive programme of reform of the empire, the Tanzimat, the success of which depended on foreign investments, and placed the Empire's economy in the hands of British and French banks. From the 1860s, the Balkans drifted gradually to complete independence. Bulgaria, Montenegro, Rumania and Serbia all became sovereign states in 1878 (Jelavich, 1963; Haldén, 2013b). In 1914 the Ottoman Empire entered World War One on the side of Austria-Hungary and Germany. Despite some scattered successes, the empire was destroyed by the war and dismembered in 1920 (Fromkin, 2000).

The Sultanic Dynasty: The House of Osman

Lindholm explains the robustness of Turkic polities with the particularly hierarchical organization of kinship relations (Lindholm, 1986). This thesis, however, gives us little headway with the puzzle why the Ottomans and not some other Turkic beylik – for example the powerful Karaman dynasty in the south – established first hegemony and then empire. The structural explanation also runs into difficulties with the empirical evidence of the tendency of Turkic polities to disintegrate due to the egalitarian and performance-oriented forms of succession among the ruling family. In contrast, the Ottoman dynasty was extremely stable; it survived in unbroken form for six and a half centuries. By Arabic, European and Turkic standards this is a singular achievement. We will now proceed to investigate how this was brought about.

The Ottomans pursued marriage strategies in their relations with the weakened Byzantine Empire as well as with the other Turkish principalities of Anatolia. The Ottomans had many kinds of relations with Byzantium, they were on different occasions kingmakers, allies, parasites and rivals (Fleet, 2010). Ottoman marriage strategies included sultans marrying the daughters of other principalities as well as marrying off their sons and daughters to other rulers (Fleet, 2010:316). These marriages with other dynasties, both Muslim and Christian, were purely political liaisons. Since Sultan Murad I (1362–89), sultans did not reproduce with their spouses but only with the slave concubines of the harem (Imber, 2009:80, 92–3; Fleet, 2010:316). Originally, Ottoman marriage alliances had been conducted with equals, but during the reign of Murad I, they became means to transform the dynasty that married their daughters to the Ottomans into a vassal power or to acquire their territory (Imber, 2009:93). During the interregnum, Ottoman princes conducted marriage alliances that were designed not to benefit the dynasty as a whole but to give them advantages over their brothers (Imber, 2009:94). Thus, marriages as much as diplomacy and conquest explain the rise of the Ottomans from one of many small principalities in Anatolia to being the only empire (Fleet, 2010).

When the Ottomans conquered Constantinople their self-image as well as their political strategies changed. Now that they were truly the heirs of the Byzantine Empire, Islamic caliphs and Turkish sultans, the Ottoman rulers perceived themselves not as one of many dynasties in the world but as the supreme dynasty. This self-image generated consequences for biopolitics and for the political order as a whole. No other dynasty in the world could be their equal and thus be worthy of marrying Ottoman princes, princesses or sultans. As a consequence, sultans ceased marrying altogether. Reproduction, as before, was conducted with concubines (Blake, 2011). Before the mid-fifteenth century, the Ottomans married off princesses into foreign dynasties but later they were married into the leading Ottoman families (Imber, 2009:95ff). According to Islamic law only males could inherit the throne, which meant that there was a substantial pressure on sultans and princes to produce male heirs. It also meant that the Ottoman Empire had no official queens (Imber, 2009:88). Islamic law does not require women to bring a dowry, but women of the imperial household could, however, exercise considerable political influence unofficially (Peirce, 1993). Particularly in the sixteenth and seventeenth centuries, queen mothers were very powerful (Imber, 2009:90–1).

In accordance with Turko-Mongol notions about political order, the legitimacy of the dynasty was never questioned. The deepest source of legitimacy of the dynasty was its descent from its first ruler, Osman. The House of Osman was not a dynasty marked by stable agnatic succession or by primogeniture as in the European monarchies. The Ottomans conformed to the Turkic-Mongol tradition that sovereignty is vested in the ruling family as a collective. Consequently, all males in the dynasty were considered eligible to inherit the title of sultan and none had precedence over the other. Furthermore, the territory of the dynasty was considered absolutely indivisible: it could not be partitioned among the rival brothers (Barkey, 2008:98, 100). Thus, although the dynasty itself was stable, there was considerable turbulence within it. Like most Turko-Mongol polities, succession to the throne of the Ottomans was of a father-son type. With some notable exceptions, it was Ottoman custom to limit the number of sons to one concubine, which meant that, as a rule, all princes had different mothers. They were raised separately and around the age of eleven sent to one of the provinces to gain political training and in time assume governorship and build a base for their future contest for the throne (Barkey, 2008:92).

Every succession between 1362 and 1574 was marked by executions of rival claimants or by violent challenges to succession. In the fourteenth century, the Ottomans followed the main Turko-Mongol cultural pattern of institutionalized civil war among the sons of the old sultan in order to decide who was the strongest, ablest and most legitimate ruler. Violent succession struggles weakened the polity and allowed external enemies to exploit the chaos but bestowed a form of charismatic legitimation upon the victor. Mehmet the Conqueror (r.1444–6 and r.1451–81) put an end to the institutionalized wars of succession by making it lawful for the Sultan to execute his brothers. As his law code stated: 'For the welfare of the state, the one of my sons to whom God grants the sultanate may lawfully put his brothers to death. A majority of the *ulema* consider this permissible' (quoted in Blake, 2011:220). However, the actual practice of institutionalized fratricide only lasted half a century. It was unpopular with the public as many were understandably unnerved by seeing small caskets being carried out of the imperial palace. Killing many potential legitimate rulers also entailed risks of the dynasty's extinction. From the seventeenth century onwards, fratricide only took place when there was a real risk of a coup by a brother of the sultan (Peirce, 1993:101–3; Imber, 2009:108). Instead of killing his siblings, it became customary to imprison them in the harem, shielding them off from the world. This way, eligible heirs could be kept in reserve without the fear of rebellion. An undesirable side-effect of this practice was that sultans often came to the throne wholly unprepared, having had no experience of ruling. From the time of Osman I only the eldest son served as a governor in the provinces (Imber, 2009:108). In the second half of the sixteenth century the principle of succession shifted from father-son to a practice of seniority, the eldest male of the dynasty succeeded to the throne, sometimes the brother of the sultan, sometimes nephews and once a cousin (Peirce, 1993:99–101).

The empire survived this period and the primacy of the ruling house was never questioned. The shift from a father-son pattern to the pattern where the eldest male of the royal house inherited the throne might tempt one to conclude that the Ottomans solved the tension between kinship and the state, to the benefit of the latter. This conclusion might be particularly appealing when the decline of older Turko-Mongol forms of succession is placed alongside the strength and sophistication of the centralized 'state' apparatus of the Ottoman Empire and the 'neutering' of the old warrior aristocracy in favour of an army and administration dominated by slaves. Such a conclusion would, however, return us to binary categories and the heritage of nineteenth-century anthropology and political science. It also obscures a number of significant aspects of the later Ottoman Empire.

The strategy of abandoning legal marriage for the sultans and instead choosing to reproduce with concubines seems like a genial solution to the problems and vagaries of dynastic politics. One obvious benefit was genetic, given that the pool of available women was far larger than that of marriageable princesses available to a European prince and the risks of inbreeding with its attendant risks of sterility, madness or birth defects were much smaller. A second benefit was that the closure of the dynasty to other dynasties, either of inferior or equal rank, protected its patrimony from dissolution through inheritance. This was also a concern when Ottoman princesses were married off, hence their husbands had a clearly marginal status in the imperial household (Bouquet, 2015:329). This closure from other dynasties in particular shielded the empire from foreign powers and connections. Maybe one could conclude that making the House of Osman a closed system in terms of political marriage (but not biological reproduction) contributed to its longevity. However, closure was not without its drawbacks. It meant that the dynasty could not connect other important power groups to it. We will now take a closer look at such groups.

Meritocratic and Aristocratic Elites in the Imperial Centre

The Ottoman Empire was not one single unit (Brett, 2010; Faroqhi, 2010:366–410; Fuess, 2010:620; Masters, 2010:425–6), like many empires it consisted of many autonomous units with different kinds of government, capabilities and relations to the Ottoman government, called the Sublime Porte or 'the Porte' (Inalcik, 1954:103–29; Stavrianos, 1958:101–3; Motyl, 1999:124; Quataert, 2000:25–7, 31–4). Although it was the most centralized and bureaucratic of the three great post-Timurid empires (the Ottoman, the Safavid and the Mughals), it never attempted to create a unified state. Instead, 'extensive territories remained in the control of nomadic tribes and local rulers' (Lapidus, 2012:437). Brett argues that originally, the Ottomans tried to unite the composite of provinces, domains, vassals and subordinate peoples by means of dynastic marriages, which had the effect of tying elites to the sultan but not to each other (Barkey, 2005:93; Brett, 2010:563). In contrast, Todorova emphasizes that integration was not the political purpose of the Ottoman Empire (Todorova, 1997:45–7). In such a diverse and cosmopolitan setting management of people was important to imperial affairs, in particular with respect to the elites.

Before analysing elite recruitment, let us consider Ottoman ideas of social order. Findley identifies two opposing and contradictory organizational principles, an egalitarian principle and a stratified one. He argues that Middle Eastern polities in general (and the Ottoman Empire was no exception) oscillated between these two principles. The egalitarian principle was materialized in the idea that all inhabitants were the subjects or slaves of the sultan and as such potentially equal in the face of the absolute ruler. The notion of equality in this scheme was, however, compromised by the bi-partite division of society into (a) a ruling class that was considered the slaves of the sultan and (b) a subject class (*reaya*), that was his flock (Findley, 1989:41ff). As we saw in Chapter 8, earlier Turkic and Mongol societies were also characterized by a bi-partitite division of society into rulers and ruled. Despite the idea that everyone was equal as the slaves of the sultan, Ottoman society was strictly stratified in terms of classes. Upward mobility, for example from the ranks of the taxpaying subject (*raya*) to the elite, was theoretically frowned upon but in principle possible in times of crisis (Faroqhi, 1997:549). The Ottoman ruling class was stratified according functional differentiation into four parts: (1) the imperial class (*mülkiye*), in charge of governing the empire; (2) the military class (*seyfiye*), in charge of defending and expanding the empire; (3) the administrative class (*qalemiye*); and (4) the religious class (*diniye*) in charge of Ottoman religious law and local administration

(Shaw, 1963:59). Traditional 'kinship or household networks and the religious communities or other groupings that existed among the subject classes were supposed to be excluded from the exercise of political power by definition, since they were excluded from the ruling "class"' (Findley, 1989:42).

In contrast to this system imposed from above, which inspired Wittfogel to see the Ottomans as a precursor of modern totalitarianism, we find a tendency to organize society according to forms of stratification and groups belonging outside of the theoretical framework and control of the government (Wittfogel, 1957). This tendency has been summed up by the term *ayan* system, which was a kind of social self-organization from the bottom up in contrast to the imposed top-down state organization of society. Ayan means 'notable' and periods that were characterized by social self-organization were marked by the dominance of local notables who based their power upon 'kinship solidarity, wealth ... the important social positions attainable through advanced religious education, or the ability to wield armed force' (Findley, 1989:43, 2005:69). Many of these ayan exercised power as local judges (*kadi*) or as military commanders (amirs). As we shall see below, the rule of ayans was more prominent in the provinces where autonomous local dynasties existed.

Unlike European realms, the Ottoman Empire did not have hereditary nobility and no corporate noble estate (Faroqhi, 1997:550). Nevertheless the Empire contained numerous hereditary elite groups. The status of some of these groups was partly or wholly hereditary and some of them resembled the warrior aristocracies of Europe in their origins, habitus and functions. Other groups were quite different in terms of the origins of their status, what their status consisted of and their relation to the sultan. However, a common denominator of all elite groups was that their relation to the organizational and ideational centre of the empire was different than that of their European counterparts. As a result the political order became differently configured.

In the fourteenth and early fifteenth centuries, Turkoman warrior elites that were organized as dynasties played an important role for warfare and politics (Rahimi, 2004). Turkic society in Anatolia appears to have been organized in a stratified way with warrior 'noble' families on different levels. Some families were allies and followers of the early Ottoman sultans, others were princes (*beys*) in their own right and possessed rival principalities. This society contained many different peoples and creeds (Barkey, 2005:59). One of the principal advantages of the Ottomans over their rivals seems to have been their skill in making connections, through marriage and alliances, with many different actors, including Christians, to create a syncretistic polity. The latter group included hereditary war leaders.

In the early Ottoman Empire, the old Turkic aristocracy, members of the ruling families of the beyliks of Anatolia, were very important. They played significant military roles in conquering the Balkans. The Porte wanted to secure their loyalty by incorporating them in the system. To do this, aristocratic families were given lands in the Balkans. In the fourteenth and early fifteenth century they had become dominant in the empire and the Ottoman sultans sought to diminish their power (Shaw, 1963:64). These efforts continued in the decades after the conquest of Constantinople as a succession of sultans attempted to centralize the empire. The Porte turned against the old landed Turkoman warrior nobility and systematically sought to curtail its power and influence. Since they possessed military power and legitimacy in the localities over which they ruled, they posed a threat to the Ottomans. Interestingly, they found it much harder to accept the ascendancy of the Ottomans and the creation of an empire than the conquered Byzantine and Balkan families did (Barkey, 2005:87). A key element in the strategy of curtailing the power of the old elite was to seize the lands of the Turkic noble families and turn them into prebends (*timars*). Naturally, the process met with resistance, often violent.

New elite groups were pragmatically brought in to service the growing empire. These attempts resulted in a circulation of elites. To replace the old families, men of low rank and members of the old Byzantine and Balkan ruling families and aristocracies rose to high positions in the military and civilian administration (Barkey, 2005:75–80). With the exception of Serbia, whose aristocracy was wiped out during the Ottoman conquest, Balkan rulers and aristocrats readily accepted at first Ottoman suzerainty and then an active role in the Empire as *sipahi* cavalry (Jelavich and Jelavich, 1977:247; Minkov, 2004:98ff). Heath W. Lowry demonstrated that during the first centuries after the conquest of the Balkans, members of Christian aristocratic and princely families had few problems rising in the ranks of the Ottoman civil and military administration, even to the highest offices such as admiral, beys of provinces or even *beylerbey* (chief of the beys) over entire regions, like Rumelia or Grand Vizir (Prime Minister/

Chancellor) (Lowry 2003:115–30). After the fall of Constantinople, several high ranking members of the Byzantine imperial dynasty made astounding careers in the Ottoman Empire, even rising to the office of Grand Vizir (Lowry, 2003:115–17).

The organization of provincial government offers insights into the organization of the Ottoman polity and its elites that help us to go beyond the interpretation of the empire as a patrimonial-bureaucratic monolith. Earlier ruling dynasties often retained their positions under the condition that they contributed troops to the Ottoman army. Such pragmatism in combination with the longevity of the first generations of rulers, contributed to the meteoric rise of the Ottomans. Although not formally required to do so, many members of the Byzanto-Balkan aristocracy had converted to Islam by the end of the fifteenth century (Lowry, 2003:132). One reason for their choice in conversion was that their career opportunities were diminishing as the *devshirme*-raised elites began to monopolize government positions. The army also began to rely more and more on the Janissaries, who were also products of the devshirme.

Devshirme, the collection of boys, lasted between 1300 and the 1700s (Imber, 2009). It was a continuation of the old Muslim practice of raising armies of slaves (*mamluk*, *ghulam*). Originally, the Ottomans used youths captured on their campaigns to man their armies and navies. From the fourteenth century, the practice of devshirme supplemented the supply of slaves taken in battle. This was a tax on the Christian population of the Balkans, which they had to pay by sending the sultan a certain number of young boys who were sent to live with Turkish families in Anatolia to be socialized into Turkish culture. Upon maturity they were sent to Constantinople and were either selected for the army or for service in the palace. Devshirme recruits made up the elite infantry corps, the Janissaries.[2] In time the Janissaries became not only a military organization but also one of the crucial parties in the state. The sultans originally used them to serve as a counterweight to the old nobility and the administrative elite. Successive sultans, from Bayazid I (1389–1402) to Suleyman I (1520–66) varied in their support of the respective factions and attempted to play them off against each other. From the reign of Suleyman, the slave party and more precisely the Janissaries, won the upper hand and became the principal locus of

---

[2] Janissary is an anglicization of *yeni ceri*, which means the new army (Ágoston, 2010:115ff).

power (Lapidus, 2012:438–9). The Janissary system broke down in the early seventeenth century as regiments became increasingly autonomous and powerful which made the sultanate turn to and subsequently become dependent upon 'provincial magnates, warlords, officials, and chieftains for military manpower' (Lapidus, 2012:479). These elites did not seem to have been politically integrated – indeed there was no system of political participation into which they could have been integrated, such as a corporate nobility or representative institutions. The lack of such factors in the Ottoman Empire further underscores their importance for the development of European polities.

Another, older, military force was the provincial cavalry, the *siphar*, which was supported and organized in a patrimonial way that could be interpreted as creating a class of atomized individuals that depended only on the sultan and thus confirm a interpretation of the empire as hostile to inherited power and kinship. Hence we need to investigate it more closely. The siphar was supported by the *timar* system, introduced in 1368 by Sultan Murad I (r.1362–89) (Fuess, 2010) that was based both on the Muslim Iqta and on the Byzantine *proinea*. In return for the grant of a farm, the owner of a timar had to perform military service as a mounted and armoured cavalryman together with his armed retainers. Unlike a European fief, stewardship of a timar did not give the holder (*timariot*) any jurisdiction over the peasants that cultivated the land, but he was expected to take responsibility for public order within his territory. A timar could not be inherited. Instead, the idea was that a timar could revert back to the Porte, either at the death of a timariot or it could be revoked, for example if the holder failed to perform military service (Fuess, 2010:622). Over time and as the system declined timars became more hereditary. But by then it was no longer warriors who held them but members of the civilian administration (Fuess, 2010:624). Michael Brett, however, argues that the timar system transformed the ethnic Turkish sipahi into a hereditary caste (Brett, 2010:571). As the expansion of the Empire halted, the timar system deteriorated into tax farming and the army became increasingly based on infantry regiments, either belonging to the Janissaries or to peasant levies (Faroqhi, 2010:395ff). Officially the timar system was supposed to counteract the formation of hereditary elites and reinforce the idea of all subjects as beholden only to the sultan. However, kinship forms of stratification crept into the system as appointment to a timar was in principle only open to sons of timariots. Hence, in a pattern that we will see repeated in the civilian administration, although offices were not hereditary, positions in a caste-like system where kinship played a major role were.

The circulation of elites in in the fourteenth and fifteenth centuries illustrates the relation between the early Ottoman Empire and its kinship elites. If we only consider the devshirme system and the suppressing of traditional landed dynasties we might be tempted to read the formation of the mature Ottoman Empire as a reiteration of the pattern of state formation by breaking kinship elites. However, two important qualifications must be made: first, recruitment through devshirme did not always sever the ties between people who entered Imperial service and their families. It did so in many cases, but not in all and evidence exists that Balkan noble families wanted their sons to enter the devshirme system in order to make careers. Second, it was not only young boys without lands, means, or connections that populated the imperial administration and military. As we saw above, members of the Balkan and Byzantine dynasties entered directly into the system and over time became Ottomanized (Lowry, 2003). When they entered into the central administration they did not become atomized individuals only obedient to the sultan but retained their family structure and connections (Lowry, 2003:123–5), in fact, they were sometimes encouraged to do so by their rulers. Hence we cannot conclude that there really was a principled opposition between Ottoman political order and kinship as a principle of social organization per se. Kinship was, however, not allowed to become a formalized and open principle of political order. We will now investigate the matter of lineages and households in the civilian administration more closely.

The Bureaucracy and Its Dynasties

The Ottoman Empire was a formation with a well-developed bureaucracy, in particular in comparison with the contemporary Safavid (Iran) and Mughal Empires (India). A far-flung conglomerate consisting of a large number of provinces (*sanjaks*) and sub-provinces had to be administered by a staff both at the centre in Constantinople and in place in the provinces (Özoğlu, 2004:51). The empire had a corps of judges (*kadi*) that administered justice centrally, and in the provinces a *kadi* always ruled in tandem with a governor (*bey*). The judges also examined cases in the central administration. Like in medieval and early modern European realms, subjects who felt they had been treated wrongly by neighbours or the authorities filed complaints. The legal administration examined such complaints and it has been demonstrated that they were often quite responsive and worked to uphold a certain degree of rule of law; both Islamic (sharia) and Turkic-dynastic (*kanun*) (Jennings, 1978:141ff; Imber, 2009). Furthermore, it has been demonstrated that the administration grew increasingly professional over time (Findley, 1980, 1989).

The central administration consisted of a council of vizirs (chancellors), presided over by a Grand Vizir (imperial chancellor). Below the council level the empire was organized into a number of departments (*divan*). When we thus view the empire as a formal organizational chart it appears to us as a highly advanced and impersonal form of rule with clear traits of 'stateness'.[3] In theory the staff of this administration was recruited according to egalitarian and meritocratic principles. The use of the devshirme system to staff the civilian administration as well as the military underscored the egalitarian tendency (Mardin, 1973). If these theoretically open and egalitarian principles for recruitment, including an interpretation of the devshirme as producing atomized individuals loyal only to the sultan, are added to our image of the Ottoman Empire then they underscore the conclusion that it had traits of the ideal-type of the state and was hostile to kinship as a principle.

However appealing, this neat image must be corrected. In reality kinship as an organizational principle was present in the administration in several different ways. The truly 'gelded' elite, the court eunuchs, performed important duties and had significant access to political and personal information but they were never as important civil servants as their counterparts in imperial China (Toledano, 1984; Tezcan 2012:103–4). Although access to the bureaucracy was in principle open to persons from all classes and categories of subjects, sons of established bureaucrats were considered the most suitable for service. Hence an almost caste-like social stratum was developed from which officials were recruited (Findley, 1989:46; Faroqhi, 1997:556). The devshirme system was, as we have seen, not entirely meritocratic. Prominent families in the Balkans tried to ensure that their sons were taken and recruited into the highest ranks of the Ottoman civil service (Brett, 2010:571). The existence of edicts forbidding recruiters to take

---

[3] For the concept of stateness see Nettl, 1968.

boys from 'good families' can be interpreted partly as official policy that attempted to enforce egalitarian principles of recruitment, partly as evidence that actors on the inside as well as on the outside of the system actively sought to circumvent formal principles (Imber, 2009). In the fifteenth and sixteenth centuries Byzantine and Balkan aristocracy, even royalty, entered more or less directly into the highest positions of the Ottoman administration.

From the seventeenth century onwards we see the formation of administrative dynasties in the Ottoman Empire: families that dominated the highest offices for several generations. The most famous and successful dynasty is the Köprülü family. Between 1656 and 1703 members of the Köprülü family served as important viziers and Grand Viziers. The dominance of the family was so considerable that the period is often referred to as the Köprülü era (*Köprülüler Devri*) (Faroqhi, 2000:61–2; Finkel, 2005:253–88). Two additional points of interest regarding the Köprülü family stand out: its founder was a product of the devshirme but nevertheless managed to establish a formidable dynasty; and while the period 1656–1703 is also known as an era of centralization of government functions we must note that this time of 'state- building' was overseen by a single dynasty of grandees. Hence dynasty formation and state formation went hand in hand in the empire, as in many European realms. The era of the Köprülü dynasty came to an end only when it was eclipsed by that of another dynasty, that of Shikhuliilsma Feyzullah Efendi. This was one of many scholarly dynasties, the ulama, which came to dominate the Ottoman administration during the eighteenth century. The ulama were crucial in the administration, legal system and in advising the government in matters of war and peace. The development of the scholarly aristocracy in the seventeenth and eighteenth centuries constitutes a second round of elite circulation whereby kinship-organized elites came to dominate the empire, the first round having taken place in the fourteenth century when the Turkoman aristocracies were replaced. The scholarly elite was not independent but controlled by the Porte and hierarchically ordered and registered. Each rung on the career ladder was supposedly meritocratic as in theory advancement required mastery of more and more advanced texts (Zilfi, 2006:209–25; Lapidus, 2012:440). However, during the eighteenth century a number of great families came to dominate the highest legal and scholarly offices for several generations.

Thus we see the establishment in the Ottoman Empire of a new kind of aristocracy, not centred on warfare but on learning and bureaucracy. These families became central to the administration of the empire and, conversely, they owed their positions not to any independent status but to their place in the state structure. Individuals that belonged to the ulama controlled the religious foundations (*waaqf*) that in turn controlled landed estates. These could not be partitioned and so constituted a source of power and wealth, particularly in the Arab provinces. The ulama were also legally privileged in the sense that they were able to transmit their estates to their heirs (Zilfi, 2006:557–8). Other elite groups had to constantly consider the possibility that their positions or estates could be confiscated and given to other of the Sultan's ruling slaves. Over time the growth of dynasties of scholarly families created a kind of 'religious aristocracy' of a small number of families that monopolized important posts. This development was part of the transformation of the empire during the eighteenth century into a more negotiated kind of polity. The emphasis of Ottoman statecraft shifted more towards bargaining and brokerage between different power holders and groups on several different levels, both in a centre-periphery manner and between different social movements. We saw above that the reformers in the beginning of the nineteenth century destroyed the Janissaries as a step in creating a more monolithic or centralized state. Having done so, the reformers turned on the ulama in order to remove a rival centre of power.

Still, we cannot talk of an unequivocal conflict between the most state-like part of the empire, the administration, and kinship principles or groups since the latter permeated the former. Contradictions that did exist were on a principled or ideational level since the official line was that the administration was a part of the egalitarian Ottoman order in which all subjects were equal before the sultan. There was thus a disconnect between official and institutionalized procedures and de facto forms of organization. Kinship formations existed in the political order, but they were not of it. This forms a contrast to the corporate organization and status of noble descent-based groups in Europe. The political system was not hereditary in the same way as in Europe, but people nevertheless organized themselves in terms of families and lineages. Now that we have examined the elites that were active in the imperial centre we shall turn to the elites of the peripheries.

Elites of the Provinces

Throughout this book I have stressed that kinship is found as a principle of organization and legitimacy in many different kinds of social formations: tribes, dynasties and aristocracies. The Ottoman Empire lacked a formalized aristocracy but it contained many informal types of nobility, in the shape of durable groups of families with a special claim to legitimate rule that they are able to enforce. In the Middle East, tribalism and nobility co-existed.

The Ottomans appointed indigenous leaders to manage the affairs of many local communities and to interact with the central government. The Kurds occupy a special position in this regard as the Porte explicitly affirmed the hereditary positions of their ruling dynasties. Kurdish society is often described as tribal but as Özoğlu points out, Richard Tapper's concept of a tribal confederacy provides a more fitting description of Kurdish formations. A tribal confederacy consists of a heterogeneous group of tribes that is politically unified under a central authority (Özoğlu, 2004:45). As a type, a Kurdish tribal confederacy (emirate) consisted of a number of groups, nomadic and settled, and was led by an emir (Özoğlu, 2004:46). In order to manage and integrate the strategically important Kurdish regions, the Ottoman government relied on the Kurdish nobility. At the time of the Ottoman conquest, 'Kurdistan' was fragmenting into smaller tribal units. The authority and position of the ruling stratum was reinforced as an effort to create a more ordered society consisting of hierarchically ordered tribal confederacies (Özoğlu, 2004:52).

The hereditary positions of local beys over the Sunni Kurdish tribes in eastern Anatolia were affirmed by imperial decree (*firman*) around 1533. Of the eleven provinces that made up the province of Diyarbekir, eight were assigned the status of family domains, *ocalik* or *yurtluk*, and given to Kurdish lords whose possessions and status were hereditary (Özoğlu, 2004:56; Barkey, 2008:92; Imber, 2009:188–9; Seyhun, 2015:113). Other provinces of the area were given the status of *Hükûmet* sanjak, provinces under state control but with local self-rule. In return for autonomy, the Kurdish lords and the chieftains of the Türkmen tribesmen promised military service in times of war (Agoston, 2009). Significantly, although the Ottoman documents categorize the hereditary sanjaks as granted by the Porte, it seems that the local chiefs were already in possession of the province and the Ottomans let them keep their place. Rulership of a hereditary sanjak passed from father to son or to other relatives. The Porte could only seize the territory if there were no relatives alive that belonged to the ruling family. In such rare cases, the territory could only be given to someone from the region that the other *emirs* could agree upon (Özoğlu, 2004:54; Agoston, 2009:20).

It is significant for the argument of this book that the Ottomans recognized the prestige and legitimacy of the descent of the ruling families of the Kurdish regions. The ever-pragmatic Ottomans saw that the charismatic power of the prestigious lineages could serve to unite the ethnically, linguistically and tribally diverse inhabitants of a strategic region (Özoğlu, 2004:54). Imperial policy towards this area had two sides: on the one hand the traditional ruling families (and the ideology of kinship that legitimated them) were supported and on the other the region was granted significant autonomy in a number of areas such as being free from imperial troops and taxation and having their own leaders. 'Embeddedness' rather than 'integration' seems to be the most appropriate label for this arrangement. The strategy of balancing policies of deep structural influence and non-intervention seems to have paid off well for the Ottomans. Towards the eighteenth century, the Porte increased its authority over the Kurdish emirates, at the same time as it preserved their political infrastructure (Özoğlu, 2004:59).

In the Middle East, we find numerous examples of hereditary ruling positions and of kinship groups holding on to their status for generations. The Middle East had been brought into the Ottoman Empire during the sixteenth century. It was strategically, economically and culturally important. However, the Porte always ruled with a light hand, using local notables and elites as intermediaries. Theoretically, this form of rule was legitimated as the a'yan system, an heir of the previous amir a'yan system. Under the millet system, Sunni Muslims were allowed to be ruled by their own leaders as long as they pledged allegiance and paid taxes to the Porte (Winslow, 1996:13). The millet system was the organization of religious and national groups of the Ottoman Empire into separate, self-organizing entities (Barkey, 2005:15–19). Hereditary sanjaks headed by leaders of Arab tribes also existed in the provinces of Aleppo (Syria), Baghdad and Mosul (Agoston, 2009:20). In many key cities such as Aleppo, Baghdad, Basra, Damascus and Mosul governors managed to establish local dynasties during the eighteenth century (Lapidus, 2012:485). Another category of hereditary power holders in the Arab provinces were families claiming ashraf status

(Arabic, *sharif*): nobility by virtue of descent from the Prophet Mohammad. In the province of Aleppo ashraf factions challenged the rule of Janissaries in the eighteenth century. Not unlike would-be nobles in Europe, not all who claimed ashraf status were genuine. At first the authorities attempted to investigate the genealogies of claimants but in the eighteenth century, titles could be bought. Ashraf families possessed military means and held substantial households and retinues (Hathaway, 2008:91ff). Indeed, the ayan dynasties, or *hanedan*, were crucial providers of military manpower in the provinces and monopolized tax farming – two of the activities that we most commonly associate with state power (Philliou, 2010:25). During the eighteenth century, in parts of Anatolia but also in the Balkans and certain Arab-speaking provinces, local provincial power holders 'seized former state-owned lands and managed sometimes successfully, to transfer them to their heirs' (Faroqhi, 1997:552). Barkey describes how powerful networks of large families in Anatolia and in the Middle East established themselves in the provinces and were active in trade, tax farming and politics. They established networks of clients and developed narratives of legitimacy. Provincial notables created networks across their territories (Barkey, 2008:226). Christian and Jewish merchants also created business networks over long distances that were based on kinship ties (Barkey, 2008:241). There were distinctions between more powerful and lesser ayan families and the latter were often bound up in patron-client networks of the former (Barkey, 2008:251). However, they cannot be considered a class because their relations with the state varied considerably (Barkey, 2008:242, 244).

The Kurdish chiefs and Arab ayans were not the only lords with hereditary rights in the Ottoman Empire: when the Ottomans conquered the small Georgian kingdoms in the sixteenth century they kept the original ruling families in charge. Initially they retained their Christian religion but eventually they converted in order to ensure that their lands could remain hereditary (Agoston, 2009:22). In the Balkan heartlands of the Empire we find a number of hereditary elites. Beginning in the fifteenth century, we find the marcher lords of Rumelia (e.g., Bulgaria). Other magnate families held possessions in what is today Greece and Macedonia. In 1463, the Malkoch family was granted hereditary governorship of newly conquered Bosnia. Inalcik notes that the old nobility of Bosnia were able to keep their position and maintain their hereditary lands until the twentieth century (Inalcik, 1954:116–17). In the fourteenth century, the sanjaks of the empire were divided into two categories, the sovereign's sanjaks and those that were governed by his sons. In the fifteenth and sixteenth century, many of the frontier sanjaks came under direct rule by the Porte (Imber, 2009). To the north of the Danube, four tributary principalities formed a ring around the empire: the Khanate of Crimea, Moldavia, Wallachia and the Kingdom of Transylvania. They were all ruled by hereditary dynasties.

Another powerful group was the Phanariots. Their development and standing is of considerable relevance since it illustrates some of the ways in which the Ottoman Empire operated with respect to its hereditary elites. Phanariots were a Greek-speaking orthodox Christian elite that came to serve in the Ottoman bureaucracy as governors, tax farmers, administrators and diplomats from the eighteenth century onwards (Philliou, 2010). Like ayans and Janissaries, Phanariots were not a formal institutionalized phenomena but rather evolved in an improvised and ad hoc fashion (Philliou, 2010:8). This fact further leads us to relativize the image of the Ottoman Empire as a centralized bureaucratic state. Originally the Phanariot families had been wealthy merchants, a vocation that supplied them with language and cultural skills that allowed them to forge links and communicate with Austrian, Italian and Russian elites. Their Christian identity restricted their access to careers in some parts of the Ottoman state, but it was an asset in dealing with Europeans. Phanariot families received titles in the central bureaucracy; the most important of which was the office of the grand dragoman and *voyvod* (ruler) of the 'Danubian principalities', Moldavia and Wallachia. The Danubian principalities were lucrative to the governors, strategic to the empire and of considerable diplomatic importance since much diplomacy with the Western powers was conducted through their borders. The thrones of Moldavia and Wallachia were not hereditary; instead several Phanariot families competed over them as well as over other offices (Philliou, 2010:14). Thus membership in a Phanariot dynasty as a centrally placed elite group with extensive networks was hereditary but not the offices that members of a dynasty occupied at any point in time. Male relatives of the reigning *voyvodas* were kept as hostages in Istanbul but staying in the capital meant that they could convey information to their relatives, thus almost acting as ambassadors between the principalities and the Porte. Furthermore,

Phanariot networks knitted together many different organizations and actors in the Western part of the Empire and in the Levant.

Over the course of the eighteenth century, Phanariots formed households akin to the provincial ayan families called *hanedan* – a Persian concept meaning great tribe or dynasty. As a means of strengthening their cohesion and base they 'borrowed kinship practices – and terminology – from their vezir and ayan counterparts' (Philliou, 2010:10). As in medieval Europe, formation of concepts and of a social formation went together. Hanedan was at this time also a recognized concept, denoting 'nobility' (Philliou, 2010:29). We find the term *hanedanzadelik* – 'descended from a hanedan' in Ottoman documents. It was more commonly used to describe the royal dynasty, the House of Osman (*handanı Osmanlı*) but during the eighteenth century both ayan and Phanariot families began to be termed hanedan in official documents. As a consequence, both kinds of families changed their surnames in the eighteenth century, adopting *zade* and *oglu* suffixes, which became synonymous with belonging to the nobility; a parallel to the *de*, *von* and *zu* prefixes that denote French and German nobility. Thus during the eighteenth and early nineteenth centuries we can see a development that looks strikingly like the establishment of officially recognized nobilities in the Ottoman Empire. However, this trend never developed into the formation of a European-style aristocracy. The lack of institutionalization (compared to Europe) meant that these groups – like the provincial nobility – could not form the same kind of cohesive gel that European nobilities became. Instead of being public and transparent they were elusive and extra-constitutional which meant that routinized politics with different households or groups became difficult.

Furthermore, Phanariots were isolated rather than integrated in a larger system. Although the sultans valued their Phanariots they also distrusted them since they often seemed to serve their own interests, they were not known and transparent objects of governance. Instead there is evidence that sultans and their advisers struggled with understanding the phenomenon. Sometimes the Phanariots were in collusion with foreign powers. Hence, they chose a form of 'exit' since they lacked opportunities for 'voice'. All three factors is a sign of a hereditary elite that since it lacked institutionalization, integration and a public nature could not serve as a further vehicle of integration in the Empire (Hirschman, 2004). The Phanariots were not registered in any official document or register in Constantinople. It is indeed curious and telling that in a supposedly bureaucratic empire a group that was one of the most important trans-regional elites was not subject to any kind of official registration. Also, they were never the subject of any major work of political theory in the empire that could have explained their role or integrated them in a conceptual scheme. Indeed it seems that in the optic of the state they were not invisible but opaque and shadowy, and thus hard to act both against and with (Philliou, 2010:18–19). They stand in stark contrast to the increasingly visible and public aristocratic elite families of Europe that were analysed in Chapters 4 and 5. Given their shadowy status within the sprawling empire and that the lack of Ottoman political institutions did not provide arenas for what Hirschmann calls 'voice' or 'loyalty', the strategies of some Phanariot families to ally with foreign powers can be seen as a rational form of pseudo-exit (Hirschman, 2004). Thus we can talk of a symbiosis in the sense that both the sultans and the Phanariots were dependent upon each other but it was not a dependency upon which further synergies and institutions could be built. This forms a contrast to the creation of parliaments out of the routinized interactions between kings and nobles in Europe.

Although there were similarities between the Phanariot and ayan families, there were important differences. While an ayan dynasty was based in a single province over which it ruled for generations, its Phanariot counterpart was transregional and cosmopolitan and did not exercise hereditary rule although the status as *hanedanzadelik* was inherited (Philliou, 2011:184). Instead, its members would occupy different positions of power in the empire within the same generation as well as over several generations. Another difference was that military power was central to the rule and power of ayans. Although Phanariots could occasionally raise armies and militias, they did not have access to a formally sanctioned military force. Their historical destinies also differed. The Phanariots were robbed of their power base in several stages, first when the Balkan principalities became independent one by one and second when the cosmopolitan Ottoman Empire was dissolved and its remaining centre turned into a Turkish national state. The Phanariots were the creation of a multi- or trans-ethnic cosmopolitan empire and as such could not survive in a world of nation states.

In sum, although there was a lack of institutional embedding of hereditary elites in the provinces, there was no principled aversion to elites with hereditary privileges, property, or rulership. The only group with hereditary powers that the Ottomans campaigned actively to curtail was the landed Turkmen elite in Anatolia (Barkey, 2008). The Ottomans kept traditional rulers whose status and possessions were hereditary rather than putting a new hereditary elite in place. This means that the power of the original rulers was firmly entrenched and that their hereditary power was accepted in their communities. Earlier Ottomanists either ignored or denigrated the status of the provinces; placing the 'centre' as the privileged locus of status and government. More recent attempts to create theoretically informed descriptions of the empire have revised the traditional centre-periphery distinction and demonstrated how networks and relations criss-crossed the empire (Barkey, 2008). If we consider the international environment of the Ottomans we recognize that the provinces were not backwaters but important points of contact with and defence against other powers. Some strategic sanjaks were controlled directly by the Porte, for example the ones along the main lines of Ottoman advance into central Europe. Others, like Diyarbeykir along the Ottoman-Safavid border, were in the hands of local Kurdish rulers (Özoğlu, 2004:48ff). In sum, with some exceptions, the frontiers of the empire were in the hands of hereditary elites. When we consider this fact, we can hardly claim that the empire only privileged meritocratic or patrimonial (e.g., appointed by the sultan) elites and saw hereditary power and kinship groups as leftovers or peripheral to their system of rule.

Conclusions

An old trope among European observers of the Ottoman Empire is that its inhabitants were all slaves of an all-powerful Sultan. This trope is connected to and reinforces the idea that for a political order to be successful it has to break the power of kinship-based groups. Modern Ottomanists however argue that the Empire was polycentric, contained many different (often kinship-based) elites and that the ability to co-opt and co-operate with them was one of the factors behind the Empire's viability. Thus, the Ottoman Empire seems to confirm rather than disprove my thesis that successful orders co-operate with kinship-based elites. Still, the position of the different elites of the Ottoman Empire was different from that of their Arab, European and Turko-Mongol counterparts. This offers us the chance to compare these different political orders with each other. All chapters have asked whether the relation between the central organizations and kinship elites was mainly co-operative or conflictual. The Porte's relation with central elites was characterized by cyclical elite circulation – and thus conflict. Long periods of collaboration ended with conflicts that resulted in the introduction of a new elite group. The conflict-collaboration dichotomy is not sufficient to describe the many different relations of the Empire.

Regarding the question of conflict or co-operation between the central organizations and kinship elites we see that the Porte replaced old elites with new ones on several occasions. Conflicts between the Porte and different aristocratic elites tended be cyclical. Periods of collaboration ended with conflicts that resulted in the introduction of a new elite group. First the Porte tried to curtail the hereditary Turkic nobility on which it initially depended by introducing the devshirme system of recruitment. Interestingly, Balkan elites took advantage of the devshirme to introduce their sons into the military system of the empire. Second, conquered princely dynasties were removed from their native provinces and replaced with appointees of the sultan. However, on no occasion until the 1830s did the Porte engage in wholesale purges of aristocratic elites, they rather replaced old ones with new ones. The dichotomy between conflict and co-operation is not sufficient to describe the many different relations that existed in the empire. Primarily, there was limited integration of elites within the political order.

An extraordinary willingness and capacity to integrate different elites characterized the early empire. In contrast to the Arab empires and even to European realms, the Ottomans were willing to integrate the aristocratic and royal dynasties of their conquered enemies even in the top military and administrative positions. Religion was no obstacle; Christians and Jews were accepted, although conversion to Islam often followed within a couple of generations. During the late phase, we find both collaboration and separation. Scholarly Arab dynasties from the Middle East (the ulama) reached high positions in the civil administration but other Arab dynasties, the ayans, and the Kurdish dynasties largely operated in the provinces and did not reach the central military or civilian bureaucracy or intermix with other elites. The relation between the Porte and the hereditary provincial lords was one of collaboration, but not institutional symbiosis. Clearly the Porte needed autonomous elite groups for manpower, income and local governance.

Conversely, belonging to a larger polity protected local Arab, Balkan, Druze and Kurdish lords gave them prestige.

The purpose of this chapter was not to analyse the viability of the Ottoman Empire in detail. However, it is possible to sketch some conclusions. It is tempting to conclude that because the empire eventually crumbled, all of its traits must have contributed to its decline and demise. However, as Karen Barkey argues, the fluid character of its political order might have been beneficial to its survival (Barkey, 2005). When the Ottoman Empire and its relations with kinship-based aristocratic elites are compared to those that pertained in the Arab empires then the fluidity of the former seems better than the rigidity of the latter. The Ottomans adapted to the situation that they found themselves in; ruling loosely over many very different social groups that were used to a high degree of self-rule. In order to create a stable empire, the Ottomans had to develop an order based on networks and negotiated rule. The Ottoman Empire also differed from both the Umayyad and Abbasid caliphates that frequently circulated and replaced elites, creating a permanently revolutionary situation in which elites gradually abandoned central politics rather than attempting to secure a stake in the political order. In Hirschman's terms, they chose exit over voice and loyalty (Hirschman, 2004). To a certain extent the same can be said of the ayan dynasties in Anatolia and the Middle East. However, given the lack of embedding institutions, there was little opportunity to exercise 'voice'. Instead, they had a degree of 'loyalty' to the sultan but were left outside the central governing apparatus, while some families governed as a kind of sub-contractor to the empire.

There was very little in terms of uniformity among the many different categories of elites in the empire. Even within a single group there was very little uniformity regarding the relations with the central government. There was no constitutional template and hence quite fluid relations between the centre and elite groups (Phillips and Sharman, 2015). As Inalcik and colleagues argue '[w]hile European nobilities had their privileges and obligations sanctioned by law, Ottoman "Estates" functioned in a purely non-official manner' (Faroqhi, 1997:552). European elite groups were sometimes unclear too. In early modern France and Spain there was no absolute definition of nobility. Rights and duties vis-à-vis the state could vary considerably but many elite privileges and obligations were held corporately as a group. Corporate organization reinforced a common collective identity for the noble elites from the different parts of the European kingdoms. It is difficult to ascertain how deeply entrenched an identity was but the organization of elites into estates gave them a common trans-local arena to formulate common interest and forge alliances, both political and matrimonial. Some dynasties were indeed recognized as *hanedan*. But many other kinship-based elites operated unofficially. This produced several consequences for the empire, which was flexible but also divided – like many other empires.

There were no arenas where different elites of the empire could meet officially, neither centrally nor provincially, but despite this there was a considerable amount of unofficial networking. The European kingdoms had public arenas in which norms could be formulated and enforced, thus reinforcing cohesion and the central values of the political order. Parliaments and diets were not the only arenas in which elites acted in public, the royal (and in earlier periods, provincial) courts were also important in this respect. The public sphere of the court was an important arena where the twin processes of surveillance and self-surveillance that were so important in creating homogeneity and orientation towards central values were played out. The Phanariot dynasties that ruled the Balkans in the latter phase of the empire had a peculiar relation to the Porte, a mixture of collaboration and subterfuge. Naturally, they collaborated with their sultanic masters but the Phanariots also engaged in subterfuge to the extent that they hedged their bets by collaborating with the European powers with which they were in frequent contact. However, the most peculiar aspect is the fact that there were partly invisible to the Porte. This did not result from a conscious strategy on their part but rather from a structural trait of the empire: the lack of embedding institutions that would have rendered all of the kinship-based elite groups visible to the centre and to each other as well as placing them in contact with one another. The prohibition on consanguineous marriage and extensive definition of blood relations up to six degrees in Europe also forced elites from different regions to integrate. To find marriage partners who were not relations, families had to cast the net ever wider and thus expanded their kinship networks over generations. In Europe collective arenas created inter-elite trust. Acting in a public context where all elite groups that mattered on the level of the realm were present created a more transparent situation. In the Ottoman Empire there was not a single arena, neither court nor parliament, that gathered all significant elites (or their representatives).

Not only did this create fewer opportunities for contacts and action it also created more uncertainty as regards the configuration of power.

Corporate organization was connected to representation. Traditionally, as seen in Chapter 5, political scientists have seen representation as a way for pre-existing groups to formulate interests and engage in a political process of bargaining and negotiation. Several scholars have stressed that the reciprocal bargaining between estates and princes over taxation and in some cases about which forces could be used in foreign wars was beneficial to state formation. Not only did it allow high levels of taxation with relatively little resistance and rebellion, it also granted liberties, privileges and co-government to the elites that created vested interests and investments over time in the polity as a whole. The rights and privileges of the hereditary European elites (which they could defend by withholding public goods desired by the prince) also gave them a more secure future and a wider horizon of expectation than their Ottoman counterparts. While this is undoubtedly important, more recent research has emphasized a more fundamental effect of representation, namely to bring about not only the representing collective, but also that which is represented. Through acts of performativity the collective identities as well as the realm that they represented – and to which the collective noble identities were connected – were brought about. Therefore corporate representation symbolically created embedded social groups as well as the embedding framework.

Finally, when we look at the ruling dynasty we note that its semantics, biopolitics, kinship structure and its internal wars affected the political order profoundly. The void between different elite groups was mirrored by the absence of semantics of rule that bound elite groups to each other and to the ruling dynasty. In Europe, aristocracies and monarchs legitimated each other and were thus co-dependent upon the level of concepts and ideas. In the Ottoman form of rule, the dynasty had a more elevated and thus isolated status, particularly during the latter phase of the empire. Its splendid isolation was due to a combination of ideas, lack of institutions and its biopolitics. Early on, the Ottomans had married freely with other dynasties, Muslim and Christian, Turkic, Balkan and Byzantine, in order to gain status, wealth and influence. From the seventeenth century onwards, sultans ceased to marry and relied on concubines for reproduction. This strategy avoided many the biological and political problems (such as inbreeding) but it also meant that the House of Osman could not tie other aristocratic dynasties to it by means of marriage.

Principles of legitimate political order were symbiotic with principles of legitimate kinship and descent. The House of Osman was the centre of the political order of the empire that was its unquestioned patrimony for 600 years. The main legitimating idea was that the Empire was the indivisible property of the House of Osman. It was unthinkable for Ottoman princes to try to carve out new and independent realms of their own. The position and character of the Ottoman dynasty exerted a constitutive influence on some of the internal wars of the empire. The centrality of the Ottoman dynasty did not preclude violence, and some of the most devastating internal conflicts were the institutionalized wars of succession between the Ottoman princes. Due to the Turkic conception that all members of the ruling house shared its charisma, wars between the princes was a means to determine the most suitable successor. In the seventeenth century, the wars ceased as the order of succession changed. However, wars of succession demonstrate that conflicts are not necessarily negative for a political system. Quite the opposite, they can show that all parties were oriented towards the centre. We saw this condition in the analysis of the Frankish realm in Chapter 3. The alternative to competition for power is not necessarily peaceful acceptance that another group rules but actually secession. That this never took place testifies to the strength of the idea of a political order. The legitimacy of the house enabled the Ottomans to break the curse of Turkic polity formation that had existed since the early Middle Ages: the tendency of empires to fragment into smaller polities ruled by princes or their regents (atabegs) (Findley, 2005:71). The dependence of the political order on the dynasty is attested by the fact that the rules and ideas of the dynasty stabilized a far-flung empire that was otherwise subject to numerous centrifugal forces. In sum, the traditional image of the Ottoman Empire is a colossal Leviathan lording over a weak society. But the image presented in this chapter, based on new advances in Ottoman scholarship, is that of a political order that was loosely coupled with a number of vibrant and sprawling societies. It was also a political order based on kinship as a legitimating principle, primarily in the shape of the Ottoman dynasty, and to which kinship-based elites were essential.

10 CLANS AND DYNASTIES IN THE MODERN MIDDLE EAST
Somalia and Saudi Arabia

Introduction

We have now arrived at the last empirical chapter of this book. Its first subject is whether families/kinship groups, regardless if we label them clans, dynasties or tribes, are incompatible with political order in today's Middle East and North Africa. Its second subject is to answer the question if kindreds are drivers of armed conflict. If they are, in what ways? My first answer is that kinship groups can indeed be components of viable political orders today, as demonstrated by Somaliland and Saudi Arabia. My second answer is more complicated. One cannot claim that Somali kinship groups have caused wars. Of course, clans have constituted one of the bases of military and political mobilization in the many conflicts of Somalia, however, the evidence that clans 'lead' in a structural fashion to wars is weak. In the Saudi case, the royal dynasty controls high politics and in that sense, it is the actor that initiates the use of armed force. Still, evidence demonstrates that the House of Saud and other Arab monarchies tend to do so much more rarely than leaders of other kinds of regimes in the Middle East and North Africa (MENA).

In Somalia, different actors have used the symbolic or semantic figure of the clan as a unit for the creation of military force and polities. The influence of clans thus is the result of conscious and strategic manipulation to gain power rather than the result of structural determination. In order to illustrate the role of actors, the empirical sections of this chapter are mainly chronological in character. I claim that these societies and their wars, like all others, have to be understood dynamically and diachronically, not in a static or structural way. Clans and dynasties do not cause wars, but they sometimes give conflicts a particular dynamic since they constitute the base of military and political mobilization. In Saudi Arabia certain dynastic traits are visible in its foreign policy and warfare, such as the need for new rulers to build personal legitimacy through action.

Somalia and Saudi Arabia manifest the combined questions of polity formation, kinship and modernity. Are the Somali clans and the Saudi royal dynasty premodern or even anti-modern formations? I will demonstrate that they are modern creations. Both have been deeply shaped by processes and entities that are modern, not least of which is state formation. Arab dynasties are quite modern in their adaptable, mutating behaviour and strategies on how they came to power at the end of World War One. The capacity of Arab dynasties to adapt to changing circumstances is reminiscent of the capacities of their European counterparts up until 1919. Three wider considerations exist in the debate whether clans and dynasties are premodern or modern: first, the validity of stage theories of state formation, second, the idea of a conflict between kinship formations and the state and third, by implication, conflictual relations and coercion vis-à-vis consent and embeddedness in polity formation and, ultimately, in the nature of political order. Chapter 11 will return to these three considerations.

My purpose is not to investigate which kind of regime causes the most war or is most stable, that would be an entirely different study (Fjelde, 2010). My purpose is to analyse countries where kinship-based formations exist and are important and analyse to what extent they underlie state collapse, state formation and war. I have chosen not to study the monarchy of Morocco, or Iraq, Libya or Syria and their orders and wars. Choosing Somalia and Saudi Arabia has the advantage that they are two countries in which kinship is particularly important but very different. In Somalia, family structures are not formalized (and written) and they are imprecise, but in Saudi Arabia where the royal dynasty is large, it is demarcated and has a special position vis-à-vis other important families.

Somalia and Somaliland: Diffuse Kinship in Diffuse Polities

Since the 1990s, Somalia has entered political and academic imagination as the prototypical failed state. Seemingly endemic violence, no state, suffering civilians and roaming militias are ingredients that have produced a cocktail of horror in academia, the media and popular culture. A social structure based on clans has added the final element to an image of anarchy and primitivism. Many observers have not only found Somalia frightening but also incomprehensible. Is it a 'premodern' state, as Robert Cooper claims (Cooper, 2004)? Are its clans primordial forces of violence? Such claims have been common, but they are of dubious value. Somalia is a crucial case in this book that investigates the relation between kinship groups, political order and war: does Somali history support the idea that 'clans' are incompatible with political order? Or does it support my assertion that we cannot draw such conclusions and that formalization of kinship groups can embed them in a political order and thus provide stability? I will argue that any analysis of Somali politics must consider clans but that they are not unequivocally negative or incompatible with political order.

Kinship in Somalia

What is a Somali clan? Anthropologists and political observes usually begin by describing the basic building blocks of Somali clan society (Lewis, 2008; Zoppi, 2017). Viewed schematically, Somali society consists of three major clan-families, Saab, Irir and Darod. Below that level we find the groups Digil, Rewin, Dir, Isaaq, Hawiye and Harti. Further below, we find further sub-divisions. For example, the Harti consists of the Dolbahanti, Mijirteen and Warsangali. Clans can be further disaggregated into sub-sub-groups down to individual families – Abbink distinguishes six levels (Abbink, 1999). It must be pointed out that the word 'clan' itself is not indigenous to Somalia, instead the Somali word for patrilineal kinship is *tol*. To avoid confusion I will, however, use the English term.

Within Somali culture, clans are defined genealogically. Each clan family, group or clan traces their ancestry patrilineally to a mythical ancestor. Thus, Somali clans are not based on biological kinship but on fictive kinship. However, Western scholarly interpretations of what a clan is, tend to start out from its function. Marco Zoppi argues that the Somali clan 'can be seen as a conglomeration of extended families coming together under those specific agreed arrangements called in their entirety *xeer*' (Zoppi, 2018:58). *Xeer* is often translated as customary law or *foedus*. Lewis argues that the smallest formation is the group of closely related kin that accepts the solidarity of blood vengeance and pays and receives blood money for offences committed against the group. Such communities are often referred to with the prefix of *diya* which is Arabic for blood, or *mag*, the Somali word (Abbink, 1999:2). Furthermore, there is sometimes an unclear distinction between clan and lineage (*reer* – 'people of').

Both genealogical and functionalist perspectives tend to impose a false picture of stability. It is wrong to see *diya* communities or clans as a primordial or even as fixed groups. The system of lineages and clans is both flexible and fluid and 'subject to dynamic changes of time' (Zoppi, 2017:58). It has seemed simple to fit this society into the neat models and assumptions provided by segmentary lineage theory. However, once we examine real politics, the categories start to get messy. As Abbink points out: 'The various groups distinguished on the basis of kinship are neither corporate nor cohesive localized groups, except perhaps a certain number of lineages' (Abbink, 1999:3). Not all of the above groups are of equal political importance. For example, the different groups of the Darod clan family have displayed greater solidarity and identity than other clan groups. In contrast, the Isaaq have a strong intra-group solidarity distinct from the Hawiye (both belong to the Irir clan family) whereas the Hawiye have known some cohesion but also considerable sundering.

In reality, clan has been quite flexible. In precolonial times many Somalis lived pastoral lives in an arid, unforgiving environment. In that setting groups had to form alliances to survive. These alliances could be cross-clan or cross-lineage based on patrinileal or uterine ties (the mother's line), marriage ties, friendship or religious orientation (Hoehne, 2016). Exogamy, marriage outside one's own lineage group (either within the same clan or with a member from another clan), was common (Hoehne, 2016). Hence, fluidity rather than rigidity characterized these formations. A further complicating factor is the *Shegat* – a patron-client relation between two sub-clans in which a clan can temporarily merge into another one but perhaps at a later stage re-emerge as an entity of its own (Abbink, 1999:1; Hoene, 2016:1389). Abbink (1999:2) usefully summarizes clan genealogy as a 'metaphoric, symbolic construct' but 'it is constantly referred to' (Abbink, 1999:2).

Although flexible and fluid, clans have important social effects. Clans are important markers of identity and arenas for the creation of order. Although the clan structure is important, other kinds of group identity, like class, ethnicity and race, are also important for collective action. Clan elders can work as effective conciliators and the meetings of elders (*guurti*) as arenas for creating consensus. An informal leader (*aaqil*) who is an authority with an 'influencing, negotiating and chairing role, rather than [an] ... incumbent authoritative power' usually represents mag groups (Walls, 2009). This system gives considerable autonomy to mediators and facilitators but is generally unfavourable against individuals who try to assume direct authority in order to receive obedience. Like their Arab counterparts, clans 'are weak at imposing order, especially on those who are willing to ignore or abuse the system' (Leonard and Samantar, 2011:569). Thus clans do not always operate as cohesive units of collective action. Somali society is characterized by strongly egalitarian discourses and practices. This means that clans and sub-clans are not hierarchical. Instead, elders occupy important roles as mediators and negotiators but their positions are not hereditary (Richards, 2014:73–4). Because of their importance, clan institutions have been penetrated and instrumentalized by warlords and the business elites. Clan has become a powerful category for political mobilization since it has been used so much. There is also an element of self-fulfilling prophesy since clan was used as a political category during as well as after the Barre regime; leading people to fear that clans will be used to mobilize and that they will be targeted on the basis of clan belonging. Thus, clan as a political category has sparked something of a security dilemma.

Analysts and anthropologists agree that clans are important, but debate their role in violence before and after the state collapse as well as the collapse itself. Some analyses in the aftermath of the international interventions in the 1990s focused on the Somali clan system as an explanatory factor. Shultz and Dew claim that when US troops went into Mogadishu in 1993, they lacked an understanding of the violent Somali culture, which 'derives from its nomadic and pastoral foundation', and they were therefore surprised by the force of the irregular warfare conducted by Somali clans (Schultz, 2009:187).

However, the idea that Somali culture is inherently violent, as well as the existence of 'clan warfare' in Somalia is hotly debated. Two conflicting positions can be seen in the literature, the 'primordialists' and the 'modernists'. Primordialists view clans as central to conflict as well as conflict prevention and resolution (Helander, 1996; Lewis, 1998). They further argue that the fundamental problem is the changes taking place during and after colonization, which destroyed existing mechanisms of mediation. Anderson points out that the central tenant in the primordialist argument is that if you 'reassert traditional authority and traditional practice within clans ... you will better control and more easily prevent conflict' (Andersson, 2011:12ff). Primordialists emphasize the importance of tribal warfare in Somalia but modernists argue that the role of tribes and clan in Somali society is exaggerated, and when discussing violence and state failure in Somalia, other factors are more relevant. The primordialist position that traditional clan structures are the root cause of the endemic violence in Somalia derives largely from the writings of I. M. Lewis. He describes Somali society as a segmentary, martial culture with an inherent 'culture of confrontation' (Lewis, 2002). Thus, Lewis claims that kinship is still the primary source of identity in Somalia and that a vast majority of violent conflicts in the country occurs along clan and tribal lines. The civil war of the 1990s was a continuation of what Somalis 'always have done' (Lewis, 2002:101).

In contrast, modernists recognize the existence of clans but argue the relationships within and between clans has also fundamentally been transformed by economic and political changes that have created new aims and motivations for conflict (Besteman, 1998, 1999; Andersson, 2011). Thus, it makes no sense to consider them premodern, instead they are thoroughly modern creations and their contemporary shapes and roles represent a postcolonial modernity (c.f. Eisenstadt, 2002). We should remember that the concept tribe is a European invention from the nineteenth century, originating with Henry Maine (Mamdani, 2012). As Porter has shown, the very idea of tribal warfare is heavily indebted to nineteenth century notions of cultural essentialism and constitutes a kind of 'military orientalism' (Porter, 2013:68–71). The invention of the concept of the tribe had a political purpose: to separate the modern from the natives. Although Somalists do not talk about tribes but about clans, the term serves the same purpose. Bruton argues that many warlords of today are not driven by traditional motivations, but have begun to engage in economic activities, such as in quasi-legitimate businesses (Bruton, 2012:48). It is argued that traditional practices 'are no longer functional' and traditional conflicting interests and mobilization of clans no longer cause conflict in Somalia. Therefore, to reach stability, the solution must be found elsewhere (Andersson, 2011:12ff). Catherine Besteman claims that other factors such as class and race are of greater importance than kinship in today's Somalia, and that they are the true causes of instability and conflict. She criticizes previous researchers for ignoring these categories and argues that previous descriptions of conflict caused by differences between lineages are insufficient to explain continuous warfare (Besteman, 1998:110). She also emphasizes that economic corruption, massive military and civilian aid and foreign intervention have strongly influenced Somali society and politics. Because of their fluidity and malleability the role of clans in Somali politics has to be studied diachronically. Far from being primordial and unchanging, they were shaped by the predatory state of the 1960s, Siad Barre's patrimonial dictatorship, the civil war during the 1990s and by subsequent violence and (often externally driven) state-building attempts (Ingiriis, 2016; Besteman, 2017; Zoppi, 2017).

From Statehood to Statelets: Somalia 1960–2018

In 1960, Italian Somalia and British Somaliland became independent from their respective colonial masters. After five days, the two countries merged into the republic of Somalia. Soon a spoils system emerged. Membership in the regime offered the possibility of enrichment; shrewd actors erected patrimonial structures on the basis of clan and personal contacts. In the elections of 1969 clans had supported their respective candidates and expected to be reimbursed with rewards from the state (Haldén, 2008:23). Meanwhile, external actors started to intervene. In the strategic Horn of Africa, Ethiopia and Somalia soon emerged as rivals. In Cold War fashion, the Soviet Union began to sponsor Somalia with guns, equipment and money. In October Major-General Siad Barre seized power and began a programme of modernization called 'scientific socialism' and declared that clans were obstacles to modernizing the country. Consequently, all expressions of clan identity were banned. To underscore the point, an effigy of the clan identity was burned at a ceremony in Stadium Banaadir (Ingiriis, 2016:168).

Although the ban was never very effective it did offer the Barre regime a way to denounce its opponents and anyone who criticized or even mentioned Barre's own policies of clan favouritism. While outwardly hostile to clans, Siad Barre built a regime that was patrimonial and clannish. His regime was based on favouring members from three clans that belong to the Darood clan families: the Marehan, the Ogaden and the Dhulbahante. Barre chose these three clans because of his own family affiliations: Marehan was his immediate clan, Ogaden was the clan of his mother and Dhulbante was the clan of his principal son-in-law (Ingiriis, 2016:168). This policy shows that clans are not static entities that operate as closed systems.

Barre's state favoured these three clans in different ways: first, officers of Marehan descent overwhelmingly commanded the army. The rest of the state apparatus also underwent a process of 'Marehanization'. Second, Barre reorganized Somalia into eighteen regions that favoured Darood clans and disfavoured Hawiye, Isaaq and Digil/Mirifle clans. Since the new division into regions concerned land resources, the reforms had a direct economic impact on the Somalis. Third, after the disastrous Ogaden War against Ethiopia of 1977–8 refugees belonging to the Ogaden clan fled into Somalia. Barre supported and resettled them in the north-western areas inhabited by the Isaaq clan. The regime's discrimination against the Isaaq led to the formation of an Isaaq-dominated guerrilla movement called the Somali National Movement (SNM) as well as the formation of the Somali Democratic Salvation Front (SSDF) (Ododa, 1985). After the fall of the Barre regime in 1991, the SNM and the SSDF created two autonomous entities, Somaliland and Puntland. Immediately after the Ogaden War a group of colonels that belonged to the Majerteen clan made a failed attempt at a coup d'état and the regime retaliated with collective punishment against all members of the clan. This episode demonstrates that there is no automatic solidarity within clan groups.

However, it would be a mistake to see clans as solid organizations and affiliations. Barre's regime was not only clannish but intensely familiar in character. The real way to gain influence and position was to connect to the Barre family network by marrying into it, or marrying a relative into it or making your wife into one of Barre's concubines. In the 1980s, the politics of Marhan rule had narrowed down to the rule of Reer Dini (Barre's sub-clan), then Reer Kooshin (sub-sub-clan), then Reer Hasan Kooshin (his sub-sub-sub clan) and finally into Reer Barre

Abdulle Yusuf (his sub-sub-sub clan) (Ingiriis, 2016:190). Hence, Barre created a kind of unstable dynasty unsupported by any institutions or legitimating semantics. We may pause and consider the Barre state in comparison to the far more successful family-based political orders in Europe's past. In comparison, we see clearly what is lacking in Somalia: there were no embedding institutions, there was no transparency and certainly no semantics that attempted to legitimate the real political order – factors that turned out to be important to the success of the European polities.

Towards the end, Barre's regime was increasingly isolated and leaned heavily on his immediate clan circles. The ironic circle of starting out by outlawing all clans and ending up depending on one's own is not an exclusively Somali phenomenon. In fact, the trajectory that Barre's regime followed has clear parallels elsewhere in the region. In retrospect one can see uncanny parallels between the regimes of Siad Barre in Somalia and Muhammar al-Gaddafi in Libya. Both came to power through military coups, tried to launch ambitious programmes of modernization and social change in quasi-socialist fashion with severe internal repression and failed expansionism through external war but left countries torn by sectarian civil war and ruined political orders. The Gaddafi regime was the most experimental, trying to create a new kind of society that would combine Islam and a radical socialism with strong traits of syndicalism and direct democracy (Vandewalle, 2011a). A final trait unites both dictators: they ruled societies where kinship groups were significant elements. They tried to handle the situation by suppressing clans and tribes but ended up ruling through their own kinship groups. Towards the end, both dictators were isolated and relied heavily on their own extended family network.

Libya's recent history offers clear parallels to Somalia's. Although clans and tribes could have constituted a cornerstone in Libya, the Gaddafi regime vehemently tried to suppress their influence. In the twilight years of the regime al-Gaddafi began to realize that the country was ungovernable without them and started to use them in his rule, but very cautiously and piecemeal. Since co-operation with tribes violated Libya's constitution, it was pursued informally and clandestinely. The result was to undermine trust in society. To make matters worse, towards the end al-Gaddafi relied more and more on his own clan, the Quaddaffa, narrowing his support base and spreading more distrust (Mattes, 2011; Vandewalle, 2011b:234). In the comparative light of this book, a tragic and ironic parallel between modern and premodern regimes is that al-Gaddafi relied on mercenaries from Chad, Mali and Niger in order to avoid having a strong army and officer corps that might challenge his rule. The similarity with the ill-fated Abbasid caliphate and its *mamluk* (*ghulam*) slave soldiers encountered in Chapter 6 is striking.

Foreign influence contributed to the volatile situation in Somalia. In the 1970s, Somalia switched Cold War patrons from the Soviet Union to the United States. The US and its allies supplied financial support, weapons and military hardware that allowed Barre to build Africa's largest army (Besteman, 2017). The country also received very large amounts of aid from the US, the EU and the World Bank, fuelling Barre's patrimonialism. Foreign support not only helped the regime to survive and to create a system of cleptocracy, the country became completely dependent on foreign aid. When the Cold War ended, American support ceased as Somalia was no longer an important partner. The economy collapsed at the same time as Barre's patrimonial state did. However, the considerable arsenal of small arms and heavy equipment was still in the country. As the quasi-state crumbled, the weapons were scattered to the winds and allowed a proliferation of well-armed militias.

Barre's regime fell in 1991 partly under the pressures of its own crumbling resource base and partly because it was under attack by the forces of the SNM and the SSDF. The fall of the regime sparked intense and large-scale fighting between large clan-based groups (Menkhaus, 2003:410). Although the armed groups may have recruited from a clan base, it was not the cause of the violence. The desire of the strongmen leading the different factions to gain power and resources that they could distribute in a classical patrimonial fashion to their followers was a main driver of the fighting in 1990–5, not clan identity (Duyvesteyn, 2005:109). However, clan identity was instrumentalized as a way to mobilize forces and as a consequence, scores of people were murdered, maimed and raped because of their clan (Kapteijns, 2012).

However, some conflicts pitted townspeople against rural populations, or were characterized by simple banditry and racist violence against marginalized minorities in the south. In her analysis of the civil war in the 1990s Duyvesteyn points to the flexible nature of clan identity. There were numerous clan alliances, many of which were temporary and cut across clan divisions (Duyvesteyn, 2005:61). There are no unequivocal patterns in alliance making. Siad Barré based his rule on the Marehan, Ogadeni and Dolbahante clans, which are all part of the Darood clan family. However, post-1991 fighting focused on combat between factions based on Hawiye clans.

Between 1995 and 2005, fighting became less intense. Extended families fought each other but fighting now took place within clan families, not between them (Menkhaus, 2004:410). External actors continued to intervene, not militarily but through state-building diplomacy. Under the leadership of the IGAD group the Transitional Federal Government (TFG) was created in 2004.[1] Lacking power, it was quickly seen as a tool for Darod interests. Interestingly, the Kenya peace process had tried to mould a stable Somalia on the basis of clan representation. Dir, Darod, Hawiye and Rewin representatives were to each send sixty members to the Federal parliament and minority clans were to select thirty members. This scheme further politicized clans as group identities and stands in sharp contrast to the more embedding solution found in Somaliland. However, Abdullahi Yussuf, a Majerteen leader, dominated the TFG by picking allies loyal to his group from other clan families (International Crisis Group, 2006:3). Thus, external state builders had misinterpreted how the clan 'system' works; believing its components to be more solid than they actually were. The failure of the TFG demonstrated that personal ties and clientelism were more important than clan affiliation.

In 2005 a new force entered Somali politics. The Union of Islamic Courts (UIC) was originally a coalition of eleven Hawiye sub-clan courts. It established a modicum of stability among the multitude of militias and gangs in the south and attempted to create an order based on Islam instead of clan and family affiliations (Barnes and Harun Hassan, 2007:154–5). However, the early 2000s was not a good time for Islamist state building. The United States began supporting a coalition of 'warlords' that had formed in opposition to the UIC. Supported both by the slender forces of the TFG and the more muscular assistance of the United States, Ethiopia invaded in the summer of 2006 to fight the UIC. The UIC were defeated, only to morph into the more radical Jihadist group, al-Shabaab, that has been active in the country ever since. Some of the fighting al-Shabaab has been involved in lends

---

[1] IGAD is a regional co-operation between Djibouti, Ethiopia, Kenya (nominally), Somalia, Sudan and Uganda.

further support to the argument that kinship in Somalia is no automatic guarantee of support. When the al-Shabaab militia attacked the seat of the nominal government (TFG) in Mogadishu in 2009 even the closest kinsmen of President Sharif Ahmed refused to defend him (Pham, 2011:139). Hence, clans appear to be more important semantically than organizationally. Having dealt with both the structural and historical reasons for the difficulties of polity formation in relation to the clan structure of Somalia I will now proceed with a brief investigation of Somaliland, an independent but unrecognized part of Somalia where a relatively stable order has been created.

Somaliland

Several authors have pointed out that numerous local and regional political orders exist in the territory nominally occupied by the Republic of Somalia (Bøås, 2013; Menkhaus, 2014). Somaliland is the most successful since it is not only stable and peaceful but has also managed to achieve democratic transition of power (Höhne, 2012:340). It was established through a series of peace conferences in the early 1990s. The participants were the elders of the Issa, Gadabursi, Dhulbahante and Warsengeli clans and leading members of the SNM. While not recognized internationally, Somaliland has been celebrated as the well-ordered exception to disorder in the rest of Somalia. Could it also be seen as evidence in favour of the argument that clan societies can form stable polities? To a certain degree, yes. Clans have been given a transparent and evident role in Somaliland politics and in the formation of its parliaments. The clan element was intertwined into the political order in a more sophisticated way than in the post-1991 state-building attempts in the south.

Is the success of Somaliland simply because clans were given an explicit and transparent place in the polity, instead being forced underground and simultaneously reinforced as in Somalia under the Barre regime? Well, other factors have also contributed to the comparative stability of Somaliland. As with several other postcolonial African polities, it was founded by a single political guerrilla movement: the SNM. The cohesion of the SNM, established during years of camp life and guerrilla struggles, was an important foundation of Somaliland as a state. The fact that the Isaaq are numerically superior to the other clans is also a contributing factor, as is the decision to give the polity a territorial base. The polity has grown out of local initiatives, whose participants represented interests and groups in the area (Walls, 2009). These factors are a marked contrast to the many externally sponsored peace conferences for the rest of Somalia, which have been rushed affairs whose participants were not representative of major groups.

Still, Somaliland did see a clan-based civil war between November 1994 and October 1996. Balthasar argues that Egal, Somaliland's president, instigated the war to consolidate the state by defeating some rivals and co-opting others (Balthasar, 2013). Its forces have also fought Puntland over the control of the border regions Sanaag and Sool in 2007 and the domestic Warsengeli and Dulbahante clans in Sanaag/Mahakir state. Thus, while Somaliland has been relatively stable it has not been peaceful and the civil war between 1994 and 1996 could have wrecked the fledgling polity. Thus, one must take care not to interpret the current stability as teleologically ordained due to more astute handling of structural factors. Instead, this could have gone differently. State building in Somaliland seems to owe a certain debt to the factors once identified by Charles Tilly as central to state formation: external war, first against Siad Barre, then against Puntland and other insurgents, helped create a national identity and more efficient state structures.

However, the embedding of the clans into the political order is a distinct feature of Somaliland. Somaliland was founded in 1991 at the clan conference in Borama. Its political system revolves around a two-chamber system. The upper house (*Guurti*) consists of elders who represent their clans. The elders have been credited with negotiating political settlements and mediating between clans and other political actors. The Guurti is the continuation of the clan council that the SNM created (Richards, 2014:111–12). Its members represent their clans and the Guurti acts as a 'clan council and as a parliamentary body'. All legislation must pass through the Guurti and it is also responsible for the 'maintenance of peace and security' and reconciliation between the people and the government. Furthermore, only three parties are allowed and these must represent all clans in Somaliland (Richards, 2014:113). The point is to have clans and parties intertwined to avoid a division of the party system along clan lines. The arrangement stands in sharp contrast to the externally sponsored state building projects in the South. In most incarnations, these have assigned proportional representation on the basis of clan affiliation. Such arrangements tend to deepen and politicize clan divisions rather than transcend them. In sum, Somaliland has embedded clans into the state and the party system and has achieved a relatively stable state albeit a democracy with limits.

Diffuse Kinship, Diffuse Institutions

The historical narrative shows it is fruitless to search for patterns in abstract schemes of clan classification and try to map them to patterns of polity formation and conflict. The schemes are abstractions and as such obscure the fluidity, cross-clan (and sub-clan, etc.) alliances, marriages and networks. The clans are practices, not a system in the strict, formal sense due to the absence of regular principles of operation.[2] Hence, there are no patterns to be found. The significant exception is Somaliland, whose leaders have embarked on a conscious policy of organizing Isaaq identity into something approximating a national identity. Instead, in order to make sense of the relation between the clan phenomenon and political order in Somalia we must view the former in a broader comparative light.

We have seen analogous patterns in earlier chapters of this book. In early medieval Europe, kinship networks could be the basis of both alliances and armed groups and the arenas for fighting between groups composed of 'friends, family and followers' (cf. Althoff, 2004). But kinship was not an unequivocal guarantee for alliances or solidarity. It is interesting that the ambiguous and causally indeterminate nature of clans is puzzling to Western researchers. I believe that the idea or even image of clans as close-knit communities, united by mechanistic solidarity that enables its members to stand by each other through thick and thin, gets in the way of understanding. Perhaps Somalia's problems could be sought not in the solidity of the clans but in their fluidity. As Duyvesteyn notes, prior to independence, Somali social structure was 'relatively loose' and the different groups of the country did not have a strong tradition of chieftaincies (Duyvesteyn, 2005:62). Moreover, most Somalis had relations to more than one clan. An individual could be linked to the clan of his mother or his wife in addition to the clan affiliation he inherited from his father (Duyvesteyn, 2005:39). As I have argued elsewhere, clans also have a tendency 'to fragment into smaller units that still remain capable of collective action' (Haldén, 2008).

---

[2] For a European analogy, see the argument about the Carolingian imperial aristocracy in Chapter 3.

Thus, Somali clans seem to be strong markers of identity, but weak as a basis for organization. The differences (such as size and semantics) notwithstanding, this complicated situation is reminiscent of the early medieval situation covered in Chapter 3. In, say, the ninth century a man might well choose to emphasize his affiliation with his mother's family is it had higher status than that of his father's and, furthermore, his wife's or mother's relatives might be valuable allies against his patrilineal relatives who would be dangerous rivals.

The complexity of Somali 'clan' and kinship structure and its fluidity may or may not be a sui generis phenomenon, in Africa and globally. However, it is a sign of a society that has not been subject to the processes of institutionalization and formalization of social life that compress it into a political order. Among the pastoral peoples of the Horn of Africa there have not been strong rules, orders or ideologies that have been interested in or capable of doing so. Thus, not only do parallels with Europe help to illuminate the Somali situation, the reverse is also true. The example of Somaliland thus illustrates how important it was to formalize social relations in order to create elaborate and durable political orders in European history.

Arab Monarchies

The chapter now turns to investigate the monarchies of the Arab world in general and Saudi Arabia in particular. For the purposes of this book three questions stand out: how were the monarchies established, are they old survivals from a premodern era or are they modern entities? The question of age is related to the question of durability. The purpose of this book is to investigate if family rule is compatible with political order. If Arab monarchies are survivals from 'bygone eras' then one could argue, as modernization theorists do, that they will succumb to an inevitable contradiction between family rule and political order. But if they are new and adaptable entities, then the case for the aforementioned contradiction is weakened and the prospects of survival are greater. The third question is how are Arab monarchies run? Does the monarchy permeate the political system? Does it rule in co-operation and dialogue with other groups or is it largely separated from them? I will address these issues below.

Kingship has old roots in Islamic societies, but contemporary Arab monarchies are strikingly modern – most monarchies were established at the beginning of the twentieth century as a means of making Arab societies modern. As Christopher Bayly has shown, many European states throughout the colonial era preferred to rule through noble and royal dynasties in the conquered countries (Bayly, 2004). At the end of World War One, the Ottoman Empire was dismantled and Iraq, Jordan, Lebanon, Libya, Saudi Arabia and Syria were created as British or French protectorates. In all cases the imperial powers recruited elite families as monarchs (Lucas, 2004:106). Monarchy was not seen as outdated but as the most prestigious form of rule. Hence in order to gain further recognition from international actors, many leaders in the Muslim countries abandoned the traditional titles such as Sultan, Emir, and Sharif, and adopted the previously rejected title 'King' (Tor, 2013:533–4). During the struggles for independence, the title *Malik* was adopted by the rulers of Morocco, Jordan, Libya, Egypt and Saudi Arabia to 'proclaim independence and, equally important, to project a degree of equality among fellow Arabian and Muslim rulers' (Kéchichian, 2008:26). Thus the royal dynasties are modern in the sense of the time as well as in the way in which they came to power. Far from being ancient, these monarchies are the results of early twentieth-century international social engineering (Anderson, 1991).

After World War Two, pan-Arab nationalist movements challenged monarchy and managed to overthrow the kingdoms of Egypt, Iraq and Libya. In the 1970s, communist and Islamist leaders toppled the monarchies of Afghanistan and Persia (Iran) and their fall led many observers in the West to declare that the days were numbered for the remaining monarchies in the region (Huntington, 1966). However, by the 1990s, the resilience of the remaining monarchies had proved modernization theorists wrong (Aarts, 2007). Anderson argues that one explanation for their resilience is their capacity to adapt (Anderson, 1991) which has clear parallels to their European counterparts in the nineteenth century discussed in Chapter 6. After the 'Arab Spring' of 2011, scholars have tried to explain why monarchic regimes have been far more stable than their non-monarchic counterparts (Fjelde, 2010; Knutsen and Fjelde, 2013; Moller Sondergaard, 2017). Oil wealth and superpower support have, for example, often been emphasized as important factors for the resilience of the Gulf monarchies (Kostiner, 2000:7). Bank and colleagues conclude that there is no single explanation for why Arab monarchies are so resilient (Anderson, 1991:4; Bank,

Richter and Sunik, 2015:5). However, some endogenous traits of monarchies seem beneficial to stability. Menaldo points to the capacity of monarchies to promote stability, limits on authority and cohesion between regime insiders (Menaldo, 2012:709). These traits are a marked contrast to the often despotic policies of non-monarchs in the Arab world – a contrast that further supports this book's argument that elite co-operation is central to stable polity formation. Of course, plenty of coercion and violence is being exercised against segments of the population at large. Still, I believe that it is important to see beyond it and the many ways in which Arab monarchies do not conform to parliamentary democracy in order to understand why they have remained viable. For instance, Kéchichian argues that the parliaments of the Arab monarchies are powerless and hence the monarchs always exercise 'absolute authority' (Kéchichian, 2008:2). It is too simplistic to limit the investigation of different power groups to an opposition between monarch and parliament. This opposition superimposes an interpretation from Europe's nineteenth century onto an alien setting. Pluralism in monarchies exists in the relations between different court factions or sub-groups of the royal family. To summarize, political order and family rule are not incompatible in the Arab world. From Morocco in the West to Oman in the East, different monarchies sustain their rule. I will now investigate and exemplify these trends by analysing Saudi Arabia.

Saudi Arabia

Saudi Arabia is the most powerful Arab monarchy today. In many ways it embodies the tendencies discussed in the previous section. It was established between 1902 and 1932 and is thus a very new state. It is modern not only in the sense of being new but also because of the capacity of its dynasty to adapt and change. In Saudi Arabia, the political order and the monarchy are largely synonymous. It is not an 'absolutist' state in the sense that a king rules without having to consult other groups and actors. Instead, politics are negotiated and decided among the different factions of the numerous al Saud family. Dynastic and political interdependence is also institutional since the monarchy and its members control all main political institutions and areas.

This section argues that there is thus no principled contradiction between family rule and political order in Saudi Arabia. But is this picture of harmony really correct? What opposition to the rule of the al Saud dynasty and to the monarchy as such exists? There are two forms of opposition: a small collection of democratic factions and a much larger collection of Islamic or 'Islamist' ones. The latter is the more important and ranges from sections of the established community of religious scholars and specialists, the ulama, to small terrorist groups. The first collection of opposition groups turns its criticism upon the monarchy as such but the ire of the second mainly concerns the perceived deviations of the monarchy's policies from the path of righteous Wahabite Islam. Below, I will analyse Saudi Arabia chronologically, which allows us to chart the development of its political order through its successive kings and their strategies. Saudi Arabia is a closed political system, where decisions are made in secrecy and within the circles of the royal dynasty, which makes exact study of decisions and reasons difficult (Ahrari, 1999). One needs to bear this in mind when analysing and making estimations about the country.

In the late nineteenth century, the British Empire began competing with the Ottoman Empire in the Middle East. The Sauds soon began exploiting the situation. However, they were not without rivals. The other two main competitors for control over Arabia were the Rashids and the Ashraf dynasty of Sharif Husayn. Each group had its distinct power resources. The Rashids were strongly associated with the Shammar tribal confederation, which was initially useful as it provided them with a military base (Al-Rasheed, 2002:25–9). As the Rashids expanded, the close association with a single tribal confederation became a liability, since it made it difficult to gain the support of other tribal groups. The Ashraf dynasty could claim holy descent from the Prophet Muhammad, which was a major asset in creating legitimacy. They could also act as mediators between important social groups, nomads and non-nomads and sedentary and non-sedentary populations. The Saudi's were not part of any dominant tribal group. At first, this was a disadvantage since they lacked manpower. However, it turned out to be an asset in the long run since it did not taint them with particularistic associations. Instead, it allowed them to act as mediators just like the Ashraf (Al-Rasheed, 2002:9). This trait shows that dynasty formation is not dependent on tribal affiliation. It also demonstrates that Saudi Arabia is not a tribal monarchy and not a 'survival' from pre-modern times but a peculiarly modern construction.

However, religious legitimacy alone does not build polities. In the early twentieth century Ibn Saud embarked on a campaign of conquest in which province after province fell to his forces. During this phase he ousted the other main rival dynasty, that of Sharif Husayn. This took place with British aid and subsidies. Sharif Husayn's sons, Faysal and Abdullah, became the kings of the newly created kingdoms of Trans-Jordan and Iraq. The four provinces Najd (the homeland of the Saudi dynasty), Hasa, Hijaz and 'Asir were unified by conquest between 1902 and 1932, when Kingdom of Saudi Arabia was declared.

In combination with the military triumphs, the old association with Wahabi preachers and ritual specialists, the Mutaww'a, proved to be the trump card of the Saudis. This organization was highly active in subduing the population and elites of Arabia both to their austere brand of Islam and to the rule of the al Saud. It also laboured intensively to create and manage the Ikhwan, a semi-permanent military force of Bedouin tribesmen that provided the manpower for the conquests of the Saud (Al-Rasheed, 2002:61). The Ikhwan were important in the wars of conquest but their vision of a good society eventually clashed with that of Ibn Saud. The latter wanted to create a durable state that would not fall victim to tribal disintegration and feuding. In 1929 Ibn Saud turned against the Ikhwan, prompting a full-scale rebellion and with the help of the British, Ibn Saud defeated the Ikhwan and thus eliminated them as a political force. From the 1930s, the major kinship element in the politics of the Kingdom would be that of the House of Saud, not that of tribes (Kostiner, 1985; Mabon, 2016:142–54). The recent revival of tribal identities seems largely to concern social rather than political questions (Maisel, 2014).

The Mutaww'a also provided the Saudis with a legitimating discourse. It appointed Ibn Saud Imam, suggesting that he was a religious leader and not a tribal *shayk* or military amir. Throughout the period of polity formation, Ibn Saud took on new titles, step by step. In 1921 he declared himself Sultan. This title signalled a position of dominance over Arabia to the British, who had become an important patron to the new polity. In 1932, Ibn Saud took the new step of declaring himself king and his polity a kingdom (Al-Rasheed, 2002:61). The first generation of polity building was characterized by intense biopolitical moves. Family management – producing offspring, settling marriages and regulating matters of succession – was tantamount to building the foundation of the new political order. First, Ibn

Saud pruned his kinship network and created a royal line. Between 1932 and 1953 Ibn Saud marginalized collateral branches of the Al Saud and consolidated his line of descent. He had previously fought off rebellions from his relatives, first from his paternal cousins and then from their maternal kin (Al-Rasheed, 2002:69). The order of succession was changed to ensure that his own sons would inherit him rather than relatives of his own generations. A second aspect of Ibn Saud's biopolitics was his extraordinary sexual relations. His astounding number of wives and concubines gave birth to no fewer than forty-three sons and more than fifty daughters, who – together with their offspring – make up the royal family. A third aspect of Saudi biopolitics were the marriages themselves, some of which were contracted with Arabian noble and religious families. Al-Rasheed points out that these marriages (most of which were serial in nature) were not ordinary alliances between powerful houses, being too short-lived or interrupted by divorces and remarriages to represent any kind of permanent relation (Al-Rasheed, 2002:75–7, 122). Moreover, most took place once the families had been militarily defeated. Finally, there was no reciprocity of wife-taking and wife-giving as the daughters of the Saudi family were married endogamously among paternal cousins. The only conclusion is that the marriages served, apart from the obvious means of procuring offspring, as a means of exerting and demonstrating dominance over militarily subdued groups.

Religious legitimacy, astute family management and foreign protectors were important power sources but in the 1930s a fourth source was discovered: oil. With the revenues they could construct patronage networks on a more intensive and extensive scale than anything seen before in Arabia. Oil enabled the regime to purchase weapons from abroad and to project influence elsewhere in the Arab world. This is not the place to detail the oil business or industry. However, suffice it to say that 25 per cent of the world's crude oil is found in Saudi Arabia. By comparison, Russia, another major exporter, holds 4 per cent (Aarts, 2007:251–67). This one crucial resource for the twentieth century world economy also enabled the Saudis to construct relations of mutual dependence to the point of symbiosis with the United States of America, the dominant great power of the twentieth century (Aarts, 2007). United States sponsorship of and support for the regime – dramatically demonstrated in the first Gulf War in 1991 – is a crucial asset.

With Ibn Saud's death in 1953 a new generation acceded to the throne of the kingdom. With the succession of his son Sa'ud a new round of biopolitical moves were necessary. Matters of succession are always problematic in dynastic polities but even more so in Islamic ones that lack primogeniture. Succession in Arab kinship groups can take two forms, horizontal and vertical. In the first case, leadership passes to the most powerful actor in the same generation, usually to a brother or cousin (Mouline, 2010:127). In the second, the oldest or favourite son succeeds the ruler. Saudi Arabia has practiced horizontal succession throughout most of its existence. All its kings, including the reigning king Salman (r.2015–) have been sons of the founder, Ibn Saud.

When Ibn Saud died his son Sa'ud succeeded him. His reign only lasted eleven years until his brother Faysal ousted him. One of Sa'ud's mistakes was to try to exclude his brothers and cousins from power and instead place his own sons at the centre of the polity (Al-Rasheed, 2002:104). During Faysal's reign the Saudi political system began to set. This system, or set of practices, which Nabil Mouline calls 'multi-domination' consists of power-sharing between the main princes and their families. Each prince controls a portion of the state, such as a ministry, and exercises considerable liberty in ruling it together with his sons (Mouline, 2010:212ff). In this family compact, the king is not an absolute ruler and must not aspire to become one. Rather, he is a mediator and a *primus inter pares*. The centre of decision-making is the royal family council (*majlis al-'â'ila*). Thus, Saudi Arabia is not a theocracy but its monarchy aligns its actions and language of legitimation with Islamic jurisprudence and political thought and makes symbolic acts intended to signify divine sanction (Al-Atawneh, 2009). Al-Atawneh calls this polity a 'theo-monarchy'. Without delving too deeply into typologies, given the system of domination and multi-domination in Saudi Arabia the label 'absolute monarchy' is misleading. True, the core of the state rests on what could perhaps translate as an approximation of the European term 'royal prerogative' but the position of the Saudi king is different from a European one (Al-Rasheed, 2002:212ff).

The state does revolve around royal prerogative in a looser sense of the word as politics are the prerogative of the members of the royal family, which was dominated by seven of the sons of Ibn Saud, the so-called Sudayrî-s. Given this fact, it may seem redundant to ask, as this chapter does, whether kinship groups (in this case the Saudi network)

cause war and conflict since they are the prime movers of the state. In
a sense, the question is already answered: reasons of state and reasons of
dynasty are indistinguishable. It was in the interests of the Saudi family
to attempt to seize leadership of the Arab world by imposing an oil
embargo on the West after the Arab-Israeli War of 1973. However,
there are some instances where specific kinship relations have determined polity. For instance Saudi antagonism towards Iraq and Jordan in
the 1950s was because their Hashemite dynasties enjoyed a much
greater legitimacy in the Arab world due to their descent from the
Prophet Muhammad than did the House of Saud (Al-Rasheed,
2002:111). Although Saudi Arabia is currently engaged in fighting in
Yemen it must be noted that a general trend among countries in the
Middle East and North Africa has been that monarchies tend to be less
involved in violent conflicts than republics (Menaldo, 2012). Since Arab
monarchies have been steadily more peaceful internally and externally,
the war in Yemen is rather an exception to this trend.

Saddam Hussein's invasion of Kuwait in 1991 set off a chain of
events that included the most serious challenges to the rule of the Saudis.
The Saudi rulers realized that they could not defend themselves and
invited the United States to garrison the country and use it as a launching
pad for their subsequent liberation of Kuwait (Al-Rasheed, 2002:159–
60). The massive presence of foreign and non-Muslim troops provoked
public opinion in the kingdom. Not only was the country evidently not
capable of self-defence but had to suffer having large numbers of non-
believers on holy soil. As a consequence, the Ulama's criticism of the
way the Saudi dynasty ruled the country escalated (Al-Rasheed,
2002:161–2).

Like European monarchies almost two centuries before them,
the Saudis countered radical protests with reforms from above. In 1992
a Basic Law of Government was promulgated. In Chapter 6 we saw how
European monarchies in the nineteenth century created constitutions as
a means of placating opponents as well as to cement power. Dynastic
preoccupations are central to the Basic Law of Government. It sets out
the following principles: it allows succession to pass to the next generation, the grandsons of Abdul Aziz, and states that each king should
name his heir apparent, a practice that was common in early modern
European monarchies to forestall succession struggles. It also excluded
the collateral branches of the royal family, by not naming them (Ahrari,
1999:17). In biopolitical terms, the last move represents yet another

pruning of the family network; narrowing it down to the main branch. We saw above that such 'pruning' occurs cyclically. The first one was made by Ibn Saud himself between the 1930s and 1950s and the latest might be underway at the time of writing this book (2019).

A decade after the Gulf War, the next series of external shocks rocked the kingdom; in turn sparking internal reforms. On 11 September 2001, hijackers flew two planes into the World Trade Center in New York City, a third into the Pentagon and a fourth – probably intended for the White House – crashed into a field in Stony Creek, Pennsylvania. Of the nineteen hijackers, fifteen came from Saudi Arabia. The origins of the majority of the hijackers led to serious external criticism of the kingdom and a temporary cooling of Saudi-US relations. The fact that al-Qaeda's notorious leader, Usama bin Laden, was a Saudi Arabian millionaire did not improve public relations. Saudi Arabia was no stranger to Islamist terrorism, the bombing of the housing complex Khobar Towers in 1996 was the first attack on Saudi soil. Since then al-Qaeda and the Saudi dynasty have repeatedly exchanged blows, including assassination attempts against members of the royal family (Hegghammer, 2006; Aarts and Roelants, 2015:129). Not only violent Islamist movements threaten the Saudi monarchy. Islamism of the kind represented by the Muslim Brotherhood, is a direct threat to Saudi rule since it advocates democracy and free elections. Also, it does not recognize the monopolization of Islamic legitimacy by a single dynasty (Aarts and Roelants, 2015:112). Although the Islamic State enjoyed some early popularity among Saudi youth, as of 2015, the latter have largely turned away from Islamist extremism but the regime faces the risk of considerable social protests that some experts claim might cause its downfall (Aarts and Roelants, 2015:118). Social discontent is considerable even though political opposition to the House of Saud is feeble. Whether the former may eventually generate the latter remains to be seen.

A certain and recognized threat to the stability of the kingdom is, however, the problem of succession. To counter this, the regime continued to modernize. In 2007 King Abdullah created the Committee of Allegiance, an institution designed to settle the succession to the throne. Its thirty-five members are sixteen sons and nineteen grandsons of Ibn Saud who meet in secret to select the king. Other elites of the kingdom and the ulama are excluded from the committee. Instead, their role is to confirm the choice made by the royal electors

(Al-Rasheed, 2002:258–9; Mouline, 2010:139–44). Although the creation of the committee seemed to confirm the de facto principles of selecting a new king and establish their alignment with Islamic jurisprudence and political theory, practice soon deviated from the template.

The death of the long-reigning and popular King Abdullah in 2015 sparked speculation, and soon intrigue, concerning the succession. At the initiative of king Abdullah, the family had designated Prince Salman – one of Ibn Saud's sons – as the successor as well as Salman's successor, namely Prince Muqrin – Ibn Saud's youngest son. This procedure of naming two successive crown princes was unusual and a breach of the Basic Law. Still, the principle of horizontal succession was maintained. However, once installed as king, Salman replaced Muqrin with his own favourite son Muhammad bin Salman as the crown prince. The elevation of MBS, as he has become known, introduced agnatic succession (father-son) for the first time since 1953, which caused some controversy (*Financial Times*, 2017). Like his father, MBS moved quickly to consolidate his position with mass purges. He targeted dozens of the kingdom's most influential figures, including eleven royal cousins (*New York Times*, 2017). He established control over the military, the internal security services and the National Guard – posts that were previously held by other princes in the royal family. Previously control over these posts were distributed throughout branches of the House of Saud, but now they are concentrated in the hands of MBS. Further crackdowns targeted the business community and the clerical establishment and those detained were all charged with corruption (Kirkpatrick, 2017).

Lately, Saudi Arabia has become much more active strategically in the region. Since 2015 the kingdom has embarked on a war against the Houthi rebels in Yemen as the leader of a coalition of Arab states. In 2017 the Saudis began intervening in Lebanon, a country where Iran wields influence through its Hezbollah client. It pressured Prime Minister Saad Hariri to resign in order to expose Iranian influence (Miller and Sokolsky, 2017). The current foreign and military policies of Saudi Arabia – and their anti-Iranian thrust – are sometimes interpreted as the latest incarnation of a Sunni-Shi'a rivalry that stretches back to the seventh century (Kazemzadeh, 2018). The fear of a 'Shiite crescent' stretching from Iran, through a Shi'a-dominated Iraq, to the client states of Syria and Lebanon is often invoked as an explanation of Saudi actions. Doubtless, such Realist interpretations of regional power games have their explanatory value (Barzegar, 2008). However, recognizing Saudi Arabia's character as a dynastic power allows for yet another facet of understanding. All Arab authoritarian systems emphasize that dynastic legitimacy is not enough, but it must be supplemented by personal legitimacy. Each time a new king comes to power (or a king hands over effective power to the Crown Prince) the new ruler must build a personal legitimacy of his own (Ahrari, 1999). This particular fact of the norms of succession in Arab monarchies allows us to understand the actions of MBS much better. Going to war in order to establish the legitimacy of one's reign is a trait that we have encountered several times in this book. We saw it in Frederick the Great's invasion of Silesia as a young king in 1740, eager to win reputation and glory[3]. But we also saw it in the Ottoman Empire, where the sons of the old sultan fought each other in order not only to knock rivals out of the conquest but actually to prove that they were legitimate rulers.

Crown Prince Mohamad bin Salman's programme of reform and centralization has received a lot of international attention. Previous chapters of this book have highlighted that it is perilous to centralize with coercion. Indeed, attempts to press pluralistic dynastic societies into an absolutist frame have often been the downfall of empires in the Islamic world and in Europe. Analysts ought to ask if the Crown Prince's series of moves is too much of a break with the balance between different centres of power in the Saudi political system. In other words, is he attempting to press the Saudi Arabian form of elite pluralism into a too centralized frame – an attempt that is likely to cause a backlash (*Washington Post*, 2017)? Or, will he be able to increase the efficiency of the monarchy and thereby limit the criticism that it has been exposed to? Only time will tell. This chapter cannot speculate on the outcomes, but given the wealth of similar attempts and how they ended in defeat for the aspiring 'absolutist' ruler, the pace and intensity of change does not bode well for Saudi stability.

Conclusions

Returning to the main questions of this book, do the examples of Somalia and Saudi Arabia demonstrate that kinship-based formations and political orders, in particular the state, are incompatible? In

---

[3] See Kunisch, 2004, chapter 2.

southern Somalia, there seems to be a certain degree of incompatibility between the modern state, based – ideal typically – on a sovereign as a single, unitary fountainhead of authority and its many kinship-based groups. There is not, one has to add, a conflict between political order in a wider sense and kinship groups since there are plenty of local varieties of political rule. It should be clarified that the conflict, or contradiction, between kinship-based groups and the state that developed in the twentieth century revolves around a particularly predatory, dictatorial variety of the state that did not attempt to build an order on the consensual, negotiated traits of Somali culture. Instead it perpetuated the divide and rule politics of the colonialists. It is this kind of rapacious Leviathan that many Somali actors turn against and prefer statelessness over. However, it is important to stress that it was not a primordial 'clan system' that caused the collapse of the Republic of Somalia but the contradictions and weaknesses of a predatory 'quasi-state' (Jackson, 1990). Somaliland is a case in point. Its genesis lies in a carefully negotiated process that took the pluralism of the area into account and valued consensus over coercion and its continued stability in the close embedding of kinship (or *tol*)-based formations and institutions taken from the modern state template. Thus, we see that kinship-based formations and principles of legitimacy are compatible with the modern state as long as the latter is flexible enough.

The example of Saudi Arabia demonstrates that it is indeed possible to combine monarchy, that is, hereditary rule, with modernity. It is of course not the liberal, democratic version of modernity. Rather, it is one akin to the survival strategy of reform that European monarchies embraced in the nineteenth century. Saudi Arabia is by no means a democracy and indeed monarchy, a ruling aristocracy or the oligarchic rule of a network of princely families is incompatible with democracy based on universal suffrage. Saudi Arabia is a very young political order and that makes it difficult to draw conclusions about the development and maintenance of political order on the basis of its brief history. However, it is noteworthy that it has not been ruled autocratically but rather through consent and collaboration within the ruling al Saud family network – or rather between the families that make up the network. On certain occasions, the king has run roughshod over collateral branches as well as over other elite families, but so far the political order has not seen any seriously threat of elite revolts of the kind that European polities experienced as an effect of autocratic centralizing measures. Whether this is due to particular circumstances of these specific episodes or to the buffering effects of oil wealth is beyond the scope of this book to investigate. However, the example of Saudi Arabia does lend support to the main arguments of this book: family rule is not incompatible with political order or even with modernity, and stable orders often build on consent and collaboration among the ruling elites.

11 CONCLUSIONS
Implications for State Theory, Power and Modernity

Introduction

Having finished the empirical chapters, the time has now come to inquire into the meaning of their results. I will do so first by summarizing and synthesizing the results of the historical-sociological analysis of the position of families and ideas of inherited power and position as legitimate in the different political orders dealt with in this book. Then I will deal with two other questions that the results of this book touch upon: the nature of power in society and the nature of modernity. As Chapter 2 demonstrated, the idea of an opposition between kinship and political order is deeply embedded in the social sciences. Disproving that idea and substituting it with a historical-sociological analysis that demonstrates that kinship, in the shape of organizations and ideas, was central to political order has consequences for these two themes. They were not part of the book's original problem, but the results of the empirical chapters nevertheless impact upon these core themes of social theory.

The section on Power and Political Orders discusses the fact that there is a strong strand in state theory that focuses on the coercive aspects of the state and the need for a monopoly of violence. A corresponding idea in wider sociology is the conflict theory of society. The contrasting tradition emphasizes that power can also be about collaboration and acting in concert – and that societies depend on equilibria and consensus, not just conflicts between groups. I argue that a synthesis between conflict and consensus sociology is necessary for a comprehensive understanding of society as a human phenomenon. This section is mainly forward-looking in character and points towards the need for further theoretical development. However, it also speaks to a topic that has been a major security and strategic concern in Western thinking in the last three decades: 'state-building' – the idea that states can and should be built in unstable regions in order to create national and international security. This strategy and in particular its execution has depended heavily upon what has been called a neo-Weberian view of the state and upon establishing military preponderance over insurgents rather than negotiating with them (Jones, 2013). My argument calls this strategy into question by pointing to the evidence amassed by an analysis of stable and unstable political orders in Eurasian history. On the basis of my study, it seems clear that a project of order that mainly depends on conquest and declines to negotiate with enemies and rivals that nonetheless are very powerful has slim chances of surviving.

The second theme my study touches upon is the nature of modernity. The idea that a break with kinship-based or kinship-influenced forms of social and political organization as central to modernity is important in most of theories and stories told about modernity. However, this book has demonstrated that kinship-based forms of organization, such as dynasties and clans, are compatible with modern societies but just not with a particular variant of what I call the modern template, namely the liberal democratic one. This insight necessitates some rethinking about what modernity is. Other scholars, such as the late and great S. N. Eisenstadt, have already done some of it through the idea of 'multiple modernities'. My argument, however, is that a common template of modernity as a civilization or epoch can be established and then a plurality of variants can be discerned. Thereafter one can periodize varieties of modernity in time and pair that typology with one that localizes different kinds of modernity in distinct social formations.

Kinship and Political Order

Each chapter of this book asked three questions. (1) Can we really see a conflict between kinship and political orders? (2) What kinds of symbiosis between kinship and political order are visible in the societies and periods studied in this book? (3) What arrangement of kinship principles and structures accounts for stability and legitimacy of a political order?

At no time between 500 AD and the end of the eighteenth century were families incompatible with political order in Europe. The same conclusion applies to the realm of ideas, conceptions that inherited power was legitimate dominated the continent. In various forms kinship was a constitutive element of politics, institutions and warfare and acted as a means to stabilize political orders. An alternative vision about political order, empty of kinship elements, began to be formulated at the end of the eighteenth century. This vision did not break through completely until the early twentieth century. Meanwhile, it was possible to create modern states and societies that had kinship at the very core of their political orders. Furthermore, the historical chapters demonstrate that integration of powerful families was a precondition of stability and cohesion in the political order. Of course, historians have documented plenty of coercion and violence but without co-operation between family-based elites and their legitimacy, no polities would have survived the vicissitudes of the centuries. Taking a broad sweep of European history we can see that there is a correlation in time between the increasing solidification of political order and the increasing formalization of elite families into the category of nobility. These families and their claims to pre-eminence were oriented towards the political order, its institutions and central values. They derived their standing from inherited power but also from their privileged position in politics and the political order was legitimated by the existence of elite families with hereditary power, both royal and aristocratic. From an early stage a co-dependence can be observed between elite families, kingship and the abstract figure of the realm. Each 'pole' in this figuration depended on the other. A unique factor in the European development was that the groups of elite families became public and transparent, and thus visible to themselves and to the king and the organs of rule. This made ruling easier and probably facilitated inter-elite trust, but it also made the monarchical-aristocratic formation a more visible target for critics who become increasingly vocal in the eighteenth century and increasingly powerful in the nineteenth.

The Arab, European, Ottoman and Turko-Mongol chapters yielded similar results with regard to successful, that is, stable, polity formation: political orders were successful to the extent that they managed to integrate and embed kinship groups. However, they demonstrated that attempting to break these formations and impose centralized and hierarchical rule was a dangerous strategy that often backfired. This pattern was clear in Turkic polities, in the caliphate of the Umayyads and in medieval European realms. Thus the admonition of Thomas Hobbes, which is echoed in some twentieth-century state theory, that one must break the importance of (elite) kinship groups in order to establish a political society, seems wrong. What is required is rather effective embedding into institutions and sets and semantics of ideas of legitimacy and rule as well as effective mechanisms of co-rule and collaboration. This book has demonstrated that kinship and its relation to the political order is a very flexible thing. It can be, and has been, shaped by political actions and ideas. In Europe, a number of institutional and ideational innovations made elite kinship into a category and a concept, nobility, that was structured, formalized and public – a development that proved to be a considerable asset to the formation of stable political orders. In the Arab empires registers existed but the policies of the Umayyads and Abbasids marginalized the proto-nobility into irrelevance. In the Turko-Mongol and Ottoman Empires no such formalization took place.

The investigation of this book stepped into an old divide between two traditions in political science and sociology. The first hailed originally from Aristotle and considered families and other associations natural parts of the political order. The second had its origins in the early modern natural law tradition and argued that the basic building-block of society is the individual who enters into a relation with the state (Bobbio, 1993). If these two traditions are viewed as normative arguments about how political order ought to be structured, then I cannot adjudicate between them. However, if they are seen as alternative ways of reasoning, then I can. It is clear that the former is a more accurate description of what political order looked like until the early 1900s, while the normative programme of the latter managed to some extent to re-mould political order during the twentieth century. As Norberto Bobbio describes them, the two traditions also differ with regard to how they reason. The first, Aristotelian, was based on historical-sociological inquiry and thus on empirical studies whereas the latter was based on theoretical reasoning on the basis of abstract models. I believe that the former is a better and sounder foundation for theoretical reasoning. Its advantages are particularly clear when we analyse societies that do not conform to the pattern envisioned by the natural law theorists, whether in Europe's past or outside of Europe. It is difficult to apply an originally normative ideal type to countries or periods that were organized very differently. I can only concur with Mamdani's argument that one must build theoretical models on the basis of conditions prevailing in non-European countries that one wants to study, rather than on late-modern European conditions (Mamdani, 2012). The same argument applies to attempts to build theoretical and synthetical models to understand societies in the past, in Europe and elsewhere. A normative ideal-type from the eighteenth or nineteenth century – that is, the sovereign state dealing with individuals – makes a poor fit if it is applied to early societies or used, implicitly or explicitly, as a macro concept of political order. Not only social scientists but also historians are sometimes prone to this habit. My concept of 'political order' that was discussed in Chapter 1, the introduction to this book, is an attempt to introduce a wider, more neutral concept.

In the introduction and in Chapter 2 I stated that this book is partly a 'postcolonial' analysis of Eurasian history. I meant this in the sense of trying to go beyond concepts and conceptions that denigrated societies, periods and traits that did not conform to the normative pattern of modern politics. This ambition entailed studying traits that are usually seen as anti-modern and anti-political – family-based institutions and orders – and highlighting their importance for stability and political development. We may not like it but political orders were made by elites who collaborated and bonded through, among other ways, kinship ties (e.g., synchronic and diachronic ties) and made rule in concert and over others possible through the symbolic medium of hereditary power, which in turn was connected to sacred power (c.f. Shils, 1975).

Power and Political Orders: Coercion or Collaboration?

Theories of the state and state formation are impossible without theories of power. However, most state theorists have focused on the coercive or, in Michael Mann's terms, distributional theories of power. Max Weber's definition of the state, which has become almost canonical in the social sciences, emphasizes coercive power by stressing the need to successfully '[uphold] the claim to the *monopoly* of the *legitimate* use of physical force in the enforcement of its order' (Weber, 1978:54). Possessing a monopoly on legitimate violence and supreme capabilities thereof in order to defeat external foes and internal rivals is central to state formation theories due to the roles played by the competitive international system and endemic warfare as a driver of state formation(Hintze, 1962b; Tilly, 1990; Ertmann, 1997). This understanding is not without its critics. Ernest Gellner called attention to the fact that not all states have had an interest in or the means to enforce a monopoly of violence (Gellner, 2008:3). Furthermore, the focus on the monopoly of violence in the Weberian tradition (although not as exclusively by Weber himself) obscures other important characteristics of the state (Kaspersen, Strandsbjerg and Teschke, 2017). Giddens has criticized Weber's concept of the state as being too based on historically specific circumstances that are projected backwards in time (Giddens, 1985:18, 27). Instead of focusing on the monopoly of force, Gellner writes that the state is engaged in upholding order. We can understand order in two principal ways: first, in the sense of ensuring conformity with existing laws or relations of rule and punishing dissent and challenges to the rulers (which means that armed parties may be tolerated as long as they do not challenge the latter). Second, we can understand order in the sense of 'arrangement', as the result of ordering activities. This understanding is inspired by pre-eighteenth-century uses of the concept 'constitution' not as a written document but as the arrangement, order and condition of political relations (Mohnhaupt, 1990). Doing so alerts us to the role of the state as the agency that gives shape to social relations and sometimes the identity and nature of actors under its sway. In this reading, the state is more of an ordering and organizing body.

Less 'Realist' and more Marxist or 'Marxomorph' theories also emphasize coercive power, which is primarily inter-class rather than inter-state, in upholding stratification, property relations and the possession of the means of production (Anderson, 1974; Teschke, 2003). Although these aspects of power in the state and in its formation are formidable and cannot be overlooked our focus on them has overshadowed the importance of consensus and collective power. These theories reduce the state to an apparatus for coercion, accumulation and regulation. Taking a very long historical view, James C. Scott argues that the emergence of sedentary societies – as opposed to hunter-gatherer societies – was an essentially coercive process (Scott, 2017). Intuitively, it is easy to agree with Weber's definition of power as the power to issue commands or to understandings power as the ability to withhold knowledge or forestall ways of thinking (Weber, 1978:53; Lukes, 2005; Gramsci, 2010). But, important as this definition is, it is not exhaustive.

My long-term historical analysis demonstrated that a common theme – at least between elite groups – has been co-operation, interwoven identities and mutual interests. At least on this level of society, which John Hall identified as the politically active one in pre-industrial societies, there was rarely a centre that exercised coercive power over other power groups (Hall, 1986). Societies that have depended on consent and co-rule among elites have been more stable throughout history. The empirical chapters show how attempts to rule a realm without counsel from the important elites have generally resulted in revolts, civil wars or breakdowns. This tendency is visible in the Arab empires of the Umayyads and Abbasids, the Seljuk Empire, and in the early medieval, high medieval and early modern periods in Europe. Evidence of collaboration from the latter period is of particular interest since the dominant ideology in almost all realms stated that the king did not need consent to govern. More recent empirical research has shown that wise rulers nevertheless sought and gained consent. This has strongly revised the earlier image of the so-called absolutist state – an image that remains a staple in social science. The image of absolutism has been undermined in the French case, which was seen as its paradigmatic incarnation for a long time. Perhaps more importantly, even in the Russian case, the image of absolutism or autocracy has been undermined. These advances have led to a re-evaluation of our understanding of the state in Europe during this important period. What remains for social science is to draw the theoretical conclusions of the changes in historiography.

In order to understand the symbiosis between kinship and political order in a theoretical way we must turn to theories of power as collaboration. Drawing upon Parsons, Michael Mann argues that social formations cannot manage with only despotic or distributive power but they also need infrastructural or collective power (Mann, 1986:6–10). Collective power is when 'persons can enhance their joint power over third parties or over nature' (Mann, 1986:6). We can interpret 'nature' either literally, as when a group of people build a bridge over a stream. However, we can also interpret it figuratively as a collective winning over the absence of organization. People living at the beginning of the twenty-first century are accustomed to highly elaborate organizational environments where organizational innovation often seems to improve upon previously existing modes of collective action. We can, however, observe several examples in world history of pristine organizational innovation that opened up wholly new possibilities of collective action. Mann rightly points out that in any social formation collective and distributional forms of power co-exist and intertwine. All forms of organization enable collective action but they also entail super- and subordination within the group and possibilities to exercise distributive power over other groups (Mann, 1986:6–10). Even more precise is Arendt's definition of power as the 'capacity to act in concert' (Arendt, 1972:143–55). This view stresses that power depends on a group, on consent, and on legitimacy.

The idea of collective power, or power as acting in concert, means that power is not just a one-sided 'resource' that is employed by one party to a relation. Some forms of power undoubtedly take that shape, but collective power emphasizes the necessity for mutuality and interdependence in order to bring about results. Mutual dependence and autonomy, respectively, can be seen as different qualities in a figuration and what quality dominates determines to a large extent what kind of figuration is established. Indeed, the essence of Elias' idea of a figuration is the interdependence of actors in a single whole that would not exist without its parts (Elias, 2012).

An older tradition in political thought distinguished between different kinds of political communities on the basis of what relations of power dominated the polity. Two of the greatest political thinkers of the late Middle Ages, Marsiglio of Padua (c.1275–1342) and Fortescue (1394–1476), distinguished between polities that were *dominium regale* and those that were *dominium politice et regale* (Fortescue, 1997a:83–90). The former was close to tyranny since kings who did not ask for or require consent ruled them autocratically. The latter were 'political' entities because they were based on consultation and consent. Theories of the state with a one-sided emphasis on coercion are closer to a view of the state as *dominium regale* and include too little of the idea of a *dominium politice* in how they see the core of the state. My intention at present is not to discuss concrete cases at this stage but to re-introduce collective power at the heart of how we understand political orders. In any formation collective power exists alongside coercive power and the two will presuppose each other in intricate ways. As the empirical chapters suggest, a theory of the formation of political order will have to take both into account as very few societies, if any, can function only based on coercion. Instead of coercion, one of the chief drivers of state formation is rather the need to collaboration and collective action. Successful formations depend on embedding and the shaping of symbiotic relations.

Dealing with the relation between kinship-based elites and political order takes us into the core of social theory: is equilibrium or conflict the most important characteristic of a social system? Some readers might have expected a book on hereditary ruling elites to focus on the overt or tacit conflicts between these elites and other groups. A society with hereditary elites is by definition a stratified one and stratification is, almost per definition, a form of domination.[1] Without disregarding conflict and domination, the question of equilibrium and stability must also be brought into the equation. Collaboration between elites and their shared norms and values account for much of the stability of societies and indeed for their formation. Stability and longevity become part of the relation between kinship-based elites and political order because the pattern of organizing society on the basis of hereditary power was so long-lived. In fact, it was the norm for much of human history (Oakley, 2006). Somewhat puzzlingly, we face a mode of organization that could be described as collaboration and manufactured consent under hierarchy. Since consent seems to point towards equality but hierarchy towards inequality, a synthesis between concepts of power is apparently necessary.

In the history of sociology, stability and conflict form the two pillars on which two different traditions were formed. The tendency to identify social systems with stability and equilibrium ultimately hails from Émile Durkheim and was significantly expanded upon by Talcott Parsons. Conflict theory was formed as a counter-reaction to the Parsonian emphasis on stability and shared norms as the bedrock of a society (Joas and Knöbl, 2009). It was formed around mid-century in America but its intellectual forerunners and sources of inspiration were earlier thinkers like Karl Marx, Max Weber, Georg Simmel and Otto Hintze. Modern thinkers like Ralf Dahrendorf, Reinhard Bendix and Randall Collins all used the insights of such forerunners but significantly expanded upon and modified their thought. Many of the significant contributors to research on the historical formation of political orders,

---

[1] For an overview of forms of differentiation, including stratification, see Buzan and Albert, 2010.

such as Charles Tilly and Thomas Ertman, can also be associated with conflict theory more broadly. It is important to note, however, that some early conflict theorists noted the need to combine the 'Parsonian theory of integration' and 'Weberian-Marxist conflict theory'. For example, David Lockwood and John Rex argued that integration theory and conflict theory were actually complementary (Joas and Knöbl, 2009:181–3). Michael Mann attempted to combine the two in his magisterial theoretical-historical work *The Sources of Social Power* (Mann, 1986, 1997). Once we analyse developments over longer periods of time, we have to engage with both stability and conflict.

I do not wish my account to be read as an attempt to neglect the role of conflict and warfare in the formation of political order but I would like to highlight a role beyond the material-accumulative function that Tilly and others emphasize: the role of creating collective meaning and community. In Chapter 4 I discuss the fact that warfare was a communal activity that wove elites closer together, with their king, with each other and with the political order. Warfare was a meaningful and meaning-creating activity that allowed them to represent their political order (and thus their roles in it) and thereby to conjure it into existence. This feature also came to the fore in Chapter 3 that illustrates that warfare was not just an activity that led to material gain but was also an important part of elite identities. In this light, then, power seems Janus-faced. Coercion and co-operation work hand-in-hand in a virtuous circle – at least from the viewpoint of social integration. Collaboration and consent are necessary to exercise coercion and collective violence and the exercise of coercion in concert enables further collaboration. A similar mechanism has been suggested by Randall Collins (Collins and Sanderson, 2009:175). In theoretical terms, the integrative effects of fighting together demonstrate that the validity of a distinction between 'power to' (coercive power) and 'power over' (collaborative power) and that the two can be co-constitutive.[2]

My focus on the early and high Middle Ages in this respect emphasizes that it was during this period that the idea, feeling and habit of participating in a political order appears and solidifies – certainly with the aid of other institutions and practices like royal elections, rituals and council government. Often the early modern

---

[2] For a recent review of the debate over the relation between 'power to' and 'power over', see Haugaard, 2017; Battegazzorre, 2017:274–85.

period (c.1500–1800) is considered the take-off period of state formation and it was certainly then that a partly new political order evolved and when the great material, administrative and military growth took place. Still I would like to emphasize, through my study of the family-based elites, that the (admittedly long) Middle Ages was a more fundamental period for the evolution of political order.

This discussion of collaboration and community brings us to the question of the balance between collaboration and coercion. It is not possible to have ruling social formations without coercive power. For authority to rule it must be able to take the form of law. In turn, the characteristic of a law, as opposed to other normative prescriptions, is that it contains the possibility of sanction (Kelsen, 2002). Sanction, in turn, requires force. However, ruling formations and politics as an activity cannot be reduced to this facet alone. Zero-sum theories of power perform a conceptual severing of the relations that a society consists of and construct them as autonomous or rather atomistic entities. Distributive power is by definition zero-sum; for A to gain power, B must lose some. It is also not without ontological consequences as it constructs A and B as autonomous entities, joined only by the dominance of A over B. The Hegelian Master-Slave (*Herr-Knecht*) dialectic can be cited as a theoretical formulation of a power relation in which both parties are parts of a configuration, that constructs both of them, rather than pre-existing actors whose identities are independent from their relation (Haldén, 2018:6–7). In more recent social theory, Norbert Elias has scathingly criticized the very idea of atomistic individuals (Elias, 2012). Viewing power thus leads to the idea that some party must have power resources in order to create a durable figuration. It also has ontological consequences in the form of a view of the state as autonomous and automatically in conflict with other centres of power. The conception of power as zero-sum and the view of society as possible to disaggregate into pre-existing autonomous components have, I believe, contributed to our tendency to avoid seeing political orders as configurations of interdependent and co-constitutive parts, and in particular to overlook the symbiosis of kinship groups and political order.

I would like to conclude that control over and the exercise of collective violence and coercion are necessary but not sufficient for the formation and maintenance of political orders. Linking the historical-sociological analysis of this book to theories of power one could say that there are three broad categories of power: coercive, hegemonic and collective – all of them necessary elements in a political order. As I said in Chapter 1, I have not endeavoured to write a complete history or formulate a complete theory of political order. First, such a task would necessarily be a multi-volume book as the seminal work of Michael Mann demonstrates. Second, that would require an in-depth examination of coercive and hegemonic forms of power and how they have been used between elite groups and between elite and non-elite groups. What this work has done is to outline a neglected aspect of the formation of political orders through a historical-sociological analysis of the relation between, on the one hand, kinship ideas and organizations and, on the other, political order in Arab, European and Ottoman history.

The results of this book also have bearing on one of the most costly and ambitious security strategies of the last three decades: 'state-building'. The United States and most European states have in some way or another tried it in Africa, Asia and Europe to a great cost in blood, time and treasure. Since this book has demonstrated the need to foster collaboration and consensus among elite groups, whatever their ideological preferences are, it is probably more effective to build the capacity of 'fragile' or 'failed' states to do so than to emphasize and construct a state monopoly of violence. Shutting the door on negotiations with key elite groups, such as the Taliban, may be normatively just but, judging from historical evidence, it may not be conducive to long-term stability. Also, the role of negotiating and brokering deals has to be developed internally. If outside actors take over the role of doing so, then the state may be fatally weakened. Finally, establishing a political community is more important than getting a formal apparatus, a set of coercive and redistributive institutions in place. Rather than looking at efficiency of state institutions in providing public goods, we should be looking for institutions and ideas that create community. Rather than effective supply chains, any political community needs ideas about that community that are believable and institutions that can foster them. How these insights from a neglected aspect of European history could be translated into current policy is, however, beyond the scope of this study.

A further implication for contemporary politics can be drawn from the insights about the communal and community-generating aspects of warfare that were assembled in Chapters 3, 4, 7 and 8. The chapters on the Arab and Turkic empires (Chapters 7 and 8, respectively) demonstrate the grave problems that the introduction of slave soldiers (mamluk, ghulam) instead of indigenous fighters brought to political order. Chapter 10 also briefly discusses Muhammar al-Gaddafi's strategy of employing mercenaries instead of building up a proper army. When the regime was shaken, the mercenaries departed and there was no one left to fight for it; as the mercenaries were marginalized in the military business, they were also marginalized in the political. In Hirschmann's terms they were forced to a kind of 'exit' rather than a possibility to exercise 'voice' or 'loyalty'. Chapters 3 and 4 demonstrate that in medieval Europe warfare was important in creating a sense of loyalty and responsibility to and for the political order. Now, with some exceptions, there are few real slave soldiers in the world today. However, there are many kinds of foreign fighters that have been imported or invited by other governments or intervened in places that lack effective state structures and/or political orders: these range from American and European troops in Afghanistan and Iraq (until their recent withdrawal); EU troops in Mali; other soldiers engaged in 'peace enforcement' or 'peace support' operations in various parts of the world; paid and invited soldiers that range from mercenaries to private military companies; the foreign volunteers in Ukraine and Syria; to Hezbollah fighters in Syria. None of these are of course slaves, and they differ vastly in terms of capacity, motivation and legitimacy, but they all have a similar effect on the countries in which they are active: displacement of potential and actual indigenous fighters.

The elites and the population in countries with a substantial element of foreign fighters do not fight for their countries to the extent that they otherwise would. Since they do not do so, the political order (however nascent it might be) also misses out on the integrative effect of mobilization of its population for war. Now, state-building or nation-building are of course not the only motives for importing foreign soldiers or for foreign powers to intervene in a country – sometimes destabilization or other destructive intentions are at play. Still, foreign armed presence might be an effective and unintended way to undercut the formation of political order. It is well known that Machiavelli cautioned against the use of mercenaries and spoke of the need for a republic to have its own troops or *arme proprie* (Machiavelli, 1993:93–8, 103–8, 1990). Machiavelli points out that mercenaries are unreliable and not as effective in the field as troops raised within the republic itself. Some mercenaries have been very effective in combat but others have failed. It is certainly the case today that foreign troops, like the Americans and Europeans in Afghanistan, were better in combat than those of the Afghan National Army. I think, however, that Machiavelli's emphasis on the need for a republic to have its own troops points to something deeper: not only is it better for a republic that is already formed to employ its own people, but for a political order to arise and solidify it needs to employ people who will be a part of it. The latter point, of course, is of particular importance for the considerable number of African and Asian polities that could be described as nascent or even embryonic, such as Afghanistan.

A greater point that I want to emphasize is the integrative and community-creating effects of warfare. The connection between warfare and political order is not just about battlefield effectiveness or about the accumulation of material capabilities or sheer numbers. But the 'utility of force' also goes beyond the battlefield and consists in whether the use of force will be beneficial or detrimental to the solidity and durability of the political order itself. As Chapters 3 and 4 demonstrate, fighting together had a cohesive-creating effect on the warrior aristocracy of Europe, making it more loyal to the political order itself. Naturally, one cannot neglect the context of the institutions and ideas in which this took place, which was very conducive to cohesion (such as the ideas of the realm and kingship). As argued in Chapter 4, political representation in assemblies is a deeply performative way to create abstract entities. In a similar way fighting together and thus representing the political order is a deeply performative act (resting on and supporting the idea of the realm) and as such a way of bringing the political order into being.

Re-interpreting Modernity

Modernity can be a description of the economic, political, social and technological changes that have taken place the last centuries, but it can also be a normative vision. Sociology as a modern science has for a long time reified modernity as an objectively existing thing. Therefore, the idea of 'multiple modernities' formulated by S. N. Eisenstadt and his associates was a significant breakthrough. By demonstrating that modernity can assume different guises in different parts of the world and that even movements that describe themselves as anti-modern in fact are modern, Eisenstadt and others made it possible to distinguish between modernity as institutional and technical innovations and modernity as a cultural paradigm or – in Niklas Luhmann's terms – a self-description. Unpacking modernity clearly illustrates how movements and society have embraced some aspects of what was long thought of as an indivisible whole (like technology and administrative reforms) while rejecting others, like liberal democracy. This new view of non-Western modernity also enables another understanding of European modernity.

The gradual and piecemeal advent of different kinds of modernity was certainly a watershed in history and that break is visible in the subject matter of this book. At the beginning of the twenty-first century, wars are no longer fought in the West in order to increase or defend the possessions, claims or honour of a particular dynasty – nor do dynasties wage wars. Political order does not require hereditary hierarchies in order to be legitimate. In fact, political orders that do contain such elements are widely regarded in the West as suspect or illegitimate. Still, this book demonstrates that political order in the epoch or civilization of modernity is not unequivocal. It also demonstrates that political development does not necessarily culminate in the establishment of liberal democracies (Fukuyama, 2014). China is today one of the globe's great powers and a hypermodern country in many respects, but it is not a democracy. To speculate if a similar development would have been possible in Europe takes us into the realm of counterfactual history. I will not do so at length but maintain my argument that, theoretically, it would have been a possible development for two main reasons: first, if Napoleon would have succeeded in making his empire durable then someone might have had to write a very different book about political order and kinship-based elites at the beginning of the twentieth century. Second, if World War One had not taken place or taken place differently, then monarchies and aristocracies in some form might still have been in place in some parts of Europe and the world. In those alternative histories, we would have had a hierarchical modernity with kinship elements existing alongside the liberal one during the twentieth century, much like it did during the nineteenth. That these two alternative histories did not become realities is in large part due to the outcomes of major wars. The fact that both were the compound results of many contingent, complex and non-linear events means that it becomes difficult to construct deterministic trajectories of political order.

Still, as Reinhardt Koselleck and others have demonstrated, modernity in the sense of a new view of the malleability of society, the possibility and/or inevitability of change and the acceleration of time is a significant transformation in social and political thinking that took place in the period, roughly, between 1750 and 1850. These features would seem to be the basic pattern of modernity of which several different variants exist. A careful analysis of nineteenth-century development that integrates the substantial role played by contingent events demonstrates that the shift to the kind of modernity that we identify as our own took place later and was uncertain, perhaps improbable, rather than pre-destined. Hence we should talk about different modernities, or variants of modernities, not just in space but also in time. For example, America represented or incarnated a democratic-meritocratic version of modernity, Wilhelmine Germany an authoritarian monarchical-aristocratic one. Until the end of World War One, it was not clear which one would prevail in Central Europe.

Finally, then, how should we consider the relation between politics in premodern and modern times? From a state formation perspective, I would claim that without the foundations of political order that were erected during the different premodern eras we would never have had modern states and countries. The political order that rested on hereditary power stabilized relations after the fall of Rome in the West and enabled stable realms to be constructed, from which in turn first states, then modern states and finally – after crises and wars – liberal states could arise. How one should understand or explain how political and social forms can arise from their ideological and organization antithesis is beyond the scope of this book. Suffice it to note that this problem occupied the minds of Marx and Hegel, two of the great thinkers of the modern era.

Concerning the Middle East, I have noted that its development has been different to that of Europe. The importance of monarchical-aristocratic formations, for example, elite families, in some countries and kinship formations (e.g., clans and tribes) in almost all countries of the region, partly rests on a different structural heritage than in Europe but it also rests on contingent events. Since they were created largely under European influence, Arab monarchies are the last pieces of the heritage of the idea that monarchy was crucial to a hierarchical modernity of the nineteenth and early twentieth century. In European history, we saw that large wars, in combination with the ideas of the

Enlightenment and revolution, caused the downfall of the political order that rested on families. However, its downfall was not always the result of intentional action. The revolutionaries that toppled the Russian and German thrones certainly intended to do so but they would never have succeeded if the monarchies themselves had not gone to war, with entirely different aims in mind. In countries like Afghanistan, Iran and Libya, monarchs were also toppled by force. But if we consider the long wars of Afghanistan, Iraq, Libya and Somalia we see that other kinship-based formations have been strengthened. It must be said that the heavy-handed attempts to impose modern liberal democracies have failed. Hence we can conclude that neither war nor modernization leads to generalizable or predictable consequences for political order. Instead, the historical-sociological analysis of this book highlights the role that unpredictable events and consequences have for political development, in particular in connection with warfare.

So, to summarize, this book has demonstrated that: (1) kinship-based groups and ideas of kinship have been central to political order for a millennium and a half, (2) polities that were very successful managed to embed kinship-based elites through institutions and cultural practices and to make them public and transparent, (3) political orders have to be built on co-operation and concert, not just coercion and monopolized violence. That is the Janus-faced nature of political power. Finally, this book has generated a puzzle: what is the role of kinship – ideas and organizations – in industrialized societies in the West today (e.g., from 1920 to 2018)? I have hinted that one clue might be to investigate concepts of the nation and of the welfare state. But that will have to be another book.

BIBLIOGRAPHY

Aarts, P. (2007). Longevity of the House of Saud. In O. Schlumberger, ed., *Debating Arab Authoritarianism: Dynamics and Durability in Nondemocratic Regimes*, Stanford, CA: Stanford University Press, pp. 251–67.

Aarts, P. and Roelants, C. (2015). *Saudi Arabia: A Kingdom in Peril*, London: Hurst & Company.

Abbink, J. (1999). The Total Somali Clan Genealogy: A Preliminary Sketch. ASC Working Paper 41/1999 African Studies Centre Leiden, the Netherlands.

Adams, T. (2012). Between History and Fiction: Revisiting the *Affaire de la Tour de Nesle*. *Viator*, 43(2), 165–92.

Āghā, S. S. (2003). *The Revolution Which Toppled the Umayyads, Neither Arab nor 'Abbāsid*, Leiden: Brill.

Agoston, G. (2009). A Flexible Empire. Authority and Its Limits of the Ottoman Frontiers. *International Journal of Turkish Studies*, 9(1&2), 17–29.

Agoston, G. (2010). Empires and Warfare in East-Central Europe, 1550–1750: The Ottoman-Habsburg Rivalry and Military Transformation. In F. Tallett and D. J. B. Trim, eds., *European Warfare, 1350–1750*, Cambridge: Cambridge University Press, pp. 110–34.

Ahrari, M. E. (1999). Political Succession in Saudi Arabia: Systemic Stability and Security Implications. *Comparative Strategy*, 18(1), 13–29.

Airlie, S. (2002). The Nearly Men: Boso of Viene and Arnulf of Bavaria. In A. Duggan, ed., *Nobles and Nobility in Medieval Europe*, Woodbridge: Boydell Press, pp. 25–41.

Airlie, S. (2006). The Aristocracy. In R. McKitterick, ed., *c.700–c.900*. Vol. II of *The New Cambridge Medieval History*, Cambridge: Cambridge University Press, pp. 431–50.

Alatas, S. F. (2006). Ibn Khaldūn and Contemporary Sociology. *International Sociology*, 21(6), 782–95.

Al-Atawneh M. (2009). Is Saudi Arabia a Theocracy? Religion and Governance in Contemporary Saudi Arabia. *Middle Eastern Studies*, 45(5), 721–37.

Al-Azmeh, A. (2004). Book Review: The Revolution which Toppled the Umayyads. Neither Arab nor 'Abbasid. *The Medieval History Journal*, 7(2), 327–33.

Al-Haj, M. (1995). Kinship and Modernization in Developing Societies: The Emergence of Instrumentalized Kinship. *Journal of Comparative Family Studies*, 26(3), 311–28.

Allman, C. (1998). Conclusions. In C. Allmand, ed., *c.1415–c.1500*. Vol. VII of *The New Cambridge Medieval History*, Cambridge: Cambridge University Press, pp. 831–40.

Allsen, T. T. (2006). *The Royal Hunt in Eurasian History*, Philadelphia, PA: University of Pennsylvania Press.

Almanach Royal. (1700–1791). 91 vols. Paris: Laurent D' Houry. For the years 1700–1791, see National Library of France, https://gallica.bnf.fr/ark:/12148/cb34454105m/date.r=almanach+royal.langFR, accessed 26 July 2018.

Al-Rasheed, M. (2002). *A History of Saudi Arabia*, New York: Cambridge University Press.

Althoff, G. (2000). Saxony and the Elbe Slavs in the Tenth Century. In T. Reuter, ed., *c.900–c.1024*. Vol. III of *The New Cambridge Medieval History*, Cambridge: Cambridge University Press, pp. 267–92.

Althoff, G. (2004). *Family, Friends and Followers: Political and Social Bonds in Medieval Europe*, Cambridge: Cambridge University Press.

Altorki, S. (1980). Milk-Kinship in Arab Society: An Unexplored Problem in the Ethnography of Marriage. *Ethnology*, 19(2), 233–44.

Alvarez, G., Ceballos, F.C. and Quinteiro, C. (2009). The Role of Inbreeding in the Extinction of a European Royal Dynasty. *PLoS ONE*, 4(4), 1–7.

Anderson, M. S. (1995). *The War of the Austrian Succession, 1740–1748*, London: Longman.

Anderson, B. (2003). *Imagined Communities. Reflections of the Origin and Spread of Nationalism*, London: Verso.

Anderson, L. (1991). Absolutism and the Resilience of Monarchy in the Middle East. *Political Science Quarterly*, 106(1), 1–15.

Anderson, P. (1974). *Lineages of the Absolutist State*, London: N.L.B.

Anderson, P. (2013). *Passages from Antiquity to Feudalism*, London: Verso Books.

Andersson, D. M. (2011). Clan Identity and Islamic Identity in Somalia. In D. Last, and A. Seaboyer, eds., *Clan and Islamic Identities in Somalia*, Defence R&D Canada – Toronto Contract Report. Royal Military College of Canada, Kingston Ontario, pp. 3–19.

Angstrom, J. and Widén, J. (2015). *Contemporary Military Theory: The Dynamics of War*, New York: Routledge.

Anthony, S. W. (2013). 'Utman b. 'Affan (ca.579–656). In G. Böwering, P. Crone and M. Mirza, eds., *The Princeton Encyclopedia of Islamic Political Thought*, Princeton, NJ: Princeton University Press, pp. 584–5.

Arendt, H. (2004). *The Origins of Totalitarianism*, New York, NY: Shocken Books.

Arendt, H. (1972). On Violence. In H. Arendt, ed., *Crises of the Republic*, New York: Harcourt Brace Jovanovich, pp. 105–98.

Aretin, K. O. von (1997a). *Kaisertraditionen und österreichische Grossmaktpolitik 1684–1745*. Vol. II of *Das Alte Reich, 1648–1806*, Stuttgart: Klett Cotta.

Aretin, K. O. von (1997b). *Das Reich und der österreichisch-preussische Dualismus (1745–1806)*. Vol. III of *Das Alte Reich, 1648–1806*, Stuttgart: Klett Cotta, Stuttgart.

Aristotele. (2013). *Aristotle's Politics*, Chicago, IL: University of Chicago Press.

Árnason, J. P. (2003). *Civilizations in Dispute: Historical Questions and Theoretical Traditions*, Leiden: Brill.

Árnason, J. P. and Raaflaub, K. A. (2011). *The Roman Empire in Context: Historical and Comparative Perspectives*, Chichester: Wiley-Blackwell.

Árnason, J. P. and Wittrock, B. (2004). *Eurasian Transformations, Tenth to Thirteenth Centuries: Crystallizations, Divergences, Renaissances*, Leiden: Brill.

Arnold, B. (1991). *Princes and Territories in Medieval Germany*, Cambridge: Cambridge University Press.

Austen, R. A. and Jansen, J. (1996). History, Oral Transmission and Structure in Ibn Khaldun's Chronology of Mali Rulers. *History in Africa*, 23, 17–28.

Bachrach, B. S. (1972). *Merovingian Military Organization, 481–751*, Minneapolis, MN: University of Minnesota Press.

Bagehot, W. (1875). *Physics and Politics, or Thoughts on the Application of the Principles of Natural Selection and Inheritance to Political Society*, London: Henry S. King.

Baldwin, J. W. (1991). *The Government of Philip Augustus: Foundations of French Royal Power in the Middle Ages*, Berkeley, CA: University of California Press.

Balthasar, D. (2013). Somaliland's Best Kept Secret: Shrewd Politics and War Projects as Means of State-Making. *Journal of Eastern African Studies*, 7(2), 218–38.

Bang, P. F. and Kołodziejczyk, D. (2012). *Universal Empire: A Comparative Approach to Imperial Culture and Representation in Eurasian History*, Cambridge: Cambridge University Press.

Bank, A., Richter, T. and Sunik, A. (2015). Long-Term Monarchical Survival in the Middle East: A Configurational Comparison, 1945–2012. *Democratization*, 22(1), 179–200.

Barfield, T. J. (1989). *The Perilous Frontier: Nomadic Empires and China*, Oxford: Basil Blackwell.

Barfield, T. J. (1991). Tribe and State Relations: The Inner Asian Perspective. In P. S. Khoury and J. Kostiner, eds., *Tribes and State Formation in the Middle East*, Berkeley, Los Angeles, CA, and London: University of California Press, pp. 153–82.

Barkey, K. (2005). Islam and Toleration: Studying the Ottoman Imperial Model. *International Journal of Politics, Culture, and Society*, 19(1–2), 5–19.

Barkey, K. (2008). *Empire of Difference: The Ottomans in Comparative Perspective*, Cambridge: Cambridge University Press.

Barnard, A. (2000). *History and Theory in Anthropology*, Cambridge: Cambridge University Press.

Barnes, C. and Hassan, H. (2007). The Rise and Fall of Mogadishu's Islamic Courts. *Journal of Eastern African Studies*, 1(2), 151–60.

Bartelson, J. (1995). *A Genealogy of Sovereignty*, Cambridge: Cambridge University Press.

Barthélemy, D. (2009). *The Serf, the Knight, and the Historian*, Ithaca, NY: Cornell University Press.

Barthélemy, D. and White, S. D. (1996). The 'Feudal Revolution'. *Past & Present*, 152(1), 196–223.

Bartlett, R. (1994). *The Making of Europe. Conquest, Colonization and Cultural Change, 950–1350*, London: Penguin.

Barudio, G. (1998). *Der teutsche Krieg, 1618–1648*, Berlin: Siedler.

Barzegar, K. (2008). Iran and the Shiite Crescent: Myths and Realities. *Brown Journal of World Affairs*, 15(1), 87–99.

Bates, D. (2000). West Francia: The Northern Principalities. In T. Reuter, ed., *c.900–c.1024*. Vol. III of *The New Cambridge Medieval History*, Cambridge: Cambridge University Press, pp. 398–419.

Battegazzorre, F. (2017). Some Reflections on the Power To/Power Over Debate. *Journal of Political Power*, 10(3), 274–85.

Bauman, Z. (1991). *Modernity and Ambivalence*, Ithaca, NY: Cornell University Press.

Bazelmans, J. (1999). *By Weapons Made Worthy. Lords, Retainers, and Their Relationship in Beowulf*, Amsterdam: Amsterdam University Press.

Bayly, C. (2004). *The Birth of the Modern World 1780–1914*, Oxford: Blackwell.

Beik, W. (1985). *Absolutism and Society in Seventeenth-Century France: State Power and Provincial Aristocracy in Languedoc*, Cambridge: Cambridge University Press.

Bendix, R. (1976). The Mandate to Rule: An Introduction. *Social Forces*, 55(2), 242–56.

Bendix, R. (1978). *Kings or People: Power and the Mandate to Rule*, Berkeley, CA: University of California Press.

Bendix, R. (1984). *Force, Fate, and Freedom: On Historical Sociology*, Berkeley, CA: University of California Press.

Berdahl, R. M. (1972). Conservative Politics and Aristocratic Landholders in Bismarckian Germany. *The Journal of Modern History*, 44(1), 2–20.

Bernard, P. P. (1965). *Joseph II and Bavaria. Two Eighteenth Century Attempts at German Unification*, The Hague: Martinus Nijhoff.

Bernstein, H. (1971). Modernization Theory and the Sociological Study of Development. *The Journal of Development Studies*, 7(2), 141–60.

Besteman, C. (1998). Primordialist Blinders: A Reply to IM Lewis. *Cultural Anthropology*, 13(1),109–20.

Besteman, C. (1999). A Response to Helander's Critique of 'Violent Politics and the Politics of Violence'. *American Ethnologist*, 26(4), 981–3.

Besteman, C. (2005). Why I Disagree with Robert Kaplan. In C. Besteman and H. Gusterson, eds., *Why America's Top Pundits Are Wrong: Anthropologists Talk Back*, Berkeley, CA: University of California Press, Berkeley, pp. 83–101.

Besteman, C. (2017). Experimenting in Somalia: The New Security Empire. *Anthropological Theory*, 17(3), 404–20.

Betts, R. K. (2000). Is Strategy an Illusion? *International Security*, 25(2), 5–50.

Beyerchen, A. (1992). Clausewitz, Nonlinearity, and the Unpredictability of War. *International Security*, 17(3), 59–90.

Biddle, S. D. (2004). *Military Power: Explaining Victory and Defeat in Modern Battle*, Princeton, NJ: Princeton University Press.

Biran, M. (2004). The Mongol Transformation: From the Steppe to Eurasian Empire. In J. Arnason and B. Wittrock, eds., *Eurasian Transformations, Tenth to Thirteenth Centuries: Crystallizations, Divergences, Renaissances*, Leiden and Boston, MA: Brill, pp. 339–61.

Bisaha, N. (2004). *Creating East and West. Renaissance Humanists and the Ottoman Turks*, Philadelphia, PA: University of Pennsylvania Press.

Bisson, T. N. (1994). The 'Feudal Revolution'. *Past & Present*, 142(1), 6–42.

Bisson, T. N. (2015). *The Crisis of the Twelfth Century. Power, Lordship, and the Origins of European Government*, Princeton, NJ: Princeton University Press.

Blake, S. P. (2011). Returning the Household to the Patrimonial Bureaucratic Empire: Gender, Succession, and Ritual in the Mughal, Safavid and Ottoman Empires. In P. F. Bang and C. A. Bayly, eds., *Tributary Empires in Global History*, Basingstoke: Palgrave Macmillan, pp. 214–26.

Blanning, T. C. W. (2015). *Frederick the Great: King of Prussia*, London: Allan Lane.

Blaufarb, R. (2008). The Creation of the Imperial Nobility. *Napoleonica. La Revue*, 2(2), 16–27.

Blickle, P. (1997). *Resistance, Representation and Community*, Oxford: Clarendon Press.

Blickle, P. (2004). *Die Revolution von 1525*, Munich: R Oldenbourg Verlag.

Bloch, M. (1924). *Les rois thaumaturges*, Strasbourg: Istra.

Bloch, M. (1949). *Strange Defeat: A Statement of Evidence Written in 1940*, New York, NY: W.W. Norton.

Bloch, M. (1989). *Feudal Society*, 2nd edn., London: Routledge.

Bøås, M. (2013). Somalia. State 'Failure' and the Emergence of Hybrid Political Orders. In R. Egnell and P. Haldén, eds., *New Agendas in Statebuilding: Hybridity, Contingency and History*, London: Routledge, pp. 55–69.

Bobbio, N. (1993). *Thomas Hobbes and the Natural Law Tradition*, Chicago, IL: University of Chicago Press.

Bobbitt, P. (2002). *The Shield of Achilles: War, Peace, and the Course of History*, London: Allen Lane.

Böckenförde, E.-W. (2006). Der deutsche Typ der konstitutionellen Monarchie im 19. Jahrhundert. In E.-W. Böckenförde, ed., *Recht, Staat, Freiheit*, Frankfurt a.M.: Suhrkamp, pp. 273–305.

Bodin, J. (2010 [1576]). *On Sovereignty*, Cambridge: Cambridge University Press.

Boretivs, A., ed. (1883). *Monumenta Germaniae Historica. Capitularia regum francorum* Hannover: Hahn.

Bosworth, C. E. (1975). The Early Ghaznavids. In R. N. Frye, ed., *The Period from the Arab Invasion to the Saljuqs*. Vol. II of *The Cambridge History of Iran*, Cambridge: Cambridge University Press, pp. 162–97.

Bosworth, C. E. (2011). The Steppe Peoples in the Islamic World. In D. O. Morgan, ed., *The Eastern Islamic World, Eleventh to Eighteenth Centuries*. Vol. III of *The New Cambridge History of Islam*, Cambridge: Cambridge University Press, pp. 21–77.

Bouchard, C. (2001). *Those of My Blood: Creating Noble Families in Medieval Francia*, Philadelphia, PA: University of Pennsylvania Press.

Bouquet, O. (2015). The Sultan's Sons-in-Law: Analysing Ottoman Imperial Damads. *Journal of the Economic and Social History of the Orient*, 58(3), 327–61.

Bozeman, A. (1976). *Conflict in Africa: Concepts and Realities*, Princeton, NJ: Princeton University Press.

Brett, M. (2010). State-Formation and Organization. In M. Fierro, ed., *The Western Islamic World, Eleventh to Eighteenth Centuries*. Vol. II of *The New Cambridge History of Islam*, Cambridge: Cambridge University Press, pp. 549–85.

Briggs, C. F. (1999). *Giles of Rome's* De Regimine Principum: *Reading and Writing Politics at Court and University, c.1275–c.1525*, Cambridge: Cambridge University Press.

Brooks, N. (1971). The Development of Military Obligations in Eighth and Ninth Century England. In O. von Feilitzen, D. Whitelock, K. Hughes and P. Clemoes, eds., *England Before the Conquest: Studies in Primary Sources Presented to Dorothy Whitelock*, Cambridge: Cambridge University Pres, pp. 69–84.

Brubaker, L. and Smith, J. M. H., eds. (2004). *Gender in the Early Medieval World: East and West, 300–900*, Cambridge: Cambridge University Press.

Brunner, O. (1959). *Land und Herrschaft: Grundfragen der territorialen Verfassungsgeschichte Österreichs im Mittelalter*, 4th edn., Vienna: R. M. Rohrer.

Bruton, B. (2012). Clan and Islamic Identity in Somalia. In A. Seaboyer, ed., *CEADS Papers*, 2 Somalia. Canada, Europe, America Dialogue on Security. Ontario, Canada.

Bührer-Thierry G. (1992). La reine adultère. *Cahiers de civilization médiévale*, 35 (140), 299–312.

Bulst, N. (2005). Rulers, Representative Institutions, and Their Members as Power Elites: Rivals or Partners? In W. Reinhardt, ed., *Power Elites and State-Building 13th–18th Centuries*, Oxford: Oxford University Press, pp. 41–58.

Bush, M. L. (1983). *Noble Privilege*. Vol. I of *The European Nobility*, Manchester: Manchester University Press.

Bush, M. L. (1988). *Rich Noble, Poor Noble*. Vol. II of *The European Nobility*, Manchester: Manchester University Press.

Buzan, B. and Albert, M. (2010). Differentiation: A Sociological Approach to International Relations Theory. *European Journal of International Relations*, 16(3), 315–37.

Buzan, B. and Lawson, G. (2015). *The Global Transformation: History, Modernity and the Making of International Relations*, Cambridge: Cambridge University Press.

Cahen, C. (2001). *The Formation of Turkey: The Seljukid Sultanate of Rūm: ELeventh to Fourteenth Century*, London: Routledge.

Cannadine, D. (1990). *The Decline and Fall of the British Aristocracy*, New Haven, CT: Yale University Press.

Cannon, J. (2007). The British Nobility 1660–1800. In H. M. Scott, ed., *The European Nobilities in the Seventeenth and Eighteenth Centuries*. Vol. 1, *Western and Southern Europe*, 2nd edn., Basingstoke: Palgrave Macmillan, pp. 61–93.

Carlsson, S., Cornell, J. and Grenholm, G. (1966). *Medeltid, 1319–1520* [The Middle Ages, 1319–1520]. Vol. 2 of *Den svenska historien* [The Swedish History], Stockholm: Bonniers.

Carneiro, R. L. (1987). Cross-Currents in the Theory of State Formation. *American Ethnologist*, 14, 756–70.

Carpenter, D. A. (1999). The Plantagenet Kings. In D. Abulafiaed. *c.1198–c.1300*. Vol. V of *The New Cambridge Medieval History*, Cambridge: Cambridge University Press, pp. 314–57.

Carver, M. (1992). *The Age of Sutton Hoo: The Seventh Century in North-Western Europe*, Woodbridge: Boydell Press.

Ceballos, F. C. and Álvarez, G. (2013). Royal Dynasties as Human Inbreeding Laboratories: The Habsburgs. *Heredity*, 111(2), 114–21.

Chapra, M. U. (2008). Ibn Khaldun's Theory of Development: Does It Help Explain the Low Performance of the Present-Day Muslim World? *The Journal of Socio-Economics*, 37(2), 836–63.

Charny, G. de (2005). *A Knight's Own Book of Chivalry*, Philadelphia, PA: University of Pennsylvania Press.

Cheyette, F. L. (2002). Georges Duby's Mâconnais After Fifty Years: Reading It Then and Now. *Journal of Medieval History*, 28(3), 291–317.

Christian, D. (2018). Inner Eurasia from the Mongol Empire to Today, 1260–2000. Vol. II of A History of Russia, Central Asia and Mongolia, Malden: Wiley Blackwell.

Çirakman, A. (2002). *From the 'Terror of the World' to the 'Sick Man of Europe': European Images of Ottoman Empire and Society from the Sixteenth Century to the Nineteenth*, New York: Peter Lang.

Clark, C. M. (2007). *Iron Kingdom: The Rise and Downfall of Prussia, 1600–1947*, London: Penguin.

Clark, C. M. (2013). *The Sleepwalkers: How Europe Went to War in 1914*, London: Penguin.

Clark, I. (2005). *Legitimacy in International Society*, Oxford: Oxford University Press.

Clausewitz, C. von (1976). *On War*, Princeton, NJ: Princeton University Press.

Cohn, H. J. (2006). The Electors and Imperial Rule at the End of the Fifteenth Century. In: B. K. U. Weiler and S. MacLean, eds., *Representations of Power in Medieval Germany 800–1500*, Turnhout: Brepols, pp. 295–318.

Colby, H. (1927). How to Fight Savage Tribes. *American Journal of International Law*, 21(2), 279–88.

Collins, K. (2004). The Logic of Clan Politics: Evidence from the Central Asian Trajectories. *World Politics*, 56(2), 224–61.

Collins, J. B. (2009). *The State in Early Modern France*, 2nd edn., Cambridge: Cambridge University Press.

Collins, R. and Sanderson, S. K. (2009 [1975]). *Conflict Sociology: A Sociological Classic Updated*, Boulder, CO: Paradigm Publishers.

Contamine, P. (1998). The European Nobility. In C. Allmand, ed., *c.1415–c.1500*. Vol. VII of *New Cambridge Medieval History*, Cambridge: Cambridge University Press, pp. 87–105.

Cooper, R. (2004). *The Breaking of Nations: Order and Chaos in the Twenty-First Century*, New York, NY: Grove Press.

Costambeys, M., Innes, M. and MacLean, S. (2011). *The Carolingian World*, Cambridge: Cambridge University Press.

Cowell, A. (2007). *The Medieval Warrior Aristocracy. Gifts, Violence, Performance and the Sacred*, Woodbridge and Rochester, NY: Boydell and Brewer.

Crone, P. (1980). *Slaves on Horses: The Evolution of the Islamic Polity*, Cambridge: Cambridge University Press.

Crone, P. (1986). The Tribe and the State. In J. A. Hall, ed., *States in History*, Oxford: Basil Blackwell, pp. 48–77.

Crone, P. (1989). *Pre-Industrial Societies*, Oxford: Basil Blackwell.

Crone, P. (1993). Review: Tribes and States in the Middle East. Reviewed Work(s): Tribes and State Formation in the Middle East by Philip S. Khoudry and Joseph Kostiner. *Journal of the Royal Asiatic Society*, 3(3), 353–76.

Crone, P. (1999). The Early Islamic World. In K. A. Raaflaub and N. S. Rosenstein, eds., *War and Society in the Ancient and Medieval Worlds: Asia, the Mediterranean, Europe, and Mesoamerica*, Cambridge, MA: Harvard University Press, pp. 309–32.

Crone, P. (2005). *Medieval Islamic Political Thought*, Edinburgh: Edinburgh University Press.

Crouch, D. (2002). *The Normans: The History of a Dynasty*, London: Bloomsbury Academic.

Crouch, D. (2005). *The Birth of Nobility: Constructing Aristocracy in England and France, 900–1300*, Harlow: Pearson Education.

Crouch, D. (2010). *The English Aristocracy 1070–1272. A Social Transformation*, New Haven, CT: Yale University Press.

Dakin, D. (1973). *The Greek Struggle for Independence 1821–1833*, Berkeley and Los Angeles, CA: University of California Press.

Dale, S. F. (2010). *The Muslim Empires of the Ottomans, Safavids, and Mughals*, Cambridge: Cambridge University Press

Dam, R. van (2006). Merovingian Gaul and the Frankish Conquests. In R. McKitterick, ed., *c.700–c.900*. Vol. II of *The New Cambridge Medieval History*, Cambridge: Cambridge University Press, pp. 193–231.

Davies, N. (1981). The Origins to 1795. Vol. I of *God's Playground: A History of Poland in Two Volumes*. Oxford: Clarendon Press.

Davies, N. (2011). *Vanished Kingdoms: The History of Half-Forgotten Europe*, London: Allen Lane.

Davies, R. R. (1995). Presidential Address: The Peoples of Britain and Ireland 1100–1400 II Names, Boundaries and Regnal Solidarities. *Transactions of the Royal Historical Society*, 5, 1–20.

Davies, R. R. (2009). *Lords and Lordship in the British Isles in the Late Middle Ages*, Oxford: Oxford University Press.

Delogu, P. (2008). Lombard and Carolingian Italy. In R. McKitterick, ed., *c.700–c.900*. Vol. II of *The New Cambridge Medieval History*, Cambridge: Cambridge University Press, pp. 290–319.

Dewald, J. (1996). *The European Nobility, 1400–1800*, Cambridge: Cambridge University Press.

Di Cosmo, N. (2010). Black Sea Emporia and the Mongol Empire: A Reassessment of the *Pax Mongolica*. *Journal of the Economic and Social History of the Orient*, 53(1/2), 83–108.

Downing, B. M. (1988). Constitutionalism, Warfare, and Political Change in Early Modern Europe. *Theory and Society*, 17(1), 7–56.

Downing, B. M. (1989). Medieval Origins of Constitutional Government in the West. *Theory and Society*, 18(2), 213–47.

Downing, B. M. (1992). *The Military Revolution and Political Change: Origins of Democracy and Autocracy in Early Modern Europe*, Princeton, NJ: Princeton University Press.

Drew, K. F. (1991). *The Laws of the Salian Franks*, Philadelphia, PA: University of Pennsylvania Press.

Drew, K. F. (1972). *Burgundian Code: Book of Constitutions or Law of Gundobad*, Philadelphia, PA: University of Pennsylvania Press.

Drew, K. F. (1973). *The Lombard Laws*, Philadelphia, PA: University of Philadelphia Press.

Drew, K. F. (1988). The Family in Frankish Law. In Katherine Fischer Drew, *Law and Society in Early Medieval Europe: Studies in Legal History*, London: Variorum Reprints, pp. 1–11.

Drews, W. (2009). *Die Karolinger und die Abbasiden von Bagdad: Legitimationsstrategien frühmittelalterlicher Herrscherdynastien im transkulturellen Vergleich*, Berlin: Akademie Verlag.

Drew, K. F. (1952). Class Distinctions in 8th Century Italy. *Rice Institute Pamphlet*, XXXIX(3), 61–95.

Duby, G. (1993). *The Knight, the Lady and the Priest: The Making of Modern Marriage in Medieval France*, Chicago, IL: University of Chicago Press.

Duby, G. (1977). *The Chivalrous Society*, London: E. Arnold.

Duchhardt, H. (1990). *Altes Reich und europäische Staatenwelt: 1648 – 1806*, Munich: R. Oldenbourg Verlag.

Duchhardt, H. (1997). *Der Herrscher in Der Doppelpflicht: Europäische Fürsten Und Ihre Beiden Throne*, Mainz am Rhein: von Zabern.

Duchhardt, H. (2003). *Europa am Vorabend der Moderne 1650–1800*, Stuttgart: Eugen Ulmer.

Duchhardt, H. (2007). *Barock und Aufklärung*, Munich: R Oldenburg Verlag.

Duindam, J. (2010). Early Modern Europe: Beyond the Strictures of Modernization and National Historiography. *European History Quarterly*, 40(4), 606–23.

Dunbabin, J. (1999). West Francia: The Kingdom. In T. Reuter, ed., *c.900–c.1024*. Vol. III of *The New Cambridge Medieval History*, Cambridge: Cambridge University Press, pp. 372–39.

Dunning, C. S. L. (2004). *A Short History of Russia's First Civil War*, Philadelphia, PA: The Pennsylvania State University Press.

Durkheim, É. (1966). *The Division of Labor in Society*, 6th edn., New York, NY: Free Press.

Duyvesteyn, I. (2005). *Clausewitz and African War: Politics and Strategy in Liberia and Somalia*, London: Frank Cass.

Eiden, H. (1998). Joint Action Against 'Bad' Lordship: The Peasants' Revolt in Essex and Norfolk. *History*, 83(269), 5–30.

Einhard. (2008). The Life of Charlemagne. In D. Ganz, ed., *Two Lives of Charlemagne*, London: Penguin Classics, pp. 3–44.

Eisenstadt, S. N. (1968). Introduction. In Max Weber, ed., *On Charisma and Institution Building: Selected Papers*, Chicago, IL: University of Chicago Press, pp. ix–lvi.

Eisenstadt, S. N. (2002). Multiple Modernities. In S. N. Eisenstadt, ed., *Multiple Modernities*, New Brunswick, NJ: Transaction Publishers, pp. 1–30.

Eisenstadt, S. N. (2003). *Comparative Civilizations and Multiple Modernities: A Collection of Essays*, Brill Academic Publishers.

Elias, N. (2000). *The Civilizing Process: Sociogenetic and Psychogenetic Investigations*, rev. edn., Oxford: Blackwell.

Elias, N. (2012). *What is Sociology?* Dublin: University College Dublin Press.

Elliott, J. H. (1992). A Europe of Composite Monarchies. *Past & Present*, 137(1), 48–71.

Engel, P. (2001). *The Realm of St. Stephen: A History of Medieval Hungary, 895–1526*, London: I. B. Tauris.

Engels, F. (1985 [1884]). *The Origin of the Family, Private Property and the State*, Harmondsworth: Penguin.

Englund, P. (2000). *Den Oövervinnerlige: Om den svenska stormaktstiden och en man i dess mitt* [The Invincible: On the Swedish Imperial Age and a Man in Its Midst], Stockholm: Atlantis.

Erbe, M. (2000). *Die Habsburger: 1493–1918: eine Dynastie im Reich und in Europa*, Stuttgart: Kohlhammer.

Ertman, T. (1997). *Birth of the Leviathan*, Cambridge: Cambridge University Press.

Ertman, T. (2005). State Formation and State Building in Europe. In T. Janoski, R.R. Alford, A. M. Hicks and M. A. Schwartz, eds., *The Handbook of Political Sociology: States, Civil Societies, and Globalization*, Cambridge: Cambridge University Press, pp. 367–83.

Eulau, H. F. (1941). Theories of Federalism Under the Holy Roman Empire. *The American Political Science Review*, 35(4), 643–64.

Evergates, T. (1997). The Feudal Imaginary of Georges Duby. *Journal of Medieval and Early Modern Studies*, 27(3), 641–60.

Faroqhi, S. (1997). Part II. Crisis and Change, 1590–1699. In H. İnalcik, ed., *1600–1914*. Vol. II of *An Economic and Social History of the Ottoman Empire*, Cambridge: Cambridge University Press, pp. 411–636.

Faroqhi, S. (2000). *Geschichte des Osmanischen Reiches*, Munich: C.H. Beck.

Faroqhi, S. (2010). The Ottoman Empire: The Age of 'Political Households' (Eleventh–Twelfth or Seventeenth–Eighteenth Centuries). In M. Fierro, ed., *The Western Islamic World the Eleventh to Eighteenth Centuries*. Vol. II of *The New Cambridge History of Islam*, Cambridge: Cambridge University Press, pp. 366–410.

Fehrenbach, E. (1984). Reich. In R. Koselleck, ed., *Pro-Soz*. Vol. V of *Geschichtliche Grundbegriffe: historisches Lexikon zur politisch- sozialen Sprache in Deutschland*, Stuttgart: Klett-Cotta, pp. 423–508.

Ferguson, N. (2011). *Civilization: The West and the Rest*, London: Allen Lane.

Ferguson, R. B. and Whitehead, N. L. (1992). *War in the Tribal Zone: Expanding States and Indigenous Warfare*, Santa Fe, NM: School of American Research Press.

Ferguson, Y. H. and Mansbach, R. W. (1996). *Polities: Authority, Identities, and Change*, Columbia, SC: University of South Carolina Press.

Ferguson, Y. H. and Mansbach, R. W. (2008). *A World of Polities: Essays on Global Politics*, London: Routledge.

Financial Times. (2017). Saudi King Replaces Crown Prince with Favoured Son, 21 June 2017, www.ft.com/content/173d0148-5637-11e7-80b6-9bfa4c1f83d2, accessed 15 August 2018.

Findley, C. V. (1980). *Bureaucratic Reform in the Ottoman Empire: The Sublime Porte, 1789–1922*, Princeton, NJ: Princeton University Press.

Findley, C. V. (1989). *Ottoman Civil Officialdom: A Social History*, Princeton, NJ: Princeton University Press.

Findley, C. V. (2005). *The Turks in World History*, New York, NY: Oxford University Press.

Finkel, C. (2005). *Osman's Dream: The Story of the Ottoman Empire 1300–1923*, London: John Murray.

Finnemore, M. (2003). *The Purpose of Intervention: Changing Beliefs About the Use of Force*, Ithaca, NY: Cornell University Press.

Fischer, K. D. (1991). *The Laws of the Salian Franks (Lex Salica) Translated and with an Introduction by Katherine Fischer Drew*, Philadelphia, PA: University of Pennsylvania Press.

Fjelde, H. (2010). Generals, Dictators, and Kings: Authoritarian Regimes and Civil Conflict, 1973–2004. *Conflict Management and Peace Science*, 27(3), 195–218.

Fleckenstein, J. (1979). *Early Medieval Germany*, Amsterdam: North-Holland Company.

Fleet, K. (2010). The Rise of the Ottomans. In M. Fierro, ed., *The Western Islamic World the Eleventh to Eighteenth Centuries*. Vol. II of *The New Cambridge History of Islam*, Cambridge: Cambridge University Press, pp. 313–31.

Flori, J. (2004). Knightly Society. In D. Luscombe and J. Riley-Smith, eds., *c.1024–1098*. Vol. IV(1) of *The New Cambridge Medieval History*, Cambridge: Cambridge University Press, pp. 148–84.

Forbes Manz, B. (2010). The Rule of the Infidels: The Mongols and the Islamic world. In D. O. Morgan, ed., *The Eastern Islamic World, Eleventh to Eighteenth Centuries*. Vol III of *The New Cambridge History of Islam*, Cambridge: Cambridge University Press, pp. 128–68.

Fornara, C. W. (1983). *The Nature of History in Ancient Greece and Rome*, Berkeley, CA: University of California Press.

Fortes, M. and Evans-Pritchard, E., eds. (1987 [1940]). *African Political Systems*, London: KPI in association with the International African Institute.

Fortescue, J. (1997a). The Governance of England. In S. Lockwood, ed., *Sir John Fortescue: On the Laws and Governance of England*, Cambridge: Cambridge University Press, pp. 83–123.

Fortescue, J. (1997b). Appendix A: Extracts from the Laws of Nature [*de Natura Legis Naturae*]. In S. Lockwood, ed., *Sir John Fortescue: On the Laws and Governance of England*, Cambridge: Cambridge University Press, pp. 133–6.

Fouracre, P. (2002). The Origins of the Nobility in Francia. In A. J. Duggan, ed., *Nobles and Nobility in Medieval Europe: Concepts, Origins, Transformations*, Woodbridge: The Boydell Press, pp. 17–24.

Fouracre, P. (2005). Francia in the Seventh Century. In P. Fouracre, ed., *c.500– c.700*. Vol. I of *The New Cambridge Medieval History*, Cambridge: Cambridge University Press, pp. 371–96.

Frankki, J. L. (1990). *The Concept of Triuwe in the Nibelungenlied: Hagen and Sifrit*, Thesis Mississippi State University, MS. Department of Foreign Languages.

Fried, J. (1995). The Frankish Kingdoms, 817–911: The East and Middle Kingdom. In R. McKitterick, ed., *c.700–c.900*. Vol. II of *The New Cambridge Medieval History*, Cambridge: Cambridge University Press, pp. 142–68.

Friedensvertrag von Oliva (Warschau) [Peace Treaty of Olivia, Warsaw]. (1660). www.ieg-friedensvertraege.de/treaty/1660%20V%203%20Friedensvertrag% 20von%20Oliva%20(Warschau)/t-1473-1-de.html?h=1, accessed 17 October 2016.

Friedrich der Grosse. (1986 [1752]). *Das Politische Testament von 1752*, Stuttgart: Philipp Reclam.

Froissart, J. and Brereton, G. (1978). *Chronicles*, Harmondsworth: Penguin Books.

Fromkin, D. (2000). *A Peace to End all Peace: The Fall of the Ottoman Empire and the Creation of the Modern Middle East*, 2nd edn., London: Phoenix.

Fukuyama, F. (2012). *The Origins of Political Order: From Prehuman Times to the French Revolution*, London: Profile Books.

Fukuyama, F. (2014). *Political Order and Political Decay: From the Industrial Revolution to the Globalization of Democracy*, London: Profile Books.

Fuller, J. F. C. (2011). Från 1789 till 1870. Vol. III of *De avgörande slagen* [From 1789 to 1870. Vol. III of *The Decisive Battles of the Western World and Their Influence on History*]. Lund: Historiska media.

Fuess, A. (2010). Taxation and Armies. In M. Fierro, ed., *The Western Islamic World, Eleventh to Eighteenth Centuries*. Vol. II of *The New Cambridge History of Islam*, Cambridge: Cambridge University Press, pp. 607–31.

Ganz, D. (2008). Introduction. In D. Ganz, ed., *Two Lives of Charlemagne*, London: Penguin Classics, pp. ix–xv.

Gat, A. (2006). *War in Human Civilization*, Oxford: Oxford University Press.

Geary, P. J. (1988). *Before France and Germany: The Creation and Transformation of the Merovingian World*, New York: Oxford University Press.

Geijer, E. G. and Lundvall, C. J. (1836). Till K. Carl X Gustaf. Vol. 3 of *Svenska folkets historia* [To Karl X Gustaf. Vol. III of *The History of the Swedish People*]. Örebro: N. M. Lindh.

Gellner, E. (1981). *Muslim Society*, Cambridge: Cambridge University Press.

Gellner, E. (1998). Trust, Cohesion, and the Social Order. In D. Gambetta, ed., *Trust: Making and Breaking Cooperative Relations*, 2nd edn., Oxford: Basil Blackwell, pp. 142–57.

Gellner, E. (2008 [1983]). *Nations and Nationalism*, 2nd edn., Ithaca, NY: Cornell University Press.

Gentry, F. G. (1975). *Triuwe and Vriunt in the Nibelungenlied*, Leiden: Brill.

Giddens, A. (1984). *The Constitution of Society: Outline of the Theory of Structuration*, Cambridge: Polity Press.

Giddens, A. (1985). The Nation-State and Violence. Vol. II of *A Contemporary Critique of Historical Materialism*, Berkeley, CA: University of California Press.

Giddens, A. (1990). *The Consequences of Modernity*, Stanford, CA: Stanford University Press.

Gierke, O. (1990). *Community in Historical Perspective: A Translation of Selections from Das Deutsche Genossenschaftsrecht* [The German Law of Fellowship], Cambridge: Cambridge University Press.

Gil, X. G. (2002). Republican Politics in Early Modern Spain. The Castilian and Catalan-Aragonese Traditions. In M. van Gelderen and Q. Skinner, eds., *Republicanism and Constitutionalism in Early Modern Europe*. Vol. I of *Republicanism: A Shared European Heritage*, Cambridge: Cambridge University Press, Cambridge, pp. 263–88.

Gilman, N. (2003). *Mandarins of the Future. Modernization Theory in Cold War America*, Baltimore, MD: Johns Hopkins University Press.

Glenn, J. (1997). The Interregnum: The South's Insecurity Dilemma. *Nations and Nationalism*, 3(1), 45–63.

Glete, J. (2002). *War and the State in Early Modern Europe: Spain, the Dutch Republic and Sweden as Fiscal-Military States, 1500–1600*, London: Routledge.

Göksel, O. (2016). In Search of a Non-Eurocentric Understanding of Modernization: Turkey as a Case of 'Multiple Modernities'. *Mediterranean Politics*, 21(2), 246–67.

Golden, P. B. (2008). The Karakhanids and Early Islam. In D. Sinor, ed., *Cambridge History of Early Inner Asia*, Cambridge: Cambridge University Press, pp. 343–70.

Goldoni, M. (2013). Montesquieu and the French Model of Separation of Powers. *Jurisprudence*, 4(1), 20–47.

Gorski, P. (2003). *The Disciplinary Revolution: Calvinism and the Rise of the State in Early Modern Europe*. Chicago, IL: University of Chicago Press.

Gorski, P. and Swaroop Sharma V. (2017). Beyond the Tilly Thesis: 'Family Values' and State Formation in Latin Christendom. In L. B. Kaspersen and J. Strandsbjerg, eds., *Does War Make States? Critical Investigations of Charles Tilly's Historical Sociology*, Cambridge: Cambridge University Press, pp. 98–122.

Gotthard, A. (2005). *Das Alte Reich 1495–1806*, Darmstadt: Wissenschaftliches Buchgesellschaft.

Grab, A. I. (2003). *Napoleon and the Transformation of Europe*, New York: Palgrave Macmillan.

Graeber, D. and Sahlins, M. (2017). *On Kings*, Chicago, IL: Hau Books.

Gramsci, A. (2010). *Prison Notebooks*, 3 vols. New York, NY: Columbia University Press.

Gregory of Tours. (1974). *The History of the Franks*, London: Penguin.

Grewe, W. G. (2000). *The Epochs of International Law*, Berlin: de Gruyter.

Haj, S. (1991). The Problems of Tribalism: The Case of Nineteenth-Century Iraqi History. *Social History*, 16(1), 45–58.

Haldén, P. (2008). *Somalia: Failed State or Nascent States-System?* Stockholm: Swedish Defence Research Agency.

Haldén, P. (2011). *Stability Without Statehood: Lessons from Europe's History Before the Sovereign State*, Basingstoke: Palgrave Macmillan.

Haldén, P. (2012). From Empire to Federation and Commonwealth: Orders in Europe 1200–1800. In P. F. Bang and D. Kołodziejczyk, eds., *Universal Empire: A Comparative Approach to Imperial Culture and Representation in Eurasian History*, Cambridge: Cambridge University Press, pp. 280–303.

Haldén, P. (2013a). Republican Continuities in the Vienna Order and the German Confederation (1815–66). *European Journal of International Relations*, 19(2), 281–304.

Haldén, P. (2013b). A Non-Sovereign Modernity: Attempts to Engineer Stability in the Balkans 1820–90. *Review of International Studies*, 39(2), 337–59.

Haldén, P. (2014). Reconceptualizing State-Formation as Collective Power: Representation in Electoral Monarchies. *Journal of Political Power*, 7(1), 127–47.

Haldén, P. (2017a). The Realm as a European Form of Rule. In L.-B. Kaspersen and J. Strandsbjerg, eds., *Does War Make States? Critical Investigations of Charles Tilly's Historical Sociology*, Cambridge: Cambridge University Press, pp. 154–80.

Haldén, P. (2017b). Heteronymous Politics Beyond Anarchy and Hierarchy: The Multiplication of Forms of Rule 750–1300. *Journal of International Political Theory*, 13(3), 266–81.

Haldén, P. (2018). Organized Armed Groups as Ruling Organizations. *Armed Forces & Society*, 44(4), 606–25.

Halim, A. A., Nor, M. R. M., Ibrahim, A. Z. B. and Hamid, F. A. F. (2012). Ibn Khaldun's Theory of 'Asabiyyah and Its Application in Modern Muslim Society. *Middle-East Journal of Scientific Research*, 11(9), 1232–7.

Hall, J. A. (1986). *Powers and Liberties: The Causes and Consequences of the Rise of the West*, Harmondsworth: Penguin Books.

Halsall, G. (1999). Reflections of Early Medieval Violence: The Example of the 'Blood Feud'. *Memoria y Civilizatión*, 2(1), 7–29.

Hamerow, H. (2005). The Earliest Anglo-Saxon Kingdoms. In P. Fouracre, ed., *c.500–c.700*. Vol. I of *The New Cambridge Medieval History*, Cambridge: Cambridge University Press, pp. 263–88.

Hanson, P. R. (2009). *Contesting the French Revolution*, Oxford: Wiley-Blackwell.

Härd, J. E. (1993). Inledning [Introduction]. In *Nibelungensången* [The Lay of the Nibelungs], Stockholm: Natur och Kultur, pp. 7–34.

Harrisson, Neil E. (2006). Thinking About the World We Make. In N. E. Harrison, ed., *Complexity in World Politics: Concepts and Methods of a New Paradigm*, Albany, NY: State University of New York Press, pp. 1–23.

Harste, G. (2013). The Improbable European State: Its Ideals Observed with Systems Theory. In R. Egnell and P. Haldén, eds., *New Agendas in Statebuilding: Hybridity, Contingency and History*, London: Routledge, pp. 95–121.

Hathaway, J. (2008). *The Arab Lands Under Ottoman Rule, 1516–1800*, Harlow: Pearson Education.

Haugaard, M. (2017). Power-To, Power-Over, Resistance and Domination: An Editorial. *Journal of Political Power*, 10(3), 271–3.

Hawting, G. R. (2000). *The First Dynasty of Islam: The Umayyad Caliphate AD 661–750*, 2nd edn., London: Routledge.

Hechberger, W. (2004). *Adel, Ministerialität Und Rittertum Im Mittelalter*, Munich: Oldenburg.

Hegel, G. W. F. (1966). Die Verfassung Deutschlands. In G. W. F. Hegel, ed., *Politische Schriften*, Frankfurt a.M.: Suhrkamp.

Hegghammer, T. (2006). Terrorist Recruitment and Radicalization in Saudi Arabia. *Middle East Policy*, 13(4), 39–60.

Hehl, E.-D. (2004). War, Peace and the Christian Order. In D. Luscombe and J. Riley-Smith, eds., *c.1024–1098*. Vol. IV(1) of *The New Cambridge Medieval History*, Cambridge: Cambridge University Press, pp. 185–228.

Heinig, P.-J. (2009). Solide bases imperii et columpne immobiles? Die geistlichen Kurfürsten und der Reichsepiskopat um die Mitte des 14. Jahrhunderts [Solide bases imperii et columpne immobiles? The Ecclesiastical Electoras and the Imperial Bishopry in the Mid-14th century]. In U. Hohensee, M. Lawo, M. Lindner, M. Menzel and O. B. Rader, eds., *Die Goldene Bulle: Politik, Wahrnehmung, Rezeption* [The Golden Bull: Politics, Perception, Reception], Berlin: Akademie-Verlag, pp. 65–91.

Helander, B. (1996). Power and Poverty in Southern Somalia. *Working Paper No. 5*, Department of Cultural Anthropology, Uppsala University.

Henel, A. J. von (1730). *Det anno M DCC XXIX. florerande Swerige, eller fullkommelig beskrifning om den mycket kloka och högst-berömmeligste regeringens författning, inrättning och beskaffenhet uti riket* [The Flourishing Sweden in the Year MDCC XXIX, Or a Complete Description of Constitution, Establishment and Nature of the Very Wise and Most Commendable Government]. Leipzig: Christophorus Zunkel.

Henshall, N. (1992). *The Myth of Absolutism: Change and Continuity in Early Modern European Monarchy*, London: Longman.

Henshall, N. (2010). *The Zenith of European Monarchy and Its Elites: The Politics of Culture, 1650–1750*, Basingstoke: Palgrave Macmillan.

Herbst, J. (2000). *States and Power in Africa: Comparative Lessons in Authority and Control*, Princeton, NJ: Princeton University Press.

Hilton, R. (2003). *Bond Men Made Free. Medieval Peasant Movements and the English Rising of 1381*, 2nd edn., London and New York: Routledge.

Hintze, O. (1962). *Gesammelte Abhandlungen. 1, Staat und Verfassung: gesammelte Abhandlungen zur allgemeinen Verfassungsgeschichte* [Collected Works, 1: State and Constitution: Collected Works on General Constitutional History]. Göttingen: Vandenhoeck & Ruprecht.

Hintze, O. (1962a). Typologie der ständischen Verfassungen des Abendlandes [Typology of the Estate-Based Constitutions of the West]. In G. Oestreich, ed., *Otto Hintze. Staat und Verfassung*. Vol. I. of *Gesammelte Abhandlungen zur Allgemeinen Verfassungsgeschichte*, 2nd edn., Göttingen: Vandenhoeck & Ruprecht, pp. 120–39.

Hintze, O. (1962b). Staatsverfassung und Heeresverfassung [State Constitution and Army Constitution]. In G. Oestreich, ed., *Otto Hintze. Staat und Verfassung*. Vol. I of *Gesammelte Abhandlungen zur Allgemeinen Verfassungsgeschichte*, 2nd edn., Göttingen: Vandenhoeck & Ruprecht, pp. 52–83.

Hintze, O. (1962c) Weltgeschichtliche Bedingungen der Repräsentativverfassung [World-Historical Conditions of Representative Constitutions]. In G. Oestreich, ed., *Otto Hintze. Staat und Verfassung*. Vol. I of *Gesammelte Abhandlungen zur Allgemeinen Verfassungsgeschichte*, 2nd edn., Göttingen: Vandenhoeck & Ruprecht, pp. 140–85.

Hirschmann, A. O. (1978). Exit, Voice, and the State. *World Politics*, 31(1), 90–107.

Hirschmann, A. O. (2004 [1970]). *Exit, Voice, and Loyalty: Responses to Decline in Firms, Organizations, and States*, Cambridge, MA: Harvard University Press.

Hirschmann, N. C. (2016). Hobbes on the Family. In A. Martinich and K, Hoekstra, eds., *The Oxford Handbook of Hobbes*, New York, NY: Oxford University Press, pp. 242–63.

Hobden, S. (1998). *International Relations and Historical Sociology: Breaking Down Boundaries*, London: Routledge.

Hobbes, T. (2008). *Leviathan*, Oxford: Oxford University Press.

Hoehne, M. V. (2016). The Rupture of Territoriality and the Diminishing Relevance of Cross-Cutting Ties in Somalia After 1990. *Development and Change*, 47(6), 1379–411.

Höhne, M. V. (2012). Herrschaft und Ordnung jenseits des Staates in Somalia [Authority and Order Beyond the State in Somalia]. *Peripherie*, 126/127(32), 321–49.

Hollister, C. W. and Keefe, T. K. (1973). The Making of the Angevin Empire. *Journal of British Studies*, 12(2), 1–25.

Holmbäck, A. and Wessén, E. (1962). *Magnus Erikssons landslag* [The Land Law of Magnus Eriksson], Stockholm: Nord. bokh.

Hont, I. (1994). The Permanent Crisis of a Divided Mankind: 'Contemporary Crisis of the Nation State' in Historical Perspective. *Political Studies*, 42(1), 166–231.

Hosking, G. (2000). Patronage and the Russian State. *The Slavonic and East European Review*, 78 (2), 301–20.

Howard, M. (1969). *The Franco-Prussian War: The German Invasion of France, 1870–1871*, New York, NY: Collier.

Howell, M. (2009). Marriage in Medieval Latin Christendom. In C. Lansing and E. D. English, eds., *A Companion to the Medieval World*, Malden: Wiley-Blackwell, pp. 131–59.

Hui, V. T. (2005). *War and State Formation in Ancient China and Early Modern Europe*, Cambridge: Cambridge University Press.

Hudson, J. and Rodríguez López, A. (2014). *Diverging Paths? The Shapes of Power and Institutions in Medieval Christendom and Islam*, Leiden: Brill.

Huntington, S. P. (1966). The Political Modernization of Traditional Monarchies. *Daedalus*, 95(3), 763–88.

Huntington, S. P. (1996). *The Clash of Civilizations and the Remaking of World Order*, New York: Simon & Schuster.

Hussey, R. D. and Bromley, J. S. (1970). The Spanish Empire Under foreign pressures, 1688–1715. In J. S. Bromley, ed., *The Rise of Great Britain and Russia, 1688–1715/25*. Vol. VI of *The New Cambridge Modern History*, Cambridge: Cambridge University Press, pp. 343–80.

İnalcik, H. (1954). Ottoman Methods of Conquest. *Studia Islamica*, 2, 103–29.

İnalcik, H. (1997). *1600–1914*. Vol. II of *An Economic and Social History of the Ottoman Empire*, Cambridge: Cambridge Univ. Press.

Ingiriis, M. H. (2016). *The Suicidal State in Somalia: The Rise and Fall of the Siad Barre Regime 1969–1991*, Lanham, MD: University Press of America.

Inkeles, A. (1975). *Becoming Modern: Individual Change in Six Developing Countries*, London: Heinemann Educational.

Innes, M. (2000). *State and Society in the Early Middle Ages: The Middle Rhine Valley, 400–1000*, New York, NY: Cambridge University Press.

International Crisis Group. (2006). Can the Somali Crisis Be Contained? *Africa Report*, no. 116.

Imber, C. (2009). *The Ottoman Empire 1300–1650*, 2nd edn., Basingstoke: Palgrave.

Isidorus of Seville. (2005). *The Etymologies of Isidore of Seville*, Cambridge: Cambridge University Press.

Jackson, R. A. (1971). Peers of France and Princes of the Blood. *French Historical Studies*, 7(1), 27–46.

Jackson, R. A. (1972). Elective Kingship and *Consensus Populi* in Sixteenth-Century France. *The Journal of Modern History*, 44(2), 156–71.

Jackson, R. H. (1990). *Quasi-States: Sovereignty, International Relations and the Third World*, Cambridge: Cambridge University Press.

Jackson, R. (2013). Authority. In G. Böwering, P. Crone and M. Mirza, eds., *The Princeton Encyclopedia of Islamic Political Thought*, Princeton, NJ: Princeton University Press, pp. 50–6.

James, E. (1988). The Northern World in the Dark Ages, 400–900. In G. Holmes, ed., *The Oxford Illustrated History of Medieval Europe*, London: Guild Publishing, pp. 63–114.

Janssen W. (1982). Krieg. In R. Koselleck, ed., *H-Me*. Vol. III *of Geschichtliche Grundbegriffe: Historisches Lexikon Zur Politisch- Sozialen Sprache in Deutschland*, Stuttgart: Klett-Cotta, pp. 567–615.

Jansson, P. (1997). Identity-Defining Practices in Thucydides' *History of the Peloponnesian War*. *European Journal of International Relations*, 3(2), 147–65.

Jelavich, C. (1963). *The Balkans in Transition: Essays on the Development of Balkan Life and Politics Since the Eighteenth Century*, Berkeley and Los Angeles, CA: University of California Press.

Jelavich, C. and Jelavich, B. (1977). *The Establishment of the Balkan National States, 1804–1920*, Seattle, WA: University of Washington Press.

Jennings, R. C. (1978). Kadi, Court, and Legal Procedure in 17th C. Ottoman Kayseri: The Kadi and the Legal System. *Studia Islamica*, 48, 133–72.

Joas, H. and Knöbl, W. (2009). Conflict Sociology and Conflict Theory. In H. Joas and W. Knöbl, eds., *Social Theory: Twenty Introductory Lectures*, Cambridge: Cambridge University Press, pp. 174–98.

Jochens, J. M. (1987). The Politics of Reproduction: Medieval Norwegian Kingship. *The American Historical Review*, 92(2), 327–49.

Johnson, C. H. (2011). *Transregional and Transnational Families in Europe and Beyond: Experiences Since the Middle Ages*, New York, NY: Berghahn Books.

Jones, L. (2013). State Theory and Statebuilding: Toward a Gramscian Analysis. In R. Egnell and P. Haldén, eds., *New Agendas in Statebuilding: Hybridity, Contingency and History*, London: Routledge, pp. 70–91.

Jones, E. L. (2003). *The European Miracle: Environments, Economies, and Geopolitics in the History of Europe and Asia*, Cambridge: Cambridge University Press.

Jones, R. E. (1993). The Nobility and Russian Foreign Policy, 1560–1811. *Cahiers du monde russe et soviétique*, 34(1–2), 159–69.

Kadi, W. and Shahin, A. (2013). Caliph, Caliphate. In G. Böwering, P. Crone and M. Mirza, eds., *The Princeton Encyclopedia of Islamic Political Thought*, Princeton, NJ: Princeton University Press, pp. 81–6.

Kalyvas, A. (2002). Charismatic Politics and the Symbolic Foundations of Power in Max Weber. *New German Critique*, 85, 67–103.

Kaminsky, H. and Van Horn Melton, J. (1992). Translators' Introduction. In O. Brunner, ed., *Land and Lordship. Structures of Governance in Medieval Austria*, Philadelphia, PA: University of Pennsylvania Press, pp. xiii–lxiii.

Kantorowicz, E. H. (1954). Inalienability: A Note on Canonical Practice and the English Coronation Oath in the Thirteenth Century. *Speculum*, 29(3), 488–502.

Kantorowicz, E. H. (1997 [1957]). *The King's Two Bodies: A Study in Mediaeval Political Theology*, Princeton, NJ: Princeton University Press.

Kaeuper, R. W. (1988). *War, Justice, and Public Order: England and France in the Later Middle Ages*, Oxford: Clarendon Press.

Kaeuper, R. W. (1999). *Chivalry and Violence in Medieval Europe*, Oxford: Oxford University Press.

Kaplan, R. D. (2000). *The Coming Anarchy: Shattering the Dreams of the Post Cold War*, New York, NY: Random House.

Kapteijns, L. (2012). *Clan Cleansing in Somalia: The Ruinous Legacy of 1991*, Philadelphia, PA: University of Pennsylvania Press.

Kaspersen, L. B., Strandsbjerg, J. and Teschke, B. (2017). Introduction. State Formation Theory: Status, Problems, and Prospects. In L. B. Kaspersen and J. Strandsbjerg, eds., *Does War Make States? Critical Investigations of Charles Tilly's Historical Sociology*, Cambridge: Cambridge University Press, pp. 1–22.

Kasten, B. (1997). *Königssöhne und Königsherrschaft: Untersuchungen zur Teilhabe am Reich in der Merowinger- und Karolingerzeit* [Sons of Kings and Royal Authority: Investigations on Their Partaking of the Realm in the Merovingian and Carolingian Periods], Hanover: Hahn.

Kayhan, B. (2008). Iran and the Shiite Crescent: Myths and Realities. *Brown Journal of World Affairs*, 15(1), pp. 87–99.

Kayserlicher Und Königlicher Wie auch Ertz-Hertzoglicher Und Dero Residentz-Stadt Wien Staats- und Stands- Calender. (1702–1806). Several different publishers http://alex.onb.ac.at/shb.htm, accessed 2 May 2019.

Kazemzadeh, M. (2018). The Sources of the Middle East's Crises and American Grand Strategy. *Comparative Strategy*, 37(1), 56–72.

Kéchichian, J. A. (2008). *Power and Succession in Arab Monarchies: A Reference Guide*, Boulder, CO: Lynne Rienner.

Keeley, L.H. (1997). *War Before Civilization*, Oxford: Oxford University Press.

Keen, M. (2000). Chivalry and the Aristocracy. In M. Jones, ed., *c.1300–c.1415*. Vol. VI of *The New Cambridge Medieval History*, Cambridge: Cambridge University Press, pp. 209–21.

Keen, M. (2005). *Chivalry*, New Haven, CT: Yale University Press.

Kelsen, H. (2002 [1967]). *Pure Theory of Law*, Union, NJ: Lawbook Exchange.

Khaldūn, I. (2005). *The Muqaddimah: An Introduction to History*, Princeton, NJ: Princeton University Press.

Khoury, P. S. and Kostiner, J. (1991). *Tribes and State Formation in the Middle East*, Berkeley, Los Angeles, CA, and London: University of California Press.

Kilcullen, D. (2009). *The Accidental Guerrilla: Fighting Small Wars in the Midst of a Big One*, Oxford: Oxford University Press.

King, P. D. (1987). *Charlemagne: Translated Sources*, Lambrigg: P. D. King.

Kirkpatrick, D. (2017) 'Saudi Crown Prince's Mass Purge Upends a Longstanding System', 4 November. www.nytimes.com/2017/11/05/world/middleeast/saudi-crown-prince-purge.html, accessed 16 April 2019.

Kirschstein, B. and Schnulze, U. (2010). *Swesterkint-Zwîvelrede*. Vol. III of *Wörterbuch der mittelhochdeutschen Urkundensprache: auf der Grundlage des Corpus der altdeutschen Originalurkunden bis zum Jahr 1300* [Dictionary of the Language of Medieval German Sources: On the Basis of the Corpus of the Old German Original Sources Until the Year 1300], Berlin: Erich Schmidt Verlag.

Kivelson, V. A. (1999). Cartography, Autocracy and State Powerlessness: The Uses of Maps in Early Modern Russia. *Imago Mundi,* 51(1), 83–105.

Kivelson, V. A. (2005). Culture and Politics, or the Curious Absence of Muscovite State Building in Current American Historical Writing. *Cahiers du monde russe,* 46(1), 19–28.

Klevnäs, A. (2015). Abandon Ship! Digging Out the Dead from the Vendel Boat-Graves. *Norwegian Archaeological Review,* 48(1), 1–20.

Knutsen, C. H. and Fjelde, H. (2013). Property Rights in Dictatorships: Kings Protect Property Better than Generals or Party Bosses. *Contemporary Politics,* 19(1), 94–114.

Koenigsberger H. G. (1971). *Estates and Revolutions. Essays in Early Modern European History*, Ithaca, NY: Cornell University Press.

Koenigsberger H. G. (1975). Monarchies and Parliaments in Early Modern Europe. In K. Möckl and K. Bosl, eds., *Der moderne Parlamentarismus und seine Grundlagen in der ständischen Repräsentation* [Modern Parliamentarism and Its Origins in the Estate-Based Representation], Berlin: Duncker & Humblot, pp. 43–68.

Kokkonen, A. and Sundell, A. (2012). Delivering Stability: Primogeniture and Autocratic Survival in European Monarchies 1000–1800. *Working Paper Series,* 2012(2), Department of Political Science, University of Gothenburg, Sweden.

Kolkey, J. M. (1995). *Germany on the March: A Reinterpretation of War and Domestic Politics over the Past Two Centuries*, Lanham, MD: University Press of America.

Konter, L. (2002). *A History of Hungary. Millennium in Central Europe*, Basingstoke: Palgrave.

Koran. (2014). London: Penguin Classics.

Koselleck, R. (1992a). Historia magistra vitae. Über die Auflösung des Topos im Horizont neuzeitlich bewegter Geschichte [Historia Magistra Vitae: The Dissolution of the Topos into the Perspective of a Modernized Historical Process]. In R. Koselleck, ed., *Vergangene Zukunft: zur Semantik geschichtlicher Zeiten* [Futures Past. On the Semantics of Historical Time], 2nd edn., Frankfurt am Main: Suhrkamp, pp. 38–66.

Koselleck, R. (1992b). Historische Kriterien des neuzeitlichen Revolutionsbegriffs [Historical Criteria of the Modern Concept of Revolution]. In R. Koselleck, ed., *Vergangene Zukunft: zur Semantik geschichtlicher Zeiten*, 2nd edn., Frankfurt am Main: Suhrkamp, pp. 67–86.

Kostiner, J. (1985). On Instruments and Their Designers: The Ikhwan of Najd and the Emergence of the Saudi State. *Middle Eastern Studies*, 21(3), 298–323.

Kostiner, J. (2000). Introduction. In J. Kostiner, ed., *Middle East Monarchies: The Challenge of Modernity*, Boulder, CO: Lynne Rienner, pp. 1–12.

Kradin, N. N. (2002). Nomadism, Evolution and World-Systems: Pastoral Societies in Theories of Historical Development. *Journal of World-Systems Research*, VIII(III), 368–88.

Krieger, K.-F. (1992). *König, Reich und Reichsreform im Spätmittelalter* [King, Realm and Reform in the Late Middle Ages], Munich: R. Oldenbourg.

Kunisch, J. (1986). *Absolutismus: europäische Geschichte vom Westfälischen Frieden bis zur Krise des Ancien Régime* [Absolutism: European History From the Peace of Westphalia Until the Crisis of the Ancien Régime], Göttingen: Vandenhoeck & Ruprecht.

Kunisch, J. (2004). *Friedrich der Grosse: der König und seine Zeit* [Frederick the Great: The King and His Age], Munich: Beck.

Kuper, A. (1982). Lineage Theory: A Critical Retrospect. *Annual Review of Anthropology*, 11, 71–95.

Lafages, C. (1992). Royalty and Ritual in the Middle Ages: Coronation and Funerary Rites in France. In J. G. Péristiany and J. A. Pitt-Rivers, eds., *Honor and Grace in Anthropology*, Cambridge: Cambridge University Press, pp. 19–49.

Lakoff, G. (1987). *Women, Fire, and Dangerous Things: What Categories Reveal About the Mind*, Chicago: University of Chicago Press.

Lambton, A. K. S. (1968). The Internal Structure of the Saljuq Empire. In J. A. Boyle, ed., *The Saljuq and Mongol Periods*. Vol. V of *The Cambridge History of Iran*, Cambridge: Cambridge University Press, pp. 203–82.

Landau-Tasseron, L. (2013). Umayyads (661–750). In G. Böwering, P. Crone and M. Mirza, eds., *The Princeton Encyclopedia of Islamic Political Thought*, Princeton, NJ: Princeton University Press, pp. 582–3.

Langewiesche, D. (2013). *Die Monarchie im Jahrhundert Europas. Selbstbehauptung durch Wandel im 19. Jahrhundert* [The Monarchy in the European Century. Self-Assertion Through Change], Heidelberg: Universitätsverlag Winter.

Lapidus, I. M. (2012). *Islamic Societies to the Nineteenth Century. A Global History*, Cambridge: Cambridge University Press,

Lasswell, H. D. (1958). *Politics: Who Gets What, When, How: With Postscript*, New York, NY: Meridian Books.

Latour, B. (1993). *We Have Never Been Modern*, New York, NY: Harvester Wheatsheaf.

Lattimore, O. (1940). *Inner Asian frontiers of China*, New York: American Geographical Society.

The Lay of Hildebrand. www.pitt.edu/~dash/hildebrand.html, accessed 7 Jamuary 2016.

Le Jan, R. (1995). *Famille et pouvoir dans le monde franc VIIe-Xe siècle*, Paris: Publication de la Sorbonne.

Le Jan, R. (2002). Continuity and Change in the Tenth Century Nobility. In A. J. Duggan, ed., *Nobles and Nobility in Medieval Europe: Concepts, Origins, Transformations*, Woodbridge: Boydell Press, pp. 53–68.

Lebow, R. N. (2008). *A Cultural Theory of International Relations*, Cambridge: Cambridge University Press.

Lebow, R. N. (2010). *Forbidden Fruit: Counterfactuals and International Relations*, Princeton, NJ: Princeton University Press.

Lebow, R. N. (2018). *The Rise and Fall of Political Orders*, Cambridge: Cambridge University Press.

Lebra, T. S. (1993). *Above the Clouds: Status Culture of the Modern Japanese Nobility*, Berkeley, CA: University of California Press.

Leister, G. (2010). The Turks in Anatolia Before the Ottomans. In M. Fierro, ed., *The Western Islamic World the Eleventh to Eighteenth Centuries*. Vol. II of *The New Cambridge History of Islam*, Cambridge: Cambridge University Press, pp. 301–12.

Leonard, D. K. with Samantar, M. S. (2011). What Does the Somali Experience Teach Us About the Social Contract and the State? *Development and Change*, 42(2), 559–84.

Lerski, G. J., Wróbel, P. and Kozicki, R.J. (1996). *Historical Dictionary of Poland, 966–1945*, Westport, CN: Greenwood Press.

Lévi-Strauss, C. (1995). *The Story of Lynx*, Chicago: University of Chicago Press.

Lewis, D. L. (2008). *God's Crucible: Islam and the Making of Europe, 570 to 1215*, New York, NY: W.W. Norton.

Lewis, I. M. (1998). Doing Violence to Ethnography: A Response to Catherine Besteman's 'Representing Violence and "Othering" Somalia'. *Cultural Anthropology*, 13(1), 100–8.

Lewis, I. M. (2002). *War and Ethnicity: Global Connections and Local Violence*, Rochester, NY: Boydell Press.

Lewis, I. M. (2008). *Understanding Somalia and Somaliland: Culture, History, Society*, New York, NY: Columbia University Press.

Lexer, M. (1992). *Mittelhochdeutsches Taschenwörterbuch*, Stuttgart: S. Hirzel Verlag.

Lind, G. (2005). Great Friends and Small Friends: Clientelism and the Power Elite. In W. Reinhard, ed., *Power Elites and State Building*, 2nd edn., Oxford: Oxford University Press.

Lindholm, C. (1986). Kinship Structure and Political Authority: The Middle East and Central Asia. *Comparative Studies in Society and History*, 28(2), 334–55.

Lindholm, C. (2013). Kinship. In G. Böwering, P. Crone and M. Mirza, eds., *The Princeton Encyclopedia of Islamic Political Thought*, Princeton, NJ: Princeton University Press, pp. 298–9.

Ljungkvist, J. (2005). Uppsala högars datering: och några konsekvenser av en omdatering till tidiga vendeltiden. *Fornvännen: Journal of Swedish Antiquarian Research*, 100(4), 245–59.

Lockwood, S. (1997). Introduction. In S. Lockwood, ed., *Sir John Fortescue: On the Laws and Governance of England*, Cambridge: Cambridge University Press, pp. xiv–xxxix.

Louis XIV. (1970). *Mémoires for the Instruction of the Dauphin*, New York: The Free Press.

Lowry, H. W. (2003). *The Nature of the Early Ottoman State*, Albany, NY: State University of New York Press.

Lucas, R. E. (2004). Monarchical Authoritarianism: Survival and Political Liberalization in a Middle Eastern Regime Type. *International Journal of Middle East Studies*, 36(1), 103–19.

Luhmann, N. (1968). *Vertrauen; ein Mechanismus der Reduktion sozialer Komplexität* [Trust: A Mechanism for Reducing Social Complexity], Stuttgart: F. Enke.

Luhmann, N. (1995). *Social Systems*, Stanford, CA: Stanford University Press.

Luhmann, N. (1997). *Die Gesellschaft der Gesellschaft* [The Society of Society], Vol. 2, Frankfurt am Main: Suhrkamp.

Luhmann, N. (1998). Familiarity, Confidence, Trust: Problems and Alternatives. In D. Gambetta, ed., *Trust: Making and Breaking Cooperative Relations*, 2nd edn., Oxford: Basil Blackwell, pp. 94–107.

Lukes, S. (2005). *Power: A Radical View*, 2nd edn., Basingstoke: Palgrave Macmillan.

Lyon, J. R. (2012). *Princely Brothers and Sisters: The Sibling Bond in German Politics, 1100–1250*, Ithaca, NY and London: Cornell University Press.

McChesney, R. D. (2011). Islamic Culture and the Chinggisid Restoration: Central Asia in the Sixteenth and Seventeenth Centuries. In D. O. Morgan, ed., *The Eastern Islamic World, Eleventh to Eighteenth Centuries*. Vol. III of *The New Cambridge History of Islam*, Cambridge: Cambridge University Press, pp. 239–65.

McHaffie, M. W. (2015). Review of Livingstone, Amy. Out of Love for My Kin: Aristocratic Family Life in the Lands of the Loire, 1000–1200. Ithaca, NY: Cornell University Press, 2011. *Early Medieval Europe*, 23(2), 255–8.

Mabon, S. (2016 [2013]). *Saudi Arabia and Iran: Soft Power Rivalry in the Middle East*, 2nd edn., London: I. B. Tauris.

Machiavelli, N. (1990 [1965]. *The Art of War*, 2nd edn., New York, NY: Da Capo Press.

Machiavelli, N. (1993). *The Prince*, Ware: Wordsworth.

Madariaga, I. de (2007). The Russian Nobility in the Seventeenth and Eighteenth Centuries. In H. M. Scott, ed., *Northern, Central, and Eastern Europe*. Vol. II of *The European Nobilities in the Seventeenth and Eighteenth Centuries*, 2nd edn., Basingstoke: Palgrave Macmillan, pp. 311–76.

Madelung, W. (1997). *The Succession to Muhammad: A Study of the Early Caliphate*, Cambridge: Cambridge University Press.

Maddox, D. and Sturm-Maddox, S. (2005). Erec et Enide: The First Arthurian Romance. In N. J. Lacy and J. T. Grimbert, eds., *A Companion to Chrétien de Troyes*, Rochester, NY: D. S. Brewer, pp. 103–19.

Mager, W. (1984). Republik. In R. Koselleck, ed., *Pro-Soz*. Vol. V of *Geschichtliche Grundbegriffe. Historisches Lexicon zur politish-sozialen Sprache in Deutschland*, Stuttgart: Klett-Cotta, pp. 549–651.

Magna Carta. (2015). London: Penguin Classics.

Maine, H. S. (2012 [1861]). *Ancient Law: Its Connection with the Early History of Society, and Its Relation to Modern Ideas*, Cambridge: Cambridge University Press, Cambridge.

Maisel, S. (2014). The New Rise of Tribalism in Saudi Arabia. *Nomadic Peoples*, 18(2), 100–22.

Malešević, S. (2010). *The Sociology of War and Violence*, Cambridge: Cambridge University Press.

Malešević, S. (2017). *The Rise of Organised Brutality: A Historical Sociology of Violence*, Cambridge: Cambridge University Press.

Mamdani, M. M. (2012). *Define and Rule: Native as Political Identity*, Cambridge, MA: Harvard University Press.

Mann, M. (1986). *A History of Power from the Beginning to A.D. 1760*. Vol. I of *The Sources of Social Power*, Cambridge: Cambridge University Press.

Mann, M. (1987). Ruling Class Strategies and Citizenship. *Sociology*, 21(3), 339–54.

Mann, M. (1993). The Rise of Classes and Nation-States, *1760–1914*. Vol. II of *The Sources of Social Power*, Cambridge: Cambridge University Press.

Mardin, Ş. (1973). Center-Periphery Relations: A Key to Turkish Politics? *Daedalus,* 102(1), 169–90.

Marlow, L. (2009). Surveying Recent Literature on the Arabic and Persian Mirrors for Princes Genre. *History Compass,* 7(2), 523–38.

Masters, B. (2010). Egypt and Syria Under the Ottomans. In M. Fierro, ed., *The Western Islamic World the Eleventh to Eighteenth Centuries.* Vol. II of *The New Cambridge History of Islam,* Cambridge: Cambridge University Press, pp. 411–35.

Mattes, H. (2011). Formal and Informal Authority in Libya Since 1969. In D. J. Vandewalle, ed., *Libya Since 1969: Qadhafi's Revolution Revisited,* Basingstoke: Palgrave Macmillan, pp. 55–81.

Mayall, J. (1990). *Nationalism and International Society,* Cambridge: Cambridge University Press.

Mayer, A. J. (2010). *The Persistence of the Old Regime: Europe to the Great War,* London: Verso.

Meehan-Waters, B. (1971). The Muscovite Noble Origins of the Russians in the Generalitet of 1730. *Cahiers du Monde russe et soviétique,* 12(1–2), 28–75.

Meier, C. (1980). *Die Entstehung Des Politischen Bei Den Griechen,* Frankfurt am Main: Suhrkamp.

Menaldo, V. (2012). The Middle East and North Africa's Resilient Monarchs. *The Journal of Politics,* 74(3), 707–22.

Menkhaus, K. (2003). State Collapse in Somalia: Second Thoughts. *Review of African Political Economy,* 30(97), 405–22.

Menkhaus, K. (2004). *Somalia: State Collapse and the Threat of Terrorism,* Adelphi Paper 364 New York: Oxford University Press.

Menkhaus, K. (2014). If Mayors Ruled Somalia. Policy Note 2, Uppsala: The Nordic Africa Institute.

Merkins, J. E. (2014). Unintended Democracy. Electoral Reform in the United Kingdom. In K. Grotke and M. J. Prutsch, eds., *Constitutionalism, Legitimacy, and Power: Nineteenth-Century Experiences,* Oxford: Oxford University Press, pp. 351–70.

Meron, T. (1995). The Authority to Make Treaties in the Late Middle Ages. *American Journal of International Law,* 89(1), 1–20.

Mettam, R. (2007). The French Nobility 1610–1715. In H. M. Scott, ed., Western and Southern Europe. Vol. I of *The European Nobilities in the Seventeenth and Eighteenth Centuries,* 2nd edn., Basingstoke: Palgrave, pp. 127–55.

Meynert, H. (1846). *Die Geschichte Österreich's, seiner Völker und Länder, und der Entwicklung seines Staatenvereins, von den ältesten bis auf die neusten Zeiten* [Trust: A Mechanism for Reducing Social Complexity], Pesth: Verlag von Conrad Adolph Hartleben.

Michaud, C. (2000). The Kingdoms of Central Europe in the Fourteenth Century. In M. Jones, ed., *c.1300–c.1415*. Vol. VI of *The New Cambridge Medieval History*, Cambridge: Cambridge University Press, pp. 735–63.

Mill, J. S. (2003). *On Liberty*, New Haven, CT: Yale University Press.

Miller, A. D. and Sokolsky, R. (2017). Donald Trump has unleashed the Saudi Arabia we always wanted and feared. *Foreign Affairs*, November 10. http://foreignpolicy.com/2017/11/10/donald-trump-has-unleashed-the-saudi-arabia-we-always-wanted-and-feared/, accessed 11 April 2018.

Minkov, A. (2004). *Conversion to Islam in the Balkans. Kisve Bahasi Petitions and Ottoman Social Life, 1670–1730*, Leiden: Brill.

Mitteis, H. (1944). *Die deutsche Königswahl: ihre Rechtsgrundlagen bis zur Goldenen Bulle* [The German Electoral Monarchy: Its Legal Basis Until the Golden Bull], 2nd edn., Brünn: R. M. Rohrer.

Mohnhaupt, H. (1990). Verfassung [Constitution]. In I. R. Koselleck, ed., *Geschichtliche Grundbegriffe. Historisches Lexicon zur politisch-sozialen Sprache in Deutschland*, Vol. 6 St-Vert, Stuttgart: Klett-Cotta, pp. 831–62.

Møller, J. (2012). *Statsdannelse, regimeforandring og økonomisk udvikling* [State-Formation, Regime Change and Economic Development], Copenhagen: Hans Reitzels Forlag.

Moller, F. S. (2017). True Blood or Blue Blood: Why Are Levels of Intrastate Armed Conflict So Low in Middle Eastern Monarchies? *Conflict Management and Peace Science*. First published ahead of print 20 July 2017 http://journals.sagepub.com/doi/10.1177/0738894217714716#articleCitationDownloadContainer, 1–28.

Montesquieu, C. L. (1989). *The Spirit of the Laws*, Cambridge: Cambridge University Press.

Moore, B. (1969). *Social Origins of Dictatorship and Democracy: Lord and Peasant in the Making of the Modern World*, Harmondsworth: Penguin.

Mosca, G. (1939). *The Ruling Class*, London: McGraw-Hill Book Company.

Motyl, A. J. (1999). *Revolutions, Nations, Empires: Conceptual Limits and Theoretical Possibilities*, New York, NY: Columbia University Press.

Mouline, N. (2010). Pouvoir et transition générationelle en Arabie Saoudite [Power and Generational Transition in Saudi Arabia]. *Critique International*, 46, 125–46.

Mousnier, R. (1972). *Peasant Uprisings in Seventeenth-Century France, Russia, and China*, New York, NY: Harper & Row.

Müllen-Mertens, E. (2000). The Ottonians as Kings and Emperors. In T. Reuter, ed., *c.900–c.1024*. Vol. III of *New Cambridge Medieval History*, Cambridge: Cambridge University Press.

Müller, K. (1964). *Die Goldene Bulle Kaiser Karls IV: 1356*, Bern: Lang.

Murdoch, B. (1996). *The German Hero: Politics and Pragmatism in Early Medieval Poetry*, London and Rio Grande, OH: Hambledon Press.

Myers, A. R. (1975). *Parliaments and Estates in Europe to 1789*, London: Thames and Hudson.

Näf, W. (1951). *Herrschaftsverträge des Spätmittelalters: Die Goldene Bulle Andreas' II von Ungarn 1222, die aragonischen Privilegien von 1283 und 1287, die Joyeuse Entrées von Brabant 1356, Der Vergleich des Markgrafen Albrecht von Brandenburg 1472, Der Tübinger Vertrag von 1514*, Bern: Herbert Lang & Cie.

Nasstrom, S. (2011). Where Is the Representative Turn Going? *European Journal of Political Theory*, 10(4), 501–10.

Nelson, J. (2008a). Kingship and Royal Government. In R. McKitterick, ed., *c.700–c.900*. Vol. II of *The New Cambridge Medieval History*, Cambridge: Cambridge University Press, pp. 381–430.

Nelson, J. (2008b). Rulers and Government. In T. Reuter, ed., *c. 900–c.1024*. Vol. III of *The New Cambridge Medieval History*, Cambridge: Cambridge University Press, pp. 95–129.

Nettl, J. P. (1968). The State as a Conceptual Variable. *World Politics*, 20(4), 559–92.

Neues Genealogisches Reichs- und Staats-Handbuch. (1766–1797), 32 vols. Frankfurt am Main: Varrentrapp u. Wenner.

Neumann, I. B. (1996). *Russia and the Idea of Europe: A Study in Identity and International Relations*, London: Routledge.

Neumann, I. B. and Wigen, E. (2013). The Importance of the Eurasian Steppe to the Study of International Relations. *Journal of International Relations and Development*, 16(3), 311–30.

Neumann, I. B. and Wigen, E. (2018). *The Steppe Tradition in International Relations. Russians, Turks and European State-Building 4000 BCE–2017 CE*, Cambridge: Cambridge University Press.

New York Times. (2017) 'Saudi Arabia Arrests 11 Princes, Including Billionaire Alwaleed bin Talal', 4 November. www.nytimes.com/2017/11/04/world/mid dleeast/saudi-arabia-waleed-bin-talal.html, accessed 15 August 2018.

Nexon, D. H. (2009). *The Struggle for Power in Early Modern Europe: Religious Conflict, Dynastic Empires, and International Change*, Princeton, NJ: Princeton University Press.

Nicholas of Cusa. (1991). *The Catholic Concordance*, Cambridge: Cambridge University Press.

Nicholson, H. J. (2003). *Medieval Warfare: Theory and Practice of War in Europe, 300–1500*, Basingstoke: Palgrave Macmillan.

Niles, J. D. (2015). The Myth of the Feud in Anglo-Saxon England. *Journal of English and Germanic Philology*, 114(2), 163–200.

Nithard. (1972). *Historia*. In B. Scholz, W. Bernhard and B. Rogers, eds., *Carolingian Chronicles: Royal Frankish Annals and Nithard's Histories*, Ann Arbor MI: University of Michigan Press, pp. 129–74.

Noble, M. (1804). *A History of the College of Arms, and the Lives of all the Kings, Heralds, and Pursuivants. From the Reign of Richard III, Founder of the College, Until the Present Time*, London: J. Debrett.

Nordström, J. J. (1839). *Bidrag till den svenska samhällsförfattningens historia: efter de älde lagarna till sednare hälften af 17: deseklet* [A Contribution to the History of the Swedish Constitution. From the Older Laws to the Latter Half of the Seventeenth Century], Helsingfors: J. C. Frenckell & Son.

Oakley, F. (2006). *Kingship. The Politics of Enchantment*, Malden: Blackwell Publishing.

Oakley, F. (2010). *Empty Bottles of Gentilism: Kingship and the Divine in Late Antiquity and the Early Middle Ages (to 1050)*, New Haven, CT: Yale University Press.

Oakley, F. (2015). *The Watershed of Modern Politics: Law, Virtue, Kingship, and Consent (1300–1650)*, New Haven, CT: Yale University Press.

Ododa, H. (1985). Somalia's Domestic Politics and Foreign Relations Since the Ogaden War of 1977–78. *Middle Eastern Studies*, 21(3), 285–97.

Ohlander, E. (2009). Enacting Justice, Ensuring Salvation: The Trope of the 'Just Ruler'. *The Muslim World*, 99(2), 237–52.

Onuf, N. G. (1989). *World of Our Making: Rules and Rule in Social Theory and International Relations*, Columbia, SC: University of South Carolina Press.

Ormrod, W. M. (1990). The Peasants' Revolt and the Government of England. *Journal of British Studies*, 29(1), 1–30.

Osiander, A. (2001). Before Sovereignty: Society and Politics in Ancien Régime Europe. *Review of International Studies*, 27(5), 119–45.

Osiander, A. (2007). *Before the State: Systemic Political Change in the West from the Greeks to the French Revolution*, Oxford University Press, Oxford.

Osterhammel, J. (2010). *Die Verwandlung der Welt: eine Geschichte des 19. Jahrhunderts* [The Transformation of the World: A History of the Nineteenth Century], 5th edn., Munich: C. H. Beck.

Ostrowski, D. G. (2000). Muscovite Adaptation of Steppe Political Institutions: A Reply to Halperin's Objections. *Kritika: Explorations in Russian and Eurasian History*, 1(2), 267–304.

Ostrowski, D. G. (2002). The Façade of Legitimacy: Exchange of Power and Authority in Early Modern Russia. *Comparative Studies in Society and History*, 44(3), 534–63.

Owens, P. (2016). International Historical What? *International Theory*, 8(3), 448–57.

Özoğlu, H. (2004). *Kurdish Notables and the Ottoman State: Evolving Identities, Competing Loyalties, and Shifting Boundaries*, Albany, NY: State University of New York Press.

Paine, T. (1998). *Rights of Man, Common Sense, and Other Political Writings*, new edn., Oxford: Oxford University Press.

Papal Letter. (1829). 56, 116–1181 (K.h. 2:621 n: 022). In J. G. Liljegren, *Svenskt Diplomatarium. Bd 1, Åren 817–1285*, Stockholm, pp. 83–5.

Papal Letter. (1829). 142, November 7, 1211 (K. m. 2:560 An. 14. Ep.121). In J. G. Liljegren, *Svenskt Diplomatarium. Bd 1, Åren 817–1285*, Stockholm, p. 165.

Paravicini, W. (1994). *Die ritterlich-höfische Kultur des Mittelalters* [The Knightly-Courtly Culture of the Middle Ages], Munich: R. Oldenbourg.

Pareto, V. (1968). *The Rise and Fall of Elites*, Totowa, NJ: The Bedminster Press.

Parker, G. and Smith, L. M. (1997). *The General Crisis of the Seventeenth Century*, 2nd edn., London: Routledge.

Peace of Westphalia (Münster). (1648). www.pax-westphalica.de/ipmipo/index .html, accessed 14 October 2016.

Peace of Westphalia (Osnabrück). (1648). www.pax-westphalica.de/ipmipo/ index.html, accessed 14 October 2016.

Peirce, L. P. (1993). *The Imperial Harem: Women and Sovereignty in the Ottoman Empire*, Oxford: Oxford University Press.

Peletz, M. G. (1995). Kinship Studies in Late Twentieth-Century Anthropology. *Annual Review of Anthropology*, 24(1), 343–72.

Pham, J. P. (2011). Somalia: Where a State Isn't a State. *Fletcher Forum of World Affairs*, 35(2), 133–50.

Philliou, C. M. (2010). *Biography of an Empire. Governing Ottomans in an Age of Revolution*, Berkeley, CA: University of California Press.

Philliou, C. M. (2011). Families of Empires and Nations: Phanariot Hanedans from the Ottoman Empire to the World Around It (1669–1856). In C. H. Johnson and H. Christopher, eds., *Transregional and Transnational Families in Europe and Beyond: Experiences Since the Middle Ages*, New York, NY: Berghahn Books, pp. 177–99.

Phillips, A. (2010). *War, Religion, and Empire: The Transformation of International Orders*, Cambridge: Cambridge University Press.

Phillips, A. and Sharman, J. C. (2015). Explaining Durable Diversity in International Systems: State, Company, and Empire in the Indian Ocean. *International Studies Quarterly*, 59(3), 436–48.

Pitkin, H. F. (1967). *The Concept of Representation*, Berkeley, CA: University of California Press.

Poag, J. F. (1962). Heinrich von Veldeke's 'Minne'; Wolfram von Eschenbach's 'Liebe' and 'Triuwe'. *The Journal of English and Germanic Philology*, 61(4), 721–35.

Poggi, G. (1978). *The Development of the Modern State: A Sociological Introduction*, London: Hutchinson.

Porter, P. (2013). *Military Orientalism: Eastern War Through Western Eyes*, New York, NY: Oxford University Press.

Poulsen, B. and Netterstrøm, J. B. (2007). *Feud in Medieval and Early Modern Europe*, Aarhus: Aarhus University Press.

Quataert, D. (2000). *The Ottoman Empire, 1700–1922*, New York, NY: Cambridge University Press.

Quillet, J. (1988). Community, Counsel and Representation. In J. H. Burns, ed., *The Cambridge History of Medieval Political Thought*, Cambridge: Cambridge University Press, pp. 520–72.

Qutbuddin, T. (2013). Husayn b. Ali (626–80). In G. Böwering, P. Crone and M. Mirza, eds., *The Princeton Encyclopedia of Islamic Political Thought*, Princeton, NJ: Princeton University Press, pp. 227–8.

Rahimi, B. (2004). Between Chieftaincy and Knighthood: A Comparative Study of Ottoman and Safavid Origins. *Thesis Eleven*, 76(1), 85–102.

Randelzhofer, A. (1967). *Völkerrechtliche Aspekte des Heiligen Römischen Reiches nach 1648* [International Legal Aspects of the Holy Roman Empire After 1648], Berlin: Duncker & Humblot.

Ranum, O. (1993). *The Fronde: A French Revolution, 1648–1652*, New York, NY: W.W. Norton.

Rapport, M. (2009). *1848: Year of Revolution*, New York, NY: Basic Books.

Reifenschied, R. (2006). Karl V. In K. R. Schnith, W. Hartmann and G. Hartmann, eds., *Die Kaiser: 1200 Jahre europäische Geschichte* [The Emperors: 1200 Years of European History], Wiesbaden: Matrix Verlag, pp. 477–509.

Reinhardt, W. (1996). *Power Elites and State Building*, Oxford: Oxford University Press.

Reinle, C. (2003). *Bauernfehden: Studien zur Fehdeführung Nichtadliger im spätmittelalterlichen römisch-deutschen Reich, besonders in den bayerischen Herzogtümern* [Peasant Feuds: Studies on Non-Noble Feuds in the Late Medieval Roman-German Realm, in Particular in the Bavarian Duchies], Stuttgart: Steiner Verlag.

Repgow, E. von and Eckhardt, K. A. (1955–66). *Sachsenspiegel*, 2 vols., 2nd edn., Göttingen: Musterschmidt Verlag.

Reus-Smit, C. (1999). *The Moral Purpose of the State: Culture, Social Identity, and Institutional Rationality in International Relations*, Princeton, NJ: Princeton University Press,

Reus-Smit, C. (2001). Human Rights and the Social Construction of Sovereignty. *Review of International Studies*, 27(4), 519–38.

Reuter, T. (1992). *Ninth-Century Histories*. Vol. 2, *The Annals of Fulda*, Manchester: Manchester University Press.

Reuter, T. (1997). The 'Feudal Revolution'. *Past and Present*, 155(2), 177–95.

Reuter, T. (1999). Carolingian and Ottonian Warfare. In M. H. Keen, ed., *Medieval Warfare: A History*, Oxford: Oxford University Press, pp. 13–35.

Reynolds, S. (1983). Medieval *Origines Gentium* and the Community of the Realm. *History*, 68(224), 375–90.

Reynolds, S. (1984). *Kingdoms and Communities in Western Europe, 900–1300*. Oxford: Clarendon Press.

Reynolds, S. (2004). Government and Community. In D. Luscombe and J. Riley-Smith, eds., *c.1024–1098*. Vol. IV(1) of *The New Cambridge Medieval History*, Cambridge: Cambridge University Press, pp. 86–112.

RI IV,1,1 n. 440, in: Regesta Imperii Online, www.regesta-imperii.de/id/1135-05-26_1_0_4_1_1_440_440, accessed 24 March 2014.

RI V,2,4 n. 10642, in: Regesta Imperii Online, www.regesta-imperii.de/id/1200-07-28_1_0_5_2_4_24_10642, accessed 24 March 2014.

RI IV,2,2 n. 620, in: Regesta Imperii Online, www.regesta-imperii.de/id/1158–11-00_4_0_4_2_2_62_620, accessed 24 March 2014.

RI II,4 n. 1754a, in: Regesta Imperii Online, www.regesta-imperii.de/id/1012–01-00_1_0_2_4_1_473_1754a, accessed 24 March 2014.

RI II,4 n. 1570a, in: Regesta Imperii Online, www.regesta-imperii.de/id/1004–06-17_1_0_2_4_1_207_1570a, accessed 24 March 2014.

RI II,4 n. 1760 m, in: Regesta Imperii Online, www.regesta-imperii.de/id/1012–00-00_1_0_2_4_1_497_1760m, accessed 24 March 2014.

RI XIV,1 n. 1966, in: Regesta Imperii Online, www.regesta-imperii.de/id/1495-06-22_1_0_14_1_0_1970_1966, accessed 24 March 2014.

RI XIV,1 n. 2251, in: Regesta Imperii Online, www.regesta-imperii.de/id/1495-08-07_4_0_14_1_0_2255_2251, accessed 24 March 2014.

Ribalta, P. M. (2007). The Impact of Central Institutions. In W. Reinhard, ed., *Power Elites and State Building*, Cambridge: Cambridge University Press, pp. 19–39.

Richards, R. (2014). *Understanding Statebuilding: Traditional Governance and the Modern State in Somaliland*, Farnham: Ashgate.

Riddarhusordning. (1626). Available at www.sok.riksarkivet.se, accessed 26 July 2018.

Rigaudière, A. (2008). The Theory and Practice of Government in Western Europe. In M. Jones, ed., *c.1300–c.1415*. Vol. VI of *The New Cambridge Medieval History*, Cambridge: Cambridge University Press, pp. 17–41.

Ringmar, E. (2008). *Identity, Interest and Action: A Cultural Explanation of Sweden's Intervention in the Thirty Years War*, Cambridge: Cambridge University Press.

Roach, L. (2013). *Kingship and Consent in Anglo-Saxon England, 871–978: Assemblies and the State in the Early Middle Ages*, Cambridge: Cambridge University Press.

Roberts, M. (1991). *From Oxenstierna to Charles XII: Four Stu*dies, Cambridge: Cambridge University Press.

Robinson, C. F. (2010). Introduction. In C. F. Robinson, ed., *The Formation of the Islamic World, Sixth to Eleventh Centuries*. Vol. I of *The New Cambridge History of Islam*, Cambridge: Cambridge University Press, pp. 1–16.

Robinson, C. F. (2013). *Civil War*. In G. Böwering, P. Crone and M. Mirza, eds., *The Princeton Encyclopedia of Islamic Political Thought*, Princeton, NJ: Princeton University Press, pp. 99–101.

Rogers, C. J. (1995). *The Military Revolution Debate: Readings on the Military Transformation of Early Modern Europe*, Boulder, CO: Westview Press.

Rogers, J. D. (2012). Inner Asian States and Empires: Theories and Synthesis. *Journal of Archeological Research*, 20(3), 205–56.

Rokkan, S., Flora, P., Kuhnle, S. and Urwin, D. W. (1999). *State Formation, Nation-Building, and Mass Politics in Europe: The Theory of Stein Rokkan: based on his collected works*, Oxford and New York: Oxford University Press.

Romanus, Aegidus. (1997). *The Governance of Kings and Princes: John Trevisa's Middle English Translation of the De regimine principum of Aegidius Romanus*, New York, NY: Garland Publishing.

Rosen, L. (2005). Theorizing from Within: Ibn Khaldun and his Political Culture. *Contemporary Sociology*, 34(6), 596–9.

Rosman, H. (1897). *Rasmus Ludvigsson som genealogy* [Rasmus Ludvigsson as Genealogist], PhD Diss. Uppsala: University, Stockholm: Almqvist & Wiksell.

Rostow, W. W. (1960). *The Stages of Economic Growth: A Non-Communist Manifesto*, Cambridge: Cambridge at the University Press.

Rubiés, J.-P. (2005). Oriental Despotism and European Orientalism: Botero to Montesquieu. *Journal of Early Modern History*, 9(1), 109–80.

Ruggie, J .G. (1982). International Regimes, Transactions, and Change: Embedded Liberalism in the Postwar Economic Order. *International Organization*, 36(2), 379–415.

Ruggie, J. G. (1993). Territoriality and Beyond: Problematizing Modernity in International Relations. *International Organization*, 47(1), 139–74.

Rumschöttel, H. (2011). *Ludwig II. von Bayern*, Munich: C. H. Beck.

Runciman, W. G. (1982). Origins of States: The Case of Archaic 351–377 Greece. *Comparative Studies in Society and History*, 24(3), 351–77.

Runciman, D. (2011). A Theoretical Overview. In Q. Skinner, ed., *Families and States in Western Europe*, Cambridge: Cambridge University Press, pp. 11–17.

Rush, M. (2007). The Decline of the Nobility. In M. Cotta and H. Best, eds., *Democratic Representation in Europe: Diversity, Change, and Convergence*, Oxford: Oxford University Press, pp. 29–50.

Sabean, D. W. and Teuscher, S. (2007). Kinship in Europe: A New Approach to Long-Term Development. In D. W. Sabean, S. Teuscher and J. Mathieu, eds.,

Kinship in Europe: Approaches to Long-Term Developments (1300–1900), New York: Berghahn Books, pp. 1–33.

Sabean, D. W., Teuscher, S. and Mathieu, J. (2007). *Kinship in Europe: Approaches to Long-Term Developments (1300–1900)*, New York: Berghahn Books.

Saenger, P. (1977). Burgundy and the Inalienability of Appanages in the Reign of Louis XI. *French Historical Studies*, 10(1), 1–26.

Sahlins, M. (2011a). What Kinship Is (Part One). *Journal of the Royal Anthropological Institute (N.S.,)* 17(1), 2–19.

Sahlins, M. (2011b). What Kinship Is (Part Two). *Journal of the Royal Anthropological Institute (N.S.,)* 17(2), 227–42.

Said, E. W. (2003 [1979]). *Orientalism*, Penguin: London.

Samuel, A. E. (1988). Philip and Alexander as Kings: Macedonian Monarchy and Merovingian Parallels. *The American Historical Review*, 93(5), 1270–86.

Saunders, J. J. (1971). *The History of the Mongol Conquests*, New York, NY: Barnes & Noble.

Saxoferrato, B. de (1883). *Bartoli a Saxoferrato Tractatus de Insigniis et Armis: Mit Hinzufügung Einer Uebersetzung Und Der Citate Neu Herausg. von F. Hauptmann*, P. Hauptmann: Bonn.

Scales, L. (2012). *The Shaping of German Identity: Authority and Crisis, 1245–1414*, Cambridge: Cambridge University Press.

Schlyter, C. J. and Collin, H. S. (1869). *Codex iuris communis Sueciae Christophorianus, cum notis critics, variis lectionibus, glossario et indice nominum propriorum: Konung Christoffers landslag* [The Common Law of Sweden with Critical Notes, Various Lectures, Glossary and Index of Proper Names], Lund: Berlingska boktryckeriet.

Schmidt, G. (1999). *Geschichte des alten Reiches: Staat und Nation in der Frühen Neuzeit. 1495–1806* [History of the Old Realm: State and Nation in the Early Modern Period], Munich: C. H. Beck.

Schmidt, U. (1987). Königswahl und Thronfolge im 12. *Jahrhundert*, Cologne and Vienna: Böhlau.

Schmitt, C. (2007). *The Concept of the Political*, Expanded edn., Chicago, IL: University of Chicago Press.

Scholz, B. W. (1972). *Carolingian Chronicles: Royal Frankish Annals and Nithard's Histories*, Ann Arbor, MI: University of Michigan Press.

Schroeder, P. W. (1994). *The Transformation of European Politics 1763–1848*, Oxford: Clarendon Press.

Schroeder, P. W. (2004a). Did the Vienna Settlement Rest on a Balance of Power? In P. W. Schroeder, D. Wetzel, R. Jervis and J. S. Levy, eds., *Systems, Stability, and Statecraft: Essays on the International History of Modern Europe*, New York, NY: Palgrave Macmillan, pp. 37–57.

Schroeder, P. W. (2004b). Alliances 1815–1945: Weapons of Power and Tools of Management. In P. W. Schroeder, D. Wetzel, R. Jervis and J. S. Levy, eds., *Systems, Stability, and Statecraft: Essays on the International History of Modern Europe*, New York, NY: Palgrave Macmillan, pp. 195–222.

Schroeder, P. W. (2004c). Containment Nineteenth Century Style: How Russia Was Restrained. In P. W. Schroeder, D. Wetzel, R. Jervis and J. S. Levy, eds., *Systems, Stability, and Statecraft: Essays on the International History of Modern Europe*, New York, NY: Palgrave Macmillan, pp. 120–33.

Schroeder, P. W. (1972). World War I as Galloping Gertie: A Reply to Joachim Remak. *The Journal of Modern History*, 44(3), 320–45.

Schochet, G. J. (1967). Thomas Hobbes on the Family and the State of Nature. *Political Science Quarterly*, 82(3), 427–45.

Schubert, E. (1977). Königswahl und Königtum im spätmittelalterlichen Reich [Royal Elections and Kingship in the Late Medieval Realm], *Zeitschrift für historische Forschung*, 77(3), 257–338.

Schück, H., Bengtsson, I. and Stjernquist, N. (1992). *Riksdagen genom tiderna* [The Swedish Parliament Through the Ages], 2nd edn., Stockholm: Sveriges Riksdag.

Schulze, H. K. (1978). Reichsaristokratie, Stammesadel und Fränksiche Freiheit. Neuere Forschungen zur frühmittelalterliche Sozialgeschichte. *Historische Zeitschrift*, 227(2), 353–73.

Schumpeter, J. A. (1991). The Crisis of the Tax State. In R. Swedberg, ed., *Joseph Schumpeter. The Economics and Sociology of Capitalism*, Princeton, NJ: Princeton University Press, pp. 99–141.

Scott, H. M. (2007). Conclusion: The Continuity of Aristocratic Power. In H. M. Scott, ed., *Northern, Central, and Eastern Europe*. Vol. II of *The European Nobilities in the Seventeenth and Eighteenth Centuries*, Basingstoke: Palgrave Macmillan, pp. 377–99.

Scott, H. M. and Storrs, C. (2007). Introduction: The Consolidation of Noble Power in Europe. In H. M. Scott, ed., *Western Europe*. Vol. I of *The European Nobilities in the Seventeenth and Eighteenth Centuries*, London: Longman, pp. 1–60.

Scott, J. C. (2017). *Against the Grain: A Deep History of the Earliest States*, New Haven, CT: Yale University Press.

Searle, J. R. (1996 [1995]). *The Construction of Social Reality*, 2nd edn., London: Penguin.

Secret History of the Mongols, The. (1982). Translated and edited by F. W. Cleaves. Cambridge, MA: Harvard University Press.

Sellin V. (1996). 'Heute is die revolution mona rchisch'. Legitimität und Legitimierundspolitik im Zeitalter des Wiener Kongresses ['Today the

Revolution is Monarchical'. Legitimacy and Politics of Legitimation in the Age of the Congress of Vienna], *Quellen und Forschungen aus italienischen Archiven und Bibliotheken*, 76, 335–61.

Sellin, V. (2011). *Gewalt und Legitimität: die europäische Monarchie im Zeitalter der Revolutionen* [Violence and Legitimacy: European Monarchy in the Age of Revolutions], Munich: Oldenbourg.

Sellin, V. (2014a). *Das Jahrhundert der Restaurationen: 1814 bis 1906*, Munich: Oldenbourg.

Sellin, V. (2014b). Restorations and Constitutions. In K. L. Grotke and M. J. Prutsch, eds., *Constitutionalism, Legitimacy, and Power: Nineteenth-Century Experiences*, Oxford: Oxford University Press, pp. 84–103.

Sewell, W. H. Jr. (1985). Ideologies and Social Revolutions: Reflections on the French Case. *The Journal of Modern History*, 57(1), 57–85.

Sewell, W. H. Jr. (1996). Historical Events as Transformations of Structures: Inventing Revolution at the Bastille. *Theory and Society*, 25 (6), 841–81.

Seyhun, A. (2015). *Islamist Thinkers in the Late Ottoman Empire and Early Turkish Republic*, Leiden: Brill.

Sharon, M. (1983). *Black Banners From the East: The Establishment of the 'Abbāsid State: Incubation of a Revolt*, Jerusalem: Magnes P.

Shaw, P. (2007). Introduction. In P. Shaw, ed., *Dante Alighieri. Monarchy*, Cambridge: Cambridge University Press, pp. ix–xxxiv.

Shaw, S. J. (1963). The Ottoman View of the Balkans., In C. Jelavich and B. Jelavich, eds., *The Balkans in Transition*, Berkeley and Los Angeles, CA: University of California Press, pp. 56–80.

Shils, E. (1975). Primordial, Personal, Sacred, and Civil Ties. In E. Shils, ed., *Center and Periphery: Essays in Macrosociology*, Chicago, IL: University of Chicago Press, pp. 111–26.

Shils, E. (1982). *The Constitution of Society*, Chicago, IL: University of Chicago Press.

Shu'ayb, F. (2013). Succession. In G. Böwering, P. Crone and M. Mirza, eds., *The Princeton Encyclopedia of Islamic Political Thought*, Princeton, NJ: Princeton University Press, pp. 524–6.

Shultz, R. H. (2009). *Insurgents, Terrorists, and Militias: The Warriors of Contemporary Combat*, New York, NY: Columbia University Press.

Siebmacher, J. (1772–1795). *Johann Siebmachers allgemeines grosses und volständiges Wappenbuch*, 10 vols., Nürnberg: Verlag der Rasvischen Buchhandlung.

Simidchieva, M. (2002). Kingship and Legitimacy in Nizam al-Mulk's *Siyasatnama*, Fifth/Eleventh Century. In B. Gruendler and L. Marlow, eds., *Writers and Rulers. Perspectives on Their Relationship from Abbasid to Safavid Times*, Wiesbaden: Reichert Verlag, pp. 97–132.

Skinner, Q. (2002). Renaissance Virtues. Vol. II of *Visions of Politics*. Cambridge: Cambridge University Press.

Smith, A. (1977). *An Inquiry into the Nature and Causes of the Wealth of Nations*, Chicago, IL: University of Chicago Press.

Smith, A. and Smith, A. D. (2013). *Nationalism and Modernism*, London: Routledge.

Sneath, D. (2007). *The Headless State: Aristocratic Orders, Kinship Society and Misrepresentations of Nomadic Inner Asia*, New York, NY: Columbia University Press.

Sneath, D. (2009). The Headless State in Inner Asia. Reconsidering Kinship Society and the Discourse of Tribalism. In K. M. Rio and O. H. Smedal, eds., *Hierarchy: Persistence and Transformation in Social Formations*, New York, NY: Berghahn, pp. 142–82.

Sonnino, P. (2003). *Mazarin's Quest: The Congress of Westphalia and the Coming of the Fronde*, Cambridge, MA: Harvard University Press.

Spang, R. L. (2003). Paradigms and Paranoia: How Modern Is the French Revolution? *The American Historical Review*, 108(1), 119–47.

Spruyt, H. (1994). *The Sovereign State and Its Competitors: An Analysis of Systems Change*, Princeton, NJ: Princeton University Press.

Stacey, R. (1999). Nobles and Knights. In D. Abulafia, ed., *c.1198–c.1300*. Vol. V of *The New Cambridge Medieval History*, Cambridge: Cambridge University Press, pp. 13–25.

Stavrianos, L. S. (1958). *The Balkans Since 1453*, New York: Rinehart.

Stavrianos, L. S. (2000). *The Balkans Since 1453*, London: C. Hurst.

Sterelny, K. (2016). Contingency and History. *Philosophy of Science*, 83(4), 521–39.

Stollberg-Rilinger, B. (2008). *Des Kaisers alte Kleider: Verfassungsgeschichte und Symbolsprache des Alten Reiches* [The Emperor's Old Clothes: Constitutional History and Symbolic Language of the Old Realm], München: C. H. Beck.

Stollberg-Rilinger, B. (2007). *Das Heilige Römische Reich Deutscher Nation* [The Holy Roman Empire of the German Nation], 3rd edn., Munich: C. H. Beck.

Stone, D. (2015). *The Kaiser's Army. The German Army in World War One*, London and New York: Bloomsbury.

Strachan, H. (2013). *The Direction of War: Contemporary Strategy in Historical Perspective*, Cambridge: Cambridge University Press.

Strang, D. and Meyer, J. W. (1993). Institutional Conditions for Diffusion. *Theory and Society*, 22(4), 487–511.

Strath, B. (2009). Path Dependence Versus Pathbreaking Crises: An Alternative View. In L. Magnusson and J. Ottosson, eds., *The Evolution of Path Dependence*, Cheltenham: Edward Edgar, pp. 19–42.

Strath, B. (2016). *Europe's Utopias of Peace: 1815, 1919, 1951*, London: Bloomsbury Academic.

Strath, B. and Koskenniemi, M. (2014). Creating Community, Ordering the World and Struggling for Securing Welfare, an Introduction. In M. Koskennimi and B. Strath, eds., *Europe 1815–1914: Creating Community and Ordering the World*, Helsinki: University of Helsinki, pp. 1–14. Retrievable from Available at www.helsinki.fi/erere/pages_newsevents/news_and_events.html.

Strath, B. and Wagner, P. (2017). *European Modernity: A Global Approach*, London: Bloomsbury Academic.

Strauss, L. (1952). *The Political Philosophy of Hobbes: Its Basis and Genesis*, Chicago, IL: University of Chicago Press.

Strayer, J. R. (2005 [1970]). *The Medieval Origins of the Modern State*, Princeton, NJ: Princeton University Press.

Sundberg, U. (1998). *Svenska krig 1521–1814* [Swedish War 1521–1814], Stockholm: Hjalmarson & Högberg.

Sutherland, D. M. G. (2002). Peasants, Lords, and Leviathan: Winners and Losers from the Abolition of French Feudalism, 1780–1820. *The Journal of Economic History*, 62(1), 1–24.

Swale, A. D. (2009). *The Meiji Restoration: Monarchism, Mass Communication and Conservative Revolution*, Basingstoke: Palgrave Macmillan.

Swann, J. (2007). The French Nobility in the Eighteenth Century. In H. M. Scott, ed., *Western and Southern Europe*. Vol. I of *The European Nobilities in the Seventeenth and Eighteenth Centuries*, 2nd edn., pp. 156–90.

Sylvester, C. (2013). *War as Experience: Contributions from International Relations and Feminist Analysis*. London: Routledge.

Szkilnik, M. (2005). Medieval Translations and Adaptation of Chrétien's Works. In N. Lacy and J. Grimbert, eds., *A Companion to Chrétien de Troyes*. Rochester, NY: D. S. Brewer, pp. 202–13.

Tacitus. (2005). *Germania*, Stockholm: Wahlström & Widstrand.

Tapper, R. (1983). *The Conflict of Tribe and State in Iran and Afghanistan*, London: Croom Helm.

Tapper, R. (1990). Anthropologists, Historians and Tribespeople on Tribe and StateFormation in the Middle East. In P. S. Khoury and J. Kostiner, eds., *Tribes and State Formation in the Middle East*, Berkeley, Los Angeles, CA, and London: University of California Press, pp. 48–73.

Tapper, R. (2011). *Tribe and State in Iran and Afghanistan*, London: Routledge.

Taylor, C. (2001). The Salic Law and the Valois Succession to the French Crown. *French History*, 15(4), 358–77.

Taylor, A. (2004). *Lords of Misrule: Hostility to Aristocracy in Late Nineteenth and Early Twentieth Century Britain*, Basingstoke: Palgrave Macmillan.

Tellenbach, G. (1939). *Königtum und Stämme in der Werdezeit des deutschen Reiches* [Kingship and Tribes in the Time of the Emergence of the German Realm], Weimar: H. Böhlaus Nachfolger.

Tellenbach, G. (1943). Vom karolingischen Reichsadel zum deutschen Reichsfürstenstand [From Carolingian Imperial Nobility to the German Noble Estate]. In T. Mayer, ed., *Adel und Bauern im Deutschen Staat des Mittelalters* [Nobility and Peasants in the German Medieval State], Leipzig: Koehler & Amelang, pp. 22–73.

Teschke, B. (2002). Theorizing the Westphalian System of States: International Relations from Absolutism to Capitalism. *European Journal of International Relations*, 8(1), 5–48.

Teschke, B. (2003). *The Myth of 1648: Class, Geopolitics, and the Making of Modern International Relations*, London: Verso.

Tezcan, B. (2009). The Second Empire: The Transformation of the Ottoman Polity in the Early Modern Era. *Comparative Studies of South Asia, Africa, and the Middle East*, 29(3), 556–72.

Tezcan, B. (2011). The New Order and the Fate of the Old: The Historiographical Construction of an Ottoman Ancien Régime in the Nineteenth Century. In P. F. Bang and C. A. Bayly, eds., *Tributary Empires in Global History*, London: Palgrave Macmillan, pp. 74–95.

Tezcan, B. (2012). *The Second Ottoman Empire: Political and Social Transformation in the Early Modern World*, New York, NY: Cambridge University Press.

The Definitive Treaty of Peace. (1783). http://avalon.law.yale.edu/18th_century/paris.asp, accessed 13 October 2016.

The Treaty of Paris. (1763). http://avalon.law.yale.edu/18th_century/paris763.asp, accessed 13 October 2016.

Therborn, G. (2008). *What Does the Ruling Class Do When It Rules? State Apparatuses and State Power Under Feudalism, Capitalism and Socialism*, London: Verso.

Thompson, J. A. (1985). Woodrow Wilson and World War I: A Reappraisal. *Journal of American Studies*, 19(3), 325–48.

Tilly, C. (1985). War Making and State Making as Organized Crime. In P. B. Evans, D. Rueschemeyer and T. Skocpol, eds., *Bringing the State Back In*, Cambridge: Cambridge University Press, pp. 169–91.

Tilly, C. (1990). *Coercion, Capital, and European States, AD 990–1990*, Blackwell, Oxford: Blackwell.

Tocqueville, A. de (2011). *Tocqueville: The Ancien Régime and the French Revolution*, Cambridge: Cambridge University Press.

Todorova, M. (1997). The Ottoman Legacy in the Balkans. In L. C. Brown, ed., *Imperial Legacy: The Ottoman Imprint in the Balkans and the Middle East*, New York: Columbia University Press, pp. 45–77.

Toledano, E. R. (1984). The Imperial Eunuchs of Istanbul: From Africa to the Heart of Islam. *Middle Eastern Studies*, 20(3), 379–90.

Tor, D. G. (2013). Sultan. In G. Böwering, P. Crone and M. Mahan, eds., *The Princeton Encyclopedia of Islamic Political Thought*, Princeton, NJ: Princeton University Press, pp. 532–4.

Totman, C. (1981). *Japan Before Perry: A Short History*, Berkeley, CA: University of California Press.

Toumarkine, A. (2014). The Introduction of Max Weber's Thought and Its Uses in Turkey: National Stakes and Foreign Actors. In M. Kaiser and H. Rosenbach, eds., *Max Weber in Der Welt: Rezeption Und Wirkung*, Tübingen: Mohr Siebeck, pp. 33–46.

Trautmann, T. R. (2008). *Lewis Henry Morgan and the Invention of Kinship*, new edn., Lincoln, NA: University of Nebraska Press.

Turner, S. (1840). *The History of the Anglo-Saxons: From the Earliest Period to the Norman Conquest*, Vol. 3, Paris: Baudry's European Library.

Ullman, W. (2010). *Principles of Government and Politics in the Middle Ages*, London: Routledge.

Upton, A. F. (2007). The Swedish Nobility, 1600–1772. In H. M. Scott, ed., *Northern, Central, and Eastern Europe.* Vol. II of *The European Nobilities in the Seventeenth and Eighteenth Centuries*, 2nd edn., Basingstoke: Palgrave Macmillan, pp. 13–42.

USA. (1783). *The Constitution of the United States of America.* Available at www .archives.gov/founding-docs/constitution-transcript, accessed 2 May 2019.

USA. (1776). *The Declaration of Independence.* Available at www.archives.gov/ founding-docs/declaration-transcript, accessed 2 May 2019.

Vandewalle, D. J. (2011a). Libya's Revolution in Perspective. In D. J. Vandewalle, ed., *Libya Since 1969: Qadhafi's Revolution Revisited*, Basingstoke: Palgrave Macmillan, pp. 9–53.

Vandewalle, D. J. (2011b). From International Reconciliation to Civil War, 2003–2011. In D. J. Vandewalle, ed., *Libya Since 1969: Qadhafi's Revolution Revisited*, Basingstoke: Palgrave Macmillan, pp. 215–39.

Vierhaus, R. (1982). Konservativ, Konservatismus. In R. Koselleck, ed., *Geschichtliche Grundbegriffe. Lexicon zur politisch-soziale Sprache in Deutschland Band 3 H-Me*, Stuttgart: Klett-Cotta, pp. 531–65.

Villstrand, N. E. (2011). *Sveriges historia 1600–1721* [History of Sweden 1600–1721], Stockholm: Norstedt.

Wagner, P. (2001). *Theorizing Modernity: Inescapability and Attainability in Social Theory*, London: SAGE.

Walls, M. (2009). The Emergence of a Somali State: Building Peace from Civil War in Somaliland. *African Affairs*, 104(432), 371–89.

Ward, L. (2007). Montesquieu on Federalism and Anglo-Gothic Constitutionalism. *Publius*, 37(4), 551–77.

Washington Post, (2017). 'Saudi Arabia's crown prince is getting reckless', 6 November, www.washingtonpost.com/opinions/global-opinions/saudi-ara bias-crown-prince-is-getting-reckless/2017/11/06/62401134-c325-11e7-aaeo-cb18a8c29c65_story.html?utm_term=.189d96da82e8, accessed 17 April 2018.

Watts, J. (2009). *The Making of Polities: Europe, 1300–1500*, Cambridge: Cambridge University Press.

Waurechen, S. (2013). Imagined Polities, Failed Dreams, and the Beginnings of an Unacknowledged Britain: English Responses to James VI and I's Vision of Perfect Union. *Journal of British Studies*, 52(3), 575–96.

Weber, M. (1978). *Economy and Society: An Outline of Interpretive Sociology*. Vol. 1, Berkeley, CA: University of California Press.

Weber, M. (2004). Politics as Vocation. In D. Owen and T. B. Strong, eds., *Weber, Max The Vocation Lectures. 'Science as a Vocation'. 'Politics as a Vocation'*, Indianapolis: Hackett Publishing Company, pp. 32–94.

Wemple, S. F. (1985). *Women in Frankish Society: Marriage and the Cloister, 500 to 900*. Philadelphia, PA: University of Pennsylvania Press.

Wendt, A. (1999). *Social Theory of International Politics*, Cambridge: Cambridge University Press.

Wenskus, R. (1961). *Stammesbildung und Verfassung: das Werden der frühmittelalterlichen gentes* [Tribe and Constitution: The Emergence of the Early Medieval Gentes], Köln: Böhlau.

Weyland, K. (2009). The Diffusion of Revolution: '1848' in Europe and Latin America. *International Organization*, 63(3), 391–423.

Whetham, D. (2009). *Just Wars and Moral Victories: Surprise, Deception and the Normative Framework of European War in the Later Middle Ages*, Leiden: Brill Academic Publishers.

White, S. D. (1986). Feuding and Peace-Making in the Touraine Around the Year 1100. *Traditio*, 42(X), 195–263.

Wickham, C. (1981). *Early Medieval Italy: Central Power and Local Society 400–1000*, New Studies in Medieval History, London: Macmillan.

Wickham, C. (1997). The 'Feudal Revolution'. *Past and Present*, 155(2), 196–208.

Wickham, C. (2009). *The Inheritance of Rome: A History of Europe from 400 to 1000*, London: Allen Lane.

Wilson, P. H. (2009). *Europe's Tragedy: A History of the Thirty Years War*, London: Allen Lane.

Winslow, C. (1996). *Lebanon: War and Politics in a Fragmented Society*, New York: Routledge.

Wittek, P. (1971 [1938]). *The Rise of the Ottoman Empire*, London: Royal Asiatic Society.

Wittfogel, K. A. (1957). *Oriental Despotism: A Comparative Study of Total Power*, New Haven, CT: Yale University Press.

Wittrock, B. (2002). Modernity: One, None, or Many? European Origins and Modernity as a Global Condition. In S. N. Eisenstadt, ed., *Multiple Modernities*, New Brunswick, NJ: Transaction Publishers, pp. 31–59.

Wolfram, H. (2006a). Gothic History as Historical Ethnography. In T. F. X. Noble, ed., *From Roman Provinces to Medieval Kingdoms*, London: Routledge, pp. 43–69.

Wolfram, H. (2006b). *Origio et religio*: ethnic traditions and literature in early medieval texts. In T. F. X. Noble, ed., *From Roman Provinces to Medieval Kingdoms*, London: Routledge, pp. 70–90.

Wood, I. N. (1994). *The Merovingian Kingdoms, 450–751*, London: Longman.

Wood, I. N. (2013). *The Modern Origins of the Early Middle Ages*, Oxford: Oxford University Press.

Wormald, P. (2005). Kings and Kingship. In P. Fouracre, ed., *c.500–c.700*. Vol. I of *The New Cambridge Medieval History*, Cambridge: Cambridge University Press, pp. 571–604.

Zilfi, M. C. (2006). The Ottoman Ulema. In S. N. Faroqhi, ed., *The Later Ottoman Empire 1603–1839*. Vol. III of *The Cambridge History of Turkey*, Cambridge: Cambridge University Press, pp. 209–25.

Zmora, H. (1997). *State and Nobility in Early Modern Germany: The Knightly Feud in Franconia, 1440–1567*, Cambridge, UK; New York, NY: Cambridge University Press.

Zmora, H. (2001). *Monarchy, Aristocracy, and the State in Europe 1300–1800*, London: Routledge.

Zoppi, M. (2018). Somalia: Federating Citizens or Clans? Dilemmas in the Quest for Stability. *Journal of Contemporary African Studies*, 30(1), 54–70.

INDEX